PRAISE FOR A WAR AGAINST TRUTH

"Roberts reports passionately and provocatively about his experiences of the war in Iraq. As an independent eyewitness to the invasion of the country in March 2003, he describes in dramatic detail the sufferings of ordinary people, the rivalries among political factions, and his personal outrage at the transformation of a place he loved."

— the Charles Taylor Prize jury

"*A War Against Truth* is a powerful and deeply personal record ... Roberts is engaged, ethically, emotionally, and intellectually, in what he sees ... Going ever deeper into Iraq's heart of darkness, he shows us how the shadows fall." — *Quill & Quire*

"Roberts has written an angry and sometimes funny book ... Roberts is a terrific writer and his account of being caught in the bombing ... is one of the most intense reading experiences imaginable." — *Ottawa Citizen*

"Roberts knows the terrain; he even knows Arab literature. He was present for the Persian Gulf War of 1991; he experienced the Shock-and-Awe Blitzkrieg of 2003 ... Like George Orwell's accounts ... Roberts's work attempts to convey the chaos and suffering unleashed by the machinations of the mighty, including the ghastly derangement perpetrated by aerial bombardment ... Such passages recall Wilfred Owen's sonnets about Great War trenches. [One] great passage is worthy of Yeats ... If you want to understand how and why the U.S. is in Iraq, start here." — *Halifax Chronicle Herald*

"Paul William Roberts' angry, deeply personal and finely written account of the Iraq invasion." — *Macleans*

"Roberts' focus is on the human impact of the invasion on everyday Iraqis. It is a firsthand account of what the 'embedded' journalists didn't tell you ... *A War Against Truth* is a great read, in part because Roberts is a good storyteller and in part because he has such a compelling story to tell." — *Kitchener-Waterloo Record*

"*A War Against Truth* is as much history as it is current events, unfolding in a masterpiece of imagery ... Whether to learn, laugh, cry or all of them, this is the next book you should read. Expect enlightening entertainment and a demand to involve yourself in a better world." — *Common Ground*

PRAISE FOR THE DEMONIC COMEDY: SOME DETOURS IN THE BAGHDAD OF SADDAM HUSSEIN

"A book that is at once funny, beguiling, poignant, powerful and very good indeed, [and] probably also has the unusual bonus feature of being true." — *Globe and Mail*

"A fine and wonderfully readable book: a tragic story told with antic humor and literary grace." — Lewis H. Lapham, editor of *Harper's*

"In the crucible of Iraq's ongoing agonies, Roberts discovers himself to be a man of the people, bitter about political leaders of all stripes and firmly on the side of ordinary Iraqis." — *Maclean's*

"The first great book to come out of this stupid, squalid exercise in gunboat diplomacy … comic scenes that recall Hunter Thompson at the top of his form, and portraits of civilian carnage that are worthy of Goya." — *The Vancouver Sun*

PRAISE FOR PAUL WILLIAM ROBERTS' PREVIOUS BOOKS

"I cannot recommend this book too highly: it is not only an outrageously funny travel narrative — the funniest I've read in years — but also a work of radical scholarship … Rare is the book that works so well on so many different levels."
— Pico Iyer in *Time*, on *Journey of the Magi*

"An instructive and entertaining travel book, a high comedy of cultural dissonance and a profound exploration of the three great modern religions. Mr. Roberts writes with verve."
— *New York Times* on *Journey of the Magi*

"*Empire of the Soul*, vivid and soul stirring, is worth 10 of V.S. Naipaul's books on the same subject." — *Toronto Sun*

"One of the most remarkable travel books ever written — but of course it is far more than that. It's brilliant, funny, moving, and often profound. Roberts writes like an angel. *Empire of the Soul* is the most living book about India I have ever read."
— Colin Wilson

The ruin of history. Even the air is red with blood, choking on sewage, cordite, burning oil, and my own fear.

The sounds are getting closer . . . thumping of anti-aircraft batteries all around (~~this is bad location, that~~ ~~to protect~~)

the people lost souls in _Purgatory_

Perhaps we are already dead?

Fear my family _I LOVE THEM_ ~~but I~~ ~~will get out of here this time~~ ~~SHIT~~ . . . that was too close

why am I why? (This is MADNESS — don't believe your leaders...There no justification for this

FUCK YOU GEORGE BUSH! YOU Sonofabitch! You ~~wouldn't send your~~ ~~daughters here~~ ~~no you couldn't even~~ ~~get to see yourself you fucks.~~

got to get out of here.

I MISS you ALL so much AND
       I LOVE you — ALWAYS

It is not safe.
THIS is TERRORISM, I'm terrified.
This So fad, ~~such a bad thing to do~~
       The children are crying under the red sky
It is not LIKE hell — this is ~~hell~~
The baby is dead — — They KILLED A BABY

~~gone~~ — NOW. Nothing is safe anymore
I want to hide but there is nowhere
to go. The whole world is in FLAMES
I HATE you BUSH, because you've
MADE me hate
I cannot love anymore. I hate.
And the world SHUDDERS and BURNS
because of it. Is this IT?

The women and children crying
       while the sky bleeds
       ···· the END??

A WAR
AGAINST
TRUTH

Paul William Roberts

A WAR AGAINST TRUTH

AN INTIMATE ACCOUNT
OF THE INVASION OF IRAQ

RAINCOAST BOOKS

Vancouver

Raincoast Books acknowledges the ongoing financial support of the
Government of Canada through The Canada Council for the Arts and
the Book Publishing Industry Development Program (BPIDP);
and the Government of British Columbia through the B.C. Arts Council.

Edited by Scott Steedman
Text design and typesetting by Tannice Goddard

NATIONAL LIBRARY OF CANADA CATALOGUING IN PUBLICATION DATA
Roberts, Paul William
A war against truth : an intimate account of the invasion of Iraq / Paul William Roberts.

Includes index.
ISBN 1-55192-688-1 (bound.) — ISBN 1-55192-819-1 (pbk.)

1. Iraq War, 2003. 2. Iraq War, 2003—Causes. 3. United States—Foreign relations—Iraq.
4. Iraq—Foreign relations—United States. I. Title.

DS79.76.R62 2004   956.7044 3   C2004-901972-4

LIBRARY OF CONGRESS CATALOGING-IN-PUBLICATION DATA
Roberts, Paul William.
   A war against truth : an intimate account of the invasion of Iraq / by Paul William Roberts.
     p. cm.

Includes bibliographical references and index.
ISBN 1-55192-819-1 (alk. paper)

1. Iraq War, 2003—Personal narratives, Canadian. 2. Roberts, Paul William—Travel—Iraq.
3. United States—Foreign relations—Iraq. 4. Iraq—Foreign relations—United States. I. Title.

DS79.76R63 2005   956.7044'31—dc22   2005014284

Raincoast Books
9050 Shaughnessy Street
Vancouver, British Columbia
Canada   V6P 6E5
www.raincoast.com

In the United States:
Publishers Group West
1700 Fourth Street
Berkeley, California
94710

At Raincoast Books we are committed to protecting the environment and to the
responsible use of natural resources. We are acting on this commitment by
working with suppliers and printers to phase out our use of paper produced
from ancient forests. This book is one step towards that goal. It is printed on
100% ancient-forest-free paper (100% post-consumer recycled), processed
chlorine- and acid-free, and supplied by New Leaf paper. It is printed with
vegetable-based inks. For further information, visit our website at www.raincoast.com.
We are working with Markets Initiative (www.oldgrowthfree.com) on this project.

Printed and bound in Canada by Friesens.
10 9 8 7 6 5 4 3 2

The author and publishers gratefully acknowledge permission to reprint copyright
material in this book as follows: Keith Douglas: Faber & Faber, from *Complete Poems of Keith Douglas*,
ed. Desmond Graham (1978). Robert Lowell: Faber & Faber, from *Collected Poems* (2002), for the U.K.
and Commonwealth; for North America, copyright © 2003 by Harriet Lowell and Sheriden Lowell,
reprinted by permission of Farrar, Straus and Giroux, LLC. Jaques Prévert: trans. © 1958 Lawrence
Ferlinghetti, from *Selections from 'Paroles'* (Penguin, 1965). Tadeusz Rózewicz: trans. © Adam
Czerniawski, from *They Came to See a Poet* (Anvil, 1991). Goran Simic: © English version by David
Harsent, from *Sprinting from the Graveyard* (Oxford University Press, 1997). Saadi Youssef: trans. ©
Khaled Mattawa for "Night in Al-Hambra," Graywolf Press; trans. © Khaled Mattawa for "A Vision,"
from *Without An Alphabet, Without A Face* (2002).

for David Fraser
great teacher, great friend,
and
for Arabella

CONTENTS

ACKNOWLEDGEMENTS

Without the generous assistance of the Canada Council I would not have been able to write this book. I am deeply grateful to them. I am also greatly indebted to my friend, Lewis H. Lapham, and to *Harper's* magazine, without whose help and encouragement I would have been unable to spend so long in Iraq. To Linda Pearce I owe more than I can ever repay in kindness and wisdom and poetry. To my friend Nagui Ghali I owe endless patience, countless breakfasts, and weekly updates on the Arab world. To my friend Marc Gabel, as ever, I owe perspective, sanity, laughter and a fund of rabbinical lore. To David Murray I owe understanding, trust and the considerable resources of Scotiabank. I have never enjoyed a more pleasurable creative experience than the current one with Raincoast Books, and I am profoundly grateful to Scott Steedman for his faith in this book, his patience with its writing, his wise insights, and his brilliant editorial judgements, all of which were utterly indispensable to me and are largely responsible for whatever merit lies herein. To my family, Tiziana, Elijah and Arabella, I can only apologize for the absence and the disruption that this project has brought into their lives, and offer my deepest gratitude for their love and understanding. It was not easy witnessing this latest chapter in Iraq's tragic history, and less easy still writing about it, but both tasks would have been impossible without the help and inspiration of my friends in Iraq and the spirit of the Iraqi people in general. Their courage, fortitude, kindness and humour never cease to leave me in awe. In particular, I can now never thank enough my old friend, the late Bassim Shaykh 'Abd al Karimi, his wife Rana, and their daughter Amira, all of whom died during the war, and were always at my side while I wrote this book, as was a five-year-old girl I knew only as Amina. I wish I could do more for all of you, but I can only offer this record of a tragedy and a crime whose enormity in truth defies description or comprehension. I send it off with my love.

PWR

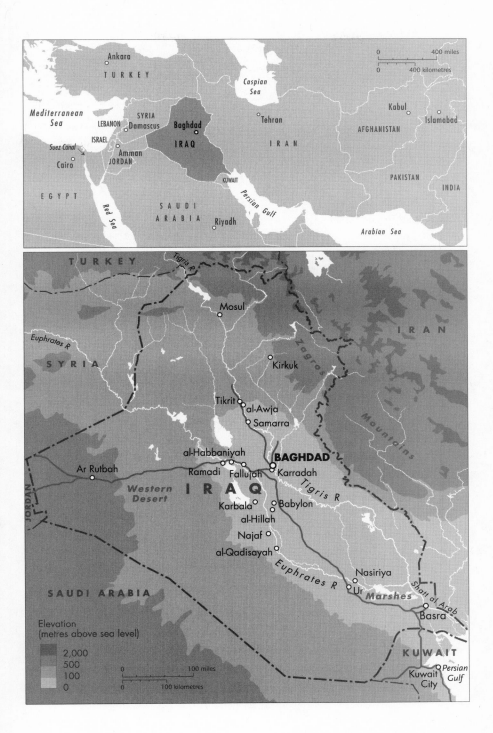

TIMELINE

3100 BC — Sumerian civilisation develops systems of irrigation, trade and writing

2600 BC — Akkadians move into Mesopotamia

1728-1686 BC — Reign of Hammurabi the Lawgiver, most famous ruler of Babylonia

669 BC — Babylon destroyed by Assyrians

1120 BC — Babylonia becomes a strong power

539 BC — Mesopotamia conquered by Persians under Cyrus the Great

331 BC — Reign of Seleucid Dynasty begins

64 BC — Seleucid Dynasty falls apart; Mesopotamia is conquered by Persians

AD 627 — Byzantine invasion

AD 680 — Shiite leader Hussein killed in Battle of Karbala; his death results in the final schism between Sunnis and Shiites

AD 750 — Abbasids overthrow the ruling caliphate family, the Ummawiys

AD 762 — The caliphate founds a new capital, Baghdad, on the river Tigris

AD 836 — Samarra becomes the new capital of the caliphate

AD 892 — Baghdad regains position as capital of the caliphate

1258 — Baghdad falls to the Mongols. The caliph is executed, signalling the end of the caliphate

1405 — Iraq falls under the control of the Turkish tribes from Anatolia

1508 — Iraq is put under Persian control

1533-34 — Iraq conquered by the Ottoman Empire; peace ensues

17th century — British, Dutch and Portuguese interests get a trade foothold in the region

1870 — Baghdad modernized, first tramways and steamship services introduced

1917 — British occupation of Baghdad begins

1914 — As a sideshow of World War 1, British forces invade southern Iraq

1921 — Prince Faisal declared king of Iraq. British forces stay in the country at the king's request

1922 — Alliance with Britain signed, October 10

1925 — Parliament elections held. International companies awarded concessions to search for oil

1932 — Iraq is declared an independent kingdom and admitted to the League of Nations

1933 — King Faisal dies; his son Ghazi succeeds him

1939 — King Ghazi dies

1941 — British regain control after a 4-week war and ensure that a pro-British government is formed

1943 — Iraq declares war on the Axis powers, headed by Nazi Germany

1950 — Strong increase in oil revenues

1953 — Parliamentary elections held; King Faisal 11 assumes throne

1958 — General Karim Kassem leads a military coup in which the king, crown prince and prime minister are killed

1963 — General Kassem overthrown by Ba'ath Party officers; Abdul Salam Arif becomes president

1968 — Arif overthrown, Ahmed Hassan al-Bakr becomes president. Iraq shuns the West and improves relations with the Soviet Union

1979 — Bakr is placed under house arrest and Saddam Hussein becomes president

1980 — Iraq invades Iran, September 22

1982 — Iran launches counter-offensive and reclaims most of the land occupied by Iraq

1988 — Iraqi aircraft shell Kurdish village of Halabja with chemical weapons, killing thousands of civilians, March 16. Ceasefire with Iran signed, August 20

1990 — Iraqi army invades Kuwait, August 2. U.N. imposes sanctions against Iraq

1991 — First Gulf War. Aerial bombardment of Iraq begins, January 17, followed by ground offensive; Kuwait is liberated, February 26. Uprisings in south and north crushed by Iraqi army. The U.N. Security Council adopts resolution 688, a historic document that calls for intervention in the internal affairs of a member state mistreating its own people

1992 — Iraq admits it has a nuclear weapons program. U.N. imposes a no-fly zone over southern Iraq, August 27. U.N. demands to eliminate the remaining weapons of mass destruction go unheeded and international sanctions remain

1993 — U.S. and Allied warplanes attack targets in southern Iraq after Iraq refuses to remove anti-aircraft missile batteries from the no-fly zone. Following further Iraqi breaches of U.N. resolutions, 119 U.S., French and British planes bomb targets in southern Iraq

1994 — Iraq moves 10,000 troops to Basra during a U.N. summit, threatening Kuwait in defiance of a U.N. resolution. President Clinton responds by moving U.S. naval fleets and army units near Iraq. Baghdad officially recognises the sovereignty of Kuwait

1995 — Defector Hussein Kamel reveals military secrets which force Iraq to admit that it has a biological weapons program. 99.6 per cent of voters back Saddam in a referendum. U.N. oil-for-food program begins

1998 — Security Council votes unanimously not to discuss lifting sanctions until co-operation with U.N. arms inspectors resumes. U.S. and Britain strike Baghdad as part of Desert Fox bombing campaign, killing many civilians. A CIA and MI6 plot to assassinate Saddam Hussein is revealed

1999 — Russia signs a deal with Iraq to upgrade the country's MIG jet fighters

2000 — The original U.N. inspections team, UNSCOM, is replaced with UNMOVIC (United Nations Monitoring, Verification and Inspection Commission), after Clinton administration admits it has received confidential intelligence reports from UNSCOM. Baghdad still refuses to let inspection teams into the country

2001 — U.S. and Britain attempt to tighten sanctions against Iraq, but their proposal for "smart sanctions" is rejected by the U.N. Security Council. President Bush authorises an air attack on the outskirts of Baghdad

2002 — President Bush names Iraq as one of the "Axis of Evil" nations, along with Iran and North Korea. Vice President Cheney reiterates America's threat of a pre-emptive strike to prevent the use of "weapons of mass destruction." U.S. warplanes bombard military and civilian targets. U.N. resolution 1441 finds Iraq in material breach of its obligations to disarm, gives it final opportunity to comply

2003 — UNMOVIC weapons inspectors led by Dr Hans Blix report limited co-operation in their search for weapons of mass destruction. U.S. and Britain call for a new U.N. resolution authorizing war; they receive backing of Spain and Bulgaria but are opposed by France, Russia, China, Germany and Syria. U.S. sends 225,000 troops to the Gulf, Britain 45,000. War commences, March 20; Saddam Hussein's regime crumbles, early April. Saddam is captured in December, hiding in a purpose-built crawl space under the yard of a Tikrit farmhouse

2003-2004 — Disastrous reign of Bush II

This Iraq will reach the ends of the graveyard.
It will bury its sons in open country
generation after generation,
and it will forgive its despot ...
It will not be the Iraq that once held the name.
And the larks will not sing.
So walk — if you wish — a long time.
And call — if you wish —
on all the world's angels
and all its demons.
Call on the bulls of Assyria.
Call on a westward phoenix ...
Call them
and through the haze of phantoms
watch for miracles to emerge
from clouds of incense.

— SAADI YOUSSEF (1934–)[1]

PART ONE

War

As I write, Baghdad lies in ruins around me. A reddish-orange fog, aftermath of a sandstorm, hangs in the air, mingling with cordite, sewage, burning oil and fear. Every few minutes, there are bomb blasts, near or far, the thump-thump-thump of anti-aircraft batteries, and the dull thud of mortar shells exploding. Twice-hit by the so-called Coalition's missiles in the past twenty-four hours, Iraqi television is back on the air, broadcasting a call to arms for the tribes of Arabia to rise up in Jihad, holy war, and help Saddam Hussein repel the infidel invaders. It is inter-cut with stirring scenes of military triumph in art ranging from the Akkadian to the British Empire. Apart from the technology, we could be at almost any time in Iraq's long, long history ...

I wrote this for the *Globe and Mail* towards the end of March 2003. But in my notebook, the first draft of the same article, written in an erratic spidery hand, reads:

The ruin of history. Even the air is red with blood, choking on sewage, cordite, burning oil, and my own fear.

The bombs are getting _closer_ ... thumping of anti-aircraft batteries all around (this is bad location, likely target) ...

the people look like lost souls in _Purgatory_.

Perhaps we are already dead?

Tell my family I love them. Don't think I will get out of here this time.

SHIT ... [the word is huge yet barely legible: a bomb had fallen nearby] ... that was too close. Why? Why? Why? (This is madness — don't believe your leaders ... there's no justification for *this* ...)

Fuck you, George Bush, you evil sonofabitch! *You wouldn't send your children here ... you wouldn't even go to war yourself, you fucki ... W-* [the letter snakes right off the page: a huge explosion had blown in the windows of my room] ...

got to get out of here.

I miss you all so much and I love you ... always ...

It is not safe.

This is TERRORISM. _I'm terrified._

This is **SO** bad, such a bad thing to do. The children are crying under the red sky.

It is not LIKE hell — this IS **HELL**. The baby is dead ... _they killed a baby_.

Apoc—*NOW*. Nothing is safe anymore.

I want to hide but there is nowhere to go.

The whole world is in flames.

I hate you Bush, because you've MADE me hate.

I cannot love anymore. I hate. And the world *shudders* and *burns* because of it. Is this IT?

The women and children crying while the sky bleeds
    ... the *END*?

I am frightened all over again when I read this.

What I wrote for the newspaper adopts a persona of calm and reason, as if the writer is narrating a documentary. It is not true. It is a lie — and we don't need any more lies about this war. I was in the history — it was also my story; I was not reading it from the safety of some faraway future. I want to convey what being in it was like. But when I look at what I wrote as hell gaped, I have nothing more to say. I cannot elaborate on it. I cannot improve it. I was writing while the bombs and missiles fell around me because there was nowhere to run, nowhere to hide; and because it kept open a line of communication back to the world I suspected I might never see again. Or lines, in fact — for it seems to be partly a letter to my daughter, partly a letter to George W. Bush, partly an open letter, and finally a letter to myself.

Never in history was a war so well documented yet so poorly *covered* by the media. Indeed, the Canadian Broadcasting Corporation stands nearly alone among English-speaking television and radio broadcasters in the sheer objectivity of its news gathering and transmission; just as the *Globe and Mail* was virtually the sole major daily newspaper in North America not to jump on the noisy bandwagon of American jingoism with its concomitant lies and deceptions. All the same, so much will be written about this war — so much already has been written — that I feel the need to justify my own contribution to these piles of paper, miles of words. Therefore I will confess that I cannot be objective. I write in a state of raging anger, and shame, about what I saw and about what I am still seeing halfway through the year 2004. So this is entirely subjective. It has to be.

CHAPTER ONE

THE ENDS OF THE GRAVEYARD

... the idea of war has to be rescued from time to time by spectacular set-pieces, such as the Gulf War or the war in Afghanistan. But the Fourth World War is elsewhere. It is what haunts every world order, all hegemonic domination — if Islam dominated the world, terrorism would rise against Islam, for it is the world, the globe itself, which resists globalization.

— JEAN BAUDRILLARD, *THE SPIRIT OF TERRORISM*

Terrorism is the privatization of war.

— PRINCE HASSAN BIN TALEL

April was the cruellest month, as always, but March felt fairly spiteful too, if you were in Iraq.

"For your safety," Bassim keeps saying, as he helps me pack. "For your safety you must hurry now."

I have been staying in suburban East Baghdad with Bassim, his wife Rana and their ten-year-old daughter Amira for the past week, but now it's time for all of us to move on. It is March 24, and the bombing has been more or less constant, day and night, for three days. The so-called Coalition is closing in and everyone thinks they know what will happen before the British and American troops enter the city: they'll raze it to the ground and kill everyone they see. But, given this uniquely pessimistic future, the average Iraqi is fairly calm. No one thinks he will miss Saddam Hussein terribly, and as long as the body count of loved ones is not too high, the clouds of war could well be lined with silver. Or at least tin.

Last night, Bassim and I were smoking cigarettes at the end of his garden, because Rana won't let us smoke in the house. We were close to the wall separating his property from a patch of overgrown parkland surrounding the ruin of a local government building that took a cruise missile during the Gulf War. There had been some bombing earlier, but it was distant, and now the night was oddly peaceful. The clouds overhead had even opened to reveal a few serene stars blinking indifferently. Bassim had been fondly recalling his student days in London, where we'd first met years ago. Then he asked me what was my fondest memory. I was wondering whether I had one when he put an urgent finger to his lips.

"Sssssh!"

He pointed at the wall, on the other side of which were heard stealthy noises. We both killed our cigarettes and crouched in the dead grass. A crack in the wall's brickwork showed the distinct khaki of military legs: the Republican Guard, I assumed. Bassim and I would be in big trouble if the authorities found me staying here — very big trouble. Although I wore a Canadian maple leaf pin, I also carried a British passport — and Britain was at war with Iraq. In fact, Britain basically *was* what made it a "coalition" and not just the United States. I somehow doubted, however, that a special RG unit had been assigned to root out stray journalists, what with Baghdad under attack from ground, sea and air. What with the promised "regime change" that would definitely put an end to a Republican Guardsman's "privileges," if not a good deal else about the life of elite-force members, including life itself. The upper echelons of this army had as much reason to fight with all their might as Saddam's sons had.

"Oi! Keef!"

Throaty, whispered, it was still the unmistakable twang of a South London accent.

"'ere!" The voice indicated something.

Bassim and I did not move, barely even breathed. The wrecked cartilage in my left knee popped, as it is wont to do, with the sensation of a red-hot tent peg driven into the joint. My heart appeared to be trying to escape from its prison through the bars of my rib cage.

There was then the faintest, cricket-like chirp of speech coming through a radio receiver, and the huddle of men passed on all but noiselessly. Dogs started barking irritably.

Moments later, there was a jowl-shuddering explosion about a kilometre away — which was about as near as you would want it to be — and all the lights went out. The cracked mud shook beneath us. I could feel my hair and skin wobbling in the percussive wave, as we were showered with debris, some of it wet. Just as we each were about to say something banal, an enormous, crunchy crash was heard, then the house next door — no more than ten metres away — sagged and, like a man on all fours whose legs have just given out, collapsed quite slowly in a wedge to its front wall. Only later did I learn that what had crushed the house was a two-ton slab of concrete hurled from the explosion.

"Allah!" yelled Bassim, bolting clumsily across the gardens.

His parents lived in that house, which was writhing, grunting and screaming like a wounded beast as concrete subsided and metal rods ground against each other.

I ran behind Bassim, who had reached a side door and now tore at it until the entire fixture came away in his hands. He carefully placed the door on its side and went to enter the house.

I had gone through that same doorway a dozen times over the past week and was thus nearly as surprised as Bassim to find, where the kitchen had been, a choking cloud of dust surrounding a mound of concrete and plaster in great chunks.

"Baba!" Bassim called out, desolately. Mummy!

We started a futile attempt to clear away the rubble, but most of it was still threaded to steel reinforcing rods, thus immovable. Bassim tried to squeeze around the mound, but there were more obstructions behind it. Something had caught fire inside, too, and was sending out a thin, acrid vapour with black tadpoles floating in it. Most ominous, though, was the fact that no human sounds came from inside.

Along with Bassim's mother and father, a great-aunt and two uncles lived in there.

Anti-aircraft batteries opened up — three or four of them — a mile or so away, throwing broken loops of light from tracer shells into the vast bruised underbelly of deep, embattled clouds. Almost immediately, a quick succession of three enormous earth-shaking explosions left my ears pulsing with static, and propped up the variegated sky with billowing pillars of black smoke fizzing with sparks. The percussive wave shattered windows all around us. Shouts and cries came from far and near. There were no more fiery beads from that defensive battery, but several others had started up much further away. I heard the low phasing effect of a Stealth bomber — which vibrates in the plexus — and immediately vomited my dinner quite neatly into a flower pot. Whenever the sky lit up one could see dozens of bulbous sooty columns that looked as if they were cascading down out of the clouds rather than pouring up from burning buildings.

"Be careful," I said.

It seemed a ludicrous statement in the face of such monumental carelessness.

"My Mummy and Daddy," Bassim explained, the strained rationality in his voice making his words sound like plastic. "I must help them ... in there ... They're in there," he added, in case I had forgotten who lived in the house.

Bassim tried climbing up the exterior wall, but his efforts just dislodged more concrete and masonry. We picked our way around to the rear, looking for a way in but finding nothing viable. The fire inside was getting worse, snapping and spitting as it gorged on kerosene and cooking oils.

Then, on the far side, we found an entire upper room exposed intact to the black night air. Its outer wall had been peeled away, like a doll's house or an architectural illustration, revealing the interior: a tiny wardrobe, a small armchair, a little writing table, a narrow pallet with a diminutive person asleep beneath pristine white sheets.

There was a noise like some giant beating on a steel door with a 200-foot-long hammer. Then came an intense roaring sound followed by a staggeringly huge explosion not far away. My cheeks flapped and lips opened involuntarily as the wave hit, shattering more glass and causing the dying house to lurch as if galvanized. Great pistons plunged through the tiny canals in my ears; I felt as if my brain was being squeezed by big soft hands.

Bassim, oblivious, had already scrambled up the brickwork and was soon cradling the little head. It was his great-aunt. She had probably died of heart failure around the time of impact.

I recalled the only thing she had ever said to me, the day before:

"You must tell Mr. Bush that this is not a good thing he does here. He thinks it is a good thing, but it is not at all good. Ask him which of his own children he would allow to die to destroy Saddam Hussein. He will not be willing to see his own child die for this. Then why must we see our children die for this madness? This is what you must write for the *Americani* to read ... is it not so?" She had turned to the others for support here.

"Aunty wants to be the next Minister of Information," Bassim had told me, gently mocking the frail old lady.

"I don't have the imagination for that any more," she had said, not missing a beat. "Mohammed Sayeed Sahaf is doing a fine job, anyway, and this is because, you see, he always wanted to be a writer of novels. The 'Mother of All Battles' was his phrase, you know?"

"This is the Mother of All Aunties," Bassim had confided to me, loudly enough for his great-aunt to hear.

"Take him back to England with you," she had asked me, suddenly very serious. "Rana and Amira too. There is no life for them here. Make him go back with you ..."

Her voice had sounded so desolate and drained that I simply nodded to her grimly — Yes, I will, I will. I promise.

"Bassim, promise you will go back with Mr. Robert. Take your family. Get out of here!"

"Oh, Aunty, don't be so grim. Look on the bright side. Everything will turn out fine — you'll see ..."

Leaving Bassim alone with his particular grief and loss, I made my way around to the front of the house, where his parents and the two uncles were at that moment standing, unharmed but in shock. They had been visiting a neighbour across the way when their house was wasted.

I felt truly, toe-curlingly awkward — the way you do when your fellow countrymen, for no good reason, have just destroyed the home of a friend's parents and killed his fiesty, beloved great-aunt.

Did George W. Bush have a great-aunt whom he loved dearly?

Rana, Bassim's wife, started gesturing at me to get inside their house. Like a robot, I obeyed, my legs feeling leaden and unpredictable, like robots' legs. Instead of opening the front door, I stepped through the shattered window into a hallway crunchy with shards of broken glass. Inside, I found Amira, still asleep but standing on the glinting stream of mirrors that flowed back into the house. She was rubbing her puffy face distractedly, her mouth frozen in a cry of utter desolation, her closed eyes sticky with old tears. I picked her up and hummed some half-remembered lullaby until she went limp in my arms. War is not very good for children.

The children of Baghdad were a heartbreaking spectacle by now, hollow-eyed and inattentive from lack of sleep, pale and restless from lack of play. They looked like little junkies, the cast of a kids' *Naked Lunch*. Sitting there in the heaving shadows of Bassim's resonant living room, I thought of cloyingly sentimental, American-style anti-war campaigns ... *for the children. What if everyone refused to fight? Don't kill his Mummy and Daddy, they're all he's got ... This was little Ahmed's home — now where will he live? "My Teddy Bear's in there ..."* War also makes one prey to foolish notions.

The howl of someone in great pain grew ever closer outside, but I was more concerned that it not wake the sleeping child than I was to seek out its cause — the sorrow of a mother whose son was bleeding to death in her arms. Then the air-raid sirens screamed in slow motion. *A little late, aren't we?* But it was I who had been premature. Once again the city lit up all around us and the earth shook below.

I was glad to hold another human being.

It was very close this time, each whistling, whining thunderclap sounding nearer.

Is this it? Lulla-lulla-lullaby ...

My mind felt paralyzed. I had to remember to breathe, my whole body tensed in an arc over Amira, instinctively offering the sleeping child all the pathetic protection it could. Adrenalin surged into my guts, drying out my mouth and making the tips of my fingers throb. I imagined I was plugged into the Baghdad grid, an effervescent tide ebbing and flowing through me as the lights powered up and down. I had to protect the child; I had to hum the lullaby; I had to tense for the next blast; I had to breathe whenever possible.

I am a protecting, humming, tensing, breathing machine ... I am soaked in the chemistry of fear ... I am close to death ...

There was something else. In those spasms of tension and adrenalin that came with each new explosion or blast, I found a blinding pool of light opening in the third eye. It had begun as a star-like peephole, but each time I saw it there was more; and it no longer seemed to be opening to me, for I was opening to the world within it. The light was almost solid in there, and although I could not see them, I knew there were dear friends, long-lost relatives, teachers and lovers waiting in there. I knew there was healing in there, too, a healing ocean of balm.

A healing bomb ...

And love ... a whole universe of love was in there. You were safe in there. Safe forever. Amira would be safe in there too. Everyone would be safe in there.

Except the killers and the liars, and the hard hearts ...

I wondered if I should attempt to go through. Then I wondered if I was actually dead and was just waiting to get adjusted to a new reality before moving on.

"We must go to hospital!" yelled Bassim. "Can you bring Amira with you?"

As Bassim's voice boomed out, what it was saying seemed to expand indefinitely, so I could edit the contents. In the same flashbulb moment, the porthole onto a universe of light closed like a camera iris. The walls were black rubber flesh.

"Coming, we're coming ..."

Sitting in the BMW's passenger seat, I soothed the rudely awoken child while watching the wholly unfamiliar streets of the City of Dreadful Night smear past the windshield.

"Ba-baaa ... Pa-paaa ... Want sleeping, Papa ..."

She opened her eyes suddenly, and finding me, not Bassim or Rana, staring back at her, Amira's face momentarily turned to stone. In her eyes was a look of pained concentration, as if she was wrestling with the nature and meaning of life itself. Then, clearly realizing how I fit into the scheme of things, her face turned, twisted and wrung out its tears like a sponge-cloth.

"No-oh-woah, no-oh ... Not YOU-hoo-ooh ... No-no-no-woah-ohhh!" Her screaming wail had that tightening, strangulated quality, like an alley-cat in heat — as if something was being twisted dangerously inside.

How much can a little girl's heart take? Could my little girl take this?

Two cars were burning near the freeway ramp, brilliant orange flames and thick, black cumulus smoke twisting out of them. As we reversed to take a side road around them, a man whose face was entirely covered in blood started beating on our hood. Eerily white eyes stared wildly through the holes in this wet, red mask. He held up his other arm while continuing to deliver great dull thumps on the metal. There was something in his upraised hand. It was another hand, a smaller hand — possibly a child's or a woman's hand.

"Bassim! We cannot stop!" This was Rana's voice.

The big car snaked back, colliding with something, then turning in an arc to growl off into total darkness. A lone tall street-lamp showed the next on-ramp. We narrowly avoided hitting a pile of concrete and were turning towards the expressway when Bassim jumped on the brakes, bringing us to a short, slithering halt.

"Allah!"

Bassim peered ahead in open-mouthed disbelief.

Why had we stopped?

It was only when Amira ceased her wriggling, relentless bid to escape from my grasp that I could see what lay ahead. Just where the ramp turned to join the expressway there was a huge, ragged hole that took up all three lanes. Bowed reinforcing rods curled down out of sight, looking like the muscles of a giant sphincter. Smashed blocks of concrete still clung to many of them, and between the rods you could see the different layers that comprised the road, some darker, some lighter.

"Shit," said Bassim, looking at me as if he'd nearly run a red light. "The *state* of these roads ..."

"Makes you wonder what you pay taxes for, don't it?" I said, as if it were a bad comedy routine we had performed long ago.

"These politicians," muttered Bassim, reversing again, and then attempting a three-point turn, "they promise you anything to get themselves elected. Then once they're in power ... they ..."

"... they build you hell and call it heaven?" I suggested.

"Call it Baghdad, you mean ..."

We zigged and zagged, hitting rubble every few seconds. Then, after we had turned onto a darkened cul-de-sac, the sky ahead was suddenly striated with chains of yellowy-white fire. Overhead, there was a blinding flash immediately followed by an over-amplified thunderclap. A kilometre or so off, something large began to burn furiously, flooding the high, black air with golden light. From where the thunderclap had come, something arced down, leaving a plume of smoke in its wake.

"My God!"

Bassim looked as if he was trying to strangle the steering wheel as he turned us around and, crashing over a debris-strewn sidewalk, careened back onto the main highway, looking back over his shoulder every few seconds.

"Which way?" he demanded.

Looking back, I realized that whatever had just been spewed from the clouds was heading towards us at an incredible speed.

"You go left," I told him. "Sorry, right ... Go right!"

The smouldering carcass of a bus blocked the way ahead.

"Shit-shit-shit!" Bassim beat on the dashboard, head bowed.

I rolled down my window and leaned out backwards so I could look directly above. The hollow whistling noise surprised me. It was extremely near. Then a long, narrow cylinder with smoke and flames pouring from its rear passed overhead not a hundred metres away. It moved strangely slowly, as if whatever misfortune had just befallen it merely increased its lugubrious weight, turning the air all around it into glue.

"T-hawk?" inquired Bassim.

"Some kind of cruiser ..."

It must have been a Tomahawk or some other kind of incoming missile that had been hit by anti-aircraft fire and was now frighteningly off target. Given our proximity and its height, the missile promised to hit ground-zero about a block away. But instead it went on falling, the smoke trail wobbling ahead like a blurred mast and sails. There was no explosion, not even the thud of a crash.

The cars outside the hospital's main entrance looked as if they'd been thrown there rather than driven and parked. Some were virtually propped against the triage unit's wall, with their doors left open, and even their engines still running. It looked as if a swarm of massive metal flies had all tried to swoop through the entrance at the same time, colliding in a dazed heap.

Inside, there were no medical personnel at Emergency Reception, nor beyond it either. Had that missile hurtled in here and reamed out the entire hall? Something big and nasty must have been this way. On both sides and down the central area, people crouched, sat or sprawled on the floor; a bare few were actually standing, or being propped up by the walls. Everyone was soaked with big damp patches of blood, some from their own wounds, some from the injuries of those they carried or supported. The walls and their posters or pictures bore countless messy handprints in brick red, and the linoleum floor was festooned with bloody footprints leading into or out of a seemingly endless succession of crimson puddles.

I don't know which was worse: the sights or the sounds. A wind tunnel of howling, a bomb shelter of screaming, an artery of crying, a subway of wailing — it was a ceaseless stream of undifferentiated despair, from which the individual scream, cry, groan or howl emerged like a passing headlight, piercing through to the core before fading back into its torrent of terror, pain and misery. I thought we would all begin to slide across the blood and off down into hell.

Bassim held his great-aunt's tiny body, which spilled like a towel from his arms, as if she had been filleted of her skeleton and muscles. No one paid any attention to us ... nor to each other. A mother whose face was blue with bruising, whose torso was plastered with mud, blood and shit, held a small boy in her thick jelly arms. His clothes had been cut away and you could see where one leg ended in a dripping bandaged stump just under the knee, and the other in a gory hollow inside the pelvis. He was blueish-white in the face and his big brown eyes stared, scarcely blinking, taking in everything but seeing nothing. The mother's eyes were simply vacant, empty, void of feeling. Every now and then she would, with infinite care and compassion, rearrange the boy's seating in her well-upholstered arms, gently tilting him back enough so he could see all around without straining himself unduly. He had lost almost all his blood and the cessation of bleeding this brought seemed like a mercy.

"Sahib ... sahib!"

Something tugged at my trouser cuffs.

Looking down, I saw an old man with a toothless concave mouth from which thin, metallic bubbles of blood would swell up, billowing out as much as ten centimetres before vanishing into mist.

"Sahib!" he said, turning his hips in order to gain a better grip on my ankles.

As he turned, the right side of his face came into view. It looked as if someone had tried very hard to shave it with an oxy-acetylene torch. Red, orange, yellow and glistening with pus, the pore-craters and the ragged little mound where an ear had been were agony's very image. Amira gawked in disbelief. How good an idea was it to bring her in here anyway? But I was not capable of thought, so I literally couldn't decide the answer. Her parents wanted her with them ... *It's up to them to tell me what to do with her ...*

Beyond the old man and curled in a fetal position in a bright red pool, a young man in his twenties lay peacefully sucking his thumb. Dead, I noticed. Peaceful and dead: the dead were the only peaceful ones in here.

The noise! It was a scraping inside my brain ...

Bassim kept asking where he could find a doctor, but people did not even reply to him. Some shook their heads, others smiled ironically, and still others rolled up their eyes then hung their faces low over the hideous floor, breathing a faint monotonous tune through their nostrils. Then a wealthy-looking woman in a silk house-coat said in perfect English:

"We have no doctors here. They're all at the front ..."

The front of what?

Along with an absence of doctors, she went on to add, the hospital didn't have bandages or antiseptic any more, either. It didn't even have any room; it didn't have anything. It could not treat anyone. It really wasn't a hospital now.

"So why are they all here?"

"Where are they going to go? Everywhere's the same. I have telephoned the other hospitals and clinics. They are all over capacity. There is no staff and no medicines or supplies. This is the End of All!"

Does she mean the end of the staff, medicine and bandages, or The End?

She looked me in the eyes and, in a stern tone, told me that America was doing an evil thing in Iraq ...

"Why they do like this? What we do to them that they hate us so? Can you tell me what crimes *we* have done ... ?"

What ... does she think I'm going to defend U.S. foreign policy here now?

Trying to head upstairs to the wards, we came across one of the vanishing doctors, hunched down in a stairwell, crying in great heaves and sobs.

"Oh my God!" he kept saying, over and over. "Oh my God!"

Bassim knew him, it seemed, and after calming him enough to get the great-aunt's corpse examined, took Amira from me. She occasionally looked back in gloating triumph, as if the loss of her wriggling eighty pounds would be what finally broke me. Kids are odd at such times, and the world so easily shrinks into a pore at the end of their nose. She had mercifully quite forgotten where we were ...

"Bury her for God's sake!" the doctor suddenly yelled, his eyes bulging and his cheeks florid. "Bury her, that's all I can do for you! Get her out of here! You don't bring the dead here! What is the matter with you?"

Bassim looked over and rolled his eyes, trying to quieten the cracking soul of the old doctor.

"She must have died from a heart failure on impact," the doctor said to no one in particular.

Amira then grasped the fact that her great-great-aunt was dead. She gazed around reproachfully for a few seconds and embarked on a prodigious gasping, crying, shuddering jag that lasted until it had wearied her into another fitful sleep. I don't remember how we got out of there. I just remember other awful scenes, in succession, like some terminal and interminable nightmare. I would rather forget them.

The next day there were rumours that a squad of British or American paratroopers had been seen in the neighbourhood and were probably responsible for blowing up a government warehouse and the local electricity station. Republican Guard units were now making a thorough search of the area. It was — for my safety — time for me to leave. Bassim and his family were also leaving, for a village an hour or so outside the city, where his parents knew some people who would take them in for the duration.

He was the first Iraqi I had ever met, an age earlier when it was America's gonzo barbarism in Vietnam that appalled us. We organized, protested, got arrested together. We shared defining moments of youth that began as souvenirs and went on to become valued treasures in memory's horde. With Bassim began my relationship with Iraq: it was a place to which I could always attach a human face. We lost touch for years, then found each other, found the friendship bright and strong as we found the terrible consequences that our choices in life had wrought. Whatever joy and light I found in Canada were always tempered by the thought of Bassim on his razor's edge in Saddam's Iraq. It was sometimes impossible for me to meet him when I came there, and this danger of a friendship causing harm gave me nightmares. Contact with foreign media was a daymare, Bassim had said, as I swore a solemn vow never to write anything using his real name. He thus has had many names, and has been many Iraqi voices.

But when I was able to escape my government minders and Bassim felt safe enough to roll the dice, we met like mad spies at tea shops or the homes of friends, laughing wildly, measuring the toll of years, then sharing the kind of news that sentenced you to death in Baghdad whether you were pitching it or catching it. We had planned to watch the end of this chapter in Iraq together, just as we had entered its pages together. I realize now that we both fantasized a celebration in which our friendship was liberated from its prison, looked forward to doing in Baghdad the kinds of things friends do in other cities. Yet our plans were suddenly unreachable, as plans so often are when their fruit is ripe upon the tree. This time had been somehow so much worse than expected, yet neither of us expressed his despair out loud; Baghdad did not need more teardrops. Instead we went about our tasks of exit. I watched us dealing with realities and thought, My God, look at us — we're men. We grew up after all.

No one had to tell me that I could not go with Bassim's family. I had intended to make my way downtown to the Palestine Hotel, yet suddenly I could not think of a single reason to do this, and in the same flash of insight I knew it was not Amira I had been carrying through the blood and fire of last night: it was my own daughter, whose love was now the only glittering prize I wanted from this world. I needed her innocence and goodness; I did not need to see the U.S. army's *son et lumière* show again. When the offer of a ride to Amman, Jordan, came up, I was only too pleased to accept the lifeline. I felt like I was going home.

Bassim seemed overjoyed at my decision, and I could not understand why. The answer only occurred to me recently: he did not want his friend to get killed. He was happy to know I would be safe. Bassim's light heart made me feel I'd joined the freedom train. We were out of here, off to safety.

It was the kind of hectic, bustling scene you associate with pleasant events, like going to the cottage. Everyone was yelling, and the pile of belongings seemed at least twice what their big Mercedes could accommodate. There was much All-right-then-I-won't-take-it, and How-long-does-he-think-this-bloody-war-will-last-he-wants-to-bring-the-kitchen-sink, but finally the seven of them were squeezed inside and nothing was left in the drive. I shan't ever forget the look of bemused despair on Bassim's face as we waved goodbye.

I don't know precisely what happened, but they're all dead now — the parents, the uncles, Bassim, Rana, little Amira. All gone. Their car was found burned out near Fallujah, and it's likely they were lit up by an American fighter jet on the lookout for fleeing members of Saddam's regime. Most Iraqis who can afford it drive the same big-engined, late-model BMW or Mercedes saloons. Both Bassim and his father were university professors. They had nothing to do with Saddam's regime.

Twelve days earlier, I had flown from Toronto to London — where Heathrow airport, massively tense, heavily guarded, edged in barbed wire, looked more like Colditz prison — then from London to Frankfurt, where I learned that Lufthansa had cancelled its flight to Amman, Jordan, fearing war was imminent. I then flew to Paris, where I found that Air France had cancelled its flight to Jordan too. There was, however, one to Athens, with a connecting flight to Beirut. I crossed Lebanon into Syria, and then travelled across the Syrian Desert to Iraq. Eight countries, three continents, one very long day.

One very long déjà vu, too. I had made almost the same trip twelve years earlier on the brink of the Gulf War. Then too the world had seemed to be bracing itself for calamity, like an old drunk skidding towards yet another car crash. The same sense of sick inevitability afflicted this impending barbarism. I must have watched twenty different news broadcasts in various countries that day, and not one of them raised the possibility of a peaceable outcome. Most news directors have their "source" at the Pentagon — it may well be the same guy — and the word had clearly been given. For most of the preceding week the focus had been on "when," not "if."

I must have had twenty conversations with the usual assortment of people a traveller meets, too, and there was only one topic on anyone's mind: the war. Unlike the 1991 war, however, everyone I spoke with was decidedly against it, though often for very different reasons. They also decidedly loathed George W. Bush. I made a note of the terms used across half the world to describe the president of the United States: hypocrite, liar, stupid, moron, cowboy, hick, fool, gunslinger, two-faced, warmonger, greedy, Zionist pawn, idiot, evil, dangerous, half-wit, trying to prove something to Daddy, blind and deaf, insane, ignorant, foolhardy, couldn't pass a grade ten history test, can't tell the difference between Iraq and Iran, makes Clinton look like a god, thinks Baghdad is two words, the myopic leading the blind, brain-dead, simpleton, a bad Christian, has watched too many movies, inhuman, a zombie, a tyrant, without conscience, lacking a soul, immoral, a greedy scoundrel, and well-intentioned but naive — this last being the most positive comment made.

With the exception of a few students, they were average people. There were no axes being ground, no ideologies on parade. I could not recall a president since Nixon who had been so universally reviled — and even Nixon evoked grudging praise for his diplomacy with China. People were personally offended by the junior Bush, it seemed. The very idea of him enraged them. That any national leader could so widely be perceived as stupid said something vitally important — if only about the calibre of White House PR.

Everyone I encountered had the same sense of inevitability: war was inevitable *because the U.S. Government wanted it.* There was something wrong with this, for a start. The reasons why it was wanted, I heard from person after person, *had nothing to do with the U.S. Government's stated objectives.* Speculation about the "real reasons" varied — oil, world domination, Israel's security — but it was very much variations on a theme.

The same negative view prevailed when the subject of U.S. foreign policy and the United Nations came up. The U.N. was only shown respect by Washington when it supported U.S. goals, many people observed, a large number adding that the U.N.'s headquarters ought to be moved to a more neutral location. There is, of course, nothing astounding or even new about such observations, yet to hear them from the lips of people who do not professionally discuss such issues made them seem like revelations. Too much of what we fancy to be open debate on current affairs is in reality a scripted simulation tailored to the requirements of television, which is more concerned with myth than it is with reality.[2] But when reality takes on the shape of formal tragedy, we planetary citizens feel impelled to become its Greek chorus, filling the sudden vacuum perceived in the media, which regard emotional outbursts and moral indignation on the news as unprofessional. Suddenly being exposed to so much unrestrained comment was like throwing open the windows in an all-night bar, and the mosaic of voices echoed around my head as I travelled across Europe to the Middle East:

George, a businessman from Leeds: "The U.S. army surrounds the country and starts bombing and threatening Saddam while the U.N. inspectors are still working and while negotiations to avoid war are still underway! — *that's* what I call negotiating in bad faith."

Len, a porter: "We hear nothing but how bad Saddam is, how many people he's killed. But who can tell you how many people the Americans have killed over the past thirty years? I bet you it's far, far more ..."

Jean-Claude, bartender: "Giving a man like Saddam forty-eight hours to leave — it's insulting! I think they try all the time to bait him ... Because he have big ego, lot of pride."

Jergen, computer analyst: "With America it is all business, bottom lines. If they cared about the suffering of the Iraqis they would have stopped their embargo — because *that* is the cause of the suffering ..."

Marie-France, public-relations executive: "Bush is a little man. He always seems way out of his depth. So why would he do this? Obviously there must be people more powerful than he is who want it."

Johannes, accountant: "This is disgraceful. I don't think ever in history there was such a big powerful country pretending that attacking such a weak, inferior nation was a war. This is not a brave or dignified thing to do. Americans should be feeling ashamed to have such leaders."

Bob, golf pro: "I'm fucking sick about the way they [the Americans] bully everyone into doing what they want. I think Bush is a lying creep ... I feel sorry for the poor Iraqis."

Hannibal, systems consultant: "It is thoroughly disgusting the way America goes on as if it had never done anything bad ... for bad reasons. Iraq, of course, has never done anything right. But when you control the media the way Washington — or the big business interests that comprise American status quo — does over there, no one else gets a look-in."

Grace, waitress: "Americans seem so badly educated on the whole — can't they see what a liar Bush is? I don't know what's the matter with that country these days. They've forgotten everything they once believed ... and now they're blind and stupid and greedy."

Tomas, engineer: "Globalization is just a euphemism for the American Empire — which will be the world. They need to control the oil because their war machine won't run on solar power."

Christina, nursing consultant: "They keep changing their reasons for war — who can believe anything they say?"

Karim, cab driver: "My people believe the Israelis want this whole region for themselves. If there is war, we are going to believe it even more strongly."

Abd, café manager: "They say Saddam work for the CIA. Possible this is his mission: to give the Americans Iraq and her oil, yes?"

This was a good one, this last one, exemplifying the Arab view in general: don't like Saddam *or* America. Or as one Syrian put it: "Like you people say: they're just different kinds of asshole ..."

The different kinds of asshole had been in especially good form while I was flying the empty skies, too. Bush had given Iraq one final ultimatum: either Saddam and his sons leave the country by midnight or we will attack. It came over as one final and cunning insult: the likelihood of Saddam packing his bags being about the same as the likelihood of a peaceful solution. For his part, Saddam appeared alongside his sons, all smirking like wolves, in a video taped down in one of the family's Gothic threat lairs, saying, Bush should leave America. Ha-ha. They were all smoking cigars the size of telegraph poles, as if they hadn't had this much fun since '91. At times like this you had to concede that Iraq's leader for the past thirty years was one helluva guy. I scrutinized this broadcast minutely, looking for signs of strain, signs of weakness, signs that Saddam was taking all this as seriously as everyone else was. There weren't any — just like the last time. If anything, he seemed more relaxed and confident than he had when I'd interviewed him back in 1990, just before he became the Butcher of Baghdad. Now he looked more like the Jolly Baker of Baghdad.

Before the threat of war emerged, if you could have secretly polled Iraqis and asked them, "Would you emigrate to the U.S.A. if you could?," Saddam and his family, along with a few members of the Revolutionary Command Council, stood to be ceded the entire country. Now, however, Iraqis were distinctly hostile to America — even given the fact that those interviewed on the subject by foreign journalists knew they'd be picking broken bottles out of their rectums if they said anything different. After years of watching Iraq, I could tell official from actual reactions. Not that anyone should find it surprising that the civilian response to a threat of massive aerial bombardment is rarely positive.

Ironically, the first casualty of the Information Age has been comprehension. Once upon a time, the content of sensitive government information — the facts — was zealously guarded from us. Statesmen like Henry Kissinger believed implicitly that government should be conducted in secrecy, because the general public were not equipped to understand the complex exigencies it entailed. Indeed, the uncovering of one lie was once sufficient to bring down an entire administration. As media proliferated, however, and the flow of information speeded up, it must have come to someone's attention that facts of a devastating nature, when leaked or otherwise coaxed from hiding, were having a less than devastating impact, because, in America at least, the public increasingly had little or no context in which to place this content. Content without context — a condition that television news has come to exemplify — is like language without imagery. It may be heard or read but it is not comprehended, it doesn't sink in. On TV the context is generally more content — factoid placed beside factoid like snowflakes in a blizzard. The effect of this is well recreated by the "Harper's Index" section of *Harper's* magazine, where factoids — polls, statistics, quotes, surveys — appear to shed light on other factoids merely by being placed next to them. Add to this blizzard the propagandizing spin of government press releases and the result is that we, the viewers, are snowed under. Fact follows fact, day after day, and many of the facts are state lies. For a lie to become truth it merely has to be repeated.

Showing an innate understanding of television's mythic substructure, the U.S. government has grown accustomed to placing its enemies or targets in a Manichaean framework of Good versus Evil. The goodness of American intentions goes as unquestioned as the boundless evil of its enemies' machinations. Take the fact that the regime of Saddam Hussein is directly responsible for the deaths of over 400,000 Iraqis. Bad. Yet placed beside the fact that since 1991 the U.S. government has been directly responsible for the deaths of over 500,000 Iraqi children alone, Saddam's crime would seem the lesser. In reality, both crimes are unpardonable. But when the corporate media are merely extensions of the state — as U.S. media largely were before and during the Iraq war — the evil remains wholly evil and the good wholly good. Any suggestion that this is not so becomes sacrilege, punishable. Voices of dissent exist, of course, but they are not usually heard, and even if they are it is in a form drastically diluted by the sheer quantity of disinformation surrounding them.

Charles Lewis, the former CBS journalist who now heads the Center for Public Integrity, has said that if the media had challenged President George W. Bush's deceptions, the invasion of Iraq might not have happened; it would have been exposed and untenable.[3] The invasion was justified by the "fact" that Saddam posed an imminent threat to both America and his own neighbours and was developing an arsenal of nuclear and biochemical weapons. This "fact" was a lie.

In Cairo, Egypt, on February 24, 2001, American Secretary of State Colin Powell said: "He [Saddam Hussein] has not developed any significant capability with respect to weapons of mass destruction. He is unable to use conventional power against his neighbors ... The [U.S.] policy of containment has effectively disarmed the Iraqi dictator."[4] On May 15, 2001, Powell added to this, saying that Saddam had not been able to "build his military backup or to develop weapons of mass destruction for the last ten years ... America has been successful in keeping him in a box."[5] Two months later, in July 2001, Bush's security adviser, Condoleeza Rice, also described a weak, divided and militarily defenceless Iraq. "Saddam does not control the northern part of his country," she said. "We aim to keep his arms from him. His military forces have not been rebuilt."[6]

It is impossible to reconcile these statements by two of the administration's most senior officials with those made by Bush and others — including Powell and Rice themselves — in the months leading up to the invasion. Powell even produced a document before the U.N. purporting to prove that Iraq had attempted to buy uranium ore from Niger; but the document turned out to be a forgery. We still don't know who forged it. The failure to locate any "weapons of mass destruction" is irrelevant, therefore, since the U.S. government clearly knew there were no such weapons to begin with. A fraud was perpetrated on the entire world. A weak and defenceless nation was attacked, invaded and occupied by the greatest superpower in history on a pretext that is a transparent deception, a lie. This should bother someone. My friend Bassim and his whole family were killed. This bothers me.

In Britain, the only other active member of the so-called Coalition, Prime Minister Tony Blair's reasons for invading Iraq have fared no better. His "dossier" on Saddam's "weapons of mass destruction" of January 2003 also proved on scrutiny to be a lie. Part of it was even plagiarized from an American student's Ph.D. thesis, preserving the same spelling mistakes, and changing terms like "opposition groups" to "terrorist groups." The rest of the dossier was refuted before the Hutton Inquiry in August and September 2003 by Blair's senior intelligence officials and even his own chief of staff. That the rationale for the deaths of more than ten thousand civilians should turn out to be nothing more than shoddily incompetent lying must also surely bother someone other than me.

As for Iraq's ties to al-Qaeda, it is highly unlikely that Saddam Hussein would have had any sort of relationship with an organization whose leader had repeatedly called for the overthrow of the Ba'athist regime in Baghdad. Indeed, just a month before the suicide attacks on the World Trade Center and the Pentagon, Osama bin Laden had urged Iraqi Muslims to rise up against Saddam, a secularist whom he viewed as an enemy of Islam. The U.S. government most certainly knew this while it was claiming the opposite to be true. If al-Qaeda has a presence within the Iraqi opposition to U.S. occupation, it is an ad hoc, post-Saddam arrangement whose existence must be blamed on the Americans themselves. When U.S. officials in Iraq refer to "foreign terrorists" it is as if the Americans have become Iraqis, or the Iraqis don't exist.

Rhetoric aside, what other justifications were there for the invasion? They amounted to the fact that Saddam was a dictator whose brutal regime had enslaved Iraq, which yearned to be free of him. That this is at least partially true no one disputes — though perhaps not all Iraqis yearned to be free of Saddam, who managed to embody a kind of nationalistic ideal. But when Colin Powell called Saddam a "dictator" in Cairo in February 2001, he was standing next to the Egyptian dictator Hosni Mubarak, whose regime, to those opposing it, is also fairly brutal and entirely undemocratic. The difference between Saddam and Mubarak is that the latter is supported by America — as are the dictators of Saudi Arabia, Kuwait, Qatar and many other countries, some of them every bit as brutal as Saddam's Iraq.

Let us not, however, fall into the linguistic trap of using or abusing certain terms without defining them, as Bush and his gang habitually do. When they use words like "freedom," "democracy," "liberty," "peace" and so on, they generally mean the opposite of what the words mean to me. Their notion of human rights also has little to do with the term's actual meaning — ask the prisoners in Guantanamo Bay how their rights are being upheld.

The difference between a dictatorship and a true democracy is that citizens of a dictatorship do not get to hold elections for the leadership every few years. In a democratic election there are typically many parties representing many aspects of the society and fielding many candidates for the leadership. In order to win such an election, one of the two or three major parties usually has to form an alliance with a few of the larger minority parties, and in doing so has to offer them meaningful roles in the future government. To form a new minority party a candidate merely has to gain a small percentage of the vote. There is often a modest sum of money deposited that will be forfeited if the candidate fails to gain enough votes, thereby protecting the process from all but the wealthiest crackpots. Such is the democratic model found in, say, Israel, Italy or Britain, indeed everywhere in the European Union, where you find the full spectrum of political thought not only represented but frequently playing an active role in government through ad hoc alliances with the bigger parties anxious to swing a close-call election. Thus the spectacle of a recent French government (1997–2002) headed by a Socialist (Lionel Jospin) and containing both Communists and Greens, with a member of the latter party holding the post of minister of the environment. You also see genuine shifts in policy — even foreign policy — such as the recent decision by Spain's Socialists, newly elected in March 2004, to withdraw the country's troops from the Coalition of the Willing in Iraq. Even Tony Blair had to argue his case for joining the Coalition himself before the House of Commons, and argue it long and hard.

Such characteristics of true democracy are unthinkable in the U.S., where voters are given the "choice" between two parties whose key policies barely differ once you peer beyond the election rhetoric. The Democrats and Republicans may differ in style and tone but, particularly since World War II, the imperial content of their world views is virtually indistinguishable, and rarely discussed in public. And the political parties are in any case merely window dressing, a distraction from the reality behind them, in which Congress, the Pentagon, the CIA and the FBI, along with a vast bureaucracy, provide the continuity of a one-party oligarchic state. This is why U.S. foreign policy remains quintessentially imperialist and exploitative, pursuing identical goals no matter who sits in the White House.

What is remarkable, however, is the extent to which the average American citizen believes what the oligarchy wants him to believe — much of which is distinctly beneficial to the oligarchs at the expense of the citizens. At the root of this is a Big Lie: that, as Ronald Reagan liked to say, America is a place where anyone can get rich. Any economist will admit that this idea is provably false. As it stands, less than five percent of the American population owns more than ninety-five percent of its wealth and assets. This five percent is in turn effectively controlled by a handful of families who, through corporate sponsorships and donations, wield considerable — if not total — control over the things that most affect them. No doubt there is fairly wide disagreement between them on these issues, but they nonetheless result in the affirmation that what is good for the oligarchs is good for America, where being poor is a kind of sin. Yet such is the level of oligarchic propaganda that even many of the poor oppose those things that would most benefit them, like access to a decent education. Let us not pretend that the United States has anything to do with freedom or democracy here. Sadly, it does not.

CHAPTER TWO

PAX AMERICANA

We have about 50% of the world's wealth but only 6.3% of its population ... In this situation, we cannot fail to be the object of envy and resentment. Our real task in the coming period is to devise a pattern of relationships which will permit us to maintain this position of disparity without positive detriment to our national security. To do so, we will have to dispense with all sentimentality and day-dreaming; and our attention will have to be concentrated everywhere on our immediate national objectives. We need not deceive ourselves that we can afford today the luxury of altruism and world-benefaction.

— GEORGE KENNAN, FORMER HEAD OF THE
U.S. STATE DEPARTMENT POLICY PLANNING STAFF
AND LEADING ARCHITECT OF U.S. FOREIGN POLICY
AFTER WORLD WAR II, FEBRUARY 24, 1948 [7]

Iraq is not a place that can be understood through events of the past few years or even the past few decades. Its peoples sit atop seven thousand years of continuous civilization, the details of which they are both aware and proud. To be ignorant of this vast context is to badly misinterpret much of what happens to Iraq today. Moreover, it is not sufficient to know the history; one must know it as Iraqis know it, which entails becoming familiar with the Arab and Persian historians. For the history we recite in the West was recorded with a European bias, and tends to posit the Arabs and Islam as The Enemy. Those who expect the Arab histories to display an opposite bias will be pleasantly surprised, for they are on the whole far more objective than their Western counterparts. Indeed, some of the Arab scholars, such as Ibn Khaldun (1332–1406), are, in Arnold Toynbee's words, "among the greatest historians we have."

We are not just ignorant of Iraq's ancient history, however, for it seems that we have conveniently forgotten even the history of America's conflict with Saddam. Since it is not possible to view the last war without an understanding of the events preceding it, I have selected here a few salient details from the past twenty years of U.S.-Iraq relations.

JUNE 7, 1981. Without any prior warning, sixteen Israeli warplanes destroy Iraq's Osirak nuclear reactor near Baghdad. The attack was especially savage, deploying cluster bombs designed to explode while rescue workers were picking through the rubble for survivors. Most of the world decried the attack, which was soon forgotten all the same. It would be ten years before Iraq responded by firing Scud missiles at Israel during the Gulf War.

DECEMBER 20, 1983. Donald Rumsfeld arrives in Baghdad as special envoy from President Ronald Reagan. According to the official notetaker at their meeting, Rumsfeld conveyed to Saddam "the President's greetings and expressed his pleasure at being in Baghdad." Saddam, it should be noted, had already established himself as a brutal dictator or, as that week's edition of *Newsweek* put it, "a murderous thug who supported terrorists and was trying to build a nuclear weapon."

America's chief concern at the time, of course, was Iran and its Ayatollah Khomeini, whom Washington portrayed as chief of demons. Iraq had gone to war with Iran, and that was the substance of Rumsfeld's meeting. Over the following five years, until the conflict finally ended, the United States supplied Saddam with economic aid and useful items such as a computerized database for his interior ministry, satellite military intelligence regarding

Iranian troop movements, tanks, cluster bombs, lethal bacteriological samples and the very same helicopters that were used to dump poison gas over Iraq's Kurdish citizens. When these atrocities finally came to light, the Reagan administration even lobbied to prevent any strong congressional condemnation of Iraq's dictator.

JULY 25, 1990, 1 P.M. Saddam takes the last official meeting he would have with a representative of the U.S. government until his capture on December 13, 2003. The American ambassador to Baghdad, April Glaspie, was summoned to discuss, among other things, the border dispute Iraq was having with Kuwait. George Bush Senior's administration had cordial relations with Iraq at that point; earlier the same year, Assistant Secretary of State John Kelley had gone so far as to call Saddam a "force of moderation" in the Middle East. When I interviewed Saddam, in May of 1990, he still viewed himself as a U.S. ally in the region, though he was painfully aware that America had also been supplying arms to Iran during the long war that saw a million dead and no clear result. The border dispute, along with money owed Iraq by Kuwait for defending the emirate against Iran, had been much on his mind then too. He had tried discussing both matters with the Kuwaitis several times but, as he told Ambassador Glaspie in the official transcript of their meeting, to no avail. They had even walked out arrogantly from the last meeting. What was more, he had recently learned that Kuwaiti oil companies were drilling diagonally through the disputed border into Iraq's oil. Enough was enough. Saddam then told Glaspie that he was contemplating military action against Kuwait and advised the U.S. not to get involved. His warning turned out to be unnecessary, though, for Glaspie next reassured him that "we have no opinion on Arab-Arab conflicts, like your border disagreement with Kuwait."[8]

A cautious man, Saddam rephrased his position vis-à-vis Kuwait twice more during the meeting, receiving each time the same formulaic reassurance: "We have no opinion on Arab-Arab conflicts ..." Glaspie even emphasized at one point that this position came directly from Secretary of State James Baker in Washington.

There would seem to be little reason to doubt that after this meeting, Saddam believed he had been given a green light to invade Kuwait.

While advising the U.S. against interfering, Saddam also said something that the events of this last war make all the more poignant:

"You can come to Iraq with aircraft and missiles, but do not push us to the point where we cease to care. And when we feel that you want to injure our pride and take away the Iraqis' chance of a high standard of living, then we will cease to care and death will be the choice for us. Then we would not care if you fired one hundred missiles for each missile we fired, because without pride life could have no value."

The transcript of this meeting is freely available, and its contents have never been disputed by either side. Why, then, is it not better known? Why is it never mentioned — or if it is mentioned, marginalized in significance and never quoted directly — in Western accounts of the Gulf War or biographies of Saddam?

It may well be that, as April Glaspie later explained in a *New York Times* interview, nobody thought "the Iraqis were going to take *all* of Kuwait ..." — from which one can infer that it would have been alright if Saddam had only taken part of Kuwait — but this hardly exonerates the administration. The fact remains that the invasion of Kuwait cannot be held against Saddam as the wanton, naked act of aggression that it is popularly conceived to have been. It provided both presidents Bush with the accusation they often levelled at Saddam, but which, given U.S. actions in the Caribbean and Central America, as well as the Israeli attack on the Osirak reactor, is sheer hypocrisy: that he was a "threat to his neighbours." To the dim sensibility of the average American presidential audience, of course, it contained the affront to Midwest values necessary to stir the mob into a mindless frenzy of bloodlust. People who could not tell you the difference between Iran and Iraq or Khomeini and Saddam were soon telling the corporate networks that Saddam should get his butt kicked. After September 11, 2001, Iraq's fate was sealed, whether it had connections to al-Qaeda or not.

Many Iraqis have told me that Saddam was a good ruler up to the war with Iran. Like most average citizens, they probably base this judgement on how well-off they were personally. Unpopular as it may be to say now, Iraq prospered under Saddam's leadership — if only because of the steep rise in oil prices during the 1970s. Unlike the rulers of Saudi Arabia, Saddam channelled the oil wealth into the nation's future, developing new businesses and building fine educational institutions that attracted students from all over the Arab world. He gave Iraq a highway system as good as anything in North America. When I first saw Baghdad in the early 1980s, it was an opulent and ostentatiously prosperous city, and fastidiously clean. It is no exaggeration to say that Saddam made Iraq into a showcase for the Arab world — and indeed U.S. ambassador April Glaspie congratulated him for doing so. She was not alone: the Saddam Gift Museum that used to be in Baghdad was filled with gifts from grateful U.S. governors, senators and congressional representatives. Whereas the oil boom made the princes of Saudi Arabia familiar figures in the playgrounds of Europe, in Iraq it established a middle class that represented a new and modern kind of Arab. It was during this period that Iraq's relationships with countries like Russia, Germany, Britain and France were first forged. On the Arab street, especially in countries such as Egypt that did not have a share in the oil boom, Saddam's reputation as a new Nasser, a leader who could potentially unite the Arab world, grew apace.

General Wafiq al-Samarrai, who was Saddam's Director of Military Intelligence, told me that Iraq's leader changed after the Israeli attack on the Osirak reactor: "He became more secretive and more paranoid. The fact that Israel was not punished by the international community for their attack also bothered him deeply. He began to suspect assassins and coup attempts everywhere, and began to spend more and more on building the army, to the exclusion of all else — except his own palaces and family."[9] Then came the long and terrible war with Iran, which inflicted massive casualties on both sides and swallowed up petro-dollars like nothing Saddam had previously experienced. Both Saudi Arabia and Kuwait had offered to reimburse Saddam for defending them against the Iranians, who had made their interests in territorial acquisition clear, yet no money was ever forthcoming.

The result was that, long before the Gulf War, Iraq was bankrupt; $40 billion is the sum Saddam told Ambassador Glaspie that he was owed by Kuwait, and she acknowledged her awareness of Iraq's financial predicament. At the close of this final meeting, Saddam asked Glaspie to convey a message to President Bush, saying it had come to his attention that certain elements with links both to the U.S. State Department and to the CIA were engaged in plots to persuade the more conservative Gulf states to cut off Iraq's economic aid. Saddam's message expediently stated that he knew President Bush and

Secretary of State James Baker (who had once been U.S. ambassador to Kuwait) could not possibly be involved with anything so wicked. Referring to the $40 billion owed by the Kuwaitis, the president of Iraq said, "Without Iraq they would not have had these sums and the future of the region would have been entirely different."

Glaspie offered no rebuttal of this, and indeed promised to convey the message to Bush.

By the time of his final meeting with U.S. ambassador Glaspie, Saddam had clearly sensed that American perfidy was afoot. He had also seen the shabby treatment meted out to his friend and fellow CIA stooge,[10] Muhammad Reza Pahlavi, the shah of Iran, when the shah was in exile in 1979-80 and wracked with cancer.[11] Furthermore, Saddam had recently been vilified by Voice of America broadcasts to the Middle East comparing him with fallen Eastern-Bloc dictators like Romania's Ceausescu. Someone had even sent him a videotape of Ceausescu's interrogation and execution at the hands of rebels, as a hint of what lay ahead. Although various American politicians had flown to Baghdad from time to time to assure him of the esteem in which he was held by Washington,[12] Saddam could read the writing on the wall. Iran had fallen to fundamentalist theocrats; Saudi Arabia looked as if it was heading in the same direction; therefore Iraq's oil was becoming increasingly vital in the eyes of those intending to call out the U.S. war machine — which had no immediate plans for conversion to solar power.

The Gulf War was what Alexander Haig, Reagan's first secretary of state, called a "demonstration war." It demonstrated that America's bite could be worse than its bark, and it allowed the Pentagon to demonstrate the deadly new hi-tech arsenal at its disposal. Any military chiefs around the world who had once entertained notions of locking horns with the U.S. were given pause. "Watch out," was the message, "you could be next." But the opportunity to remove Saddam from power that the war clearly presented was not taken, supposedly because of pressure brought to bear by the Saudi princes, who feared for their security if Iraq were to be destabilized. The security of Saudi Arabia was clearly a higher priority than the well-being of Iraqis, so Saddam was permitted to retreat back to Baghdad with much of his elite Republican Guard forces intact. Only the regular Iraqi army of poor conscripts was engaged by U.S. forces, who buried hundreds of them alive in their trenches with armoured bulldozers and slaughtered thousands more in a "turkey shoot" on the road to Basra; the final death toll was at least 50,000 men.[13] In a now familiar pattern, the figures were denied by the Pentagon until the issue was old news. When the body count was finally admitted, few noticed it, and fewer cared.

Despite his acquiescence to Saudi demands, President Bush still urged Iraq's southern Shiites to rise up against Saddam, who massacred tens of thousands of them in an attempt to keep his splintered country together.[14] The Shiites had been promised U.S. support for their rebellion, but it never arrived. This betrayal was still fresh in their minds during the 2003 invasion, where some of the fiercest fighting took place around the southern cities of Basra, Najaf and Karbala, whose populations are predominantly Shiite.

The Kurds in the north, too, were encouraged to rise up, and found themselves similarly abandoned to Saddam's bloody reprisals — as they had previously been in 1975, prompting Henry Kissinger's notorious comment that "covert operations is not missionary work."

The aftermath of the Gulf War became confused by these rebellions, making it easy to blame the many thousands of Iraqi dead on Saddam. I travelled through Iraq during the war, however, and will never forget the dead and dying lined up on roadsides after U.S. raids, waiting for ambulances that would never come. In Baghdad, the dead were mostly women, children and the elderly, since all able-bodied men were at the Kuwait front, as were most of the doctors and paramedics. But George Bush the First had promised a "clean war with no civilian casualties," and by the time the truth came out another administration was in office and no one cared that yet another ex-president had told yet another lie.

One promise Bush did deliver on was his chilling vow to "return Iraq to the pre-industrial era." Besides the missiles, three waves of B-52 warplanes carpet-bombed Baghdad every night, indiscriminately hitting schools, infant formula factories, art galleries and private homes. Air strikes deliberately targeted Baghdad's urban infrastructures, so that — in the dead of winter — power facilities, water-treatment plants, state-subsidized bakeries and grain silos were destroyed, leaving millions without food, heating or potable water. Sickness quickly spread; many thousands died long after the bombs had stopped falling. On the whole, people in the West preferred to believe Bush I's lies about the war; and by the time the truth emerged their interests were elsewhere. The former Attorney General, Ramsey Clark, set up a war crimes tribunal — in which I participated — in an attempt to indict Bush and others. But nothing came of it, and the University of Toronto even awarded the ex-president an honorary doctorate, deaf to the student voices denouncing him as a mass-murderer. There was never a clearer indication of the moral abyss separating our rulers from the rest of us.

Air attacks on Iraq continued throughout the Clinton administration, during which time the American-inspired United Nations embargo came into effect. When I visited Iraq in 1996, I was profoundly shocked by the condition in which I found Iraqis living. Galloping inflation had made their currency worthless. In the 1980s there had been three dollars to a dinar; now there were three thousand dinars to a dollar. State salaries had remained unchanged — and the state was by far the largest employer — so that someone who had earned the equivalent of a thousand dollars a month was now making the equivalent of thirty cents a month. Manufacturing industries had closed down because imported raw materials were either impossibly expensive or else prohibited by the embargo. All Iraq had was oil, so being prevented from selling it meant that no foreign currency could be earned, which meant that nothing could be imported, and Iraq imported almost everything it needed.

The majority of Iraqis were now subsisting on whatever could be grown or grazed in the flood plain between the Tigris and Euphrates rivers. Malnutrition was beginning to take its toll. Not as visually dramatic as starvation, malnutrition means the body cannot obtain the range of nutrients, trace elements and minerals it needs for cellular growth. The average age of death had fallen from 76 to 58, and between half a million and one-and-a-half million people, the majority of them children under five, died in what a U.N. report described as "a humanitarian disaster comparable to the worst catastrophes of the past decades."[15] In the south, the incidence of cancers had dramatically risen on account of the depleted uranium used by American armour-piercing bullets.[16] The pharmacies contained no medicines. People looked drained, worn, and many seemed on the brink of nervous breakdown. The once-grand city of Baghdad reflected its people; it was patched together around the rubble, reeking of sewage. Tap water ran brown; there were no light bulbs, no toilet paper. Indeed, there was no paper of any kind — the embargo prevented its importation — and even the hotels were using the reverse side of used government stationery for customers' bills. Where there had been no beggars, there were now many; and once-respectable women — sisters, mothers, wives — were sent to prostitute themselves for a dollar or two. It was a question of sheer survival.

Saddam had ceased to trust any but his immediate family and a few longtime colleagues. What wealth the country produced he kept to himself, embarking on a spree of palace-building in a grotesque and misguided attempt to stir up national pride. The education system he had once cared so much about was cut off from most of its state funding. Junior schools became little more than indoctrination courses in the glories of Saddam. In his Revolutionary Command Council the average level of education was the equivalent of grade four — as if sending out the message that learning no longer mattered. The secret police proliferated, with one unit investigating another in an attempt to root out conspiracies that left father distrusting son, brother distrusting brother. If you were not connected with Saddam's tribe, based on his home town of Tikrit, you had little future anyway. As a result, a vast "Tikrit Mafia" had grown up, with cousins and uncles of Saddam carving out abusive little fiefdoms for themselves.

Saddam was renowned for his brutality, but even he could not match the fear inspired by his eldest son Uday, whose reputation as a sadistic womanizer caused many to hide their daughters permanently from his gaze. Sent by the *New York Times* in 1996 to write about Uday, I was swiftly warned away from the subject. "They'll take you out to the desert and drive a car over you, then say you were in an accident," I was told. Besides, the appalling effects of the embargo made the story of Uday pale. In just five years, Iraq had changed beyond recognition. Its people had been reduced to sickly, fearful wretches; its cities were falling apart with neglect and decay; its leader had seemingly lost all touch with reality.

America behaved as if Saddam was responsible for these conditions. The U.N. weapons inspectors continued to turn up nothing — probably because there was nothing to turn up any more — yet the embargo was kept in place. Washington increased its demands, which grew abusive. But, though grumbling, Saddam allowed the inspectors into his palaces, where they found nothing. It was widely believed in Iraq that American demands would just increase until they were unacceptable — then the country would be attacked again. As the Iraqi information minister, Mohammed Sayeed Sahaf, told me, "They will want to inspect Saddam's asshole every morning, and still it will not be enough." Indeed, one wondered if the doctor inspecting Saddam's mouth with a flashlight after his capture was really still looking for those elusive weapons of mass destruction.

Faced with all this evidence, I think we are forced to conclude that there has been a deliberate attempt by the U.S. to undermine Iraq's stability stretching back at least fifteen years, and possibly further, to the beginning of the war with Iran, or even to the encouraging of Kurdish independence before 1975.

Some of the principal reports seen by President George W. Bush and his vice president, Dick Cheney, soon after the inauguration, especially one from the Council on Foreign Relations, directly warned that Iraq's oil should be grabbed now, before it ran out, or China seized it. That the second President Bush is also trying to "reshape the Middle East in Israel's favour"[17] seems likely, as well. The weapons inspections in Iraq had turned up nothing, and it was just a matter of time before the U.N. embargo would have had to be lifted. With the petro-dollars flowing in again, there is little doubt that Saddam would have continued to rebuild his army and his nuclear and biochemical weapons programs. It would, presumably, not have been long before Iraq and Israel clashed over something. And to play down its Israel-biased policy in the region, while still controlling it, America really needed a base of its own in the Middle East — just as it had in Germany, Italy, Japan and elsewhere. Any idea of using Saudi Arabia for these purposes must have been scuttled with the rise of fundamentalist Islam, which would never tolerate Infidel presence in the state where the holy sites of Mecca and Medina were located. An opportunity such as Iraq now presented might not come along again.

Or rather, an opportunity such as Saddam presented, because it was largely by virtue of Saddam's character that Washington could pull off this neo-imperialist grab. To say that America's post-World War II foreign policy made a habit of cultivating — or even creating — leaders like Saddam is no exaggeration. Possibly with the model of Hitler in mind, Washington's covert ops people sought out, as leaders in places for which they had an interest, men who would be particularly easy to take down when or if the need arose. The Shah, Saddam, Pinochet, Suharto, Marcos, Noriega, to name but a few, were all propped up initially or placed in power with CIA help; and they were also all corrupt and brutal dictators who oppressed their own people. Their advantage to Washington lay in the ease with which they could be deposed. The mere revelation to a gullible media of their crimes would have the West howling for their removal — which gave Washington the kind of security it needed, however things turned out. Nothing about politics in America is missionary work.

When a gang of crooks like the current administration in Washington takes power, one can expect to see some reshaping of policy to favour the individuals involved. I do not think anyone expected the degree of rapaciousness in imposing it that we have seen, however, nor the infantile understanding of the world that it entails.

Behind the propaganda and the pomp, behind the declarations of a noble purpose, behind the real grief of widows, orphans and mothers lies a squalid truth that history will not treat kindly.

> *People worry a lot about how the Arab street is going to react.*
> *Well, I see that the Arab street has gotten very, very quiet since we*
> *started blowing things up.*
>
> — DONALD KAGAN, CO-CHAIRMAN,
> PROJECT FOR A NEW AMERICAN CENTURY [18]

Iraq is a key part of a plan for world domination whose origins go back a decade to when Bush I was president. Part of it is laid out in the National Security Strategy, a document every administration is obliged to produce that outlines the approach it will take to defending the country. The Bush II administration's plan was released on September 20, 2002, and is significantly different from previous plans, a fact which it acknowledges and attributes to the attacks of September 11, 2001.

The terrorism problem is addressed in the president's report by an aggressive military and foreign policy that embraces pre-emptive attacks against perceived enemies. When referring to what it terms "American internationalism," it speaks of the need to ignore international opinion if that is what best serves U.S. interests, and asserts bluntly that "the best defense is a good offense." The doctrine of deterrence is dismissed as a Cold War relic, and in its place the report talks of "convincing or compelling states to accept their sovereign responsibilities."[19]

Basically, the document lays out a scheme for permanent U.S. military and economic domination of the entire globe, unconstrained by international treaty or concern. To make this scheme a reality, it projects a massive expansion of the U.S. global military presence. "The United States will require bases and stations within and beyond Western Europe and Northeast Asia," warns the report, "as well as temporary access arrangements for the long-distance deployment of U.S. troops."[20]

The repeated references to terrorism are somewhat misleading, however, because the approach of the new National Security Strategy was clearly not inspired by the events of September 11. The same approach can be found in much the same language in a report published in September 2000, a full year before the attacks, by an organization called Project for the New American Century, comprising a gang of conservative interventionists who are outraged by the thought that the U.S. might be passing up its shot at a global empire. "At no time in history has the international security order been as conducive to American interests and ideals," states the PNAC report. "The challenge of this coming century is to preserve and enhance this 'American peace.'"[21]

This report reads like a blueprint for the current Bush defence policy; and indeed the Bush administration has tried to implement most of what it advocates. The PNAC report urged the repudiation of the anti-ballistic missile treaty, for example, and recommended a commitment to some kind of global missile-defence system. This is precisely the course that has been taken.

To project sufficient power worldwide for the enforcement of Pax Americana, states the PNAC report, the U.S. would have to increase defence spending from 3 percent of gross domestic product to as much as 3.8 percent. The budget requested for defence for 2003 by the Bush administration was $379 billion, almost exactly 3.8 percent of GDP. As things turned out, of course, the skyrocketing cost of the Iraq invasion sent actual spending way over the requested sum. The 2004 budget is $431 billion.

The PNAC report also advocates the "transformation" of the U.S. military to meet its expanded obligations, including the cancellation of outdated defence programs like the Crusader artillery system, urging instead the development of small nuclear warheads "required in targeting the very deep, underground hardened bunkers that are being built by many of our potential adversaries." This is pretty much the route that Defense Secretary Donald Rumsfeld has travelled, and, in 2002, the Republican-dominated House of Representatives gave a green light to the Pentagon to develop a weapon called the Robust Nuclear Earth Penetrator.

The close parallel between PNAC report recommendations and current policy is not particularly surprising given the current positions held by the seven people who contributed to the 2000 document:

Paul Wolfowitz became deputy defense secretary.

John Bolton became undersecretary of state.

Stephen Cambone became head of the Pentagon's Office of Program, Analysis and Evaluation.

Eliot Cohen and Devon Cross became members of the Defense Policy Board, which advises Rumsfeld.

L. Lewis Libby became chief of staff to Vice President Dick Cheney.

Dov Zakheim became comptroller for the Defense Department.

Back in 2000, though, the authors of the PNAC report were still private citizens and could thus be a little more frank and less diplomatic than they were in drafting the National Security Strategy. For example, they clearly identified in the 2000 report Iran, Iraq and North Korea as primary short-term targets, a good while before President Bush classified them as the "Axis of Evil," criticizing the fact that "past Pentagon war games have given little or no consideration to the force requirements necessary not only to defeat an attack but to remove these regimes from power," in the case of North Korea and Iraq.

The key element in preserving Pax Americana, says the report, will be "constabulary duties" performed by U.S. forces acting as global policemen. Anticipating those who might envisage a multilateral world police force, the report adds that such policing actions "demand American political leadership rather than that of the United Nations." We are not told why this should be, but the implication is clear: America cannot entrust its safety to other nations, nor can it be ruled by the judgements of global democracy. The tenets of American exceptionalism dictate that the rest of us are forced to believe in the inherent rectitude of U.S. foreign policy — or else become one of its targets.

The 2000 report then advocates, in addition to the roughly 130 nations where U.S. troops are already deployed, a much larger military presence spread over yet more of the globe, to ensure that the responsibilities of global policing can be met and that no country dares to challenge the United States. More specifically, it is argued that permanent military bases are needed in the Middle East, in Southeast Europe, in Latin America and in Southeast Asia — places where no such bases then existed. Besides explaining U.S. actions in Iraq, this also helps explain other anomalies in the reactive aftermath of September 11, that saw the Bush administration rushing to install U.S. troops in Georgia and the Philippines, as well as sending military advisers to aid the civil war in Colombia.

The 2000 report also directs our attention by acknowledging its debt to a still earlier document, drafted by the Defense Department in 1992. The defense secretary was then Richard "Dick" Cheney, who is now Bush's vice president. The report's author was Paul Wolfowitz, who was then defense undersecretary for policy. This report similarly presents America as a global colossus, imposing its will upon recalcitrant, feckless nations and safeguarding world peace with military and economic might. However, when leaked in a final draft form, the 1992 proposal drew so much ire and criticism that the first President Bush was forced to withdraw and repudiate it.

One measure of Bush II's accomplishments is that he is able to make his father seem a wise and reasonable man by comparison. For the implications of Pax Americana are immense and dire indeed.

Take, for example, its effect on U.S. allies. Once the unilateral right to act as the world's policeman was announced to the U.N. via the invasion of Iraq, most U.S. allies receded into the background, and those that remained — largely because of economic threats or enticements — did so in most cases against the will of their peoples. It is proving singularly difficult to lure back important allies such as Germany and France, and it seems likely that the only real ally left, Britain, will suspend its allegiance when Tony Blair's term as prime minister ends. If such a situation continues, America will be forced to spend increasingly more of its wealth and blood protecting the peace of an ungrateful world while other nations redirect theirs to such eccentricities as health care and education for their citizenry.

Those who argue that no one would really mind the U.S. acting as global cop, or that it really has no choice but to act thus, should explain why the matter is not something that Bush II or others have dared discuss honestly with the American people. It represents an historic change in what America is as a nation, as well as how it has traditionally operated in the international arena. Thus, analogies to previous unpopular actions, such as Vietnam, are not particularly helpful since they only serve to suggest a continuation with the past that in reality does not exist. In the same way, President Bush's use of the September 11 attacks as a justification for America's policy shift is also misleading once we are aware of the 2000 report and the prominence of its authors in the Bush II administration, not to mention the Cheney-Wolfowitz 1992 report. It is useless to speculate on what would have happened if the September 11 attacks had not occurred, but given the personnel in Bush II's administration it is reasonable to assume that another excuse would have soon been found.

The term "empire" is avoided like the plague by all concerned with implementing Pax Americana. They hide behind jargon and academic-speak or terms like "liberty" and "freedom" to such a point of obfuscation that one is forced to wonder what it is about world domination that embarrasses them so acutely. Answer: the cost, probably. Just the amount of increase in the defence budget from 1999 to 2003 is far more than the total amount spent annually on defence by China, the next-biggest spender.

The temptation of empire is great, and history is often scarcely more than a catalogue of the horripilating crimes men have committed in its pursuit. But again, analogies with past empires are not that useful, for never before has a nation had an empire laid at its feet — twice. At the close of World War II, the dispirited populations of Germany and its two main allies were only too happy to allow the conquering Americans in and give them permanent military bases. So were Britain and its allies. For despite America's own view of its role in the war, the truth is that it cost little and gained much. Britain, on the other hand, was physically devastated and economically exhausted. The strains of empire were by then beyond its capacity, so the world's largest empire was cut loose and numerous newly independent nations appeared, all of them painfully open to anything they could get from anyone able to give it. Without always fully realizing the ramifications of their indebtedness, these fledgling nations borrowed heavily from U.S.-controlled bodies such as the World Bank and International Monetary Fund, finding themselves colonies in a new kind of empire that was controlled remotely through banks and multinational corporations.

With the end of World War III — which is what the Cold War constituted — the collapse of the Soviet empire similarly presented the U.S. with more prospective colonies, many of them part of the Soviet Union's spoils from World War II.

In the eyes of many — including the Cheney-Wolfowitz gang — September 11, 2001, marked the start of World War IV, which some view as a war against Islam, others as War on Terrorism, the rest as a Clash of Civilizations. It is none of these. It is, as the 1992 and 2000 reports unambiguously demonstrate, a war to end all wars by establishing an American global empire over which the son of George Bush, though he will never of course crown himself emperor, would nonetheless ever preside in spirit as founding father. It is also an infantile fantasy that cannot succeed and for which we shall all pay dearly — and indeed are already paying.

The Australians have paid the price for John Howard's alliance with Bush in Bali. For Silvio Berlusconi's alliance, Italians paid the price in Nasiriya. Saudi Arabia has paid many times over. Britain has paid in Turkey, twice, with bombs targeting both the British Consulate and the British-headquartered HSBC bank, while Bush was visiting London in November 2003. Spain has paid a hideous price, yet seems to be the wiser for it, with a new government that kept its promise to withdraw troops from Iraq. Canada is also on al-Qaeda's list, though at the date of this writing it has not yet seen the cost of its alliance with the American empire first-hand.

Now history seems to be cracking apart. Those leaders of America, termed by the playwright Tony Kushner "miscreants and psychopathic bandits,"[22] pursue their reckless policies that are taking the world ever closer to an assortment of apocalyptic scenarios both ecological and moral. An evil enchantment seems to have befallen men of good will, and those still awake to the peril sound increasingly like Hebrew prophets driven half-mad by the horror surrounding them, raging at the folly and mendacity of humankind with frail, crackling voices, in a language no one seems to understand. Those who once were citizens seem little more than sheep, terrified into obedience, their terror made all the more terrible by being colour-coded for them daily on the seven o'clock news. That we survived the twentieth century for this seems the cruellest cut of all, and certainly the most ironic — indeed, perhaps it is the Last Irony of an ironic age.

CHAPTER THREE

HUSSEIN THE MARTYR

Annihilate then yourselves gloriously and joyfully in me, and in me you shall find yourselves. Thereupon, the birds at last lost themselves for ever in the Simurgh — the shadow was lost in the sun, and that is all.

— FROM FARID AD-DIN 'ATTAR'S
CONFERENCE OF THE BIRDS (13TH CENTURY)

CITIES OF THE RED NIGHT

On the second day of October in the year 680, Hussein, grandson of the Prophet Mohammed, was encamped at Karbala on flat salty plains some fifty kilometres south of what would one day be Baghdad. His army — if indeed you could call it that — numbered a mere seventy-two, and this *included* the women and children. In pursuit of them was an Umayyad force of some four thousand men, highly trained in both Persian and Byzantine techniques of war. When warned that he could not hope to win against such staggering odds, Hussein replied: "O people, the Apostle of God said during his life, 'He who sees an oppressive ruler violating the sanctions of God ... and does not show zeal against him in word or deed, God would surely cause him to enter his abode in the fire.'"[23]

Mohammed had died nearly fifty years earlier without designating a successor. In the tribal world of the Bedu, pastoral nomads of the Arabian desert, such matters were traditionally settled through bloodlines or, failing that, consensus. Many felt that the leadership should be given to Ali, who was both Mohammed's cousin, his first convert and his son-in-law, being married to Fatima, the Prophet's only living child. Ali was also pious, modest, selfless, austere and, by all accounts, a spiritually inspired teacher of Islam's sacred texts. He was the logical choice. But the caliphate went to Abu Bakr, who had been Mohammed's closest confidant and was a member of the Umayyad clan, the Meccan establishment. To prevent a similar confusion on his own death, Abu Bakr designated Umar, another Meccan aristocrat, to succeed him, thus ensuring a tradition of Umayyad succession that contradicted Islam's democratic, egalitarian spirit. After Umar, the caliphate went to Uthman.

All this while, for twenty-four years, Ali had been teaching by word and deed the message of Islam to a growing horde of disciples, many of them non-Arabs from what is today southern Iran. The religion had spread rapidly during these early years, concomitant with Arab conquests of neighbouring tribes and cities, which also brought great wealth and wealth's eternal companion, corruption. The widening division of a wealthy Umayyad elite and a burgeoning caste of have-nots crying hypocrisy first became apparent during the disappointing third caliphate. This was when those who followed Ali began to designate themselves *Shia Ali*, the party of Ali, and became more militant in their advocacy of his caliphate. Uthman's reign ended in the now traditional manner — he was murdered by dissidents — and finally Ali's patience paid off. Yet his term as caliph was marred by the opposition of both Umayyads and the xenophobic Bedu, who loathed Ali's following among non-Arabs. Kept out of the closed societies of Medina and Damascus, Ali was obliged to install his capital in Kufa, Mesopotamia. He had no taste for power politics, however, and even after five years was unable to establish himself as head of the Islamic state. In 661, while leaving a mosque after the first evening prayer, Ali too succumbed to an assassin's blade. Tradition tells us that his last words were a whispered request to be placed upon a camel and laid to rest wherever it first knelt down. His tomb is in Najaf, southern Iraq.

Proclaiming Yazid caliph, the Umayyads now once more seized the leadership, but found themselves challenged by Ali's second son, Hussein, who upheld the claim of Mohammed's descendants. The two armies met on what is known today as the Plain of Sorrow and Misfortune. It cannot have been much of a battle. The four thousand Umayyad troops butchered all seventy-two of Hussein's men, women and children without mercy. Hussein's severed head was immediately dispatched to Damascus, where Yazid slashed his cane in fury across its mouth. A stunned silence followed, during which the voice of an old man was heard to say, "Alas that I should have lived to see this day, I who saw those lips kissed by the Prophet of God."[24]

Waves of grief and anger spread through the Islamic world with the news of Hussein's death, and the existing cleft in the faith ruptured entirely, forming what amount to two different religions — despite the fact that among the Prophet's very last words, according to the Hadith or apocryphal traditions, was an injunction for his followers not to succumb to schism. Though most Muslims remained within the fold of *sunna* or orthodoxy, some chose the *Shia Ali*, putting down the roots of Shia communities, mostly in southeastern Mesopotamia.

The two branches of Islam — Shia and Sunni — are often compared to the Protestant and Roman Catholic divisions of Christianity, but this is not really accurate — especially in Iraq, where Hussein's blood was spilled and where it can still seem wet upon the ground. The only comparable event in Christianity to the massacre of Mohammed's grandson and his family is the crucifixion of Jesus, which in some third-world communities still invokes the kind of immediate sorrow or tearful anger you can see at Hussein's tomb in Karbala and in the bazaars outside Iranian Shia mosques, where the biggest-selling item is a mawkish rendering on black velvet of Hussein the Martyr, his bearded manly face riven by a single teardrop. Since Christian scripture wrongly places the blame for Christ's murder upon the Jews, for a meaningful comparison with the Sunni-Shia problem one has to imagine a Judaism as huge and politically mettlesome as Roman Catholicism yet as stark as Calvinism, running concomitantly with a tiny Protestant faith adhered to largely by an emotionally volatile underclass of superstitious idolaters. The comparisons are unhelpful. The Shia in Iraq outnumber Sunnis by at least three to one today, but the country has always been controlled by its Sunni minority — *there's* the rub.

Until Iran adopted Shia Islam as the state religion in the sixteenth century, most Shia tended to live in the Arab world, principally in and around the great shrine cities of Najaf and Karbala in Iraq. Their numbers during the first thousand years of Islam were quite small — unsurprisingly, since they were relentlessly persecuted by the empire's orthodox Sunni leadership. This persecution led to Shia theologians furtively developing their own ideas about Islamic law in total isolation from the mainstream. While Sunnis believe that the Islamic community as a whole is responsible for upholding or interpreting the religion's legal tenets and general teachings, the Shia came to view this as insufficient. Rather, they felt that the divine will required a figure possessed of great wisdom and authority to interpret God's wishes for the faithful — just as it was in Mohammed's time. It was not a job for amateurs.

Hence, the whole issue of religious leadership in Shiism has always been fraught with peril and imbued with significantly more importance than it is in Sunnism. As improbable as it may seem to us in the contemporary West, the task of divine interpreter is accorded to an academic, a master of Islamic law who is charged with the interpretation of all moral questions — religious, political or social — until the arrival of the Mahdi, a kind of Islamic Saviour or Second Coming. While I know many academics who would fight their way into a line-up for this job, lamentably few possess the "profile of a just Shiite figure of authority, however temporary or fallible, who could ... follow the Quranic mandate of creating public order that would 'enjoin the good and forbid the evil.'"[25]

Such moral guides of the Shia are unmistakable, dressed in a cloak draped over an ankle-length kaftan, and a turban — black if they are "directly" descended from the Prophet, white if they are not. Their air of antiquity and authority is palpable, especially at the great Shia shrines, yet their existence is somewhat paradoxical, since Islam essentially posits the equality of all believers, whereas the Shia follow authoritarian lines that divide those who interpret the law from those who are qualified only to obey it.

Since the sixteenth century, when Shia Islam was established as the state religion, Iran has dispatched clerics to the opulent shrine cities of Najaf and Karbala, whose wealth derived from the traffic in pilgrims. It was not long before Shia clergy were being sent even further afield, to convert and minister to the Arabian tribes as well as increase clientele for the pilgrimage trade. As a consequence, much Shia theology was adapted to mesh with Bedu customs and traditions, particularly when it came to interpreting the roles played by Ali and his son Hussein. Whereas the Persian Shia tended to venerate Ali for his devotion to justice and the law, the Arab Shia found in Hussein a figure far more in keeping with the manly warrior virtues they so admired as well as the purity of bloodline lineage that obsessed them. This predilection for idolatry, combined with the Shia fondness for worship at the tombs of saintly imams and the decidedly undemocratic nature of their society, aroused scorn and hatred in the purist Sunni Muslims. As Shia numbers increased in Iraq, creating a vast underclass whose festering resentment of their lowly status owed nothing to Karl Marx, Sunni hatred turned to fear.

The annual pilgrimage to Karbala was held during the Spring of 2003 for the first time in thirty years, having been banned by the Sunni-dominated — but ideologically atheistic — ruling Ba'ath Party. The television images of bloody Shia pilgrims mortifying their flesh with whips and blades, beating their chests as they leapt towards the gold-domed shrine of Hussein in a macabre dance of empathetic death, filled Sunni and Christian Iraqis alike with terror and foreboding. For, whether the old status quo liked it or not, the Shia now held the key to Iraq's future in those blood-stained fists.

Washington has repeatedly warned Tehran to stay out of Iraqi affairs, but with the theocratic Islamic Iranian state this is as futile as attempting to keep fundamentalist Christians out of American politics. Furthermore, Iran has an interest in American-occupied Najaf and Karbala as legitimate as the Jewish, Christian and Muslim interest in Israeli-occupied Jerusalem or the Christian interest in Palestinian Bethlehem.

Because of their questionable loyalty, many Iraqi Shia religious leaders had been exiled in Iran since the Iraq-Iran War; but during April 2003, as U.S. and British troops swept up through southern Iraq towards Baghdad, they returned, some openly and to tumultuously emotional welcomes. Their goal is uncompromisingly simple, and will be simply achieved by any truly democratic one-man-one-vote election in Iraq: to create a theocratic Shia Islamic state run on the strict principles of *sharia* law, just like Iran. Anything less will be unacceptable, while anything approaching it will be unacceptable to the Sunnis and Christians of Iraq — not to mention the occupying Americans.

George W. Bush has created a problem as insolvable as the conflict between Palestinians and Israelis.

A BRIEF HISTORY OF LIES

President Tells Hussein to Leave Iraq Within 48 Hours or Face Invasion
— FRONT PAGE HEADLINE IN *WASHINGTON POST*, MARCH 18, 2003

Allies Will Move In, Even if Saddam Hussein Moves Out
— HEADLINE OF PAGE A16 STORY IN THE
NEW YORK TIMES, MARCH 18, 2003

In his March 17 speech, as it was boiled down by media accounts, George W. Bush delivered a single blunt statement: "Saddam Hussein and his sons must leave Iraq within forty-eight hours. Their refusal to do so will result in military conflict, commenced at a time of our choosing." The *New York Times* article cited above, by the newspaper's military correspondent Michael Gordon, began, however: "Even if Saddam Hussein leaves Iraq within forty-eight hours, as President Bush demanded, allied forces plan to move north into Iraqi territory, officials said today." Gordon pointed out a line in the speech that other journalists had seemingly overlooked: "It is not too late for the Iraqi military to act with honor and protect your country by permitting the peaceful entry of Coalition forces to eliminate weapons of mass destruction." In the context of Bush's speech, this statement appeared to indicate what the president hoped Iraqi commanders would do if or when his ultimatum was rejected, but Gordon insisted that it was actually a signal that, no matter what course of action Saddam chose, the U.S. would still "enter Iraq to search for hidden weapons of mass destruction and help stabilize the nation so that a new and more democratic regime could take over."

Even if the Iraqi military overthrew Saddam themselves, wrote Gordon, "a military intervention seems very likely." To back this up, he then quoted Colin Powell's March 17 statement to the effect that "the only way for Iraq to avoid an attack is for Mr. Hussein to leave the country and 'allow this matter to be resolved through the peaceful entry of force.'"

Put more straightforwardly, there was in fact nothing, then, that Iraq could do to escape invasion and occupation. Its sole option was the alternative to surrender or not surrender. A traditional enough policy — indeed, one deployed by Hulagu Khan's Mongols when they attacked Baghdad in 1258 — so why did the White House feel a need to confuse the issue by acting as if Saddam's refusal to step down was the cause for the military conflict? The only possible answer would appear to be Pentagon certainty that media would find the ultimatum drama so irresistible they would thus be obliged to present the imminent war not as a choice Washington had already made the day Bush took office, but instead as a final test of Saddam's character and will to comply with the world's wishes.

Unsurprisingly, the media swallowed this bait whole, framing their stories the following day, March 19, as "defiant" Saddam scornfully spurning his last chance for peace. "Saddam Sneers Back: Hell No, I Won't Go" brayed the New York *Daily News'* front-page headline (cunningly including an allusion to the well-known 1960's draft protesters' chant as a middle-finger to the now middle-aged anti-Vietnam war veterans who were leading a new anti-war movement and would not fail to recognize the taunt). On the cable news channel MSNBC viewers were even provided with a "Deadline" clock, visible at all times in the lower-right-hand corner of their screens, ticking away the 172,800 seconds until the meaningless deadline was up. Curiously, even the *New York Times* itself appeared not to grasp the significance of its own correspondent's report, leading on March 19 with a front-page headline that the Pentagon could well have penned for them: "War Imminent as Hussein Rejects Ultimatum." The story beneath it began, "The White House said today that Saddam Hussein was making his 'final mistake' by rejecting an ultimatum ordering him to leave Iraq or face war." The cynicism and hypocrisy entailed is more shocking and awesome than the weapons and massive destruction Washington had planned for Baghdad *no matter what Saddam did to appease them or meet their demands.*

The sole reason offered for attacking, invading and occupying Iraq was that of the threat posed to Americans and the world by a secret arsenal of chemical, biological and possibly nuclear weapons allegedly possessed by Saddam's regime. The subsequent failure on the part of U.S. and British forces to produce such weapons or even evidence of their existence was generally viewed by the media, in the aftermath of war, as evidence of either a deception or of poor intelligence reporting on the matter. But given the gravity of the situation, as well as the long history of misinformation on Iraq that I have already pointed to, the weapons of mass destruction (WMD) issue deserves greater scrutiny.

Did the Bush administration get it wrong? Did they have suspicions but no hard evidence? In other words, was it a white lie, told with the best intentions? Or was it a black lie, told with the full knowledge that it was untrue? Since many, many thousands of innocent civilians were killed or mutilated on account of this lie, not to mention tens of thousands of soldiers, it seems vitally important that we know the answer.

One clue is that, in his State of the Union Address of January 2003, President Bush cited as evidence of Iraq's perfidy a letter purporting to reveal an attempt on behalf of Saddam's regime to purchase uranium ore from Niger. The Nigerien government itself pronounced the document a forgery, even pointing out errors that distinguished it from what a genuine document would have looked like. Confronted with this in March, Colin Powell merely said that the administration had nothing to do with forging the letter. Astoundingly, the media left it at that, rather than attempting to discover who was responsible for the forgery. It certainly was not the Iraqis; nor was it the Nigeriens. Indeed, the most likely culprit was some branch of the Bush administration. But no one seemed to care who had committed the crime, just as no one seemed to care that the U.S. president had attempted to mislead the American people into sanctioning an act of war. While there are no clear precedents to go by, one would think that this ought to be regarded as a very serious offence. It also shows that the U.S. government, if it was responsible for the forgeries, did not possess the evidence it claimed to have justifying a war that would kill over ten thousand civilians[26] — *and knew it would never possess such evidence since the evidence did not exist.*

Here is the proof. In the UNSCOM report to the Security Council of

January 25, 1999, the U.N. disarmament group that had scrutinized Iraq throughout most of the 1990s stated that its whole history of weapons searches "must be divided into two parts, separated by the events following the departure from Iraq, in August 1995, of Lt. Gen. Hussein Kamel." Kamel was the senior military official in charge of Iraq's various secret weapons programs; and he was also Saddam's son-in-law. He defected with his wife, Saddam's daughter, her sister and brother-in-law, and several crates of top-secret documents relating to Iraq's past adventures in diabolical weaponry.

The defection was front-page news during the dog-days of August 1995, largely because Kamel's disclosure revealed for the first time the full horrifying extent of Saddam's pre-Gulf War biological weapons and vx nerve gas programs, proving that Iraq had been lying about them. This in turn scared Saddam's regime into handing over to U.N. inspectors millions of documents relating to the programs.

For the administration of President Bill Clinton, Kamel's revelations were useful in its efforts to prove that Saddam was still concealing vast amounts of banned weaponry. Indeed, well over two years after the defection — by which time Kamel had been executed on Saddam's orders[27] after returning to Baghdad — Defense Secretary William Cohen stated that "following the defection of his son-in-law, [Saddam] admitted they had produced more than 2,100 gallons of anthrax." Then, shifting measures somewhat confusingly, he pointed out that "if you were to take a five-pound bag of anthrax, properly dispersed, it would kill half the population of Columbus, Ohio."[28] It appears, by the way, that "properly dispersed" on this level would entail handing out anthrax inhalers to every other Columbian or herding them all into a sealed chamber.

By the time George W. Bush and his gang had taken over Washington and were making the case for war on Iraq, Hussein Kamel's story had become the stuff of legend. But a secret United Nations transcript that recorded the whole 1995 interview with Kamel also existed. It had clearly been made available to Security Council members — the U.S. is a permanent member — and contained a highly significant qualifying comment to the revelations about vast stockpiles of lethal substances: "All weapons," Kamel states in it, "— biological, chemical, missile, nuclear — were destroyed." He goes on to emphasize that "after the Gulf War, Iraq destroyed all its chemical and biological weapons stocks and the missiles to deliver them." The only things remaining were "hidden blueprints, computer disks, microfiches" and items like production moulds.

The elimination of these weapons occurred secretly during the summer of 1991, Kamel said in the transcript, in order to conceal their existence from the UNSCOM inspectors, and with the hope that one day production could be resumed when the U.N. inspectors left.

On February 23, 2003, John Barry published an account of the U.N. transcript in *Newsweek*, reporting that the CIA and its British equivalent M16 had been told the same story as the U.N. by Kamel himself, and adding that "a military aide who defected with Kamel ... backed Kamel's assertions about the destruction of WMD stocks."[29] It seems that the U.N. inspectors kept Kamel's statements quiet, Barry reported, hoping to "bluff Saddam into disclosing still more."[30]

The *Newsweek* story appeared just as the U.N. Security Council debate over weapons inspections was reaching a crucial juncture for the Bush administration's war plan, so a spokesman for the CIA, Bill Harlow, angrily denied there was any substance to it: "It is incorrect, bogus, wrong, untrue."[31] Sadly for CIA credibility, however, a complete copy of the Kamel transcript was posted to the Internet two days later (February 26, 2003) by myself and Glen Rangwala of Cambridge University.[32] It is an internal UNSCOM/IAEA document stamped "SENSITIVE."

> *In 1995, after several years of deceit by the Iraqi regime, the head of Iraq's military industries defected. It was then that the regime was forced to admit that it had produced more than 30,000 liters of anthrax and other deadly biological agents. The inspectors, however, concluded that Iraq had likely produced two to four times that amount. This is a massive stockpile of biological weapons that has never been accounted for, and capable of killing millions.*
>
> — U.S. PRESIDENT GEORGE W. BUSH, OCTOBER 7, 2002

> *It took years for Iraq to finally admit that it had produced four tons of the deadly nerve agent VX. A single drop of VX on the skin*

will kill in minutes. Four tons. The admission only came after inspectors collected documentation as a result of the defection of Hussein Kamel, Saddam's late son-in-law.

— U.S. SECRETARY OF STATE COLIN POWELL, PRESENTATION
TO THE U.N. SECURITY COUNCIL, FEBRUARY 5, 2003

The CIA's embarrassment is understandable. By the time *Newsweek*'s story was on the stands, nearly every senior foreign policy official in the Bush administration had quoted Kamel's confessions to push the argument that Saddam was sitting on a horripilating arsenal, as well as the contention that weapons inspections could never work. Many even argued that only defectors such as Kamel could point out the locations of concealed weaponry; and others frequently cited Kamel for the specific quantities of things like anthrax and vx produced by Iraq before 1991. Not one of them bothered to point out that the defector himself had also declared that these quantities had been destroyed.

When war arrived, Hussein Kamel had been forgotten entirely. Gripped by jingoistic fervour, the U.S. media took it as conventional wisdom that Hans Blix and his team of inspectors failed to uncover any weapons because they were just not smart enough to ferret them out — or that Saddam's devilish cunning could only be thwarted by the divinely inspired crusaders of the U.S. Marine Corps. But as the weeks passed and the weapons still proved elusive, there were voices in the government who began to recall and echo Kamel's message. As early as March 16, 2003, the *Washington Post* mentioned that "a senior intelligence analyst said one explanation for the difficulties inspectors have had in locating weapons caches 'is because there may not be much of a stockpile.'"

The administration in Washington would prefer now not to remind anyone of Kamel's defection, because his testimony proves that the president of the United States is a liar who led his country into a disastrous war for reasons he is unwilling to tell the citizens who placed him in office and place in him their trust. Considering the issues at stake during previous impeachment hearings, surely this is cause for impeachment.

But the Arabs are used to lies from the West.

People of Baghdad ... you have suffered under strange tyrants
who have ever endeavoured to set one Arab house against another
in order that they might profit from your dissensions. This policy
is abhorrent ... for there can be neither peace nor prosperity where
there is enmity or misgovernment. Our armies do not come into
your cities and lands as conquerors or enemies, but as liberators.
— LIEUTENANT-GENERAL SIR FREDERICK STANLEY MAUDE,
MARCH 11, 1917 [33]

Since 1908 when the vast Masjid-i-Salaman (Temple of Solomon) oil well in Iran's Zagros mountains began disgorging its precious black wealth, the British have had proprietary interests in what was destined to be the world's most zealously coveted resource. They knew their empire more thoroughly than have any imperialists in history, dispatching teams of scholars from every discipline hot on the heels of every conquering army. Thus it was not only geologists who assured the politicians and bureaucrats of London that oil on one side of the Gulf meant oil on the other side; historians, anthropologists and ethnologists also confirmed that the people of Ur had festooned their ziggurats with designs in bitumen, that the Tigris boatmen had since the dawn of recorded time sealed the hulls of their flat-bottomed barges with pitch and that the pillars of fire reported by texts — including the Old Testament — composed during the second millennium BC were almost certainly descriptions of burning surface oil. For the fossil fuel of Mesopotamia, besides its high calibre, had something else that made it uniquely attractive to those who sought to harness its energy: many subterranean oil lakes were under such high pressure that no pumps were needed to extract their contents. One simply drilled into these sunless caverns, sank a pipe, and the oil was forced up through it to the surface faster and more efficiently than any pump could manage. Today this makes Iraqi oil some five dollars a barrel cheaper to extract than the marginally more plentiful Saudi oil[34] — and means that some of the larger wells are up to $5 million a day more profitable than their Saudi equivalents;[35] and wells producing net profits of $30 million a day are far from uncommon. The richer fields have hundreds of such wells, and there are thousands of lesser ones. When it operated at full capacity, the Iraqi oil industry poured billions into its government's treasury every month — money that Saddam had once used to educate his people, build modern highways, and make Iraq *the* success story and showcase of the Arab world.

Oil is an arcane business, and it is said that only an oilman truly understands its nature. Is it any coincidence that the Bush family, which has supplied the two presidents most notably obsessed with Iraq, possesses a fortune deriving almost entirely from oil? Or that the only foreign trip George W. Bush had *ever* taken before becoming president was a very brief visit to Riyadh, capital of Saudi Arabia, a country that does not issue tourist visas?

During the first two decades of the twentieth century, oil, for Britain at least, meant fuel for a new generation of battleships that were no longer reliant on the cumbersome and inefficient energy from burning coal. The battleships were primarily required to defend the jewel in Britain's imperial crown, India, from those nations that perceived it to be the principal source of British wealth and power. In the words of Lord Curzon, a future viceroy of India, the first duty of British foreign policy should be "to render any hostile intentions futile, to see that our own position is secure and our frontier impregnable, and so to guard what is without doubt the noblest trophy of British genius, and the most splendid appendage of the Imperial Crown."[36] It was not the education system to which he referred.

Throughout the late nineteenth century and into the twentieth, Britain had watched like a chess master the moves of other empires in what was fondly called the "Great Game," the efforts towards depriving Imperial Great Britain, superpower, of its empire, wherein also resided its greatness, superiority and power. It had once been, after all, an inconsequential province of the Roman Empire, then an easy conquest or looting stopover for various northern European tribes, before finally being acquired by the Normans, who subdued its rabble of churlish tribes — something even the Romans had failed utterly to achieve. Even so, until the sixteenth century England was scarcely more than a backward annex to European civilization. Within the space of four hundred years, however, every European power dearly wished it had taken the trouble to seize the damp little island in the North Sea that now boasted the largest empire in history — with attitude to match. Yet the Europeans were well aware that Britain's strength, naval superiority, was also its weakness. And so the game commenced.

In 1879, Britain secured the western end of sea routes to India by acquiring a major share in the Suez Canal. Check. In 1903, a final concession was secured from the government of Ottoman Turkey by German financiers to construct a Berlin-to-Baghdad Railway. Once in Baghdad, it would be simple for the Germans to extend the tracks south to Basra, a deep-water port commanding the head of the Shatt al Arab waterway leading into the Persian Gulf. Once in the Gulf, Germany would possess an open door onto the Indian Ocean. Check. This was something that the Russians, then already ensconced in Persia, were also finding irresistible. Check. As were the French, who liked the look of Mosul, a city on the upper Tigris river, down which they could sail quickly through Mesopotamia to the Gulf. Check.

Suddenly all imperial eyes were on Mesopotamia. The presence of any imperial rival south of Baghdad would pose a serious threat to British naval superiority — now oil-fuelled — by menacing both the potential fossil-fuel riches of Mesopotamia and the actual fields and refineries of the Anglo-Persian Oil Company in what is now southern Iran. Big trouble had been brewing in Europe and the Ottoman Empire for the previous half century, and the Mesopotamian gambit now helped force an endgame — winner takes all. The Triple Entente of Britain, France and Russia poised on the square opposite another Triple Alliance of Germany and the empires of the Ottomans and Hapsburgs. Russia moved a pawn in the Balkans, and the whole board came crashing down.

It was the summer of 1914, and what erupted was the most terrible war the world has ever known. When it was over, some thirty-seven million people had been killed in action, wounded, taken prisoner or simply gone missing — a full fifty-two percent of all those mobilized. The figures may not be as great — or awful — as those for World War II, but the circumstances and suffering, of trench warfare in particular, perhaps made it even worse, while the psychological impact was arguably unequalled by any other event in history. By 1918, the very fabric of the world itself — the warp and woof, the *texture* — had altered beyond recognition. Of course, the misery of thirty-seven million people was deemed well worth the price of saving empires whose riches had scarcely even touched the prior nature of those people's joy. As my grandfather once remarked: "If those who fought had known for what and whom they were fighting, they would have turned to point their rifles in the opposite direction. But they were told the old lie, and they believed it. And died for it." He would have been truly dismayed to find the "old lie" still in business, still claiming the lives of those still young and uninformed enough to swallow its hook.

Imperial Britain wasted little time before implementing its darker purposes. By November 1914 Indian Expeditionary Force "D" had landed at Fao on the Shatt al Arab, moving rapidly towards Basra. It took nearly a year to secure the far south area sufficiently to permit an advance on Baghdad — compared with the three weeks it took two brigades of the British 1st Armoured Division along with the Royal Marines in March-April 2003.[37] In 1915, however, the British advance through Iraq's desert was not exactly speedy. Some days it could virtually be measured with a ruler, as sand flies and mosquitoes from the swamplands appeared to have allied themselves with the Turks. At the old Persian Sassanian capital founded by Alexander the Great's generals, Ctesiphon, about forty kilometres southeast of Baghdad, the dispirited British forces found themselves pushed back by a reinforced Ottoman army nearly two hundred harrowing kilometres to the village of Kut al-Amarah, set in a loop of the Tigris. There they held out against the savage pounding of Turkish artillery for 140 days, increasingly demoralized by disease and starvation. On April 26, 1916, the thirteen thousand still alive surrendered.

Eight months later, Major General Sir Stanley Maude arrived to resume the advance on Baghdad with fifty thousand fresh troops. He was encouraged by intelligence reports showing that a rebellion in the Shia shrine city of Najaf — resting place of Ali — had driven out the Turks, so he sent off agents to contact Shia tribal leaders in the hope of gathering allies. The failure of this mission reveals how uncharacteristically little the British then understood of the land they were attempting to add to their empire. Very few Bedu Arabs had any interest in lending their horses, their guns or themselves to an alien invader, no matter whether he hailed from London or from Istanbul. Darting out from the shelter of their swamps, the Marsh Arabs wreaked havoc indiscriminately on both Turkish and British forces, killing soldiers and looting supplies. Similarly, the nomadic desert tribes preyed like jackals on any military camp they found, ransacking stores and carrying off weapons. With both Arabs and Turks to fight off, the British inched their way north, and it was only on March 11, 1917, that they found themselves marching past the ruined tomb of Zobeida, principal wife of Harun al-Rashid,[38] and on through the crumbling gates of Baghdad. They saw the miserably decayed tents of Turkish soldiers scattered among ruined stonework, but there were no soldiers. Maude had feared that the Turkish commander, Kazim Karabekir Pasha, would flood the plains in front of the city. But Karabekir was indecisive. Initially, he had moved to meet the British troops head on; then he changed his mind, deciding to defend the railway station instead. This blunder made Baghdad's defence virtually impossible, so the Turks ordered a general retreat. More than 12,000 Turkish soldiers simply fled; some 9,000 surrendered without a fight.

Ablaze with triumph and its accompanying largesse, General Maude proclaimed to the dubious people of Iraq — as Mesopotamia came to be known — that Britain's purpose in this invasion was actually to liberate them from the oppressive rule they had endured since the last days of the Abbasid caliphate and hand them back control of their own affairs. Then he dropped dead from cholera fever. What he had handed to Iraqis, and indeed to all the Ottomans' Arab provinces, was in fact the epic struggle between European colonial interests and Arab aspirations that has continued up to this very day, and most frequently been embodied for the Arabs by the figure of a charismatic leader.

Few have been as charismatic as Hussein ibn Ali, Sharif of Mecca.

> *I am strongly in favour of using poisoned gas against uncivilized tribes.*
>
> — WINSTON CHURCHILL, ON DEALING WITH THE ARAB
> REVOLT AGAINST BRITISH RULE OVER IRAQ IN 1920 [39]

In 1917, the Ottoman Sultan was still Islam's caliph — a dismal fact of life to which Arabia's tribes had never accustomed themselves — and it was in this capacity two years earlier that caliph Abdul Hamid II had exercised his right to declare *jihad* against the Triple Entente of Britain, France and Russia. Not then such a familiar concept as it would become in the West, *jihad* was nonetheless understood by the British to be a formidable ideological weapon, and it sent them searching for a psych-warfare blade of their own with which to parry the Turks' unexpected thrust. They found it in the somewhat grandly baggy idea of pan-Arab nationalism, an unintended and rather baffling product of Ottoman occupation in Arabia, yet also one that had found a most eloquent voice in Hussein ibn Ali.

Directly descended from the Prophet through the House of Hashim, Hussein cut an imposing figure and was said to have eyes so black and piercing that they could paralyze those who came within his gaze. For four hundred years, the Middle East had been under the domination of Ottoman Turkey's empire, a vast and potent hegemony that extended across northern Africa, western Asia and eastern Europe. At its peak it had stretched from the Adriatic to Aden and from Morocco to the Persian Gulf, and its brilliant generals and fearless soldiers even reached deep into Europe to the outskirts of Vienna. Western technology, however, began to make its impact felt by the mid-nineteenth century, and, weighed down by archaic institutions and medieval social structures, the great empire began to blur at the edges. The Russian czar Nicholas first referred to Turkey as "a sick man" in 1853.

Yet even with their star on the wane, the Turks were a deadly foe with dazzling strategists and a web of intelligence assets spanning all of Europe. Thus it was not hard for the caliph to discern in Hussein ibn Ali a potential troublemaker, so he was invited to Istanbul, where Abdul Hamid kept him for fifteen years as a sort of honorary hostage in a gilded safe-house. Rightly, the caliph viewed Hussein as a two-faced schemer principally committed to ambitions of his own. But such was the persistence and force of Hussein's will and its Turkophile persona that his scheming eventually succeeded. On November 1, 1908, aged fifty-five, Hussein was granted the coveted title of Meccan Sharif, which made him the caliph's own representative as protector of Islam's two holiest cities. The office was spiritual in nature, but Hussein swiftly transformed it into a rock-solid base of political power by winning the allegiance of Arabia's tribes. Soon he was secure enough in his position to humble the Turkish governor of the Hejaz — the crucial area along the Red Sea gulf containing both the holy cities and most vital ports — by forcing him to kneel in public and kiss the hem of the sharif's robe.

Hussein was a brilliantly perceptive, almost visionary thinker, and as well informed as his Turkish captors had been on matters that concerned him.

Early in 1914, before World War 1 had even started, Hussein sent his second son, Abdullah, to meet Lord Kitchener, the British resident minister in Cairo, to hint that the sharif, if he had British support, might consider fomenting an Arab revolt against the Turks. He merely wanted in return the same deal the British maintained with the eastern coastal emirates — petty fiefdoms dotted along the Arabian peninsula, where the resident minister doled out gold coins to local sheikhs in return for any assistance they could offer the British Navy if it had to be called in to deal with the encroachment of a hostile power.

Kitchener listened, which was all he was required to do. The war broke out several months later, in August, and he began recalling his conversation with Emir Abdullah, finding its prescience somewhat remarkable. By October 5 he had sent off a secret emissary — code-named "Messenger X" — from Suez to the Red Sea port of Jeddah, whence the man travelled by mule to Mecca. In the holy city — no place for an infidel to be — Kitchener's envoy reported that "every man he met, even if he possessed an insufficiency of clothes, was armed to the teeth and bristling with weapons."[40]

It sounded promising indeed. Britain was anxious to begin hacking apart the Ottoman Empire's front on the Red Sea, effectively neutralizing Turkish ability to threaten the all-important sea routes to India — and Messenger X's account made the Arabs seem to be the right men for this job. Thus it did not take long to arrive at the decision to commit to some form of Arab independence in exchange for Sharif Hussein's promise of effective assistance from the tribes for the British war effort.

To the excellent and well-born Sayyid, the descendant of the Sharifs, the Crown of the Proud, Scion of Mohammed's Tree and Branch of the Quraishite trunk, him of the Exalted Presence and of the Lofty Rank ... the Lodestar of the Faithful and cynosure of all devout Believers ... may his Blessing descend upon the people in their multitudes.

— FROM A LETTER BY SIR HENRY MCMAHON
TO SHARIF HUSSEIN [41]

Arabic is a highly formal, ornate and hyperbolic language, especially when translated into English, yet even so one cannot help but feel that "Dear Sharif" would have sufficed if McMahon's now famous correspondence had had any substance. British high commissioner for Egypt and Sudan, Sir Henry McMahon oozed that peculiarly British blend of fawning obsequiousness and pragmatic hypocrisy in these letters which, in this reader's eyes, constitute a solemn British promise to Sharif Hussein of an independent Arab state following the defeat of the Ottoman Empire. This state included the entire Arabian Peninsula, from Alexandretta in Syria to the north, eastward to the Iranian border, and south to the Persian Gulf. The sole exceptions from these boundaries were the British port of Aden and those districts of Syria west of Damascus — Homs, Hama and Aleppo — that also contained vital ports or strategically crucial naval facilities.

It is extremely important to understand that it was this British promise, and *only* the promise, that enabled Hussein to sever the Arabs' emotional bond with the concept of universal Islam and rise up in revolt against the Ottoman caliphate. "We are Arabs before being Muslim," the sharif told his tribes, "and Mohammed is an Arab before being a prophet. There is neither minority nor majority among us, nothing to divide us. We are one body ..."[42]

These were brave words for an Islamic spiritual leader. Hussein had never been a pan-Arab nationalist ideologue, but he intuitively understood what was necessary psychologically to draw in those Arabs beyond the sphere of his own political alliances. In leading the revolt, which played the key role in cutting off Turkish access to the Gulf ports, allowing General Allenby and the British army to push north and east out of Palestine, Sharif Hussein ibn Ali risked literally all — not just his own future and that of his sons, but the future of all Arabs. For it was by no means certain that Britain and its allies would win this war, and should they lose it the Ottoman revenge for Arab perfidy was sure to be terrible. Hussein's willingness to take this high-stakes gamble alone ought to convince any skeptic that Britain's promise was made very clearly, convincingly and sincerely to the sharif. He was not an easy man to fool, and very far indeed from being a fool himself. He also kept his end of the bargain impeccably.

To betray him, to deceive and double-cross him, to lie shamelessly and even to make it seem as if he had lied to his own people, ranks among the most ignoble, disgusting and unforgivable deeds in history. And we are still paying the price for it today.

One non-Arab who was forever wracked by guilt over the shabby treatment of Hussein was T. E. Lawrence. His remorse left us one of the unquestioned masterpieces of twentieth-century literature, *Seven Pillars of Wisdom*, in which he spells out what the revolt meant and what the Arabs expected to get for it: "Our aim was an Arab government with foundations large and native enough to employ the enthusiasm and self-sacrifice of the rebellion translated into terms of peace."[43] Could it be any clearer?

If we charitably discount any promises made to the Arabs while war still raged, we are nonetheless left with two other fora where promises were made that cannot easily be dismissed. The first promise was made in June 1918, when seven Arab nationalist leaders met with British representatives in Cairo. They were promised that Arab territories that were free before the war would remain so, and that in territories liberated from Ottoman rule by the Arabs themselves, the British would officially recognize the "complete and sovereign independence of the inhabitants."[44] Governments elsewhere, it was promised, would be based on the consent of the governed. The second promise is part of the Anglo-French declaration made just days before Germany surrendered. It was an unambiguous offer of self-determination, a promise to establish governments chosen by the Arabs themselves.

Other Arab nationalists more familiar with Western attitudes towards "uncivilized tribes" had long argued that in helping the British and French oust Ottoman Turkey from the Middle East, the Arabs would merely be exchanging one form of foreign domination for another. The reason such voices of caution mostly went unheeded was that, ironic as it now may seem, the hopes of the Arab masses were suddenly raised when, in April 1917, the United States entered World War I — just in time to lay a claim to some of its spoils.

The Arabs imagined that they might get a more receptive hearing from the U.S. government for their demands of self-determination than they would from the British. For the Americans knew the oppressive nature of colonial rule, did they not? President Woodrow Wilson's Fourteen Points, advocating freedom and self-determination for races dominated by the old multi-national empires, also seemed highly encouraging.

President Wilson was, however, not the unconditional friend to the wretched of the earth that the Arabs pictured him to be. A few years earlier, in April 1914, he sent several thousand American troops into Mexico for the purpose of deposing a ruler deemed unacceptable to Washington, "to teach the Latin Americans to elect good men."[45] It was an early example of the American predilection for "regime change," just as Wilson himself was a prototype for the kind of American leader whose stubborn refusal to separate church from state leads him inexorably towards wars between the sons of light and the sons of darkness.

The "whole disgusting scramble for the Middle East" horrified Wilson's sensibilities and stood against everything he believed America represented. His views began to worry the British establishment, which believed Wilson might imperil their policy for the area. How was it possible to reconcile Wilson's commitment to the independence of Middle Eastern states with Britain's imperialist designs? The answer, some felt, might be Lawrence of Arabia.

To combat public reluctance to fight in the war, Wilson had established a Committee on Public Information headed up by a journalist, George Creel. One of Creel's first acts was to propose sending Lowell Thomas, a former newspaperman who lectured in English at Princeton, to gather stirring stories from the European front. Once there, however, Thomas quickly realized that he could find nothing heartening or inspiring in the muddy trenches and mechanized slaughter of the Western Front, so the British Department of Information, his real master, subtly guided his interest towards the Middle East, where Allenby's army was about to capture Jerusalem.

Here Thomas found the kind of yarn that he knew would grip the emotions of an American audience. In reality a mere sideshow to the harrowing conflict in Europe, the Middle East war could be transformed into a latter-day crusade to liberate the Holy Land from evil Turks and free its enslaved Arab, Jewish and Armenian communities. In no time at all Thomas had dubbed T. E. Lawrence "Britain's modern Coeur de Lion." With the newsreel photographer Harry Chase, Thomas shadowed his new Richard the Lionhearted until he had enough material for what was termed a lecture on the Middle Eastern campaign, but in fact was a multimedia variety show that eerily prefigured the way American television would handle all current affairs by the close of the century. "Come with me to lands of history, mystery, and romance," Thomas began, on a set featuring pyramids, moonlight on the Nile and three arc-light projectors that could be used simultaneously with a fade-and-dissolve facility to crank up the drama of Chase's film footage. Other highlights were the Dance of the Seven Veils, the Muezzin's Call to Prayer — adapted and sung by Mrs. Thomas — and of course Thomas' hyperbolic commentary, accompanied by a musical score played by the band of the Welsh Guards and billowing clouds of frankincense pouring from braziers of glowing charcoal.

More than a classical British hero, Lawrence was marketed as the embodiment of the new benign brand of British imperialism. The aim of this was to dispel deep-seated American suspicions that Britain was the rapacious, tyrannical force in the Middle East that it had once been in the American colonies. Thus Thomas presented the Arabs as delighted to have the British running their affairs for them, and not at all worried that they had exchanged one oppressor for another.

Lawrence himself was horrified when he finally viewed the extravaganza, which made him physically ill. It made Thomas very rich, naturally. He toured the world, eventually presenting this travesty to a total audience of some four million, most of whom found it enchanting. Lawrence once referred to Thomas as "the American who made my vulgar reputation, a well-intentioned, intensely crude and pushful fellow" — they might as well have belonged to different species. The small blond scholarly Englishman would spend the rest of his brief life trying to shed the mantle Lowell Thomas had shackled to him.

Lawrence had been just as ruthlessly betrayed as his Arabs. Long before the promises of self-determination were dangled before the Bedu tribes, Britain and France had carved up the Middle East between them in the secret Sykes-Picot Agreement of 1916, named after the representatives from London and Paris who had signed it, Sir Mark Sykes and François Georges-Picot. For his part, Sykes believed Arab independence would mean "Persia, poverty and chaos."

At the 1919 peace conference, the political clout of big business was first deployed as private oil concerns pushed their governments to back away from all wartime pledges made to the Arabs. Their advice was naturally couched in terms of the national interest, but it should have alerted someone to a previously unimagined menace lurking in the brave new world that the delegates in Paris that year were fashioning from the old one's rubble, blood and excrement.

With Faisal, Sharif Hussein's third son and the Arab Revolt's noble figurehead, Lawrence attended the peace conference. No one was entirely certain whom he represented there or even why he had come. The British delegates feared he might try to scuttle their plans for the new Arabia by arguing persuasively for Arab independence. Lawrence was by now the prototypical celebrity — famous for being famous — but although this may have obtained for him the best tables in the finest Parisian restaurants and invitations to weekends at magnificent châteaux, it counted for nothing at the conference itself, where a world was up for grabs.

The rapaciousness of Britain's prime minister, Lloyd George, became a thing of wonder. Waving aside President Wilson's high-minded fourteen-point fantasy, once embraced in the heat of war, Lloyd George went after territory for the British empire like a starving tiger set loose in a mortuary. The British had sacrificed a generation to save Europe from German militarism — thus Lloyd George demanded Egypt, Arabia, Palestine and Mesopotamia as just compensation. Clemenceau, the French premier, proved less greedy, insisting nonetheless that France hold onto Syria and southern Anatolia, and speculating that a French adviser might be placed at the elbow of Turkey's sultan, whose empire had vanished in the smoke of burning civilizations and the clouds of chlorine and mustard gas. The sultan might need a little advice.

While Lawrence and Faisal waited patiently, the fate of the Middle East was decided without them in drawing rooms, private clubs and dining rooms in rented châteaux within easy motoring distance of Paris. It was a done deal, all sewn up and in the bag by the time Faisal was permitted to speak.

The scion of Islam's most illustrious family, who, with his father and brothers, had risked everything for a dream, whose help had been instrumental in freeing Arabia from the Turks, had waited two months to be allowed a mere twenty minutes to plead his case. With great dignity, dressed in the white robes that had once captivated the imagination and the heart of the Englishman who now sat at his side, Faisal spoke in classical Arabic, explaining that he represented his father, who was requesting the right of self-determination for all Arabs and the recognition of an Arab state as an independent geographic entity. That was all. The other participants listened politely, yet even while Faisal spoke British and French cartographers hunched over maps behind closed doors were drawing the borderlines of what would soon be known as the Arab states of Lebanon, Syria, Iraq and Transjordan. In every case, these boundaries conformed to the requirements of European colonialism.

The other current that was working against Arab interests without their knowledge was Zionism, the plan to make a Jewish homeland out of Palestine. The principal British Zionist, Chaim Weizmann, a brilliant chemist who had made a significant contribution to the war effort by inventing a new process essential for the manufacture of TNT, perceived that the British government — in spite of its agreement with France for an *international* administration there — still felt that Palestine would only provide an effective buffer for the vital Suez Canal if it was a purely British protectorate. Weizmann thus assured Britain that in exchange for its support, Zionists would work for the establishment of such a protectorate there. This suited British plans far better than the arrangement made with the unreliable French.

On November 2, 1917, Arthur Balfour, the British foreign secretary, made his famous and profoundly ambiguous declaration that Britain would "view with favour the establishment in Palestine of a national home for the Jewish people ...," qualifying this promise with the assurance that "nothing shall be done which may prejudice the civic and religious rights of the existing non-Jewish communities or the rights and political status enjoyed by Jews in any other country." The question that has never been satisfactorily resolved is how this pledge to the Zionists conflicted with what had already been promised to the Arabs for their support in the war against Ottoman Turkey.

The Arabs claim that the letters between McMahon and Sharif Hussein promised Palestine among the areas in which Britain pledged to uphold Arab independence. The Zionists deny this is true, a position also assumed officially by Britain and endorsed in 1937 by the Palestine Royal Commission's report. However, a report by the British Arab Bureau, which has never been rescinded or corrected, places Palestine firmly in the area that the Arabs were promised.

At the Paris peace conference, faced with a Zionist lobby led by Weizmann and Felix Frankfurter, a Harvard Law School professor who was later appointed to the U.S. Supreme Court, the Arabs soon realized they had been outmanoeuvred. The issue seemed one of great importance to President Wilson, however, and in the interests of fairness he went out of his way to insist that a commission be formed and sent off to discover the wishes of those people actually living in the area.

The report of this commission was decidedly blunt: there could be mandates for Palestine, Syria and Iraq, it stated, but they should only be for a limited term, and independence ought to be granted as soon as possible. The idea of making Palestine into a Jewish commonwealth should be dropped. Period. One can imagine how this suggestion was greeted by Zionists, who were finally within sight of their goal. Only the Arabs were surprised when the commission's report was completely ignored, even in Washington.

There was another conference in April 1920, in San Remo, Italy, where the agreements of the Paris conference were ratified. The British and French got the mandates they had requested; the Arabs got nothing.

Their reaction to this final confirmation of utter betrayal was bitter fury. British establishments in Iraq were raided, and there were strikes at the French in Syria. Both insurrections were swiftly put down in the most ruthless manner. In Iraq the British army razed any village from which an attack was believed to have been mounted. It will come as no surprise today to learn that such tactics in no way deterred the Iraqis from continuing their assaults on British personnel and property. Lawrence had by now retreated to a fellowship at All Souls College, Oxford, from whence he ventured his opinion, dripping with irony, that burning villages was not very efficient: "By gas attacks the whole population of offending districts could be wiped out neatly; and as a method of government it would be no more immoral than the present system."[46]

Appallingly, something like this was then actually being considered. The ubiquitous Churchill, by now secretary of state for war and air, asked Sir Hugh Trenchard, chief of air staff, if he would consider taking over control of Iraq since the army had estimated the job would require eighty thousand troops and cost £21.5 million a year, which was considered to be more than the country was worth. If the Royal Air Force took on the task, suggested

Churchill, "it would ... entail the provision of some kind of asphyxiating bombs calculated to cause disablement of some kind but not death ... for use in preliminary operations against turbulent tribes." These, presumably, were nothing like as great a menace as the "uncivilized tribes" for whom he prescribed poisoned gas. But Churchill's suggestions were clearly not valued that highly, since the RAF decided to stick with conventional high-explosive bombs in the end. It was a technique of colonial governance that obviously worked for them, since the British deployed such bombs to control the Middle East well into the 1950s.

Arab humiliation is embodied by the fate of Faisal, the leader "created" by Lawrence, to whom he had conveyed the promises gushing forth from Britain like the fountains of the Palace of Versailles where they were forgotten. After the French had kicked him out of Syria, Faisal was waited on by an embarrassed delegation of British officials as he passed through Palestine, one of whom recorded the incident: "We mounted him a guard of honour a hundred strong. He carried himself with the dignity and the noble resignation of Islam ... though tears stood in his eyes and he was wounded to the soul. The Egyptian sultanate did not 'recognize' him, and at Quantara station, he awaited his train sitting on his luggage."[47]

One might wonder where Lawrence was during this. He was at his mother's home in Oxford experiencing a major crisis of conscience. According to his mother he was depressed and would often sit between breakfast and lunch "in the same position, without moving, and with the same expression on his face."

Unfortunately, this guilt made him leap at an offer to join Churchill, by this time ensconced in the Colonial Office and eager to do something about the rat's breakfast in the Middle East. The first task Lawrence was handed was to patch up things with Faisal by offering to make him king of Iraq.

The trouble with this was that it appeared far from clear whether or not the Iraqis wanted Faisal as their king. There were other claimants to the newly invented Iraqi throne, including Ibn Sa'ud, the ruler of a Saudi Arabia his family had cobbled together from the territories of tribes they had wiped out in what had resembled a gang war. Churchill, who loathed Ibn Sa'ud for reasons unknown, rejected his claim on the grounds that "he would plunge the whole country into religious pandemonium." The House of Sa'ud ruled in partnership with an hereditary priesthood provided by the House of Wahhab, whose founder had imagined himself to be Successor of the Prophet, devising an Islam so stripped down it was more like a prison's code of conduct than a religion — though far less tolerant.

Another candidate for Iraqi leader was the nationalist Sayid Taleb, whose popularity stemmed from his threat to revolt if the British did not allow Iraqis to choose freely their own leader.

But the British knew how to operate a colonial democracy better than any nation that had ever been in the business. Disapproving of Taleb — bad attitude — they handled his candidacy by kidnapping him after he left afternoon tea with the British high commissioner, then whisking him off on a freighter for a very long vacation in Ceylon. With his main rival removed, Faisal was elected king by the sort of majority — 96.8 percent — that can only be described as "suspicious."

Britain needed a tranquil, stable state in Jordan to protect Palestine, so Faisal's brother Abdullah was made king and given money and troops in return for his promise to eradicate any local anti-Zionist or anti-French activity. Their father, Hussein, with whom the Arab Revolt had begun, and who had sacrificed all to find himself betrayed by those to whom he had been unflinchingly loyal, was offered £100,000 a year not to make a nuisance of himself. This was the same amount received by Ibn Sa'ud, since the strictures of the cynical Cairo accord warned that "to pay one more than the other causes jealousy." The Saudi ruler had to agree to accept the whole settlement and not attack Hussein.

Astonishingly, Lawrence regarded all this as redemption in full of Britain's promises to the Arabs. Perhaps he needed to believe it was so. The Arabs did not, however, and have been displaying their feelings of righteous indignation ever since.

Faisal managed to obtain some measure of independence for Iraq by the time of his death in 1932. Yet British forces intervened again in Iraqi affairs in 1942, overthrowing the pro-Nazi government of nationalist leader Rashid Ali and restoring the monarchy. The kingdom of Faisal fell for the last time in 1958, in a somewhat belated response to the Suez Crisis. (Two years earlier, Egypt's ruler President Nasser had sought to test his nation's role in the vague new world of neo-imperialism by seizing control of the vital canal that linked the Mediterranean to the Red Sea and the Persian Gulf beyond. Along this route came tankers carrying most of the oil needed to keep the great wheels of Western capitalism turning. As French and British paratroopers fell like spoors of fungus from the azure skies above Port Said, it occurred to many Arabs that independence was something they could only have if they promised never to use it.)

Iraq's new leader, General Qasim, devoted his time to building a working relationship with London, whose main interest, as always, was oil. Within five years he too was dead from an assassin's bullet and another military faction seized power. This next regime also lasted less than five years, deposed in a coup in 1968 by the Arab Socialist Ba'ath (Resurrection) Party, which was to control Iraq well into the next millennium (and still rules Syria, as it has done since 1963).

While Saddam Hussein was prominent in the Ba'ath Party, feared and powerful, he kept a low profile, devoting those early years to building up the Special Republican Guard — an elite division of the army committed to him and his policies alone — and creating a secret police force through which he could spy on colleagues. This paid off in 1979 when he finally emerged on centre stage as president, a strongman who could weather Iraq's turbulent tendencies. He immediately instigated a purge of his enemies, broadcast on state TV. Videos of the individual tortures and executions were also made available to those left unpurged, in case they were inclined to think that Saddam was basically a decent guy.

France managed to hold on to Syria and Lebanon until 1946 before grudgingly evacuating its troops. That same year Britain gave up its claim on Jordan. Abdullah reigned until 1951 when he was shot dead while entering the El Aqsa mosque in Jerusalem, his assassin one of a growing number who believed the Jordanian king had betrayed the Arabs over Palestine.

In 1958 the American Sixth Fleet stood by to save Abdullah's son, by then King Hussein, from a repetition of the coup that had just toppled his cousin Faisal II in Iraq. Hussein survived, his popular rule lasting until his death in 1999, when his brother Crown Prince Hassan was passed over for the succession in favour of Hussein's son, Abdullah, whose mother was British and who barely speaks any Arabic. Many feel that the brilliant, scholarly Hassan and his charismatic son, Rashid — who bears an uncanny resemblance to his beloved late uncle — would have been a more prudent choice for the future prosperity of Jordan than the affable but uninspired and decidedly over-Westernized Abdullah, a situation that has somewhat divided friends of the nation. Yet the peaceful, elegant Kingdom of Jordan still continues, sole lasting legacy of Lawrence, whom a few old Bedu sheikhs there still claim to have known as "the man with the gold."

THE WHOLE WORLD IS WATCHING

We hear ominous tidings. We hear of a malevolent race,
withdrawn from the communion of our belief, Turks, Persians,
Arabs, accursed, estranged from God, that have laid waste by fire
and sword to the walls of Constantinople, to the Arm of St.
George ... Turks perforate the navels of God's servants, pull forth
and bind their intestines to stakes, lead them about while viscera
discolour the earth. They pierce Christians with arrows, flog the
suffering. What else can we say? What more shall be said? To
whom, therefore, does the task of vengeance fall, if not to you?
— HIS HOLINESS POPE URBAN II, 1095 [48]

Amman was cold and gloomy, exactly the way it had been during the Gulf War. But nothing else was the same in Jordan. Someone had been spending big money all over the capital. Entire suburbs had sprung up since my last visit five years earlier, every new building more attractive than the old ones, yet conforming to the city regulation that requires all structures to be made of white limestone or marble — which makes Amman by far the most charming city in the east. There were more luxury hotels now than there were in Toronto, and most were more lavishly and tastefully decorated. I had booked into the brand-new Hotel Royale, whose opulence and sheer style took my breath away. My room was a quarter of the price charged by the Holiday Inn on London's Cromwell Road for a room half the size and nothing like as nice. Uday Hussein, Saddam's Bad Boy, was evidently one of its major investors. A stone's throw away was the Marriott Hotel, built by Mohammed bin Laden, who had his own Bad Boy.

Everywhere in Amman, too, one could see the national ambivalence to young King Abdullah reflected by the portraits of him that had gone up on billboards, in offices and shops, and on the walls of government buildings. Most seemed to show him with his father, the late King Hussein, as if to reassure Jordanians that the fleshy, boyish figure was indeed legitimate heir to the throne that Hussein had occupied for as long as anyone could remember. There were still many portraits around the city that showed Hussein alone. He had been much loved and was dearly missed. The extraordinary gathering of world leaders — both in and out of power — attending his funeral was testimony to his stature as a statesman. No one minded him siding with Saddam during the Gulf War. He had always walked a tightrope between the will of Israel and the West, and the needs of his fellow Arabs, frequently doing what was prudent when his heart demanded otherwise. He had ruled a country that housed not just Jordanians and tribal Bedu but also a million or so Palestinian refugees, as well as, since 1991, many thousands of Iraqis seeking refuge from Saddam, American bombers and the cruel U.N. sanctions. To keep everyone happy was an impossible task, yet Hussein managed it as well as was humanly possible.

Abdullah did not seem to be enjoying the same success. Where Hussein had felt it better to let Amman's Palestinians vent their emotions in loud angry demonstrations marching out from the breeze-block hell of their Baka'a ghetto, Abdullah had clamped down on public gatherings. It was widely known that he had sided with America, but the fact had never been stated publicly. U.S. fighters were using Jordanian bases for raids into Iraq — I had seen F-11s and F-15s flying in low to land south of Ruweished, and the Jordanian air force does not possess the F-15 — yet this was denied outright by the government. The prime minister himself assured me Jordan would never permit the U.S. to launch attacks on Iraq from its soil.

No Arab wanted to see Iraq attacked or invaded by America, so the great-grandson of Sharif Hussein of Mecca, who had once proclaimed himself king of all Arabs from the holy city's Great Mosque, could hardly admit to aiding and abetting the slaughter of his brothers. But Jordan was a poor country. It had no oil. So when Washington offered to waive $2 billion in foreign loans and promised all manner of aid programs, Abdullah could not refuse — especially knowing that the outcome of the war was a foregone conclusion. Or seemed to be. It is unlikely that his father would have taken the same course, but Abdullah did not have the emotional ties to people and land that Hussein did. His queen was Palestinian, however, and this was probably what kept the lid on the anger in Baka'a, which is the angriest place I have ever been.

No, things in Jordan were not the same as they had been when last Saddam had made front-page news. There were not even Saddam lapel buttons for sale in the hotel kiosks, and the stock of anti-Israel literature had diminished too. Only the weather remained constant, its grey chill all there was to remind a visitor that sorrow gripped the soul of Arabs whenever they were forced to see the reality of the circumstances in which they lived.

For all the stories told around fires of camel dung under the great dome of heaven, for all the heroes and heroism, for all the great battles fought against impossible odds and, with Allah's help, won, and for all the history of a civilization that was once the summit of human achievement, they were now, once again, just a little people unable to protect themselves from any invader and totally at the mercy of powers they knew deep down despised them — and would one day destroy their whole world. Little remained of the old ways now. The tribal Bedu slowly drifted into city life down a one-way street; camels were being replaced by suvs; the *keffiyah* and *dishdasha* were exchanged for baseball caps and jeans; only old men still smoked the shisha pipe; and in place of tribal dances and songs there was television — soap operas from Egypt, MTV and even worse trash from America. It was all vanishing, to be replaced by nothing anyone could call his own. This was why Islam seemed suddenly so much more precious than it had half a century earlier. It was virtually all that was left from a thousand years of culture which owed nothing to anyone, springing forth from the desert sands and dry rocks like the brief flowers of April, when the wadis gushed with water, newborn lambs swelled the flocks and life in the bleak barren plains of dust seemed full of promise. Arabs don't like the desert; their heaven is a place of running streams, blooming flowers and shady trees. The desert is merely what they have.

It even snowed in the desert, and one day there was a blizzard as wild and blinding as any seen in Canada. It was on this snowy day that I was invited by my friend, Crown Prince Hassan — brother of the late King Hussein — to dinner at a house overlooking the Temple of Hercules in the old part of the city. Among the other guests were the French and Spanish ambassadors to Jordan. The mood was sepulchral, and I don't think anyone wanted it otherwise. We were appalled at the news reports coming in from the American advance.

Prince Hassan had a vested interest in Iraq. His uncle, Faisal II, had been the last Iraqi monarch — yet he was not gripped by what his wife, Princess Sorvath, termed "red-carpet fever." Unlike other relatives of Faisal, he had no desire to seek the Iraqi throne should it be dusted off and declared vacant, as some thought possible. Iraq has always been notoriously difficult to govern, and a parliamentary monarchy would at least provide the semblance of continuity in leadership, filling the vacuum left by Saddam while Iraqis grew accustomed to the mysteries of democratic government.

Siddi Hassan seemed careworn and sad. A barrel-chested man with sparkling eyes and curiously small legs, he normally had a deep explosive laugh that rattled chandeliers, but tonight there was nothing to laugh at. Erudite, thoughtful and compassionate where his late brother had been a pragmatic man of action, Hassan would nonetheless have made for Jordan a great king, if a very different one. He has worked tirelessly on interfaith activities that bring together representatives of the region's three great monotheisms in the belief that they, and not the politicians, hold the key to peace just as the religions hold the hearts of the population, and that as long as there is dialogue between them there is still hope. Among his close friends he numbers London's chief rabbi, and as President of the Club of Rome — a think-tank operating on the principle that politics are too important to be left to politicians — he oversees the publication of countless papers, pamphlets and books penned by men and women who, like himself, share the conviction that violence ought not to have a role in civilized diplomacy, that the only thing war prevents is peace. He is one of the most thoroughly good and decent human beings I have ever known, and I could merely imagine the sorrow that this war was now causing him, especially since his nephew the king had made Jordan a collaborator in it.

"I know him," Hassan said of Saddam, at one point. "He thought Europe would intervene with the Americans before it got to this stage. He was wrong. Again!"

He had met Saddam many times and did not like him, yet respected him for many qualities never mentioned by Western media, not least of which was his love for Iraq.

"He truly loves his country," Hassan told me. "It is his passion — no one can take that away from him. He's not a learned man but there is no aspect of Iraq's vast history he isn't intimately familiar with. That he believes he has always acted in her best interests I do not in the least bit doubt. Just as I don't doubt he is a dreadful tyrant and a brute."

He went on to tell a story about finding Saddam supervising arrangements for a state dinner with King Hussein.

"'Make sure there are napkins at every place,' he was telling the servants," Hassan said, "'Otherwise the Jordanians will think we're animals ...'" Then he added ruefully, "He always acted on instinct. He never thinks things out. He isn't a thinker. His instincts aren't always accurate, though — and that has been a problem ..."

What did he think would happen now?

"Oh God," said Hassan, wearily. "It is going to be a mess. I really think the Americans have put us all on the slippery slope ..."

He left the phrase hanging, and I suddenly had a vivid mental picture of us all holding on to each other in terror as we slowly slid behind George W. Bush down a steep incline of greased metal towards the roaring flames of some awful maw opening in the bowels of the earth.

I wondered if the war might not at least assist the Palestine-Israel peace negotiations, adding somewhat redundantly, "Where there's a will, there's a —"

"There are usually lawyers," Hassan cut in, half a laugh erupting like a mortar shell from his throat to bounce off the ceiling and set cut-glass tinkling around flickering candles.

A little later, he said: "The first Arab state to gain independence in the twentieth century becomes the first to lose it in the twenty-first century ... Could one call this 'irony'?"

His smile was the expression of an academic enchanted by structural symmetry or the beauty of an equation — some act of appreciation in which the heart is not required.

"I think 'tragedy' is the term you're looking for," said the Spanish ambassador.

"Yes," said Hassan. "Probably is."

Princess Sorvath tried to dispel the gloom by recalling an anecdote about her mother meeting King Ibn Sa'ud, but it included a mention of Faisal, which returned the table to the only subject of discussion possible under the circumstances.

The French ambassador bridled at a news report claiming the French embassy in Baghdad was aiding Saddam's regime and had issued French passports to members of the Revolutionary Command Council, Saddam's cabinet.

"We evacuated the embassy two days before the war began," he announced, exasperated. "There is no one there to do such a thing. Really! It is disgraceful how they are behaving."

He meant the Americans, of course, who were reacting with scarcely believable foolishness to France's refusal to collaborate in a war that Paris had denounced as illegal. Restaurants across America were pouring French wine down their drains and had eagerly embraced some idiot's suggestion that "French fries" be renamed "freedom fries." It had occurred to me that, as a fried potato they could buy or sell, freedom might finally become the kind of commodity Americans could truly understand.

There were no Americans present that evening, and if there had been I am sure they would have been treated courteously. Yet an American fly on the wall would have been shocked by how low an opinion everyone at the table shared of his nation.

I asked the ambassador when he thought embassy staff might consider returning.

"To whom do they present their credentials?" he asked, incredulous. "I mean, it is ridiculous. Do they go to General Franks perhaps?"

No one seemed sure who would be issuing Iraqi visas now, or even if there would be visas for Iraq. I wondered what happened to a country's embassies around the world in cases like this.

"I think they carry on functioning," the Frenchman said, not sounding too sure about it. "They do what it is possible for them ..."

"I think not," opined the Spanish ambassador. "A new government must select its own diplomats."

It was clear neither ambassador actually knew. It was not a situation they had personally experienced, nor one they expected to experience. I got the impression that the Spanish ambassador was not too pleased to find himself part of America's so-called Coalition.[49] But diplomats are nothing if not diplomatic, and the Spaniard kept his misgivings to himself and innuendo.

What had happened to Amman's Iraqi embassy?

"I think we are guarding it heavily," Prince Hassan replied. "The staff are all inside, presumably trying to get information from Baghdad. It must be dreadful for them." He wrung the neck of his napkin, then said, "When are you going back?"

This attracted the interest of both ambassadors, who requested I keep them in mind if any information that involved their respective interests came my way. And if it proved possible to communicate with the outside world from Baghdad.

"Is it going to be a Stalingrad?" someone inquired.

"Even the Israelis thought twice about going into Beirut when they were camped at its gates," someone else replied. "If *they* aren't trained for urban warfare in the Middle East, then the Americans most certainly aren't."

"They've no idea what they're in for," said Hassan. "Two snipers can hold off a regiment from one alley. They will have to flatten the city first, or take heavy casualties."

"Then we can assume that we won't see Baghdad again, can't we, dear?" Princess Sorvath told him.

"There will be no winners in this war," Hassan said, quietly. "Only losers."

Hey, diddle diddle, it's straight up the middle!

— FORMER U.S. ARMY COLONEL DAVID HACKWORTH,

COMMENTING FOR CNN ON THE AMERICAN

ADVANCE, MARCH 20, 2003

A uniformed soldier drove me back to the Hotel Royale, whose floodlit ellipsoid edifice on its hill could be seen from almost anywhere in the city. Had Uday designed it himself?, I wondered, trying to find a name that adequately defined the building's bizarre but not unpleasing style. Greco-Sumerian, perhaps? Romano-Babylonian? Neo-post-Islamic Romanesque? Post-Unusualist seemed the most apt. Weaving through the hills of Amman, I pressed my nose against the window and let my breath gradually mist the glass until everything beyond it vanished into a haze — the way I used to do when I was a kid and the adults were talking among themselves. A moonlit frosting of snow coated olive groves, fields and orchards, making them as pale as the bone-white buildings stacked in cubes like toy bricks in the steep ravines. It gave the world an appearance of having suddenly aged, turned silvery-grey with worry.

"How is Siddi Hassan?" asked the desk clerk, Abdul.

"What makes you think I'd know that?"

"His car pick you up from Royal Palace; take you old city for dinner," replied Abdul.

"Oh *yeah*? What did we eat?"

"How could I be knowing what you eat?" Abdul laughed.

"You know everything else ..."

I would not want to be a bank robber in the Middle East. Everyone *always* knows what you're doing, where you've been, *who* you're doing ...

"He is good man, Siddi Hassan," said Abdul.

"Yes, he is. Do you miss King Hussein?"

He smiled wanly, looking down, and replied, "Yes, sir. We loved him. He was our king ..."

"And Abdullah?"

"He is *son* of King Hussein."

It was the only answer he could give, yet it still said everything there was to say.

The lobby was littered with the equipment of arriving television crews from all over the world. Cameramen stood guard over the more precious items, while producers holding cellphones like poker cards worked at keeping their stress levels up to maximum torque.

"Robert *promised* me a hardside would be waiting for us, Trevor. Where the fuck is it?"

"No, the driver's name is Mahmoud *not* MacMood ..."

"I'm missing the fucking *story*, that's all, Rachel! You expect me to wait for a fucking visa while the biggest story of the decade is just fucking *happening* without me?"

"They told me lead boxes would be *here*, lovey. And they're not. They're just *not*! They are *not here*!"

A man leapt into the elevator beside me through six inches of closing door. Short and wiry, he reminded me of Eric Idle playing his nudge-nudge scoundrel character.

"Teridane," he said, holding out a hand to shake.

"No, I don't use it," I told him, assuming he was after some sort of medication. It sounded like a tranquilizer and I wondered if it was any good. His hand felt as if the skin had been removed — a skeleton's hand. I had to look down to make sure it was not.

"No, that's *me*," he said. The accent sounded Australian. "Terry Dane."

"Oh, sorry, I thought you were asking for Xanax or something ..."

"You *want* Xanax?" he asked, looking me in the eyes sincerely. "I'll get you *Xanax*. I heard you needed lead boxes too, right?"

"Wrong."

The accent was in fact New Zealand, and Terry turned out to be a disbarred lawyer from Auckland who now worked as a fixer, the kind of war profiteer who roams the planet in the wake of TV crews, for whom he found ... well, *anything*. Networks with crews missing a firewire, in need of extra flak-jackets, short of digital videotape or Marmite or the anchor's brand of clove cigarettes or a hooker willing to bugger the producer with a strap-on — *anything at all* — were willing to pay big bucks to keep their units up to speed on the Big Story. Cash. And Terry Dane could find whatever they needed, anywhere they needed it. *Whenever* they needed it. Because whatever he charged was still going to be cheaper than flying someone over with the item, since Fedex doesn't deliver to war zones.

How did he manage this?

"*Contacts*, mate. I got contacts, *don't* I?"

I was sure he did.

When he learned I was a one-man-band whose budget barely extended to room and board, he jumped out at the next floor, saying, "Bear it in mind, mate. 'Cos you *never* know, do you? If things get *hairy*, just call *Terry* ... I'll be seeing you around, eh?"

He was able to make "hairy" and "Terry" rhyme perfectly.

In my room, Sky TV was reporting live from Kuwait City. A man with a microphone was interviewing another humanoid. Both wore gas masks and the night sky behind them was red. They spoke without lips. It looked like a fetish movie. I found the images profoundly disturbing. They made me feel anxious and weary at the same time. I did not want to be alone in the room, yet I did not want to go out. I did not know *what* I wanted.

In the elevator, a producer was telling his deuce of cellphones, "The whole fucking world is watching, Brian! And *I'm* not on air because *your* assistant forgot to arrange the docs! *Forgot*? What the fuck is *that*? Forgot. Brian, *you don't fucking forget a thing like that*!"

"Relax," I told him, getting out on the third floor. "It'll be *fine*. Be happy ..."

He looked at me as if I'd tried to persuade him I was a spider from Mars. As the doors slid shut on his face like one of the transition effects in Adobe Premiere 6.00, I realized I actually *was* in a movie. It was like that moment in a dream when you realize it's a dream, then dream you've woken up and can't understand why the air feels like molasses or your limbs won't work. I was *supposed* to be in a movie, at least. A TV network I can't name for legal reasons had loaned me a Sony digicam with the idea that I might learn how to use it. I just kept forgetting to carry it around with me, because the present only ever seems interesting once it has become the past and you can't get it back again — at least, not to film it you can't. Yet.

I sat in a bar the hotel had decorated like a London gentlemen's club — leather wingbacks, bookshelves, framed engravings, a cigar humidor — where a television played the same fetish movie: *Rubber Sluts Under A Red Sky* or *Kiki Does Kuwait*. They had a better selection of single-malt Scotch whisky than the Howard Hotel in Edinburgh. Ahmed handed me the TV remote-control along with a very generous pour of Lagavulin Distiller's Edition.

"You may wish for change the program, sir," he said.

"Thanks. I may."

Flipping through the dozen or so 24-hour news channels the hotel was somehow able to provide — I only get *two* at home — I paused to watch Hugh Grant playing some recklessly handsome chap called Col. Chris Vernon, who was evidently now in charge of Basra. Basra didn't sound very much under control, though, and Hugh — or Col. Chris — looked as weary as I felt. He'd had a hell of a day by the sound of it, though his "men" had done "a fantastic job." There was still "quite a lot of mopping up to do," however, but "the morale" was "quite splendid." It turned out to be the BBC World News. Had Col. Vernon been put in charge of Basra *because* he resembled Hugh Grant — so you couldn't possibly dislike him no matter what he or his men did — or because he was the right man for the job? Seventy-eight civilians had been killed in the city that day, it seemed. The inhabitants of Basra mostly scowled at the camera from doorways, stubbornly unaware that they were now in good hands, indeed *jolly decent* hands. Except for a few mischievous five-year-old boys who kept saying, "Hullo, mister," and "Jorg Boosh good!" while wiping snot on their wrists and waving at the camera — a big no-no in TV news, because it reminds the viewer there *is* a camera, something the viewer must be shielded from knowing in order to suspend disbelief and think his box is a window through which the world can be spied upon the way King Lear wanted to spy upon it.

I flipped to the Iraqi State TV channel, where Mohammed Sayeed Sahaf, the only information minister in the world who did stand-up propaganda, was on in a replay of that morning's classic routine, *The Crusaders' Sketch*:

"Those *villains*," he said, to the five journalists left in Baghdad, "those *crusaders* now try to pretend they will soon reach Baghdad. They are just trying to fool you, to make Iraqi people be feared there is now no defence for Baghdad. They are just lying, those *villains* and invaders ... I assure you that Iraq will be their graveyard, their tanks will be their coffins ..."

Someone asked him how Saddam was doing.

"He is *good*," said Mohammed-the-Info, clearly not having a clue whether Saddam was even alive, let alone thriving. "They are all *good*, the leaders. And those *crusaders*, those *villains* will soon be seeing how we Iraqis defend our country. Soon they will taste our thirst for freedoms and the terrible weapon in store for them ..."

His English could become quite remarkable given enough time ... or rope ...

I resumed playing the couch-potato's piano with an arpeggio that flipped all the way back to Sky News, which was also at the Pentagon by now.

Donald Rumsfeld promised the Iraqi regime that it faced "certain death." The last time I'd seen his smug, irritating face, in Frankfurt, it had been going on about "the humanity" that went into building America's weapons of mass destruction these days. I think he meant that they were more accurate than they had previously been, so they were less likely to blow up the wrong buildings, therefore only civilians near the right buildings were in danger of becoming collateral damage. I wondered if anyone in Baghdad realized how humane the bombing was this time. It most certainly never occurred to me.

Still, it was good to gain a perspective on what I'd only experienced subjectively, like any other inhabitant of Baghdad. It explained why the previous Friday — March 21 — had seemed to be a reasonably good facsimile of Armageddon from my vantage point at Bassim's house. In less than 24 hours, 1,500 cruise missiles and precision-guided bombs had been hurled down on Baghdad. No wonder it was noisy. *One thousand five hundred!* Good news if you manufactured cruise missiles and PGBS, though ...

> *Today I weep for my country ... When did we become a country that ignores and berates our friends and calls them irrelevant? When did we decide to risk undermining international order by adopting a radical doctrinaire approach to using our awesome military might?*
>
> — U.S. SENATOR ROBERT BYRD, ON THE
> FLOOR OF THE SENATE, MARCH 20, 2003

That good old man, Senator Byrd. Gonzalo ... Gloucester: he could be cast as any of Shakespeare's good old men. I began reading the *Jordan Times*, while auditioning U.S. politicians for Shakespearean tragedies. Colin Powell — or *Colon Bowel* in this part of the world, since Arabic has no "P" — as Othello, with Bush as Iago. Or Bush as Hamlet, with Bush senior as the ghost of Hamlet's Dad, and Saddam as Claudius, Paris Hilton as Ophelia ... If Senator Byrd was Gloucester, with George W. as Regan and Goneril, who played Lear or Cordelia?

My head was spinning. Every time I closed my eyes I saw that hospital in Baghdad, the puddles of blood, the crying women, the groaning and wailing, people vibrating with fear and shock, their eyes staring without comprehension because the horror of their pained and wrecked bodies had become an infernal *tableau vivant* in which they both played a part and watched the other actors play theirs. Wives and mothers brought in body parts — arms, hands, legs, feet — like pieces from a gruesome jigsaw puzzle that seemed to fit anywhere ... children with burned faces that looked as if a thousand horseflies, hornets, snakes had bitten them, or a hundred spiders' eggs had hatched below the surface and larvae were eating their way out ... the flesh on an aged woman's hands was coming off like surgical gloves exposing waxy yellow bones ...

And this is a good thing?

I feared I might have said it out loud. My hands were shaking, and I could feel the creeper veins in my temples throbbing to the same sticky cushioned drumbeat that sounded a phasing effect like wet rubber bootsteps across the tympanum of each ear.

"For you, sir ..." Ahmed handed me another bevelled glass crucible of Lagavulin.

"Oh, no, no — I can't. Thank you though ..."

"This one from the hose, sir. It is grift from Misel ..."

"Misel?"

He nodded bashfully. "Yes. Mai's elves and the chief of chicken ..."

It was "on the house," a "gift" from Ahmed "himself" and the "chef," who still laboured in the "kitchen." I imagine a lot of people learning English as a second language or punishment might have trouble with "chicken" and "kitchen." I know I would.

The TV suddenly flipped itself to CNN, where Aaron Brown, the thinking man's Forrest Gump, was saying "a lot of people wondered why Iraqi TV had been allowed to stay on the air, why the Coalition allowed Iraqi TV to stay on the air as long as it did ..."

Ahmed and I both stared at the screen, which showed pretty clouds of pink and purple blooming like time-lapsed tulips and roses over Baghdad, as if Turner had been commissioned to paint *The Bombing of Baghdad*. The images in no way conveyed the noise, carnage and horror that was their reality, just as no photograph of the sun's surface communicates the vast landscape of thousand-mile-high flames and the oceans of raging gas that are the perpetual explosion comprising its normality.

"They bombed the TV station?"

"Yes," said Ahmed. "Iraq having not telluvission now ..."

"That is ... It's terrible."

CNN's correspondent Nic Robertson appeared to approve of this act, now saying that the bombing of Iraq's TV station "will take away a very important tool from the Iraqi leadership — that of showing their face, getting their message out to the Iraqi people, and really telling them that they are still in control."

Wasn't that the same service CNN — and the other networks — provided for the U.S. government?

Now a *New York Times* reporter, Michael Gordon, was giving CNN his views, which I trust he'll remember when someone blows up his newspaper: "I think the television, based on what I've seen of Iraqi television, with Saddam Hussein presenting propaganda to his people and showing off the Apache helicopter and claiming a farmer shot it down and trying to persuade his own public that he was really in charge, when we're trying to send the exact opposite message, I think, was an appropriate target."[50]

According to the Geneva Conventions it was a war crime. The conventions forbid the targeting of "civilian installations, whether state-owned or not, unless they are being used for military purposes ... it is not permissible to bomb a television station simply because it is being used for the purposes of propaganda."[51] The media were quick to cite Geneva when Iraq was accused of violating the conventions by airing footage of POWs being interrogated — something the U.S. has subsequently done several times, including when it aired humiliating images of a doctor examining Saddam's long unkempt hair and shining a flashlight in his mouth.

Just then, Michelle from Sky TV walked into the bar.

"*There* you are!" she said. " Come on, we're leaving in fifteen minutes ... Meet you in the lobby ..."

"They just knocked out Iraqi TV ..."

"Oh, fucking hell, no!" she said, on her way out again. "There really aren't any rules for them, are th—"

"I've gotta go to Baghdad, Ahmed."

He took a swig of my Scotch and winced.

"I am wisking for you safety, Mister Bawl."

"So am I, Mister Ahmed."

We shook hands in a formal, manly manner. Then hugged and kissed cheeks like the sentimental saps we were. I'd known Ahmed since the Gulf War, in four different hotels. We knew nothing about each other really, but I think he liked me as much as I liked him.

What I really wanted to do was sleep, not drive eight hundred kilometres back into the war.

CHAPTER FOUR

THE DOGS OF WAR

The three most significant political developments of the twentieth century were the growth of democracy, the growth of corporate power and the growth of corporate propaganda as a means of protecting corporate power against democracy.

— ALEX CAREY

The idea of "embedding" journalists with the U.S. military during the invasion of Iraq came from public relations wizards who work in the Pentagon. In their current strategic-planning literature,[52] journalism is described as an aspect or wing of psychological warfare operations — "psyops." Its purpose, in turn, the Pentagon tells us, is to achieve "information dominance," which itself is an aspect of "full-spectrum dominance." Translated into English, "full-spectrum dominance" means gaining the total control of all land, sea, space and information — which is the ultimate goal of the United States. This is not a secret; it is in the public domain. Anyone can look it up. And they mean full-spectrum domination of the world, too, not just their little piece of it. If you're thinking, *How come I didn't know this worrying fact?* — keep thinking it. It's a good question.

Journalists such as John Pilger, Andrew Cockburn, Martha Gellhorn and Robert Fisk, who insist on reporting the truth as they witness it, are an endangered species. Literally. Al Jazeera, the independent Arab TV outfit, had its operations in both Afghanistan and Iraq bombed by the Americans. During the invasion of Iraq, twenty-seven journalists were killed, more than in any previous war in history — almost all of them by the Americans.[53] On one day alone — April 8, 2003 — there were three separate U.S. attacks on non-embedded media, in which three journalists were killed and four more badly injured.

> *Things are gonna slide, slide in all directions*
> *Won't be nothing, nothing you can measure any more.*
> *The Vision — the blizzard of the world*
> *Has crossed the threshold*
> *And it's overturned the order of the soul ...*
>
> — LEONARD COHEN (1934–)[54]

The giant portrait in oils of Saddam wearing lederhosen and a Tyrolean hat with a feather in it, standing amid misty mountain peaks, the master of all he surveyed, still hung in the Iraqi embassy's waiting room. I had not left for Baghdad after all. To my horror, I had realized that my Iraqi visa had expired. I needed a renewal, and quickly. Big men with moustaches, curiously over-dressed in smart suits and ties, all looking as if they had recently retired from the professional torture business, sat around on every available surface smoking cigarettes and drinking thimbles of black coffee with their massive hands. Al Jazeera played recent episodes from the hit series *Anti-Aircraft Farmer*, in which a ninety-year-old Iraqi farmer blows an American Apache helicopter out of the sky with a 12-bore shotgun. The farmer now posed for photographs with one foot on the chopper's wreckage. It made me think of a photograph from the fifties I'd seen in an Indian hunting lodge showing Prince Philip with his foot on the head a dead tiger.[55] There were grunts of approval.

"*Sab al'khir ...*"

Every huge head looked up mournfully, like relatives at a funeral. Several growled something unintelligible. Whatever was said or indicated, it happened next door, not here.

Next door I found the Suppliants' Room — the ugly bank-like space every embassy keeps to remind those seeking visas that they are owed nothing.

"Yiss!"

I'd taken a numbered ticket — 637, dismayingly — from a dispenser and joined a snaking line-up of depressed Arabs who were seeing how many cigarettes they could smoke before their numbers were called, when one of the moustaches from the waiting room appeared at a vacant window to summon me over. No one complained about the preferential treatment.

"I just need my visa updating," I said, trying to make the request seem so piddling it could never be refused. "*Only that.* Sorry to be a bother."

"No visas."

"Aw, please ..."

"Nod posseeble."

"Please?"

"I zorry."

He was, too.

"Come on ... Just an update. Just stamp it ..."

"We must get abbroval from Baghdad," he said. "But vones nod working ..."

"American swine," I said. "I myself in fact live in *Canada* out of shame ... So just give me the visa and I can run along into Baghdad. You want me to take some gifts to your relatives?"

"I zorry. No visas."

"Yes visas ..."

"No."

"Yes. Yes, you can do it ..."

"Nod posseeble."

"Why? *Why* not?"

"I zorry."

"Okay, okay ... Listen. Iraq now finished ... *Pfft! Saddam* finished. *Vinished!* Understand? So *it doesn't matter what you do*, does it? You can *sell* visas and *keep* the money — you'll need it too because you don't have a job any more. See?"

"I zorry."

"How about a hundred bucks?" I showed him the money, slipped inside my passport.

"Oh-kay. *Give.*"

He took my passport, removed the $100 bill, held it up to the light, then placed it on the palm of his hand to check that the heat made it curl and, nodding acceptance, folded it neatly and placed it inside a wallet the size of a Koran that must have held ten thousand dollars in similar bills. Opening my passport to its Iraqi chapter, he slowly and meticulously inscribed something on the page.

"I wishing for you zafe drip," he said.

"Thank you very much."

On the way out I asked a wise-looking old Arab if he spoke English.

"I grew up in Sussex," he replied, sounding like my uncle Ray.

"But you read Arabic?"

"Yes, of course ..."

"What does *that* say?"

"Hmmm. It says *Visa Updated Until March 2008,* and it's signed *Ahmad al Mammiti, Iraq Embassy, Amman.* In parenthesis he's written *one hundred U.S. dollars* ... That's all."

"Great. I'm really sorry about the queue-jumping ..."

"This is a work-permit queue," he said. "No one here — except you — wants an Iraqi visa. We *are* Iraqis."

There is only one way to fight a war now. First of all, pick a much weaker enemy, one that is defenceless. Then build it up in the propaganda system as either about to commit aggression or as an imminent threat. Next, you need a lightning victory. An important leaked document of the first Bush Administration in 1989 described how the U.S. would have to fight war. It said that the U.S. had to fight much weaker enemies, and that victory must be rapid and decisive, as public support will quickly erode. It is no *longer like the 1960s, when a war could be fought for years with no opposition at all.*

— NOAM CHOMSKY[56]

Prince Rashid was intolerably handsome, with the curiously low hairline, sparkling eyes and sense of coiled, pent-up energy that his uncle the late King Hussein had possessed. He made me resent my life. I wanted his. Although I could see that I wouldn't have been able to handle his life: too much stress and intrigue. He grew up thinking he was heir-apparent to the heir-apparent, only to find he wasn't — that with every new babe springing forth from the new queen's fecund womb he grew further and further away from being heir to anything. He'd have to murder them all, and a century earlier probably would have. His aura gave off an electric sense of danger.

Killing was the theme of our conversation that day. Rashid had good sources of intelligence in Iraq. He seemed to be on quite good terms with Saddam's crew, while openly despising them. He thought the Americans were behaving like barbaric louts, however. It was during this conversation that it dawned on me that Rashid wouldn't mind ruling Iraq — something not beyond the bounds of possibility. His father didn't need that kind of agro any more, but Rashid did. Rashid did not have anything like the kind of agro he was capable of handling. It wasn't difficult to picture him riding an Arab stallion into someone's fort, hacking off heads with a scimitar.

"I'm going to smoke your cigarettes," he announced. "I left mine in the car. Is that okay?"

He was *so* well brought-up it made me want to weep.

"Of course, sir."

He was only twenty-five or so.

"I hear Uday's dead," he told me.

"How?"

"Saddam had his cousin shoot him. Uday was going nuts, firing guns at people. Saddam watched the execution. And he wept."

This was long, long before the Americans had displayed cadavers of Uday and Qusay to the media, but I still believe Rashid's version. The brothers did not like one another, for a start, and would not have been together anyway. There's no safety at all in numbers. And no host from here to Islamabad would turn over his guests to the enemy, no matter how much it paid. The U.S. badly needed cautionary symbols to display at the time, and they may have found Qusay somewhere. The bodies were not convincing, and to this day American soldiers guard the tomb where Saddam's boys were laid to rest.

"The Americans bombed a convoy taking the Russian ambassador to catch a plane," Rashid continued. "He was unharmed. But he flew to Moscow then immediately flew back to Baghdad again ..."

"Hmm."

"As if he was escorting someone there. Who could merit that level of escort?"

"You think Saddam's in *Moscow*?"

"It's not what my intelligence sources tell me, but it's possible. I'm told he's still in Baghdad."

"Then who was on the Russian plane?"

"Or *what* was on it?"

"Right."

"Two days before the war began Qusay and his mother showed up at the national bank with five trucks. They removed all the gold, dollars and euros. I'm told the money was flown in a small plane to Byelorussia."

"Hmm."

"After all, the Russians are Saddam's only friends ... The only place he's ever been outside the region is Moscow. He thought Moscow was a wonderful city ..."

"All the concrete ..."

He laughed. "When are you going back?"

"Soon as possible ..."

"Look, take my cellphone number and stay in touch, will you?"

"Of course."

"Anything interesting comes up ... Or you have trouble ... *Call me.* Hmm? If I don't answer, *don't* leave a message because I never listen to them ..."

And someone else might, I thought.

"I will."

"And you'll get in touch when you return?"

"I promised I'd see your father, too."

"Good. Make sure I know you're here, though ..."

"Right, I'll do that too."

Those born to rule have a natural way of recruiting others into their service.

"It's going to be interesting ..."

What was? Clearly it wasn't me telephoning him ...

"I wish I could come ..."

"Why don't you? You *could* ..."

"*They'd* never let me ..." He meant the royal court. "Besides, the Iraqis would kill me when they found out who I was ..."

"Right ..."

They did have a tendency to kill rulers, even potential ones. In fact, Saddam was about the first leader since Nebuchadnezzar who had hung onto the job for more than a year.

"Well, have a very safe trip," said His Royal Highness. "I look forward to seeing you when you return. Let me buy you a pack of cigarettes — I smoked all yours ..." He began to take his wallet out.

"Don't be silly. Please! It isn't necessary."

So well brought-up!

And now the wheels of heaven stop,
You feel the Devil's riding crop
Get ready for the future: it is murder.

— LEONARD COHEN [57]

"Fucking *hell*!" said Michelle Clifford, the Sky TV reporter. "It's driving me nuts. The biggest story of my life is happening in Baghdad and I'm stuck here! They won't okay us to go in. Too dangerous. Shit!"

A spiky, tomboyish young woman with short, tousled streaky-blonde hair and a permanent expression of rank disbelief — an excellent thing in journalism — Michelle had a feisty disposition that was to serve her well but right now just tightened her spring and made her swear like a rapper. She and her crew had not left. They had been told by their bosses in London that it was deemed too dangerous for them to drive to Baghdad. By "too dangerous" the bosses did not mean that they were concerned for the crew's safety so much as concerned for the show's budget: insurance for crews in war-zones is high. The CBC, for example, was forced to order its Baghdad crew out when premiums rose to $7,000 per person per week from $1,500. The official explanation was similar to that given by Michelle's bosses: too dangerous. But Sky already had a two-man crew in the Palestine Hotel — David Chater and his cameraman, who were already causing enough alarm back at the station with their reports.

> *You can hold back from the suffering of the world, you have free permission to do so and it is in accordance with your nature, but perhaps this very holding back is the one suffering that you could have avoided.*
>
> — FRANZ KAFKA

The waiting was making everyone a little crazy. Hours felt like weeks, just as they probably still did in Baghdad. At one point, I managed to get through by telephone to a friend of Bassim's in Ramadi, but whoever answered spoke no English. While they had gone to fetch someone who did, I heard children crying hysterically in the background. Then the line went dead. It heightened the feelings of helplessness and dread that fizzed in my guts like damp gunpowder.

While trying to find an adjustable wrench to tighten my camera's tripod shoe, I wandered into an area of Amman full of tiny hole-in-the-wall stores that specialized in things mechanical. Imagine my surprise when in the narrow, grimy window of one, alongside stained plastic tubs filled with oily nuts and bolts and rusting spanners, I saw, propped against a dented carburetor, a very used copy of *The Demonic Comedy: Some Detours in the Baghdad of Saddam Hussein*, my earlier book about Iraq. It was the American edition, with a dust-jacket I did not like because it bore an image of Saddam with devil's horns but no picture of George Bush senior. There are two demons in the book, not one. Since I wanted a copy to give someone in Amman, I decided to buy this one — although it looked as if a coalminers' reading circle had circulated it among themselves.

"*Salaam aleikum,*" said the young grease-monkey inside.

He sat on a frail-looking stool hunched over a choking kerosene heater in a tiny space whose uneven stone walls made it resemble a cave. It was utterly bare, apart from a crooked wall calendar for 1997 showing the Great Mosque in Mecca and the month of June. A nasty floral rag curtained off the narrow doorway to further rooms, whence came the muffled clatter of metal on metal and the sound of a heated argument in progress between several men.

"*Aleikum wah a'salaam ...*"

Perhaps it was the world's most highly specialized bookstore? In which case my arrival would be akin to *Descent of the Mothership*. It seemed to be received, however, more in the manner of an Ingmar Bergman movie, *Hour of the Wolf*, that I recalled watching on Jordanian TV with a group of Bedu near Aqaba. It was in Swedish, with Arabic subtitles over English subtitles. If I couldn't decipher its story, I was damn sure the Bedu couldn't, yet they watched in avid silence. When it finished — leaving me as clueless as I was in scene one — an old man said simply, "It have no wolf." There were snorts of agreement but, besides this criticism, everyone appeared to find it as enjoyable as *The Beverly Hillbillies*, which we had watched next.

"Book ... window ... yes?" I said, illustrating the statement with my hands. "I buy it. Okay?"

I showed the boy a five-dinar note. I wasn't about to pay a cent more.

"Book not for sale," he replied, in good English and a matter-of-fact tone.

"Why not?"

"This *boss's* book. He keep there."

I was, presumably, the only person on earth who would find this a maddeningly inadequate explanation.

"Big reader, your boss, is he? He have many book?"

"No, he have only one. That his book."

"Where boss?"

With a flick of his head, the boy indicated that source of clatter and argument beyond the floral rag.

"Get him! I must speak with him now."

I was reminded of my acting debut, as a servant in *Macbeth*. I had one line — "My Lord, the king comes here tonight!" — which I had repeated in my head so many times the words no longer made any sense. When the moment came for me to say them, they were gone, in their place a void. I stood frozen in terror, my mind clamped into this vacuum where there was no language at all and nothing else besides. Fortunately, the other actor was firing on all cylinders. "If you've come to tell me that the king is coming here tonight," he said, "I already know ..." In the wings, someone angrily beckoned for me to get off the stage. Like a robot, I backed out of the glaring lights. My underpants were wet. I was twelve.

The boy made me wonder what I'd said, if the words meant anything, exactly as I'd wondered about my one line in *Macbeth*.

"What's the problem? Get your boss, eh?"

"I not get boss," he told me. "Boss get angry if I call him ..."

"Why's that?"

The boy attempted a gesture that both indicated life's inexplicable mystery *and* his boss's irascible nature. It was not wholly successful, forcing him to add, " You want me lose job, mister?"

"No. No, of course I don't. I just want to meet your boss ... *min fadlak* ..."

The boy looked up balefully. Just then, the doorway's filthy curtain parted abruptly and a head like a cannonball jutted through it, yelling, "Ala!"

The eyes in the head met mine. There was a pause, then the expression of knotted anger melted.

"Abdel-Khaleq!" I said.

"*Mister Bool! Salaam ...*"

Abdel-Khaleq and his brother, Muhie, had taken me through Iraq along the ancient Bedu smuggling routes during the Gulf War. We had shared our humanity through many a dark and terrifying moment. I had not seen the pair since I'd paid them a pitifully inadequate $1,500 for risking their lives and they had handed me over to a Kurdish guide with whom I had walked all night through the snow and mountains to Turkey.

There were tears in Abdel-Khaleq's eyes. Bedu are refreshingly emotional men, whose friendship, once attained, survives the wreck of time. I approached the doorway, arms open. But Abdel-Khaleq remained on the other side. He looked, if anything, younger than I remembered. He was no longer balding — a luxuriant swath of black hair, immaculately combed, sat upon his huge skull — and the lines of his pencil-thin moustache were as straight and black as a circumflex. The trouble lay below the neck, and he gestured helplessly with his hands at it: five hundred pounds of torso in a soiled white *dishdasha* that would have served as mainsail for a schooner. He was too fat to get through this doorway.

On the other side, I went to embrace him, finding that my hands barely reached his shoulders. We both looked down at the ballooning expanse of oil-stained cotton stretched tight as bratwurst skin.

"I too much big," he theorized. "I too much happy see you, Mister Bool ..."

Rivulets flowed from his small weary eyes now.

"I happy too. Is Muhie here?"

"Muhie *finished*," Abdel-Khaleq said, shaking his head.

He meant dead.

The brothers had different mothers, so they bore no resemblance to each other at all. Muhie had been a wiry skeleton, full of coiled energy and life; if one of them were headed for an early grave, I would have put my money on Abdel-Khaleq, although he had carried a much trimmer four hundred pounds back then.

"How?"

Bedu did not like discussing such things, so Abdel-Khaleq dismissively replied, "Saddam soldier shooting ... *Pfft!*"

It took me a while to extract from him the dreadful news that Muhie had been killed as they returned to Jordan after leaving me in 1991.

"I am so, so sorry ..."

"No, no," said Abdel-Khaleq, tut-tutting. "You not make problem ... *La, la. Mektoub!*"

It meant something like "fate."

We ate and drank late into the night, remembering old times. Unseen women cooked in a kitchen that was still further back in the depths of a house that proved to be unexpectedly huge, handing out platters to the boy from the shop, who, I eventually learned, was one of Abdel-Khaleq's eleven sons ("but small ..."). After burying Muhie somewhere in the desert, Abdel-Khaleq had returned to Amman and given up the smuggling life. Using Muhie's share of the money I'd paid them, as well as his own, Abdel-Khaleq told me, he was able to start some sort of business that involved vehicles but was not a garage. It was impossible to get any clearer a description out of him, but I did glean that whatever it involved, I didn't want to know any more about it. He had not exactly gone straight, he had merely gone urban. But whatever it was had evidently thrived, for Abdel-Khaleq had acquired three more wives — the most recent, a cousin, was still only fifteen — and produced thirteen more children; or eighteen more if you counted the girls, which he did not. It was nice to think that his entire life had been founded upon the cash I'd paid out twelve years earlier, but I doubted it was true. It made a charming story, and no doubt had threads of truth in it, but it was the sort of courtesy yarn Bedu tell their guests — not to deceive them, but so they feel more welcome.

But how on earth had he come to get hold of my book? He did not read Arabic, let alone English. The answer to this was very convoluted, but appeared to boil down to a second cousin's relative who had emigrated to America.

"Story of Mister Bool and Muhie now *very* famous with Bedu," said Abdel-Khaleq. "Everyone he know it!"

This meant that his account of our trip and Muhie's death was familiar to other members of his family. Clearly one of them had then read my book in America and realized that there could hardly be any other brothers with the same names who had taken an Englishman into Iraq during the Gulf War. So he had mailed the book to his father in Amman, who had then given it to a cousin who could read English. This cousin then presented it to Abdel-Khaleq, who kept it in his store window to remind all who passed by that he was *the* Abdel-Khaleq ...

"You book make me too much famous man," he said, shaking his head at the thought of fame's pressures and obligations. "All big sheikhs they wanting give me daughter for wife."

He in fact meant that the heads of other families wanted their daughters to marry his sons. In short, he had come to be considered respectable, which to Bedu was the same as well-off, the kind of family with which other prosperous families wanted an alliance, a merger. Whatever the truth, it was apparent that Abdel-Khaleq had not expected to attain such a level of respectability in his life, and had certainly not come from anything approaching it. He also seemed to think I knew far more about him than I did, which was probably due to the fact that he could not read my book and thus only imagined what it might contain. All he knew for sure was that he was in it. He knew this because someone had circled every instance of his name in red marker, just as they had circled Muhie's name in green.

"You writing Muhie name many time," he remarked, somewhat diffidently, as he showed me the well-thumbed pages. "Abdel-Khaleq name you write just sheven time ..." He held up seven fingers thick as farmer's sausages.

This affront to his dignity still stung — and was obviously something someone had gone out of their way to point out to him, probably to deflate his ego down to a level it was possible to tolerate. Or with which it was possible to cohabit.

I asked if he wanted me to inscribe the book.

"Huh?"

"Shall I write my name here?" I indicated the title page, pressed into which there was half of a pistachio shell.

Abdel-Khaleq looked at me as if I had offered to wipe some shit on the page, shaking his head many times and saying, *"La, la ...!"* Most definitely not ...

I felt obliged to explain that this bizarre custom was something that Westerners expected an author to do, indeed they quite often purchased a book *only* for that purpose.

Irrational and inexplicable behaviour was something he had come to expect in Westerners, so to this extent he was able to understand my offer, and then mull it over in his mind. Until he said,

"You writing letter for Abdel-Khaleq, yes?"

"You want me to write a letter for you?"

"Ah!"

I had assumed he merely needed to communicate with someone in English, but what he actually wanted amounted to a signed affidavit stating that he, Abdel-Khaleq, had played by far the most important part in arranging and conducting my 1991 adventure in Iraq — even though his name was not mentioned as frequently as Muhie's, a fact accounted for by the sheer modesty for which he was justly famous. He summoned pen and paper, and I wrote what he dictated. More or less. Not wanting to risk any further humiliation, he had Ala read what I had written and translate it for him. Once assured of the contents, he acted as if a great burden had been lifted from him.

"Too much good, Mister Bool! I too much happy now ..."

He had been insufficiently happy earlier, it would seem. As if to emphasize his now one-hundred-percent genuine joy, he brought out a tiny key, and with it unlocked the lower door of an armoire the size of a Greek temple. From inside he produced a bottle of Johnnie Walker Blue Label — in fact the only bottle of *blue* label I had ever seen. Until tasting it, I even presumed that there *was* no blue label, that someone had ripped Abdel-Khaleq off, telling him it was impossibly rare stuff, never to be seen again. For blended Scotch, it was pretty good — though not worth $200 a bottle.

I also noticed that the boy, Ala, had not been truthful with me: mine was not the *only* book in Abdel-Khaleq's life after all. On an X-shaped reading stand purchased, I knew from the style, in Damascus, there rested the most atrociously gaudy copy of the Koran I have ever seen. Studded with pearls and fake rubies, this enormous edition of the good book was bound in white vinyl with gilded edges and dangling gold tassels that had been freed from the shrink-wrap still imprisoning the rest of it.

It was not until 4 a.m. that we got around to discussing this new war.

"Saddam *very* bad man," Abdel-Khaleq told me. "Kill *Muhie!*"

He had not cared much for Saddam *before* Iraqi soldiers had killed Muhie either.

"But the son of the Boosh *too much* bad man," he added, sucking air between his teeth at the very thought of George W. Bush's incomparable evil. "Wanting steal the Iraq oil, this son of Boosh," he confided, as if I might run out yodelling naked down the street upon hearing the news. "Killing many Moo-slim peoples, this son-of-a-Boosh. Why? Why they not like the Moo-slim, this Boosh, eh?"

This new brutal aggression did seem to be taken far more personally by Abdel-Khaleq than the earlier war had been. But in those days he had not worn the mantle of a pillar in society, someone of whom strong opinions and views on all matters were expected — nay, were *essential attributes*. I wondered if he was running for some kind of political office, but he was not. I think he had simply found the pressures of middle-class respectability rather more onerous than he'd expected. It was proving to be a war zone out there in high society, with battles for which — having no education and a medieval sensibility — he was ill-equipped to fight. He now wanted me to provide many more arrows for his quiver, if not restring the bow while I was at it.

So we sorted out questions that had plainly caused him recent anguish or even loss of face. For example: No, I told him, Bush was not Jewish, but there were a couple of Jews in the administration — and his grandfather, Prescott, had probably been a Nazi sympathizer. Also, the more important figures in Washington administrations tended to be less well known than the leaders, who were in reality more like figureheads, entirely reliant on a staff over which they had little or no control ... was that any help?

It did seem to be, and I could not help wondering how all this new information would sound by the time Abdel-Khaleq came to recycle it in his debates with other local patriarchs. It was a long way from the realities of Arab politics, where the ruler actually was the person who ruled. Until his death. How a ruler arrived at his decisions was another matter, as was which superpower he had permitted to secure him in power, and why it kept him there. Abdel-Khaleq's world view was scarcely different, I realized, from that of his distant ancestors during the Prophet's time. The West was a place for infidels and barbarians. Except for Britain. The Jews secretly controlled America, where people were irretrievably decadent, except for *Canadian Americans*. U.S. foreign policy was engineered solely to benefit Israel, which was a repository of all evils and cause of all human miseries. Why? Because the Holy Koran said so, and no man could question the word of Allah. Why then had Allah created Jews?

"Allah *not!*" cried Abdel-Khaleq. "The *shaitan* he making the Jewish ..."

It is difficult to convey the fact that such a statement can be made in the Arab world without anything like the levels of malevolence and sheer craziness that would of necessity lie behind it in the West. This is largely a direct consequence of unfamiliarity with English, an inability to perceive relative permissible levels of hyperbole between it and Arabic — this, and a genuine belief in Jews being demons. In war, alas, both sides are children of light believing each other to be the spawn of darkness.

I was too tired to raise the issue of Satan's origins — and I was not so sure I remembered Milton's take on it either — so I simply tried to look amply enlightened, and I could see that Abdel-Khaleq was pleased to be able to reciprocate the flow of knowledge. I hope he will be suitably pleased to find himself mentioned in this book far, far more frequently than his brother — with whom may Allah be pleased! I had never realized there was such rivalry between them.

By the time I tottered through the Hotel Royale's lobby it was 10 a.m. I sat in the bath, ordered breakfast from room service, then listened to my messages. Then ordered a Bloody Mary. There was only one message, from Michelle:

"There's a convoy leaving tonight," she said. "Meet in the lobby around eleven. Hoo-fucking-ray! There's not going to be any room in the hardside after all, though, but I got you a ride with a guy from the *Sunday Telegraph*. He's at the Hyatt, give him a call ..."

She gave me Philip Sherwell's room number as well as his local mobile number *and* his satellite phone number.

Until then, I was the only person I'd ever known to have a satellite phone. Mine was an Iridium, thoughtfully supplied by *Harper's* magazine, whose editor thought I might find it useful. It was not easy to use; at this stage of war and journey, I still had no idea how to operate it. I did not even know its number. It struck me that phoning another, a *fellow*, satellite phone might be a good start.

The phone rang in my hand so unexpectedly that instead of hitting the "C" button with a tiny red dot, as the handbook recommended to those wishing to receive a call, I threw the whole contraption across the room. Gathering up the pieces of my satellite phone, I used the hotel's landline to call Philip Sherwell at the Hyatt. The accent on his message was public school Yorkshire — just enough burr to take the edge off it. After all, it was the *Sunday Telegraph* for which he reported. Along with its *Daily* brother, the *Telegraphs* were so notoriously right-wing that other journalists frequently referred to them as the *Daily Fascist*. If the *National Post* was rabidly keen to see America go to war with Iraq in defiance of international laws and the unanimous will of the earth's other nations, then the *Telegraph* would be shipping its entire staff off to *fight in* the war rather than *cover* it.

Phil Sherwell expected to be back soon. I told him we were about to become close friends and to meet me in the lobby of the Royale just after 11 p.m. — at which time we would leave for Baghdad.

He arrived at 11 p.m. sharp in a chauffeured 12-cylinder Jaguar. Although it was not the vehicle I would have selected for an eight-hundred-kilometre drive through barren desert, I was nonetheless impressed.

"Glad to see the *Telegraph* keeps you in style ..."

A clerkly, somewhat introspective fellow in his thirties, Phil Sherwell had a wicked sense of humour when he allowed himself the luxury of it. Usually, he was preoccupied with the job at hand.

Parked ahead of us in the Royale's driveway was the Sky TV "hardside," a white armour-plated Landrover emblazoned on four sides and roof with the legend PRESS in huge black letters. It had been specially flown in from London, and its presence underlined the danger of its purpose. Michelle Clifford stood watching as her crew loaded in equipment, hopping from foot to foot as if she needed badly to pee.

Phil and Michelle knew each other not because they both lived in London but because they had both covered Kosovo and Chechnya. It is not difficult to get to be considered a "war correspondent" — few people want the job, although the few who do want it *really* want it. Their reasons vary from "it beats covering city hall," through various kinds of death-wish, to a genuine sense of professional or personal obligation, the need to bear witness to events the truth of which may otherwise be seriously compromised. It is a dirty job, but no one *has* to do it.

"We've got to go back to my hotel and pick up the photographer," Phil told Michelle. "Shall we all meet up at the Baghdad Café then?"

"Yeah, okay. Let's do that."

The "Baghdad Café" was a makeshift eatery frequented by the horde of media staff that had been encamped on the outskirts of Ruweished, the last Jordanian town before the Iraqi border, waiting for an American victory before they would be cleared by their editors or network executives to head for the killing sands.

The mood was subdued. We would soon be leaving all that was familiar behind and entering a world with no rules. CENTCOM, the U.S. central command, had been informed a media convoy would be crossing from Jordan en route to Baghdad, but there were no guarantees. If some pilot decided we were Syrian mercenaries on our way to reinforce Saddam's army ... well, that would just be our bad luck. The Pentagon had already issued a statement that amounted to a threat to kill journalists: the Palestine Hotel was, it said, on a list of "legitimate" targets.[58] The U.S. could not promise that anyone staying there would be safe. It was well known that the only people staying there were journalists. Only those journalists "embedded" with the military would be afforded protection by U.S. armed forces, because their reporting was virtually guaranteed by its subjective nature to be part of the war effort's propaganda offensive.[59] It was a brilliant stroke of PR — one that wholly countered media complaints regarding the limited access to "real action" during the Gulf War. By placing journalists with troops, and thus subject to military regulations that included preliminary training, however, the Pentagon effectively muzzled them. Basic psychology made it clear that something akin to the Stockholm Syndrome would cement a bond between reporters and the troops protecting them from enemy fire, making objectivity next to impossible. If journalists had also been "embedded" with the Iraqi forces it would have been different, but they were not. As a result, we only saw the U.S. military's point of view, and that is propaganda not journalism. The obvious delight of the Pentagon with its own genius, combined with the often embarrassing enthusiasm for war shown by many reporters, and the shameless jingoism of all major media at home, formed a new nadir in the history of American journalism.

Possibly the single lowest point was the work of *Boston Herald* correspondent Jules Crittenden, an embedded journalist who appears to have become a combatant in the war he was assigned to cover. In a column written for the Poynter Institute he even admitted that while the unit to which he had been appointed was on patrol outside one of Saddam's palaces he assisted in the killing of Iraqis:

> *I spotted the silhouettes of several Iraqi soldiers looking at us from the shadows 20 feet to our left. I shouted, "There's three of the fuckers right there."*
>
> *"Where are the fuckers?" [Sgt. Dan] Howison said, spinning around in his hatch.*
>
> *"The fuckers are right there," I said, pointing.*
>
> *"There?" he said, opening up with the .50 [calibre]. I saw one man's body splatter as the large-caliber bullets ripped it up. The man behind him appeared to be rising, and was cut down by repeated bursts.*
>
> *"There's another fucker over there," I told Howison.*[60]

One of the many points this piece of writing raises is that Crittenden seems to have been unaware that the use of high-calibre weapons on human targets is specifically forbidden under the Geneva Conventions, which argue that the damage caused to a body by the force of such rounds makes it an inhumane form of warfare. Sergeant Howison would almost certainly have been aware himself,[61] however, which places this incident on the stack of U.S. war crimes charges.

It is not a question of begrudging Jules Crittenden his opinions, either, or of objecting to the obvious bias of his sledgehammer prose. Indeed, I found his writing a useful insight to the U.S. military mindset, which relies on dime-novel, action-movie talk. There are, however, very precise objections to his approach to war reporting that ought to concern all journalists. Under the Fourth Geneva Convention, war correspondents are clearly designated as civilians and afforded specific protection. By picking up a weapon or assisting in the fighting *in any way*, by blurring the line separating reporters from combatants, they not only strip themselves of this protection, they also place every other journalist covering the war in serious danger. Thus far, Crittenden seems to have come under more criticism for bringing home illegal loot than for helping to kill people. Even defending himself against this charge he managed to make no distinction between himself and the military, referring to "the time-honored tradition among soldiers of bringing home reminders of some of the most intense experiences of their lives. There was no exception to that historic practice until we began arriving home."[62]

> *I'm sure there are some people who will question my ethics, my objectivity, etc. I'll keep the argument short. Screw them, they weren't there. But they are welcome to join me next time if they care to test their professionalism.*

— JULES CRITTENDEN [63]

Over at the Hyatt, I discovered the Jaguar was not in fact our transportation to the theatre of war — it had merely been a town vehicle belonging to the same company from which Sherwell had hired the standard Toyota Landcruiser. It came equipped with the standard clinically depressed driver, Kareem, an Iraqi, who now awaited us, along with a freelance shooter, Paul Hackett, assigned by the *Telegraph*'s picture editor to join Phil. A big, handsome man with an easy, ironic smile and a broad Scots accent, Hackett was immediately likeable. Sherwell you had to work at. There was something austere and uncharitable about Phil that was heightened by its proximity to his photographer's innate generosity of spirit. No doubt they had their opinions of me too.

Before long we were on our way beneath a dome of high black air spattered with raging Van Gogh stars, a place endless yet nowhere. It occurred to me that eternity might well be where I was heading — a mournful thought that proved to be first in a series, titled *It's Not Too Late To Turn Back*, that was only curtailed when Phil received a phone call. The Americans had crossed the Euphrates and were now heading for the walls of Baghdad. For the *Sunday Telegraph*, for all of us, it was a race against time and history. As General "Tommy" Franks liked to quip: "Speed kills the enemy."

We were also gambling heavily on the fact that reports of the collapse of Saddam's regime were at least true enough to open up the border. My visa, with its handwritten renewal, was at best iffy, but Paul Hackett possessed no visa at all.

After a busy spell sending short message-service text messages to various colleagues, ascertaining where they all were on the dark and empty road east, and what latest news reports revealed about the battle for Baghdad, the three of us fell in and out of fitful slumbers. Before long, we were cleared through the final checkpoint and heading towards the reddish glow of Ruweished, which spread across the horizon like a false dawn. On either side, the blackened rocks of a flat wasteland of stone stretched their moonlit shadows into mottled darkness, towards Arabia on the right and Syria to our left.

By the time we pulled off the road to park among an ocean of media vehicles in the dust and mud outside the Baghdad Café, a deep purple smear was already staining the eastern sky, where unfamiliar airplanes flew back and forth, one of them flying off course to take a closer look at the steadily growing convoy.

You entered the café through a side door that led first down a dingy corridor towards what served as a washroom area. The place was packed, its owners now clearly rich men by local standards from providing the eggs, toast and coffee simulating a Western breakfast — for Western prices — to Westerners. CNN played on an old black-and-white television. Producers and journalists worked cellphones, attempting to get updates on the war or file stories. The Americans had now entered Baghdad, it seemed, and were already at the banks of the Tigris, meeting little or no resistance from Iraqi troops. Saddam's regime had simply vanished. Victory was already being cautiously declared. But something about this information didn't seem right to me. Where was the Stalingrad we had all expected? The regular Iraqi army might have walked off the job — and who could blame them? — but the Republican Guard, especially its elite inner corps, could not simply quit. They lived apart from other units, and their fate was inextricably linked to that of the regime. They were expected to fight on. Either way, there were too many of them to just vanish. The news palpably increased frustration levels. Everyone just wanted to get there.

The Jordanians habitually opened the border at dawn. Now, however, no one knew what to expect on the Iraqi side. Had the Iraqis who were stationed there — a mixture of soldiers and Mukharbharat, secret police — been able to receive any instructions, any information at all, from Baghdad? If Saddam's government had indeed collapsed, under whose control would the border now be? No one I met recalled being in a similar situation before. What happened when a totalitarian regime collapsed without immediately being replaced by another regime?

The answer, according to the Geneva Conventions, is that from this point on, the United States became entirely responsible for running all aspects of Iraq and providing for the needs of its citizens.

Given the size of the media convoy, Sherwell, Hackett and I decided to head immediately for the border, which still lay some forty minutes' drive further east through a no-man's land that now housed a tent city of refugees attempting to flee Iraq. Most were Palestinians, for whom Saddam had provided housing in Baghdad at a fraction of the usual cost, requisitioning properties from Iraqi landlords for this purpose. Needless to say, it had not been a popular program with Iraqis. Many of the Palestinians had thus simply left their homes, knowing they would have to leave them soon anyway; others had been ordered out by landlords who knew the government was about to fall.

Saddam was one of the few Arab leaders who gave assistance to the Palestinians on a regular basis, although his concern was hardly philanthropic. Like all Arab states, Iraq's relationship with the Palestinians was essentially symbolic: their plight represented the scourge of Western imperialism, which had knocked the Arab world off the civilization charts. In Arab eyes this subjugation of East by West, which began with the Crusades, was lastly and most humiliatingly manifested by the creation of Israel. It had nothing to do with Jews, either; the Arabs saw Israel first and foremost as a European colony started at a time when colonialism was vanishing everywhere else. Then they watched as the European Jews abandoned the original agreement and made it clear that they did not intend to share the country with Palestinian Arabs (many of whom are Christian). The Sephardic Jews, who had lived side by side with the Arabs in Palestine for two thousand years, were also dismayed at the treatment meted out to Arabs. Most dismaying of all was the lack of response from the countries that had helped create the Jewish state as their original conditions for its existence were steadily violated. The Arabs felt doubly betrayed and began to view the West with increasing cynicism.

Children from the desolate tent city between the two rows of barbed-wire fencing that separated Jordan from Iraq ran out as we passed, waving. They were as happy and excited as children anywhere, and we felt guilty as we waved back, knowing how hopeless their futures almost certainly would be. Their families had not yet been admitted into Jordan, where — if they were lucky, and were granted refugee status — their lives would be harsh and bitter at best. These people were, I thought, pretty close to that first rung, pretty close to being those compared with whom no one else is worse off. They had nothing. They did not even have a country. Jordan would take them in, though, almost certainly it would. For where else could they go? Since it was the only Arab state adjoining what had once been Palestine, Jordan was seen as the natural choice for Palestinian refugees. A number of Israelis I know even express the idea that Jordan actually *is* — or *ought to be* — Palestine. The country was also viewed as a natural choice for Iraqis fleeing Saddam, as if it were some kind of dumping ground. Jordanians don't view their nation this way, needless to say, and with growing unemployment the resentment against refugees grows — even if many Iraqi refugees have now gone home.

The border had not yet opened but already there were vehicles waiting in front of the arch bearing the smiling image of King Abdullah beside his late father. There were also a large number of Jordanian soldiers around. About a kilometre further off, the Iraqi side looked deserted. We were told, however, that there had been an "incident" a little earlier. Just before abandoning their posts, apparently, the Iraqi soldiery had fired off a few rounds at Jordan — presumably by way of saying thanks for not helping us out. No one had been injured, but the event now posed a problem: was it safe to open the border? Were Iraqi snipers still lurking somewhere?

"Oh God," said Sherwell. "We could be stuck here forever while they work *this* out. The fucking war will be *over* ..."

It could not have been difficult to ascertain that the Iraqi side of the border was no longer manned, for a few minutes later the barrier post was raised. As traffic began to pass under the white concrete arch, it became apparent the Jordanians were checking that everyone had valid Iraqi visas. Normally they did not do this. Why they now felt impelled to do so was a mystery — but no one knew the correct protocol for this situation, so perhaps it was prompted by pure brotherly concern. We decided to attempt bluffing our way through the visa check. Paul Hackett slid down to the floor of the rear seat and I pushed a coat on top of him. Since I had a visa — albeit expired — and a handwritten renewal, I felt I could at least *seem* to believe I ought to be allowed entry.

"Whatever happens," said Sherwell, "I'm going in with Kareem. I hope that's understood?"

"Och-ay," said the muffled voice of Hackett. "You gotta, don't you?"

Idly, I wondered what Hackett and I would do, stranded four hours away from Amman, without either bus service or taxi rank. The Jordan-Iraq traffic was strictly one-way these days, too. But since the likelihood of this happening was slim, I gave it no more thought.

Kareem handed our passports to the guard, who began to look baffled, then tried matching passengers with passport pix.

"Where is this man?" he said, eventually.

We had neglected to remove Hackett's passport from the glove compartment. There may have been a way of answering the guard that did not involve telling the truth, but if there was, neither Sherwell nor I could think of it.

"They've seen your passport," Sherwell told his photographer, in furtive tones.

Paul Hackett pretended to be waking up from a nap over the drive shaft, rubbing his eyes and greeting the guard with a hearty Scots' *g'mornin'*.

"There is no visa," the guard said, sorrowfully. "You not have Iraq visa. Only those with visa can go ..."

He was greeted with a hail of *bullshits*. It wasn't Jordan's business if someone had no Iraqi visa ...

"There's forty thousand Brits and three hundred thousand Americans in Iraq right now without visas," I added, wondering if soldiers ever bothered to get visas from the countries they were about to invade.

"Your visa expire," the guard told me, somewhat too enthusiastically showing me the page upon which my visa lay dead.

"No, no ..." I tut-tutted, in the manner of a man wholly certain of his own rectitude. "The ambassador personally renewed it for me. See — right there ... Just before he fled the country ..."

"You write this?" asked the guard. "This no good. Not official."

"*Did I write it?* I have never been so insulted in all my life ..."

"I find *that* hard to believe," Hackett said, under his breath.

Suddenly we were all sucking in our cheeks and emitting swinish grunts like people trying very hard not to laugh. This made it still harder not to laugh.

"Telephone the embassy yourself," I said, mainly to defuse the mounting hysteria. "They'll tell you."

"You are fine," the guard told Sherwell, handing back his passport.

Then he scrutinized Kareem's ID, which resembled something from a museum exhibit: *Early Nineteenth-Century Identification Cards from Eastern Serbia.* I felt certain he was going to tear it up and order Kareem out at gunpoint, but he just scowled at the driver and gave him back the ID.

"This two men ..." The guard mimed our beheading. "Not possible without visa."

"I *have* to go on," Sherwell said to us, without a trace of remorse. "But look on the bright side: you can sit all day in the burning sun and not have to take a single note."

"Thanks, mate," Hackett said.

"Seriously," Sherwell continued, seriously, "they're bound to open the border soon. No one will be able to *get* visas now. Michelle told me some of her people don't have visas either, so you'll probably be able to catch a ride with one of them. But I do *have* to go ..."

Hackett and I unloaded our baggage, watched the Landcruiser drive off into Customs Land, then dragged everything over to the dust away from the road and sat on our coats.

"When we passed those Palestinians," said Hackett, "I were wondering what it'd be like to live out here i' the middle o-fucken nowhere ..."

"Yeah. So was I."

"Must be pretty shitty, I'd say ..."

"That would be my assessment too, Mister Hackett."

The sun was getting hotter by the minute. It may have still been winter back in Amman, but it wasn't here, at the edge of a desert larger than Ontario.

"What d'ye think we should *do*?"

"I heard the Iraqi embassy was selling actual visas on request ... if you knew the right person to ask."

"Who did *you* ask then?"

"Probably the wrong person?"

"So ye think we should go back?"

The more I thought about it, the more outrageous it seemed. "How can they make us get visas they *know* aren't legal any more?" I said. "I mean, the Jordanian government can hardly admit to a policy that supports the illegal issuing of Iraqi visas by embassy officials who pocket the money, can they?"

"Why don't you tell *them* that," said Hackett, nodding over at the border guards. "Can't do any harm ... Or you could call your pal, the prince ..."

"Call him on what? You have a phone?"

"I thought you had a sat-phone?"

"Right. I don't suppose you know how to use one, do you?"

"Give it here."

Photojournalists are good with technology. I left Paul with the Iridium satellite telephone and trudged over to the guard post. By the time I had presented a third, fourth and fifth official with the numinous logic of my argument about their Iraqi visa policy, I could see that this tactic was flogging an entirely decomposed horse.

"What did they say?" asked Hackett.

He showed me how to work the sat-phone. I got through to Prince Hassan's personal assistant with laughable ease. Although the call went via Arizona, the line was crystal clear. Until it cut out. Fortunately, I'd been able to explain our dilemma and the need for princely help. I did, however, wonder if Hassan still had any clout in the right circles of power.

"This sun is getting pretty fucken *hot*," said Hackett. "Did we think tae bring any water from the car?"

We had each purchased a case of mineral water before leaving Amman, along with several packets of Nice biscuits. The name belies the actual biscuit.

I pulled out a blue plastic bottle that now contained about three inches of tepid and somewhat murky liquid. We had both forgotten the cases of water.

"I did bring these, though," said Hackett, waving an unopened oblong of Nice biscuits. "We should be *fine* ..."

"Great."

"I guess Phil will be showering with the stuff. Whew!" Hackett mopped his flushed brow. "Let's take it i' turns tae sit in the shade under that arch thing?"

I told him to take the first turn — it *was* his idea.

Dishevelled, exhausted, thirsty, hungry and sitting in the dust, I cut a pathetic figure. There were only two kinds of people in the world: those with Iraqi visas, and those without. The media with Iraqi visas continued breezing through the arch in their air-conditioned chariots. The rest came to sit in the dust.

A young blonde woman came up. She had a backpack big enough for a dictator to hide inside and the skin around her mouth was raw, as if she had recently scrubbed something very nasty from it.

"No visa, right? Oh yeah, same boat. Ask me how I feel about *that*! I'm like, *Huh*? There's no fuckin' government, *dude*!"

"I was also like that."

"Yeah. You have any room in your car if they let us through?"

"I don't have a car."

"Get *outta* here! Wow! I guess, like I'm not talking to the right dude at all, am I?"

"Nope. I am definitely the wrong dude for you ..."

"Aw ..." She shrugged off her backpack. "Someone needs a hug. Come 'ere, c'mon ..."

Like a child, I got up. She hugged me very sincerely. She smelled of soap and tobacco.

"There! That's what we needed, wasn't it? We all need our huggy-a-day, don't we?"

"Uh-huh."

"I'm like, I needed that too," she announced, furrowing her mouth and brows, as if trying to recall something.

Then she hoisted her backpack, said, "See ya 'round! *Hello!*" and was gone.

"What did that blonde chickie want?" Hackett inquired, his watch in the shade over. "It's fucken great under there. Must be twenty degrees cooler ... I thought she were gonna gie you a blow-job there ..."

"She looked like she'd already given the day's allotment ..."

"Do ye know who she is?"

"No. Who is she?"

For a moment I thought he was going to say George Bush's daughter.

"Her name's Josie. She were wi' us in Afghanistan and Kosovo, too. She goes wherever there's a war. Always latches on to one o' the TV crews ..."

"She's a journalist?"

"Nooo," he frowned. "She's not."

"What is it, like a grisly hobby or something? A death-wish?"

"What I heard was that she goes to all these trouble spots where the Yanks are bombin' an' shootin' everyone and she gets the people compensation for injuries and property damage from the American govverment ..."

"She's with some NGO?"

"Noooo, she's not. That's the strange part. Apparently she inherited a tidy sum o' cash, and she spends it all on hot-shot lawyers to get poor people compensation for war damage."

"That's a nice thing to do ..."

"That's what I thought too."

We looked at each other with manly sincerity.

I took my moment in the shade beneath Jordan's back door. Hackett was right: it was considerably cooler there. The border guards nodded welcome. We all sat smoking.

"You are *Americani*?" asked one.

"Good Lord, no! I'm *Kanadi*, Canadian. Proud of it too ..."

There were several repetitions of *Kanadi* accompanied by various kinds of solid endorsement for the Prince of Nations.

"You har welcome to Jordan," said a guard.

"Thank you."

"Yesh, welcome, *friend*," said another.

"Thank you. I'm just going to make a quick phone call, okay?"

Now, I thought, would be a good time to call Hassan again, or be heard to call him.

"Ah, *salaam aleikum. Siddi Hassan, min fadlak* ..."

"You espeak Harabic?"

"*Swaya-swaya*," I said, holding my thumb and finger a millimetre apart.

"Oh. Okay. I'll call him back in about ten minutes, shall I?"

"Hew know *Siddi Hassan*?"

"Yes, as a matter of fact we were at school together ..."

This prompted the hoped-for ripple of translations and affirmations.

"He is *good* man, Siddi *Hassan*," said a guard.

"Yes, he is, isn't he?"

"We har like him too much. And him brother the King Hussein. Now finish. We like him too much also."

"Yes. Terribly sad. Great loss. Great man."

"Now Siddi *Hassan* not king. Abdullah king. Son of the King Hussein."

It was hard to be certain what the guards felt about their new king. Were they saying they would have preferred Hassan? Or that it was only right and proper for Abdullah to become king? Possibly, ambivalence *was* the message. Without labouring the point, I tried to convey that Siddi Hassan, my school chum, would be — perhaps even *was* at that very moment — calling their commanding officer to have me cleared through the border.

"You have passport?" a more senior guard asked.

"Absolutely." I handed it over, immediately conscious of its Britishness. "UK passport but issue from Ottawa," I explained. "See. British High Commission. Ottawa. That's the capital of Canada. Although no one knows it ..."

"Hotter-wah?"

"Yes. Bit like Ankara. You know? Ankara's the capital of Turkey, but everyone thinks Istanbul is the capital?"

"You har *Turkey*?"

"No, no ..."

At that moment a magnificent Chevy Suburban pulled up bulging with Big Media. Among those in the rear was Dan Rather. Another man held out an open cellphone, telling the guard who had waved him to stop that there was a call. The guard took the phone, holding it to his ear as if it were a loaded gun.

"Ah ... ah ... ah ... ah," the guard repeated at intervals.

Then he passed the phone to a senior officer, who walked away with it.

"For crissakes!" said the American in the Suburban. "They know you're in the car, Dan. Now they've taken the fucking phone away."

Dan looked as if he was able to decipher this much on his own. To give credit where it's due, there was no air of self-importance in his manner. You don't need it when you're surrounded by people who think you're important, I suppose. He had been the first journalist to interview Saddam since Desert Storm, Dan Rather. And since me. The bastard! I was hoping I might at least become the last journalist to interview Iraq's dictator. Not much to ask, is it? Dan's interview was as bad as mine, I have to admit. Saddam was not a good subject.

Suddenly there was a flurry of activity on all sides. The senior guard handed back the Rather minder's phone. The barrier was raised and the Suburban went on through, followed by every other vehicle. Engines roared; people scrabbled with equipment. I ran over to Paul and told him we were going in.

"How?" he asked. "I cannae carry all *this* ..."

Good point. We had no vehicle. He ran off to attempt finding us a ride, while I closed bags and hoisted tripods onto my shoulders.

"Over here, mate!"

Hackett was waving frantically next to a beaten-up Oldsmobile bearing the broad band of orange paint that indicates a Baghdad taxi.

"This gentleman has been kind enough tae offer us a ride over to the Customs area," he said. "Then we're on our tod agin ..."

The gentleman, whom dental fate had left a mere three tar-stained teeth, confirmed this. We crammed all the baggage inside and ... the car's engine died. There was a *clunk*, then nothing. The driver tortured his starter motor, pumping furiously at the gas pedal. I badly wanted to tell him to stop — he'd flood the engine, drain the battery — but I restrained myself. Amazingly, after five minutes of desperate hacking and wheezing, the thing woke up like a drowned monster given the kiss of life. It was a hot rod now. Even by Middle Eastern standards, the engine was too loud, and it burned more oil than gas.

I waved farewell to my guard friends, to king Abdullah and his Dad, to the sane world, and *zoom*, we were gone through the arch and heading towards Customs. Here I could be of some use since, if you had not been this way before, the sheer quantity of bureaucratic arcana would have you weeping and gnashing your teeth inside ten minutes. First you had to pay departure tax and receive a chit proving the fact. Then you took this to baggage inspection, where baggage was viewed, pawed through and queried. All being well, the inspector would stamp your tax chit, which you then took to Immigration, a Nissen hut with rows of benches and a wall of bank-clerk windows, Early Humiliation and Abuse style.

"You have any bomb, rogget, han grenade?" asked an inspector.

"Nope. Not this week."

"Any gun, mizzel-luncher, eflame-trower?"

"No. Couldn't find one compact enough."

"Any Ofium, narguddick?"

"No. Sadly."

"Any Jews?"

"In the bag?"

"He mean jew-ell, jewe-ell," the inspector's colleague explained. "You have any jew-ell?"

"Only my sparkling memories of your country ..."

"Open this," I was told.

It surprised me. They were never this thorough here.

"What is?" The inspector held up a jar of Multistart vitamins.

"Medicine ..."

The jar had on its label a small photograph of Dr Michael Murray, "formulator" of the vitamins, apparently, with his simulated autograph off to one side. Below it was a larger rectangular photograph of three fat, oppressively perfect apples, bearing the legend "natural factors." The inspector scrutinized this label for some minutes.

"*National fagtories?*" he eventually asked. "It means what?"

"Got apples in it."

He opened the jar and peered inside, clearly surprised to find speckled-brown caplets. "There not happles," he stated, replacing the lid and handing me back the jar.

The implication, I felt, was that I had been duped, fleeced, ripped off. There were no apples inside.

He then held up a postcard of the new king and his queen on their wedding day. I'd forgotten buying it.

"Hah!" he exclaimed. "This Jordan king and the queen ..."

"So I gather ..."

"You like heem, the king Abdullah?"

"Oh yeah. Liked his father too ... Great king ..."

"Yesh ..." I thought he was about to burst into tears. "Now finished, the Hussein ..."

"I know. I know. Very sad ..."

"I ham much happy you having picture Abdullah ... You welcome here, friend."

"Thank you. Sorry to be leaving so soon, too."

"You har Tee-Vee person?"

"Yep."

"I wish for you safety in Iraq. Very danetrush now ..."

"Thank you."

"You must take the grade careful."

"I will."

"Goodbye, friend."

We shook hands. The genuineness of his concern for my welfare had tears streaming down my cheeks. My God, I thought, we have forgotten even how to be human beings back in the West. It was easier to imagine Noam Chomsky being elected president than it was such an encounter occurring with U.S. Customs officials.

In the Hut of Humiliation, there were now about a thousand journalists and media staffers behaving like a starving mob of ancient Romans during the weekly bread hand-out. A speaker system with the audio fidelity of a Chatty Cathy doll periodically blurted out what might have been names: *Psarko Drerb ... Drerb Psarko, Franch? Myorf Skrettip ... Skrettip Myuff, Svedden?*

"Ah cannae hear a fucken *thing* he says," Hackett complained.

Nor could anyone else. This was why the entire mob surged forward waving documents every time the speakers crackled.

"But ah did learn summat useful," Hackett added. "We need to get police clearances stamped in the passports, then we have to hand them tae that guy. Otherwise we'd hae been sitting here all day for nothing ..."

"Right."

I'd forgotten that station of the cross. I was of no use, after all.

Four hours later, we were still sitting with our mound of baggage in the Hut of Humiliation. Behind the Panes of Abuse, officials were stacking files and papers, putting on jackets, chatting in an easy school's-out manner. We were the very last people to be called.

We approached the Counter of Belittlement itself.

"Roppit Bule Wirri-yams, Yoo-kay?"

"Yes, that'll be me ..."

"Hud-krett, Bule? Bool Ha-whack-it, Yoo-kay?"

"Right," said Hackett, "Thanks for a lovely day ..."

With all its starts and stops, the day had been singularly unlovely so far. Considering I had not actually *done* anything, my body felt as if I been hacking my way through the Amazon for the past twelve hours. I had managed to avoid thinking how far there was still to go until now, not wanting to jinx the next stage. But then the vastness of the desert began to gape before me, the bleached monotony of the freeway, the miles upon miles of barren, parched dust and jagged rock through which we would have to roll on burning rubber before chafing aridity was smothered in the diseased humidity, the malarial fog oozing up to join ten kinds of smoke in the airborne mud that had been as red as congealed blood over the Land Between Two Rivers when I'd seen it last. It was *so* far. So very, very far. It was a journey back to the Beginning, back to the Dawn — and it always felt like it.

If you could manage to start it.

During the interminable wait we had run into one of Sky TV's crew, a videographer named Dikon Mager, who said there was room for us in his vehicle. That had been hours earlier, though, and neither of us had seen him since. The customs area that had been packed with people and vehicles was now eerily deserted. As we began to collect our bags, the full gravity of our situation suddenly bore down upon us.

"How the fuck we going to work this?" Hackett asked.

"Miracle?"

"*Ess-kuse, sirs!*" bellowed a voice behind.

A very much more dangerous-looking and senior official stood beckoning us back with his index finger.

"Wha *now*?"

"Hew must for to essign this papers," the man said.

"What papers?"

He proffered us a sheet each.

The Government of Jordan has determined that the journey from Ruweished to Baghdad is dangerous and it cannot guarantee the safety of any persons make this journey. By signing this below, I acknowledge that Jordan Government, while concerned for safety of all visitors, is not responsible for any dangers that may befoul [sic] me while on Iraq side. I hereby absolve Jordan Government of any and all responsibilities for my safety after Leaving kingdom.
Signed,

Despite the quaint charm and idiosyncratic grammar, there was something chilling about the document. We both signed without comment, handing the sheets back.

"Police," said the man. "Hew will kindly put name of your orgnation here." He pointed to a space below our names.

"I'm *actually* freelance," Hackett said, "but I think I'll poot down *Sunday Telegraph* ..."

"I'll put *Harper's* — it'll make identification of the corpses easier ..."

"Hew har e-welcome to Jordan," said the man, as if we were leaving his restaurant.

Improbably, parked alone in the middle of a space that could hold two thousand vehicles, was Dikon and his driver, Abdul.

"Ah," he said, in the manner of someone who has waited for five minutes, "there you are!"

It was an extraordinarily generous thing that he had done.

"Listen," said Dikon, who bore an eerie resemblance to the young Martin Amis, while being, of course, much taller. "We've all decided to stop here for the night, because it will be dark soon and we don't know how safe the road is. That okay with you?"

I thought "we've all" referred merely to him and Abdul, but, as we later found, Dikon meant all the journalists who had crossed the border with us, who were now camped on the Iraqi side.

"I found this little spot here," he added, "and cleared it with the guy who runs this place. So, if it's all right with you, we'll just stay right here for the night and leave at dawn in convoy."

I have not met a more polite and thoroughly decent human being than Dikon. I did wonder, however, what he found so attractive about the centre of this giant parking lot. But this was not the "spot" to which he referred. That was a small concrete shed with windows and a door on one of the customs islands.

It was, for some reason, a joy to be able to shut the rickety door and place a brick behind it. At the back of our minds was still the morning's sniper incident. With darkness falling, primal fears and vulnerability flooded back. It was good to be safe and secure.

One of those people you hope is among those with whom you're shipwrecked, Dikon was relentlessly resourceful, always two steps ahead of the game. He had bought a case of cold beer before the Duty-Free closed; he had set up a propane stove and was ready to cook us dinner. Although it was only freeze-dried paella, food never tasted so good.

I handed Hackett a foaming beer.

"Thanks, mate, but no thanks. I'm on the wagon ..."

"A teetotalling Scot, that's novel," said Dikon. "How long's it been?"

Paul looked at his watch, saying, "Put it this way: I got five weeks three days and sixteen hours to go ..." He looked at the misted cans. "I gotta admit, though, it's awful tempting ..."

I snatched away the can.

"But we must be strong, firm. Or we'll lose all self-respect."

"Fuck off!"

It is curious how the cooking and sharing of food under odd circumstances breeds closeness, yet it does.

I must have dozed off, for Dikon had wandered over to the media camp in the meantime, and was now back with more news.

"Much as I hate to leave this cozy spot," he said, "I think we ought to spend the night over there with the rest. I don't want to risk them leaving without us ..."

The five hundred kilometres to Baghdad was not safe at night at the best of times. Sand pirates frequently set up road-blocks for anything that looked worth the trouble. A truck full of rich foreigners would be irresistible. Besides, there was no police force to worry about now. God only knew what lay out there.

As we loaded our bags into the Landcruiser, we heard, skimming across the deep purple air above like a vast stone over waves, the phasing sound of a Stealth bomber. It is a noise so far removed from anything mechanical that it seems sinister, a supernatural agent of death. To the northeast, the sky over Iraq glowed a hellish red. Although it was in fact only the sodium glare of lights in the Iraqi Customs compounds, it still added to the ominous great chord playing on the soundtrack of our lives.

"Welcome to Iraq, gentlemen," Dikon announced, as we passed the gatehouse and headed through a stretch of fenced no-man's land. "Leave your qualms at the door ..."

This area, which had once been the most impossible, time-consuming, aggravating, and boring of all Customs and Immigration arenas on earth, was hauntingly empty. Where there would have been ten guards and three inspection points — *before*, that is, you even reached the real inspection — there was no one. A white concrete arch, much like the Jordanian one, loomed up in our lights. Saddam Hussein still personally waved to each visitor from his portrait over the pale curve. Beyond it, we saw the unusual sight of bonfires and a camp where some two hundred journalists from all over the globe had parked in a comforting circle and were amusing themselves before turning in. Here and there, the odd blaze of light revealed someone doing his or her daily stand-up ... *And this is Bendt Spoonikker live at the Iraqi border* ... There were several sat-com dishes set up, and generators roared to power them.

"Not a good idea," said Dikon. "The U.S. military have said they will bomb anything transmitting to satellite from Iraq. By the way," he added, "I notice you have a sat-phone with you. Please keep it turned off, will you? Otherwise we're a target."

I looked at the Iridium satellite telephone in a new light.

"Of course. And Dikon ..."

"Yes?"

"Thanks. For everything, I mean ..."

"You're welcome." He meant it.

I had thought sleeping on the roof of the Landcruiser would be idyllic, just the stars above me ... But, as the night wore on, it got colder and colder, and a brisk wind blew. I had borrowed Dikon's ski jacket, but only had a tarpaulin over me. The wind blew through it maliciously. Even the stars looked spiky and malevolent. People seemed to be wandering around all night talking, too. And snipers kept running to different positions in order to get a clear shot at my skull. But I must have slept because I dreamed Swedish TV did a brief interview with me — along the lines of *Why are you sleeping on this vehicle's roof?*

As the angry sun stuck its furious florid head over the horizon and said *What the fuck do you want?* I saw for the first time the New Iraq. It was exactly like the old one on the surface. There was the VIP hut, where foreigners used to be sent to sit and contemplate an interior designer's hell in gold and pink while the secret police checked them six ways from Sunday — or at least pretended to. The sheer length of the wait would have deterred anyone with dodgy papers. I assumed they were reading every word I had ever written about Iraq, although they were probably just waiting for a phone call from Baghdad: *Yep, we issued him a visa. Let him through ...* Now it was achingly empty, as were the checkpoints before and beyond it, seeming all the more empty because of the suspicion and security that had once filled them. The place was utterly deserted.

"So why's everyone lining up in front o' that gate then?" asked Hackett.

The line of vehicles snaking away from our campsite through Iraqi Customs and Border Control did seem to concertina to a total stop in front of the final arch. Maybe the regime was not so finished?

When we reached our point in the queue, I ran down to see what was happening at the gate, where people had gathered around a soldier of some kind who was clearly the source of the problem. From the *keffiyah* wrapped around his head like a scarf, I thought he must be Fedayeen — Uday's elite force — or perhaps a mercenary, but as I pushed into the throng around the man, I saw his blonde moustache and the weather-beaten young face with its deadly blue eyes.

"I am United States Special Forces," he was saying, in response to someone's question. "We are now in control of this border. We will let you through, but the road is not safe. Stay together and good luck! Any more questions?"

It was unremittingly strange to see an American standing at this gate, the entrance to Iraq that I had passed through many times before after hours with the Mukharbharat. An American standing guard ...

The soldier was deluged with questions and demands, microphones shoved towards him, cameras flashing or whirring on every side. He seemed somewhat dazed by it all, like someone who has been on a desert island alone for years and then finds himself on *Survivor*!

U.S. Special Forces had been in this area of the desert for some time, it was said — certainly from well before the war began. These were men trained to be able to drop by freefall parachute into a foreign land — and vanish. They would cover themselves entirely with sand and sleep under it by day, breathing through a tube, coming out at night like predatory androids to do whatever it was they had been sent to do. They could kill without weapons, make a bomb from anything lying around, and survive without money for months. They were totally self-reliant. And if they were caught, they knew their government would not be coming to their rescue. "Deniable Ops," they're called: missions of which, if they fail, the government behind them denies all knowledge. Only one in five thousand soldiers has what it takes to be invited to join Special Forces — you don't *apply* — that peculiar mixture of fortitude, insanity, intelligence and the utter absence of any emotions or conscience. *Feelings, they are told, are for others, not you. For you, feelings are poison and death. You only do, you don't feel; and you only think about what you are doing, not why you are doing it. "Why" doesn't concern you. "Why" is for sissies and civilians ...*[64]

He was as alien as the yogis I'd seen up in isolated Himalayan caves — people who have had no interaction with other humans for years, who have forgotten how. The soldier was both shy and lethal. He had lost most human qualities. If he married, it would not last: she'd realize eventually that he had no feelings towards her[65] — that he had no feelings at all. The "company" would never let him go, either. It might make his leash quite long, but it would always want to know what he was doing, because it had trained him and knew what he was *capable* of doing. If he turned to crime, no police force on earth would be any match for him. This was *The Terminator* for real ...

He walked away from the scrum, turning to gesture that no one should follow in such a manner of icy finality that no one took another step. Special Forces may have taken over remote desert bases in Iraq before the actual war began. It is not clear, and it probably never will be. They certainly now had vehicles and tanks — which could only have been flown in — for the soldier, who wore fatigues but not a uniform as such, walked over to the tank parked by Iraq's first road sign. Its barrel was pointing our way, and someone was observing us through field glasses.

So, they really *had* taken Iraq. I knew I would never believe it until I had seen it for myself. The place where one American was a tremendous oddity now had hundreds of thousands of them — *and they were in charge ...*

At least, that was my initial perception. But Special Forces bear about as much resemblance to the main army as leopards do to field mice. Three hundred thousand of these guys would even be *too many* to take control of the entire planet. Fortunately, no country can ever find more than a handful of men who have what it takes — and are not yet serial killers.

We drove into Iraq under the watchful eyes and shrouded faces of Special Forces, aware for the first time, I think, of the enormity of what had happened in this country. A week earlier, it had still been business as usual — being bombed *was* Iraq's business, after all — but now everything had changed. The country that had been clenched tightly in a fist of totalitarian repression was just beginning to realize that the fist had been cut from its arm.

> *Things fall apart; the centre cannot hold;*
> *Mere anarchy is loosed upon the world,*
> *The blood-dimmed tide is loosed, and everywhere*
> *The ceremony of innocence is drowned;*
> *The best lack all conviction, while the worst*
> *Are full of passionate intensity.*
>
> — W. B. YEATS [66]

We needed gas. There was a huge gas station just outside the border post. To reach it you needed to drive almost all the way around the roundabout where Special Forces had their tank. Being Iraqi, Abdul, our driver, was not sure he now had the right to do this, although the vehicles ahead of us already had. To soothe him, we agreed to ask permission.

Dikon jumped out and went to approach the soldiers. Immediately, he found three automatic rifles aimed at him.

"Remain inside your vehicle!" instructed an amplified voice.

His hands in the air, Dikon shouted that we needed gas. Was it okay to get some, because the station appeared to be closed?

"The pumps are on. Take what you need and get on your way," said the voice.

Already the Americans considered Iraq's oil theirs to do with as they pleased. Although it was usually cheaper than water — literally — it was not free. With the world's second-largest deposits of fossil fuel, and possibly more (see chapter nine, "Oil," page 236), Iraq could afford to let citizens in on the bonanza. Jordanians paid many times more for a litre — so much so that Iraqi drivers viewed Jordanian gas stations with dark suspicion. But you could tell Abdul was not comfortable with simply taking the petrol. He wanted to leave the payment in an envelope, but settled for deciding to pay next time he saw the station's owner. We filled up two spare cans as well — and it was a good thing we did, because this turned out to be both the first and the last gas station between here and Baghdad.

The excellent highway linking Baghdad to the southwest was for the most part five lanes running straight as a bullet. You could land a jet on it. Normally you passed a truck or, more rarely, a car coming the other way every few minutes. That day there was nothing.

Using its roof aerial — and switching the phone off the moment we had finished calling — Hackett managed to get through to Philip Sherwell via the Iridium satellite. He was still on the road, we learned to our great surprise, trying to find a reasonably safe route into Baghdad. The convoy he was in had encountered a U.S. checkpoint on the highway somewhere near Ramadi, and decided to camp near it for the night since there was heavy fighting going on ahead of them. They had set off for Baghdad just after dawn but were having trouble finding a route that avoided areas of intense fighting or aerial bombardment, most of which was unreported by whatever news he was picking up. He sounded scared.

Using his own cellphone, Dikon spoke to various people in the convoy now establishing itself ahead and behind us. His clarity and precision in matters of important information were breathtaking. By then I knew that he lived in Jerusalem with an Israeli woman; the Middle East was his camera's beat. You did not get far there in his business by being careless.

"Abdul," he told the driver firmly, "you *have* to close the gap between us and the car ahead. Do you understand?"

Abdul thought he did.

Suddenly, the cars ahead veered sharply across three lanes. The still smouldering hulk of a burned-out coach blocked the entire width of the road on the opposite side of the highway, a few minutes from the turn-off for Syria and Saudi Arabia. Potholes a metre wide had taken out three lanes on our side.

"Let me get a few shots o' this," Hackett said.

Dikon had Abdul — who was now confused — pull over.

"Phil mentioned this," said Hackett. "The Americans said it were a busload o' Syrian mercenaries comin' tae join th' war ... So they had a plane zap it ..."

"But the Syrians, of course," Dikon added, "say the bus was just a regular service between Iraq and Syria, carrying ordinary people ..."

It certainly looked like a regular bus. I wondered who had come to remove the dead and wounded, for there were no bodies inside the blackened, twisted wreckage. You find that is a rule in war zones, however: if it is humanly possible, someone will come and take away the bodies fairly soon, affording the dead some last shred of dignity. Only those who live in the world's war zones can fathom the quotidian realities life there entails: the backbreaking labour, the eking out of resources, the vast long tedium interspersed with a brief but unimaginable intensity of horror. Most Americans could not imagine it, let alone hack it. In Iraq, from March 20, 2003 onwards, indeed to the date of this writing, every day has been September 11. If a handful of Iraqis controlled the global media, the world would know this — if anyone could even bear to watch the news any more.

Half an hour on, our convoy had to cross over to the other side of the highway for a stretch to avoid a partially collapsed overpass that had been carrying trucks America needed to attack. Over the northbound lanes, the bridge now dangled in strands of steel like ribbon, and enormous slabs of concrete blown from a gaping hole were scattered across our path like so much gravel. Two months later, that side of the highway was still blocked. The traffic had grown used to detouring across the centre island for a kilometre.

Sparsely populated though it was, this enormous desert still had outposts of humanity, a few gas stations and truck stops that had spawned a cottage industry of tire re-treading, engine repair, cigarette peddling, fast food and reasonably swift tea and coffee. Each greasy oasis trailed off into huts, kennels and tents before vanishing into the ochre sands. On my previous visits these were always hives of humanity, welcoming every traveller with enthusiasm. These watering holes for internal combustion never shut; no business was dismissed, and there was always someone to staff the fort, boil the water and fry the egg.

But now they were closed. There was no sign of anyone anywhere. Doors swung in the wind. Garbage blew in the dust. When we pulled in, as we did a couple of times, the cafés were locked, pumps turned off, and no kids ran out to sell you cigarettes and candy. For four hundred and fifty kilometres, we did not see a single Iraqi, only U.S. soldiers. It had become a ghost country. Not until we had crossed the Euphrates, and the sands had suddenly given way to palm jungles, the smeared azure skies to billowing torpid gloom, the dryness to a sickly clamminess, did we see the occasional person. They were mostly men, who looked up from the swamps with a mixture of fear and fury, then turned away, back to their crops, their animals or machines. There was no interaction out here. I wondered what they knew of the war, for what they *felt* about it was clear. Their world had been destroyed.

The stillness of death had paralyzed Iraq, it seemed. Even the high blue air above the desert was empty. You don't think you would miss air traffic, but you do. It is what I remember most about September 11, 2001: the empty skies. That same mood infected Iraq. No planes, no birds. All the birds had vanished, frightened away by the noise, lights and terror. They came back to Baghdad, but slowly. When nothing is what it's meant to be, when there is no normality, it is often hard to point to what exactly makes everything seem so strange. For me it was the birds: no sweet little songs to greet the dawn, nothing for sunset. A silence broken only by machines, by men.

As we neared the outskirts of Ramadi, itself a distant suburb of Baghdad, the convoy stopped to discuss plans. Dikon and Hackett put on flak vests and blue steel helmets with PRESS stencilled on them in white letters. They looked foolish but, though I joked about it, I felt suddenly naked, vulnerable. I did not think to ask *Harper's* for armour. Like cricketers, journalists need it now. The game has changed; it's not played by the same rules any more. Perhaps there are no rules any more?

Besides bullet-proofing, some of the larger media outlets could also afford security advisers, ex-marines or commandos who knew how to stay alive and how to talk to soldiers. John did this for the BBC, riding in the white hardside, map in one hand and phone in the other, mirrored Oakleys hanging from a chain around his neck, on top of which his shaved head seemed merely another big tense muscle. He was barely five feet tall, but you knew he could crush you like a bug if he had to. When I first encountered him I thought he had lost his temper — veins stood out in his temples, he bared his teeth — but he was always like this.

"Get the other fuckin' drivers here," John was saying. "They should fuckin' *hear* this ..."

The drivers were assembled. You could spot them easily: apart from me, they were the only people not wearing flak jackets and hard-hats. Iraqis who now lived in Jordan, they were preparing to proceed along the same route into the city that they always took. John had other plans.

"I just spoke to a fuckin' co at soc," he said. "What we got 'ere is more than a fuckin' AWE — an' that's ADVANCED WARFIGHTING EXPERIMENT, not the other fing. I'm tryin' t' get some fuckin' idea of their ASMP, see? We want to avoid goin' fru any 'ot spots — we got RTS to worry 'bout: one false fuckin' move, we're lit up. Now," he pointed northwest, "we got *jaish* over there, in Ramadi and Fallujah, we got the fuckin' SOF engaged there ... This is fuckin' MTW, it ain't no game ..."

I had no idea what he was talking about, so I am damned sure the drivers didn't; I later learned that soc is Special Operations Command, ASMP is Army Strategic Mobility Program, RTS is Rapid Targeting System, *jaish* is Arabic for "army," SOF are Special Operations Forces and MTW is Major Theater War. The military speaks and thinks in acronyms, and having spent more time and money experimenting with psychology than any other sector of the community, they know why. The further from the word you go, the further from the image you go too, and the further you go from the image, the greater the distance between you and reality. It's hard to discuss ways of killing and destroying all day long, but through the skilful deployment of acronyms, you don't have to really know that's what you're talking about. But it is, and it still gets to people — for although they are encouraged to forget it, soldiers are people too, and the suicide rate among armed forces in combat is always very high. Only in movies, it cannot be too often stressed, do people kill casually and without consequence — because in movies no one is *really* killing anyone.

John was in touch with soc and CENTCOM (Central Command), with people flying in planes so high above us we could not see or hear them, with people in tanks and tents and towns and foxholes. Yet he still could not find a route into the city that made sense.

There was a loud explosion a kilometre or so off, followed by a spinning black pinnate column of smoke. The ground shook beneath our feet briefly.

Fierce bursts of heavy gunfire erupted, .50-calibre stuff, *thump-thump-thump*, punctuated by the solid *thud* of mortars. It's a primitive business, war, and there is no great secret to success at it: the side with the best weapons almost always wins. And the side that wins always seems to be the side that should have won — because they get to tell the story, their way.

The small battle ahead explained more succinctly than John could why we did not want to continue heading that way. Dikon got through to Michelle, who had arrived at the Palestine Hotel in central Baghdad a few minutes earlier. She had her security people talk to John, and between them, they devised a route that soon had us heading off the freeway and onto the narrower but still impressively modern roads running beneath it. We were warned that units of Iraqi soldiers in civilian clothes were firing rocket-propelled grenades at any foreigners they saw. The news made every group of Iraqi men seem sinister. As we proceeded into Baghdad's squat, ugly exterior, all we seemed to see were groups of men, in cars or standing on the sidewalk, unshaven, always smoking, black eyes fierce yet frightened. Perhaps the country had retreated into the city. Occasionally, an Iraqi car would drive alongside us, four or six men, usually young, inside it, staring. Once in a while, someone would give us the thumbs up, but it was rare and they were scared, uncertain even as they made the gesture.

Now, too, we began to see looters. Small trucks, laden down with swag — huge vases, typewriters, chairs, desks, paintings, sofas, fridges, stoves, anything — careened along the collector lanes, so low in their suspension that some were grazing sparks from the blacktop. Some men pushed wheelbarrows or handcarts stacked with stuffed animals, or cash in big bundles, or coat stands, or air-conditioners. One man led two immaculately groomed prize racehorses along the sidewalk, their sculpted frames tense with fear. An old woman in a veil carried a typist's chair on her head. It was as if the largest, most opulent garage sale in history had started giving everything away. For poor Shia Muslims who lived in the sprawling slum known as Saddam City (and now as Sadr City), it was no doubt a day of days, a day to rejoice — and plunder. For virtually everyone else it was hell.

As we headed into the wealthy Mansur district, where the Americans later sent a Tomahawk missile to destroy a crowded restaurant in which they wrongly believed Saddam was holding a meeting, the full extent of Baghdad's destruction first became apparent. The whole city seemed to be smouldering, plumes of black or grey or white smoke crawling up into the deep, embattled charcoal clouds wherever one looked. Some people were not looting, I realized, they were merely rescuing whatever they could from buildings that would soon collapse or be engulfed by flames. If you saw women or children at all, they were invariably shrieking with fear or grief. When what the citizens needed was an army of doctors, fully supplied, to tend their wounds and assuage their sorrows, what they got was a caravan of journalists intent on asking them dumb questions.

As the emblems of Saddam's reign, the exotic domed palaces and Stalinesque concrete monoliths, came into view, near or far, it was obvious that they had all been hit, most within a few minutes on March 21, when three hundred cruise missiles coasted in to destroy fifty landmark buildings. The first one we saw up close was the Telecommunications Ministry. It still stood, but the interior was gutted, the floors now a forest of wires and melted steel girders. It looked as if a massive fist had punched through the side and then thrashed around until everything was crushed into a bolus of metal like spaghetti on a fork, pieces dangling, dripping, falling. Nobody spoke. From Bassim's house, I had mostly been unable to see the results of the bombing, but even in my imagination, they were not like this. Baghdad was gone. The Baghdad of Saddam Hussein had been obliterated.

Let's not talk about "precision bombing" — there is nothing precise about hurling enormous bombs into a city full of people. Let's not talk about "government targets," either — or if we must, think of it in terms of Washington. Imagine if "only government targets" were hit there: no White House, no Capitol, no Lincoln Memorial, no Pentagon ... Remove another few hundred large office complexes and you have some idea of what has happened to Baghdad. The only government buildings not hit were the Interior Ministry and the Oil Ministry — and let us not talk of irony or coincidence.

I have heard few people remark on this devastation. It is because most observers never knew Baghdad before Saddam fell afoul of his old ally, never saw the clean expansive boulevards, the swaggering monuments, the prosperous ministries, the brilliant manicured gardens, nor the obvious pride in people's faces when they showed you around. The sparkle and swagger had already gone back in 1991. The decade of sanctions and bombing that followed slowly but surely let all the remaining air out. Every bit as malignant as Bush i and ii, President Bill Clinton was merely able to put a more *reasonable* and *humane* spin on his crimes. Some part of Iraq, on average, has been attacked by Britain or the U.S. every single day since February 1991. That's at least one attack every day for more than four thousand days. Before that, for three brief years, there was peace. Then the war with Iran takes us back to 1980. A generation was swallowed up fighting it, and the generation growing up behind has known nothing but war. And we all know that, when pressure is applied to them, totalitarian regimes do not relax their hold on power. In 1996, I found a people driven to the brink of madness by deprivation and repression. The economic and military might of the United States under three administrations had been brought to bear on a small country just emerging from the medieval fog into its own version of the twentieth century. Of course the consequences were going to be dire. Nonetheless, the situation was still salvageable. There was still a chance for self-determination, until Bush ii came along with what Al Gore called his "go-it-alone, cowboy-type reaction to foreign affairs."[67]

> *O Lord our God, help us to tear their soldiers to bloody shreds*
> *with our shells; help us to cover their smiling fields with the pale*
> *forms of their patriot dead; help us to drown the thunder of the*
> *guns with the shrieks of their wounded, writhing in pain; help us*
> *to lay waste their humble homes with a hurricane of fire; help us*
> *to wring the hearts of their unoffending widows with unavailing*
> *grief; help us to turn them out roofless with their little children to*
> *wander unfriended the wastes of their desolated land in rags and*
> *hunger and thirst.*
>
> — MARK TWAIN [68]

As I looked around at what had been Baghdad, I was never more convinced that an awful crime had been committed here, a deed made all the darker by the cloak of goodness and justice in which it was disguised. No good thing has been done in Iraq by America. Not one. And the wickedness that has been done has no justification. Even if the elusive weapons are found, it will not be justifiable. And if the mass graves and torture chambers justify it, why were they not deplored two decades ago? They existed then, too. During the thirty years his regime ruled Iraq, Saddam slaughtered thousands upon thousands of his own people, true — all too true. Yet in a third of that time, the U.S. government has slaughtered many times that number of Iraqis itself. It is still slaughtering them. Yes, there is a difference between the two slaughters, and it is this: Saddam killed men — and a few women — who opposed him in some way; America's victims were and are largely civilians, old people, women and children who just happen to be in the way. Asked, "Do you feel that 300,000 dead Iraqi children is a price worth paying for the possibility of regime change in Iraq?," Clinton's secretary of state Madeleine Albright replied, "Such decisions are never easy, but yes, I think it is worth the price."[69]

When Bush II and his gang, who are mainly recycled from the most reactionary elements of the Reagan and Bush I administrations, talk about "Saddam's history" — as in "he has a history of slaughtering his own people" — it is worth remembering that these horrors are also Saddam's history and the history of Iraq.

Aghast at the damage all around me in Baghdad, at the senseless waste entailed in the deeply primitive process of war, a process that technology has simply veneered with modernity without reducing any of its brutality, always involving now the innocent, I underwent a change, a turning-about of the inner self — a small revelation, if you like. I once thought that there were both just and unjust wars — that World War II, for example, was a just war — but I no longer think this. The fifty million people who died to prevent the spread of fascism in Europe is not, I suggest, a price we would knowingly pay again for any political outcome — especially for an outcome that is by no means guaranteed. The outcome of wars is always unpredictable, but the process of war — the mass killing of human beings — is as certain as sunrise. If our response to terrorism is merely to terrorize other people in return, we are not in fact *fighting* terrorism at all, we are *creating* yet more terrorism for the future. In 1997, the American Defense Science Board reported that "historical data show a strong correlation between U.S. involvement in international situations and an increase in terrorist attacks against the United States."[70] Given that "involvement" is a standard euphemism for covert or overt military intervention, what you have here is the real explanation for terrorist acts. An event like 9/11 — the grief and suffering of which I am not marginalizing by placing it alongside other grief and pain, merely contextualizing — of course requires a response. But that response ought to involve addressing the issues that lie behind the attacks of 2001, not reproducing those attacks a thousand-fold upon largely innocent people. Silly as it may sound, the only thing war prevents is peace. The trappings of war and those of terrorism may differ, but the *modus operandi* is the same, as is the result: the mass killing of non-combatants. This is not a pacificist argument, either: self-defence may justify a concentrated act of violence to fend off a real and present danger of a specified attacker. But when you drop bombs on cities teeming with innocent people, including children, the old and the ill, any claim to this argument has long been waived.

I wonder too if those American taxpayers providing the Pentagon's annual $431 billion would find this money — hardly unwanted back home — well spent if they could see the carnage in Baghdad it has bought? Or the ongoing occupation, which increasingly mirrors in racist brutality the deplorable situation in Israel-Palestine? And will they find their taxes well spent when they witness the dozens of conflicts-in-making that will arise from plans already in progress behind the many closed doors of Washington?

The people of America ought to wake up. There is blood on their hands. They ought to think what could be done with $431 billion if it were spent on life instead of death. Most of all, they ought to *think*. Our minds are all that separate us from the beasts, and war is the bankruptcy of everything human — imagination, intelligence, compassion, wit and most of all, perhaps, the facility of speech, discussion, dialogue. War is not an option. In every other dispute, the parties are obliged to sit down and talk until a solution is found. Only politicians can legally advocate violence as a solution to anything; the only other organizations that advocate it, illegally, are criminal gangs. More Americans ought to go to Iraq, to behold what has been done in their name, even those who believe in what was done there — to see if they still believe in it.

> "Every gun that is made, every warship launched, every rocket
> fired, signifies, in the final sense, a theft from those who hunger

*and are not fed, those who are cold and are not clothed. The
world in arms is not spending money alone. It is spending the
sweat of its laborers, the genius of its scientists, the hopes of its
children."*

Who said that? Gandhi? Che Guevara? Karl Marx? Martin Luther King? It
was President Dwight D. Eisenhower[71] — who also, in his final address as
president, warned the nation to "beware the Military-Industrial complex."
During the first two minutes of the attacks on Baghdad, thirty million dollars
in cruise missiles went up in flames and smoke, destroying some fifty billion
dollars worth of Iraqi property, little of it with any military functions. Who
gains? The arms manufacturers, of course; the oil companies; and the
contractors assigned the task of rebuilding Baghdad, the Bechtels, the Boeings,
the Halliburtons, the Argyle Groups. This is what Eisenhower meant. When
what a company manufactures is missiles — each of which is like a very
expensive match: you cannot use it twice — imagine how concerned it will be
to prevent war at any cost. When that same company is actually represented in
the highest levels of the government — well, clearly they should not be. This
seems so obvious, I wonder why it needs to be pointed out. More important
is to see that it does not have to be this way. Are countries like Sweden,
or Denmark, or New Zealand — ones that do not have military forces
intervening in the affairs of sovereign nations — prey to terrorist attack or
threat? No, they are not.

Americans are not, of course, bad people. It is not a bad country. It has just
fallen under an evil enchantment and forgotten its way, forgotten what it was
about. But it was hard to see any goodness in America that day. Thinking of
all the good men and women I knew there, whose hearts would have broken
to see what their government had wrought, I felt sick to my stomach. Three
times, our convoy passed funeral processions. In the Shia manner, photos of
the deceased were carried like placards, the corpse draped in the religion's
black and green flag. Every picture showed a young man, gaunt, unshaven.
They were probably all war-related deaths, involving the poorest and most
oppressed of Baghdad's citizens, who had lived beneath Saddam's boot only
to die beneath America's. The dark scowls of the mourners when they saw

cameras pointing at their sorrow said all there was to say.

The air became acrid as we approached the city centre, close to unbreathable from all the toxic forms of smoke mingling with it from countless smouldering items in hundreds of still-burning buildings. An ill-equipped, exhausted, undermanned fire brigade in a city now mostly without electricity and running water meant that many fires put out once would smoulder back to life, sometimes weeks later. It was just one of many problems now faced in Baghdad.

Another striking difference between the Baghdad of a week before and the Baghdad of Bush II was that many men were now armed, either with pistols or, mostly, with Kalashnikov semi-automatic assault rifles — although it was not uncommon to see someone carrying a loaded rocket-propelled grenade (RPG) launcher. One old man I saw had two of them. Under Saddam — often shown himself in news footage firing guns in the air as an expression of joy or triumph — only a small elite segment of the military was allowed to carry both guns *and* bullets. Now, it seemed, every third man was openly packing. This struck me as hardly an ideal situation in a place where emotions were raw and tempers flared at the best of times.

Several times our convoy was forced to turn back by U.S. tanks blocking the way ahead. The soldiers were hostile and distinctly threatening in manner when asked for alternate routes, merely ordering us the fuck away, back across the boulevard's centre isle.

Apart from these encounters, though, there was remarkably little evidence of a U.S. military presence in a city for which it was now entirely responsible. Its obligations under international law were extensive, everything from providing security to ensuring that utilities functioned, food supplies were adequate, hospitals were properly supplied, transport services ran and children could resume their education. In two months that followed, I did not see the U.S. seriously attempt to fulfill a single one of these obligations.

Had we, on the other hand, been beamed down in Firdos Square, just in front of the Palestine Hotel, I would have sworn the U.S. military had arrived with massive force throughout Baghdad. There were, literally, more soldiers, tanks and other armoured vehicles visible from the Palestine's lawn than I had seen in the rest of Iraq, let alone the rest of Baghdad. This was helpful for the world's media now beginning to set up generators and tents, satellite dishes and chemical toilets on the lawn. It meant they would have front-row seats for the circus that was about to begin.

My first concern was to find myself a room. Dikon and Hackett were already taken care of by their people. I was suddenly on my own again. I did't have any people.

In the little street behind the Palestine I came across the Al-Arabie Apartment Hotel, a privately run place that was six floors of spotlessly clean sanctuary. It was to be home for the next few weeks, which were the most exhilarating and also the most terrifying of my life.

CHAPTER FIVE

THE GENEVA PROTOCOLS

Our forces will be strong enough to dissuade potential adversaries from pursuing a military buildup in hopes of surpassing, or equaling, the power of the United States ... As a matter of common sense and self-defense, America will act against such emerging threats before they are fully formed.

— FROM THE BUSH DOCTRINE [72]

The hubris of the Bush II administration requires no more elaboration here. Its puerile imperialist fantasies, largely the product of Rumsfeld, Cheney and, especially, Paul Wolfowitz, will yet, I am convinced, see this entire gang of criminals thoroughly discredited, if not jailed. With Bush II himself, I hope we will see an impeachment.

Because of this, and because I have and will again refer often to them, it is worth setting down here in full the most relevant clauses from the Geneva Protocols. This is international law.

"Protocol Additional to the Geneva Conventions of 12 August 1949, and relating to the Protection of Victims of International Armed Conflicts (Protocol 1)," June 8, 1977. From Chapter II, "Civilians and Civilian Population," Article 51, "Protection of the Civilian Population":

1. *The civilian population and individual civilians shall enjoy general protection against dangers arising from military operations. To give effect to this protection, the following rules, which are additional to other applicable rules of international law, shall be observed in all circumstances.*

2. *The civilian population as such, as well as individual civilians, shall not be the object of attack. Acts or threats of violence the primary purpose of which is to spread terror among the civilian population are prohibited.*

3. *Civilians shall enjoy the protection afforded by this Section, unless and for such time as they take a direct part in hostilities.*

4. *Indiscriminate attacks are prohibited. Indiscriminate attacks are:*
   a) *Those which are not directed at a specific military objective;*
   b) *Those which employ a method or means of combat which cannot be directed at a specific military objective; or*
   c) *Those which employ a method or means of combat the effects of which cannot be limited as required by this Protocol; and consequently, in each such case, are of a nature to strike military objectives and civilians or civilian objects without distinction.*

5. *Among others, the following types of attack are to be considered as indiscriminate:*
   d) *An attack by bombardment by any methods or means which treats as a single military objective a number of clearly separated and distinct military objectives located in a city, town, village or other area containing a similar concentration of civilians or civilian objects; and*
   e) *An attack which may be expected to cause incidental loss of civilian life, injury to civilians, damage to civilian objects, or a combination thereof, which would be excessive in relation to the concrete and direct military advantage anticipated.*

A violation of any one of the above sections of the international laws governing warfare is a very grave offence indeed, warranting an international tribunal and severe punishments for those convicted. I have already shown, and will continue to show, that as commander-in-chief of the U.S. Armed Forces, George W. Bush is guilty of violating *every single one* of these protocols, besides many others from elsewhere in the Conventions and international humanitarian law.[73] Unless international law is to be waived, unless America's case is considered *sui generis*, unless the world is content to lie down and become America's paddock or rodeo, there is no option but to move for the indictment on war crimes of Bush II, Cheney, Rumsfeld, Powell, Wolfowitz and many others. They are mass murderers, complicit in the deaths of thousands of civilians. Just as they have judged others, they must be judged.

CHAPTER SIX

THE GHOST OF GHENGIS KHAN

Some targets, especially late in the war, were bombed primarily to gain post-war leverage over Iraq ... Military planners hoped the bombing would amplify the economic and psychological impact of international sanctions on Iraqi society ... Because of these goals, damage to civilian structures and interests, invariably described by briefers during the war as "collateral" and unintended, was sometimes neither.

— *WASHINGTON POST*[74]

If you gained the impression, via CNN or somesuch, that the U.S. deployed mostly so-called smart bombs in its attacks on Baghdad during the 1991 Gulf War, it is because you were supposed to gain that impression. When I returned from that war hardly anyone believed my account of the civilian death-toll, which even American experts now agree exceeded 100,000 dead, with many more injured.[75] In fact, 93 percent of the 88,500 tons of bombs dropped on Iraq during the forty-three days of that war were not smart bombs — and the so-called smart bombs often missed their targets. Overall, seventy percent of U.S. bombs missed their targets [76] — or, in other words, 59,500 tons of bombs fell on something that was *not* a target. This was on the front page of the *Washington Post*, yet it is still a largely unknown fact. We ought to ask ourselves why this is.

Here is a clue: Walter Isaacson, the chief executive of CNN, told his staff during the U.S. invasion of Afghanistan in late 2001 that it was "perverse to focus too much on the casualties or hardship." [77] "Perverse"? Why is it perverse? It is perverse because the fundamental purpose of CNN is to be part of the state propaganda apparatus. When they, or any of the other networks, appear to criticize the government, you will find — as with Al Gore's "criticism" of Bush II — that what is actually said is very mild indeed. The differences are always more apparent than actual. Lewis Lapham, the editor of *Harper's* magazine, once told me that he enjoyed appearing on Canadian TV programs "because I feel I can say anything I want to say. Of course, you *can* say anything you want to say on U.S. TV, too — but you also know that, if you do, you'll never be invited back again." John R. MacArthur, *Harper's* publisher, said he felt exactly the same way. They rarely appear on television in the U.S. anyway, and almost never on the networks. Both are among the most articulate, well-informed people in the country, and their positions at *Harper's* amply warrant media attention. To ask why they are not given an opportunity to air their views before the vast audiences a network can provide — with of course a host or another guest who disagrees with their views — is like asking why the Democrats are throwing this year's election. Nobody cares what you write in *Harper's*, but somebody cares a lot what is said on U.S. network television. The revolution will not be televised, unless it is by community access channels.

> *Circus dogs jump when the trainer cracks the whip. But the really well-trained dog is the one that turns somersaults when there is no whip.*
>
> — GEORGE ORWELL

I sat drinking tea in what had once been the Palestine Hotel's bar. There was no food anywhere to be found. No stores were open, and not because it was Friday, the Muslim holy day. No stores were open the next day either, nor the week after it. Many had, like Bassim's family, simply fled the city, leaving shops boarded up and empty. I had eaten all the Nice biscuits, which were all I had eaten since Dikon's paella the night before.

The large L-shaped room was full of soldiers, the majority of them Marines. They looked like fish out of water, and I found that, for most, this was the first time they had been inside a building since leaving Kuwait City three months earlier. Their faces were tanned and scarred from the sun and blowing sands. Even holding a tea-cup seemed novel to them. I'd expected to see far more black faces, but there were hardly any. There were Philippinos, Mexicans, assorted Latin Americans, but most were white boys, and from the South more often than not. Not one resembled Sylvester Stallone or Arnold Schwarzenegger. Indeed many were quite tiny, and not a few were quite fat. Away from their tanks and monster rifles, without the hundred pounds of stuff they had to lug around, without the big steel hats and mirrored bug-eye shades, they did not look very threatening at all. Most of them looked like exactly what they were: teenaged boys from dirt-poor backgrounds.

The first time I listened to one of them talk I had assumed he was parodying good-ol'-boy-speak, perhaps telling some anecdote that involved hillbilly rednecks. There were no consonants, so it is pointless to attempt any written approximation. I had to tune in carefully before I could even get a gist of what was being said, which involved an incident earlier in the day. The soldier's unit had been told to intercept a vehicle in which high-ranking Iraqi military personnel were thought to be travelling out of Baghdad.

"We lit that fucker up real good," the soldier said. "Blew the door clean off and the fuckers clean out ... Asshole had his wife an' kid with him too. L'il girl. She were standin' there fuckin' screamin', man, an' on fire. She were fuckin' burnin', man. We was laughin' our fuckin' heads off, man ... Her face's all black an' she screamin' ... yeah! It were fuckin' tasty, I tell ya!"

I waited for some kind of punch line, but that was it: blew up the car, set the little girl on fire, stood there watching her burn and laughing. The soldiers to whom he was relating this charming little tale of heroism found it appropriately amusing too. They said things like right-on and dang, then related anecdotes of their own experiences that day, all of which involved fuckers who got whacked or lit up. They used an avalanche of acronyms, but it was not hard to get a general idea of what was said.

I took it for granted that war was a nasty, violent business in which weapons and orders played key roles. All I felt about these boys was sadness. They merely did what they were ordered to do. By the time you found yourself where they were, you had accepted this fact of life. The average CNN viewer knew more about what was going on than they did. The "need-to-know" thing is taken very seriously by the military. All that most of the grunts know is where they are supposed to position themselves and what to do when they get there. No one ever tells them why, or even what they might do next. They don't need to know that.

I had been making friendly gestures to the group, and finally one of them noticed my press ID card, which said "*Harper's* New York" on it. You could tell they were real southerners because one asked where I lived in New York, and I don't sound like someone who lives in New York. But, I quickly gathered, being a Brit was even better with this crowd (being Canadian was little better than being Iraqi).

"We sure grateful to you guys," a soldier with pale blue eyes only half an inch apart told me. "Resta those fuckers can go fuck themselves ... know what I mean?"

"Ingrates," I said. "Someone's got to defend liberty, haven't they?"

"Fuckin' ay, fella!"

They had clearly been warned about the media, but I was obviously proving myself an exception to the rule. They had not taken their CO seriously enough, though: journalists are all liars. And they lie to you as well as about you.

"So," I asked, now we were all friends, "what you think happened to the Iraqi army?"

"We killed 'em all."

"That would be an awful lot of bodies, wouldn't it?"

"Mebbe so. But we killed 'em ... eh?"

They all roared with laughter.

Soldiers freely admit that their job is "killing people and blowing things up." In a cramped room at Camp Falcon in Baghdad, I would later watch platoon Staff Sgt. Alexander Aguilastratt tell his guys from the 82nd Airborne's 2nd Brigade, 2nd Battalion, Alpha Company what they already knew. This was when they thought they were going to be leaving Iraq. "You've been close-up with the enemy," he said. The men nodded in agreement. "You looked him in the eyes and shot him in the head — but you have to turn off the switch when you get back because you're going to be dealing with American civilians. Dealing with families. We can't be the same killers we've been all this time. It's time for us to go home."

Soldiers are killing machines. When insufficiently deprogrammed, they have killed their own wives.[78] It is naive to think they would not kill the enemy's children in order to spread the terror that makes their job easier. We train them not to consider their enemies as human. Perhaps we ought to ask ourselves what the long-term effects of training so many killing machines are for our society.

I took a walk across to the Ishtar Hotel, where I had stayed in 1996. It was part of the Palestine compound really, a bow-shot away. The place looked as if they'd last cleaned it the day I left. It was black with dirt. It smelled terrible too, as if something had died inside the air-shafts a long time ago. Even the air looked filthy. It was a while before I realized the place was actually on fire. Black sooty smoke wafted over into the lobby from the mezzanine level. The lobby was gloomy and crowded, yet no one appeared unduly bothered by the smoke. I was so used to seeing the Mukharbharat sitting around, playing with their worry beads, smoothing their Saddam moustaches, waiting for the foreigners they were assigned to mind, that it only struck me later what was missing in the place, indeed missing everywhere. Not so long ago, you did not leave home without one — at least, you didn't if they could help it. It was hardly relaxed, though, the new Baghdad. Here in the Ishtar there was no electricity either. I had quite liked the hotel seven years earlier, even though it was already in a fairly advanced state of decay. The electricity had of course been working, but thanks to the embargo there were no light bulbs so the place was not much less gloomy. Like the Palestine, the Ishtar was now operating with a staff of perhaps three or four.

"Are you aware that the mezzanine floor is on fire?" I asked a sad old desk clerk.

"Yezza-yezza, we know about it."

"Okay. Good. Just checking. Got any rooms?"

"Noza-noza."

"Got any food?"

"There izza no food in all Baghdad nowza."

"What will *you* eat?"

"*Me*-za? I am not hungried."

"Nice chatting with you. Bye."

"Goods-bi-za," he said, balefully.

Everyone here had been through hell and out the other side, and then shoved back through twice again, spat on, kicked, set on fire, and now they were being starved. How did an old man like that find the will to get up in the morning and go on?

"Za?" the old man's voice said behind me.

I turned. He was beckoning me back. Maybe he had found a room?

"Yes?"

"The fire-za ..."

"Yes. What about it?"

"It izza not a beeg fire-za ..." He held his fingers half an inch apart.

"Glad to hear it. Thanks."

"You-za welcome-za. Hello!"

Many Iraqis say hello when they mean goodbye. Like the Beatles' song.

I am certain the old desk clerk was cracking a joke — about the fire not being big. Iraqis have a sense of humour that is wickedly dark, as it would need to be. I recall a story the British journalist Robert Fisk tells about being alongside a car so dilapidated it was held together with string and duct tape. This was when car theft had reached a new zenith in Baghdad. The driver of the juddering wreck nodded to Fisk, who called across the gap between them, "Well, at least you don't have to worry. No one's going to steal your car ..." The man then reached down beside him and pulled up a cheap old artificial leg, saying, "Yes, and they not going to steal the rest of me too."

If they worked out a way to export Iraqi spirit, courage and fortitude, they would not even need their oil.

I and the public know
What all schoolchildren learn,
Those to whom evil is done
Do evil in return.

— W. H. AUDEN (1907–73)[79]

As night fell that first day back in Baghdad, the soldiers seemed edgier. Looking out from my balcony on the fifth floor of the Al-Arabie I began hearing gunfire both near and far, the steady *pop-pop-pop* of semiautomatics and the *thump-thump-thump* response from more hi-tech weaponry. Occasionally something much bigger went off. Apart from this block, it seemed, the city was plunged in darkness, besides the fires burning dimly here and there. The roar of generators told me where our power came from. But where did Power come from? It suddenly seemed a vast, awesome and dangerous place, this city of the dreadful night.

I thought about what the soldiers had said about killing all the Iraqis. What would make them think they had done that? On the other hand, where were they? Where was Iraq's army? I had heard from various people that there was intense fighting still going on around the Saddam International Airport, yet the gunfire from that direction sounded no different in intensity or quantity than that from anywhere else. And nowhere was there any sign of something even approaching a battle between armies. What I was hearing were "incidents," just as likely to be firefights between looters as isolated cases of Iraqi snipers being caught getting off a few rounds at the U.S. army.

A week later, the alleged "battle" or "intense fighting" at the airport was still being used as the reason U.S. troops had blocked off the roads leading to the airport. For our "own safety," journalists were not allowed near the airport, so there is no video footage of the battle there. And, as the military know full well, when there is no picture, there is no story these days. All they have to do to keep the media from covering anything they do not want covered is to make it impossible to shoot pictures of it.

What was really going on at this time? You can be sure that whatever it was, it was not happening right in front of the Palestine Hotel. What you were *told* was the spontaneous tearing down of Saddam's statue by liberated Iraqis

149

was in fact an entirely staged event in which a group of Ahmad Chalabi's[80] militia posing as locals were helped by the army, creating the seminal image of U.S. victory in Iraq right in front of the world's media just in time for the evening news back home. If you stood on the roof of the Palestine, all you would have seen was a small group of people around the statue and a few onlookers being held back by the army. All the pictures that appeared around the world, however, were framed tightly to give the impression of a large crowd. Thus is news fabricated.

> We are not hostages, America
> and your soldiers are not God's soldiers ...
> We are the poor ones, ours is the earth of the drowned gods.
> — IRAQI POET SAADI YOUSSEF [81]

Using military and government sources that prefer to remain anonymous, I managed to get an idea of what actually occurred during the last days of Saddam's regime. Some of this is first-hand state intelligence passed on to me by senior members of the Jordanian government; some is from an Israeli intelligence unit[82] which closely monitored U.S. Central Command transmissions at the request of Washington, in order to verify information with MOSSAD agents inside Iraq; the rest is from various other sources I have always found to be reliable. Why this account of the war was kept from the general public, however, is a question to which I still have no compelling answer.

These are the salient details:

Around April 5, the seventeenth day of the war, U.S. Central Command deputy operations officer Brigadier General Vincent Brooks delivered a very brief statement announcing that special troops were seizing key points in Baghdad. What this meant was that the main focus of the invading troops was on capturing Saddam's control, command and communications centres — the brain and nerve centres of the regime — which were buried deep underground in four vast subterranean palace complexes beneath Baghdad and its suburbs.

The first of these underground palaces was reached when U.S. forces captured Saddam International Airport — now Baghdad International — on Thursday, April 3. At the far end of the outer runway, a ramp led down into a gigantic labyrinth of staggering size and complexity. A similar facility, known as the Northern Palace, was located further north within the airport perimeter; there were two others in Baghdad and one southeast of Tikrit, very near al-Awja, the village where Saddam was born. These command posts were more like self-contained underground cities, taking up areas between seven and ten square kilometres, in three or four tiers, and about thirty metres below the ground. Each had its own internal highway system comprising as much as seven kilometres of road, and every complex was linked to one or more of the others. A four-lane underground expressway connected the two airport complexes.

The other two palace-cities were set deep below Baghdad's streets. One was beneath the upscale area called Karah, and had a private airstrip attached to it. The other was located below the Dora district, a little south of the Tigris and Baghdad University. These two complexes were also linked by a highway, running underneath the river. The tanks of the U.S. 3rd Infantry and 101st Airborne Divisions, which provided classic news footage when they were filmed victoriously entering the city, but then disappeared, were in fact on their way to the Karah palace complex.

Much of the fighting occurred underground, which is why there was not much evidence of troops on the streets of Baghdad. Between Friday, April 4 and Monday, April 7, a sequence of related events occurred:

1. On Friday, Information Minister Mohammed Sayeed Sahaf stated that there would be something "non-conventional" happening. The U.S. military encouraged the media to believe this was an Iraqi threat to use weapons of mass destruction. Had this been remotely possible, the army would not have been there. The reference, however, was understood by military analysts to refer to a plan for Iraqi troops to perform a rearguard ambush, pouring out from the underground cities and attacking the American advance from behind.

2. That same day Saddam, or one of his doubles, appeared for his now-legendary Last Walkabout, ambling unhurriedly through the handpicked crowds of a working-class Baghdad neighbourhood, seemingly confident,

calm and in charge. Hearing of this performance, war commander General Tommy Franks reportedly announced to aides that it did not much matter whether or not it was Saddam and whether or not he was alive, since capture of the command and control centres would signal the war was over anyway.

3. The following day, April 5, Information Minister Sahaf announced that the "non-conventional" plan had worked, that Iraqi forces had pushed back the U.S. units and retaken the airport.

4. On the morning of April 7 an American officer was interviewed standing conspicuously outside the entrance to the Northern Palace, saying his troops were securing it and moving on to additional government centres and symbols of Saddam's regime. There was, however, little evidence of any military activity in the background. This was, many analysts believe, a ploy to fool Iraqi commanders into thinking that American units had captured the main command and control centre.

5. That same morning the 3rd Mechanized Division troops were sent to raid Saddam's official Baghdad palace. Two hours after an announcement that the compound was now in U.S. hands, War Command issued a statement declaring that the operation was merely an "armoured raid" whose purpose was "not to take ground."

6. Later on that same day, Sahaf declared that the incoming U.S. column had been "slaughtered." Speaking to media from the east bank of the Tigris, he said, "They are beginning to commit suicide at the walls of Baghdad."

American troop movements, along with a careful reading of military statements and CENTCOM innuendo, suggest that there were serious setbacks around both the airport and the official palace. However, Jordanian intelligence sources indicate that, at some point over the weekend of April 5 and 6, a deal was brokered between the U.S. and General Ahmed Hussein, the only other person apart from Saddam with total authority over all units of the Republican Guard. Ahmed Hussein ordered most of the Special Republican Guard, an elite fighting force of some forty thousand troops, to retreat into the underground complexes at the airport, whence they believed they would be airlifted along with Saddam to Syria. A smaller unit of four to five thousand guardsmen was sent to defend the Karah subterranean complex.

The Americans were taken by surprise and withdrew when they encountered the SRG forces at the airport. Instead of engaging them in battle, U.S. troops went searching for other entrances and exits to the underground complex. One was found in Saddam's opulent suite at the airport, another at the official palace. There were others. When these entrance-exit points had been sealed, and U.S. commanders were certain of the exact locations of Special Republican Guardsmen, the Americans detonated some kind of hi-tech bomb — there are rumours that it was a neutron bomb, but that seems outrageous even by their standards — in the airport's underground complex, the Southern Palace, killing everyone in it and in the Northern Palace. Estimates are in the forty thousand range. With the SRG defeated and the command and control centres destroyed, the war was, at least in General Franks' terms, essentially over.

General Ahmed Hussein is believed to have provided the Information minister with false reports of an Iraqi victory in order to draw out remaining pockets of Iraqi troops. The general himself, of course, managed to slip out of Baghdad unharmed. Evidence that some sort of deal had gone down is seen in the terms of Ahmed Hussein's surrender, a month or so later. He agreed to turn himself in for questioning on the understanding that he would not be arrested; he subsequently disappeared and is probably now living in Syria. It was widely believed by Iraqis at the time that Saddam had been betrayed. Even those who despised the Ba'ath regime and yearned for Saddam's fall wanted the end to come about honourably, and there is no honour in losing a war because of a traitor.

Every American commander knows that the strength of the U.S. military lies in its weapons, not its troops. Americans do not make good soldiers and in any prolonged battle with orthodox weapons, this weakness would become apparent. The U.S. was therefore anxious to avoid the "mother of all battles" scenario, in which the Iraqis knew they had a chance of inflicting heavy casualties that would swiftly lower American morale and weaken resolve. General Franks' war plan reflects this purpose at every turn, using air support to punch at command centres, and strategic manoeuvres to box in rather than engage the enemy. Death tends to come from the skies in American wars, and the serious battles are always over before troops appear. The army itself is only really useful for policing and "mopping up" exercises.

Based on previous patterns, the U.S. was also certain that Saddam would avoid being caught in the command and control centres: he always felt most safe when he was virtually alone. During the Gulf War, he spent nearly all of his time motoring from place to place in an orange Volkswagen Jetta, accompanied only by a driver-bodyguard. This of course made him almost impossible to hit, and therefore — except when there was reliable intelligence on his whereabouts (as on March 19, when they bombed his command complex in Dora on a tip-off; see below) — the U.S. did not even target him this time.

The notable absence of any media reports concerning Saddam's underground command centres was curious. They had been the subject of much speculation and interest over the decade prior to the war, so to see them vanish from the horizons of news coverage was baffling. The sealing-off of the airport from journalists for much of the month, combined with the apparent absence of signs indicating that a serious battle was being fought in the area, added credence to the notion that something significant had happened there. When they were questioned about the much-feared Special Republican Guard, military commanders tended to use phrases like "they just vanished into thin air" — which, if a massive bomb was employed, would not be entirely a lie.

Until the disappearance of the Special Republican Guard is satisfactorily explained — unlike the rest of the Iraqi forces, they could not have simply shed their uniforms and walked home — and until journalists and weapons experts have been able to explore the underground palace complexes, the explanation offered here will have to remain on the table, since it at least *does* explain what happened in Baghdad between April 4 and April 7, 2003. Because by Tuesday, April 8, what had been a war the last time anyone looked became merely a "mopping up" operation. Of course, no one then realized that the cleaners and their mops would be doing a far longer and infinitely more dangerous job than the soldiers and their guns had performed.

As early as April 12, Israeli intelligence sources were asking themselves, "Why has not a single officer in charge of weapons of mass destruction been caught — or come over? Why has no large-scale frontal battle been fought?"[83] They were also asking themselves, "Why did the American commanders refrain from placing Baghdad under curfew Wednesday night? — both to stop the looting and prevent the bloody settling of scores widely expected in the days to come between victims and their oppressors, member of the defeated regime and its opponents, Shiites and Sunnis, or even criminal gangs exploiting the in-between days of havoc for to [sic] occupy turf."[84] These are all good questions.

Israeli intelligence also agrees that deals were done between the U.S. and Iraqi commanders, although it differs widely on the details and names:

> ... *the keys to east Baghdad were handed over by the high commander of Iraq's elite Special Republic [sic] Guards, General Maher Safian Al-Tikriti, another of Saddam's cousins. This was the upshot of discussions that took place between him and U.S. Special Forces and CIA officers deployed undercover in the Iraqi-controlled parts of Baghdad. General Takriti [sic] agreed to let U.S. forces roll into central Baghdad unopposed across bridges that were not blown up in return for an American guarantee of safe exit from the city for his troops and a promise they would not be pursued ... [These] reports shed partial light on the ease with which the U.S. 1st Marines Expeditionary Force was able to reach the heart of Baghdad on Wednesday, April 9, without encountering substantial Iraqi resistance. In one case, the Republican Guards supposed to defend the Diyala River bridges and keep American forces out of east Baghdad suddenly stopped shooting and deserted their posts. In general, large sections of the elite SRG divisions charged with defending Baghdad melted away without inflicting or suffering casualties.*[85]

If the use of "melted away" reflects language in the intelligence reports received from U.S. sources by the Israelis, then it is yet another example of the suspicious preponderance of this imagery in discussing the SRG. Even with the finest intelligence network in the Middle East, however, the Israelis still had a lot of questions about what had occurred in Baghdad:

> *All these secret deals — especially the one with General Takriti [sic] — raise two important questions:*
> 1. *Was the Baghdad transaction the only one closed with Safian Al-Tikriti? Or was it part of a package?*

2. *Were this and any other trades approved in full or in part by Saddam Hussein or his sons? If so, what did they get in return? Does it mean that the decisive battle will take place in Tikrit after all? This would depend on whether General Al-Tikriti dealt with the Americans with the knowledge of Saddam and his sons or betrayed him — not merely to save his men but to keep the town of Tikrit and his clan's homes safe. If this is what happened, then Tikrit, like Najaf, al Kut, Karbala and Baghdad, will fall to the Americans without much real opposition.*[86]

Since Tikrit did fall without much opposition, it would seem that Saddam *was* betrayed.

Revealing new knowledge about the structure of Saddam's underground fortresses, American B-52 bombers carried out a "bunker-buster" raid on the system beneath Dora a day after U.S. troops entered Baghdad. This was the second attack on the same site, the first being the war's opening shot, on March 19, when it was termed a "target of opportunity." U.S. command believed that Saddam was in the command centre the first time — and, it seems, they were probably right. What they were wrong about was the strength of the bunkers. By early April, evidently, they knew that the only way to destroy these centres was by repeated pounding that eventually cracked the walls and caused them to cave in. Knowing this, however, they also knew that, unless they were prepared to kill hundreds of thousands of civilians and flatten much of Baghdad — which was by no means ruled out, initially — the bulk of the underground complex was effectively invulnerable. The decision to employ a horrendous hi-tech bomb is thus somewhat defensible, if the only alternative was a massive civilian death toll. Since heavy American casualties were also unacceptable, it is easy to see how the options were quickly narrowed down.

> *America, we are the dead.*
> *Let your soldiers come.*
> *Whoever kills a man, let him resurrect a man.*
> *We are the drowned ones*
> *beneath the waters at your feet,*

dear Liberty.
We are the drowned.
Let water come.

— SAADI YOUSSEF [87]

I knew none of this information as I gazed out over the dark and wounded monster of Baghdad that night. Not knowing it also made the situation seem far more ominous. I think everyone expected some sort of last and horrible surprise from Saddam. Speculation ranged from a nuclear bomb placed beneath Baghdad that would melt us, the Americans and everyone else into a vat of bubbling plasma, to a plague that would come festering forth from some Ba'athist test-tube to leave all humanity a leprous wailing rabble. Such are the consequences of an overkill propaganda campaign. We believed Saddam to be another psychopathic god like Hitler, diabolically resourceful, bent on Armageddon. This is why it became necessary to capture him, alone and dishevelled, cowering in a "spider-hole" — a term I have never before encountered but which, to give someone credit where it's due, serves admirably to convey an image of a man trapped at the centre of his own lethal web.

The fear that had ruled in Baghdad since the late eighties had now merely transmuted to fear of different things. My hands were clammy, thinking of all the horrors that might lie concealed in the belly of this beast. I had to tell myself repeatedly that the U.S. would not have so many troops here if it suspected there was any serious danger for them. Then I thought of the callous dumb kids in uniform whom I had met at the Palestine: did anyone in Washington really care what happened to them? Cannon-fodder: that was all they were. I looked across at the hotel's dark tower, imagining it like an ant farm, exposed and teeming, with all the corridors and rooms full of babbling journalists open to the night. I saw the lobby, revealed to be full of U.S. soldiers, who were also everywhere around the grounds and environs. If I were Saddam and wanted to deliver a parting shot the world would never forget, I reluctantly conceded, I would send in the suicide bombers to Firdos Square. No one would be able to kill that story.

Feeling spooked, very hungry and ill-at-ease, I began looking through a history of Mesopotamia,[88] hoping for a soothing effect from its vast span of time. I recall, while studying Latin at school back in the last millennium, reading a letter by Pliny (the Younger, I think) written during the volcanic eruption of Mount Vesuvius that buried the Roman town of Pompeii in AD 79. Pliny watched the spectacular cataclysm from across the bay in what is now Naples, and the immediacy of his account thrilled me.

History came to life and it stayed that way, in the sense that, as I later came to embellish the idea, all of human consciousness was a continuous moment, causes inextricably linked to effects, stretching backwards and forwards in an unbroken chain from Beginning to End.

The past literally is the present.

Don't think I haven't wondered how dumb the concept is, either, because I have. It is. But I still like it. Everything about Iraq has traces of paradox and oxymoron. In this, it has much in common with the world itself, for Iraq is like history's maquette: moulded from pain and futility, yet acted out and endured with such flair and panache.

No other place on Earth has been more involved for longer in civilization's history than the area now roughly encompassed by Iraq. When I first came to Baghdad, back in the 1980s, when the Iraqi dinar was worth more than the dollar and Saddam still considered himself America's good friend, the first sight that impressed itself upon me was a fifteen-metre banner draped across the arrivals' hall reading: "Welcome to the Cradle of Civilization."

What a difference the decades make, melting into one another, compounding error with malicious repetition. Baby Civilization has been kicked from his cradle and lies dead from malnutrition and bombs; one U.S. dollar can buy as many as 3,000 dinars[89] and Saddam, even in jail, is the closest thing to Satan that America has seen since Ayatollah Khomeini lay his head to rest in a golden tomb.

The West just cannot read Saddam; we don't know what to make of him. The Arabs see him far more clearly, though. The reader may recall Prince Hassan's comment about Saddam: "He truly loves his country. It is his passion — no one can take that away from him. He's not a learned man but there is no aspect of Iraq's vast history he isn't intimately familiar with."

To raise anything approaching nationalist fervour among the three distinctly different peoples who make up modern Iraq — the Kurds to the north, the ruling Sunni Muslims centred in Baghdad, and the more numerous but pitifully impoverished Shia in the marshes and wastes of the south and east — Saddam always resorted to evocations of a very distant past. It was thus fitting that his own reign concluded with an ancient and tragic symmetry, discovered looking like a mad prophet in a hole in the ground near the village of his birth, visited and taunted in prison by old enemies from his youth.

In keeping with its Manichaean nature, Iraq's recent emergence as a vital player on the world's stage came after a period of centuries during which it had never been less important. There was a time, of course, when the whole region was not only of paramount importance to the frenzy of humankind, it was the very gate of God on Earth, a garden full of paradise. The name Babylon — *Bab-El* — means just that: "the gate of God."

The arc of land between two mighty rivers, the Dijla or Tigris and the Furat or Euphrates, curving down from the mountains of Turkey to flow into the Arabian Ocean, is in fact probably the biblical Garden of Eden. It was certainly the site of Sumer, the oldest documented civilization on the planet. A full millennium before the staggering grandeur and unparalleled 3,000-year longevity of Egypt, Sumer marks the transition of humankind from nomad to city-dweller. This is recounted as myth in the story of Abel and Cain, who heads east out of Eden to take up a trade and build himself a city.

Sumerian society was dominated by two opposing qualities of the very land itself: the capricious nature of the two rivers, which at any time could unleash devastating floods capable of wiping away entire peoples; and the extreme richness of the valleys, whose soil had been deposited by thousands of years of such flooding.

The latter quality attracted migrating tribes and made possible for the first time in recorded history the growing of surplus food; whereas the former, the volatility of the rivers, necessitated a form of collective management to shore up the marshy, low-lying land against flooding. As surplus food production increased and collective management advanced, a form of urbanization evolved in which Sumerian civilization took root. The chief myth of Sumer involves a search for immortality within the tenuousness of human existence. It also recounts the destruction of the world in a massive flood, with a wise old man who survived by building an ark.

Along with the pioneering development of cereal agriculture, the Sumerians invented something else that facilitated civilization: writing.

Cuneiform, the bird's-feet-like script made by impressing a wet clay tablet with the triangular end of a chopped-off reed stylus, made it possible for them to hand down, generation to generation, their accumulated wisdom in general and such specific things as agricultural techniques. Indeed, writing evolved to keep track of property, and double-entry bookkeeping, a remarkable innovation used to this very day, was every bit as important an offshoot as the syllabic alphabet. Innovation after innovation poured from the fertile minds of Sumer: the wheel and the plow, around 3700 BC; a math system based on the number 60, still the basis for our measurement of time ... Sumerian society evolved rapidly and in ways far more conducive to our own thinking than any other ancient society. It was matriarchal, for example, and women were highly respected, holding positions of importance that were not simply ceremonial.

Private property played an unusually important role in daily life, in stark contrast to Egypt, where the pharaoh, as a god, owned everything and everyone. Sumerian kings were very human indeed, and answerable to their people, with whom they shared the same right to bargain fairly for goods. Increasingly doubling as safe repositories for stored valuables, Sumer's temples can also be regarded as the first banks. In fact, everything Sumer did was a first. There are many perquisites associated with being the first civilization, not least of which is being fairly certain that you will not be the last. History is anything but symmetrical.

Unlike the average Egyptian, who now professes scorn for anything earlier than Islam, the average Iraqi is immensely aware and proud of being a descendant of Sumer, no matter that a span of five millennia stand between him and the Dawn. Here, we have reached only 2700 BC, but already it should be easier to understand how joyously those whose ancestors gave the world writing, justice and agriculture must view an invasion by those who have given the world Mickey Mouse and the Big Mac, not to mention CNN and Hiroshima. Iraqis are an educated, sensitive, accomplished people fallen on evil times. Things have never been worse, in fact — but this, they feel, is no reason to treat them like helpless savages.

The use of writing to record the oral tradition of songs and epics was one of those great leaps of human progress without which history simply wouldn't make sense; there wouldn't be any, for a start. Not only did literature begin on the banks of the Tigris; that which survives from Sumer makes up one of the world's supreme masterpieces, an epic about a man named Gilgamesh, who ruled the city-state of Uruk around 2700 BC. It also happens to be the principal source for the biblical book of Genesis, core of the cultural myth around which Western civilization formed. Our own identity begins here.

If ancient Sumer sounds too good to be true, it was. Perhaps the last great contribution it made to collective humanity was to become living proof that there is nothing made perfect by human hands that religion cannot corrupt and destroy within a year. A parasitical high priesthood evolved and before long its members were claiming to be gods descended to Earth, sole discerners of the ineffable divine will. It was essentially downhill from there on. In 2340 BC, the Akkadian strongman with a name like industrial detergent, Sargon, stomped into Sumer and subdued its city-states into his burgeoning empire, which extended as far as Lebanon.

But — take note, America! — empires rarely last very long, and it was a mere 215 years later that Sargon's vanished forever, when the Sumerian city of Ur rose up in revolt. Ur, of course, was home to uber-patriarch Abraham, in whom the three querulous religions whose bickering makes up much of history are joined at the source.

The Sumerian civilization was reunited about six centuries later, in 1700 BC, by King Hammurabi. What had been Sumeria was now Babylonia, whose capital on the Euphrates was the greatest city of the ancient world, Babylon, the gate of God. Hammurabi was strong, just, wise and visionary — the kind of ruler you vote for but never get. During his long reign, Assyrians and Babylonians, the two cultures that compose what was next known as Mesopotamia ("between the two rivers" in literal-minded Greek), achieved complete and harmonious fusion for the only time in their history. Tireless in his supervision of irrigation and construction projects, Hammurabi is now best known for his codification of the laws governing Babylonian life, from which both Mosaic law and the modern legal system are directly descended. "An eye for an eye, a tooth for a tooth" was one of his catchphrases.

Dissent and squabbling soon tore the Assyrians and Babylonians apart, with the Assyrians gaining the upper hand and controlling Babylonia until the sixth century BC, when a series of revolts installed a new dynasty ruled by

Nabopolassar. He crushed the Assyrians. Then his son, Nebuchadnezzar II, conquered Judah, razed Jerusalem, removed every trace of Solomon's Temple and, in 597 BC, carried off the entire Hebrew ruling class, all fifteen thousand, into slavery at Babylon, beside whose rivers they sat down and wept when they remembered Zion.

But at least the Nebuchadnezzar II can take pride in being the builder of Babylon's fabled Hanging Gardens, one of the Seven Wonders of the Ancient World. They were on the east bank of the Euphrates about ninety kilometres south of present-day Baghdad, quite near where the Coalition of the Willing blew up one of its own tanks. The second Nebuchadnezzar built them for his wife, whose name was Amyitis — it was not a disease. She had been "brought up in Media and had a passion for mountain surroundings," we're told, referring to the Persian province and not a hereditary career in television.

Her husband, supposedly, was trying to recreate these mountain vistas to prevent her homesickness. The scale of Babylon's Hanging Gardens is rather terrifying, however, and reveals an obsessive streak in Nebuchadnezzar II. A contemporary observer noted that they had

> plants cultivated above ground level, and the roots of the trees are embedded in the upper terrace rather than in the earth. The whole mass is supported on stone columns. Streams of water emerging from elevated sources flow down sloping channels. These waters irrigate the whole garden, saturating the roots of plants and keeping the whole area moist. Hence, the grass is permanently green and the leaves of trees grow firmly attached to supple branches ... This is a work of art of royal luxury and its most striking feature is that the labour of cultivation is suspended above the heads of the spectators.

It's hydroponics, then. I recall seeing something similar in British Columbia, where the grass is also permanently green.

The Jewish captivity in Babylon lasted sixty years, but it couldn't have been so bad since, when it was ended by the Persian Cyrus the Great, few Israelites wanted to leave. When a group led by Zerubbabel finally did return to Zion in 538 BC, it was with what amounted to a new religion, one deepened and enriched by its prolonged contact with the profound theology of the

Zoroastrian Persians. It is to the Zoroastrians, or Parsis as they are also now known, that Judaism, Christianity and Islam owe their existence. Just as Judaism was the vehicle that took Zoroastrianism westward, Zoroastrianism was itself a vehicle in which Vedic Hinduism had travelled out of India, where all the great religions have their origin.

Around this time, a pattern or habit was established that became the template of regional activity for close to two thousand years: the Babylonians form an alliance with the Persians and stomp the Assyrians. Then the Assyrians recover, form an alliance with the Babylonians and stomp the Persians, who eventually recover and resurrect their alliance with the Babylonians ...

By the time Islam arrives to stop the cycle, one is heartily glad of it.

I could have driven to Babylon in less than an hour. Not much of it remains, although there is quite a lot there (the way things are going, there'll be much less left of Baghdad in two millennia). Ninety-five percent of what is visible today in Babylon, however, is Saddam's reconstruction. It resembles the set from a cheap 1950s biblical epic. Saddam was not as good at reconstructing the past as he was at invoking it. The mighty lion gates are about an eighth the size of the originals, whereas Nebuchadnezzar's palace is more than twice the height it would have been. This, however, might be because it is also Saddam's palace. A French architect, who was not allowed to go home during the Gulf War, told me back in 1991 that Saddam often came to stay in the ersatz palace alone, and he liked to wander around all night chatting with the ghost of Nebuchadnezzar. "They plan 'ow they gonna capture the Jews again," the architect said, chuckling. "Only this time they not gonna let 'em go ..."

It's when you find yourself near the sign in Babylon that reads "Alexander the Great died on this spot in 323 BC" that you feel those chilling inner waves that drive home Iraq's awesome past. Having conquered the known world and been hailed as a god by the Egyptian priesthood, Alexander died, broken, exhausted, worn out, aged thirty-three. It was an omen for the city, which went into decline after Alexander's general and successor in Babylonia, Seleucus Nicator, moved his capital to Antioch. In the second century BC, Babylon became part of the Persian empire, remaining in it until the seventh century AD, when an army of 18,000 Arab Muslims led by Khalid ibn al-Walid defeated the much more numerous Persians, who were said to be exhausted from ceaseless campaigns against the Byzantines and had been chained together so they could not flee. The people were offered this ultimatum:

"Accept the faith and you are safe; otherwise pay tribute. If you refuse to do either, you have only yourself to blame. A people is already upon you, loving death as you love life."

The words are chilling, and a reminder of the implacable power of Islam, a power vested equally in the mighty and the displaced or disenfranchised. *We want to die more than you want to live*: it is what every suicide bomber and freedom fighter now tells the invaders and neo-colonists of the Middle East. It was what the Chechen Islamist guerrillas told those they held hostage in a Moscow theatre for fifty-seven hours in October 2002.

The following year, the Persians rallied under their hero, Rustum, attacking the Muslims at al-Hillah, west of the Euphrates, where the Americans ran into some stiff opposition from Republican Guard units. The Persians were soundly defeated then and again the year after that, at the Battle of Buwayb. But they clearly did not understand their time was up, for another year later at al-Qadisayah, a village south of Baghdad where U.S. troops had a firefight with Fedayeen militia, Rustum was killed, and finally the Persians gave up. The story is retold in one of Iran's greatest epic poems from the classical era.

Inspired, the Muslims pushed on, but they were fighting a *jihad* and thus were regulated by religious laws that prevented looting, rape and needless killing of civilians. It was not in their economic interest to destroy unnecessarily and indiscriminately. Just like the Americans and British — this time.

In AD 750, Abo al-Abbas was established in the province of Baghdad as the first caliph, or supreme Islamic authority, of the Abbasid dynasty. Twelve years later the city of Baghdad was founded, swiftly rising to importance. By the tenth century it was the intellectual centre of the world. This is the era that Arabs always gaze back upon wistfully, when their civilization was the glory of the world, a triumph of mind and spirit unprecedented in human history, a place to which all roads led. Without it, the European Renaissance could not have occurred, for it was the Arabs who preserved and built upon the wisdom of the ancient world throughout the so-called Dark Ages. It was, however, also the peak of Islamic culture, never to be seen again. The

Crusades are largely viewed by Arabs as the cause of this demise, and are regarded, rightly, as a product of European fear and envy. When most of Western Europe had scarcely improved upon the Stone Age, there was running water and three kilometres of illuminated public roads in Seville in Arab Andalusia, where the beauty of the new mosques and palaces alone drew thousands of Christians and many Jews to embrace Islam.

Baghdad was a mere village when the second Abbassid caliph, Abu Jafar Al-Mansur (ruled 754–75), a skilled orator and administrator, decided to build his new capital nearby. In less than fifty years, the population outgrew the city's walls. By the reign of Mansur's grandson, Haroun al-Rashid (ruled 786–806), the city was second in size only to Constantinople. Al-Rashid was the caliph of *The Arabian Nights*, a highly educated, refined man of exquisite taste who actively supported and encouraged all manner of intellectual pursuits. But it was during the reign of his son, al-Ma'mun (ruled 813–33), that the city soared to heights previously undreamed of by human civilization.

Al-Ma'mun founded Bait al-Hikma, the Academy of Wisdom, which took over from the Persian University of Jundaisapur as the pre-eminent global centre for scientific research. Scholars of all races and religions were invited to the Academy. The most notable mathematician of the era, Abu Ja'far Muhammed ibn Musa al-Khwarizmi, discovered algebraic equations there, although he did not invent the mathematical concept of zero, as is commonly believed; for that innovation we have India's Hindus to thank. Al-Khwarizmi's magnum opus was called *Kitab al-jabr w'al-muqabalah* (Restoration and Balancing), which gave us the word "algebra." His books were translated into Latin and appeared in Renaissance Italy like a bolt of lightning. Since no one there knew any Arabic, his name came out as Algorismus, from which we derive algorithm, a systematic process for performing computations.

The Baghdad Academy's explosion of genius and innovation recalled the blistering achievements of Sumer. And it burned out just as swiftly. Cairo soon usurped Baghdad's position as intellectual centre of the world, luring away any scholars of promise to al-Azhar, the world's first university and still the Vatican of Sunni Islam. But without Baghdad's example to build upon, it is unlikely that al-Azhar would have aspired to what it achieved.

Early in the thirteenth century, Ghengis Khan, at the head of a mighty Mongol army said to be 700,000 strong, swept out of the east and laid waste to the cities of central Asia, often killing every living thing in them. He never reached Baghdad, but he badly wanted to, and his grandson, Hulagu Khan, did. With 200,000 Tartars, he smashed the feeble forces raised by Baghdad in 1258, and was busy killing for forty days.

Hulagu wantonly destroyed Iraq's canal head-works before he rode off. It was the kind of uncalculated act of raw destruction for which his grandfather had been famous. The waters swiftly rose, swelling over their banks, and the artistic and intellectual creations of centuries were swept away in a torrent of mud. Iraq became a neglected frontier province ruled from the Mongol capital of Tabriz in Iran, where to this day Ghengis Khan is viewed in a favourable light, as tends to be the case with any conqueror of Arabs.

With a brief respite during the rule of the Mamelukes — Turkish slaves of the Egyptian Ayyubids who rebelled and took over their masters' empire — Baghdad continued a dismal cycle of tribal warfare and ever-deteriorating urban life. By the end of the nineteenth century, travellers remarked upon its squalor, expecting to find far more trace of the glorious past than was visible in the squat, decayed sprawl and the debased existence of its inhabitants. Curiously, though, the name "Baghdad" continued to wrap itself in the exotic mystique of a long-lost time, largely thanks to stories like "Aladdin" and "Ali Baba and the Forty Thieves" from *The Arabian Nights*, which fuelled countless movies and fired the imaginations of children everywhere. No one wanted to believe that this Baghdad, the dream palace of the Arabs, had vanished without a trace.

Locked between the clashing empires of Turkey and Britain, Iraq found itself miraculously rescued from obliteration by the self-serving needs of the British, and it became the first Arab nation to achieve independence under the British mandate in the twentieth century. Sadly, as Prince Hassan observed, it has become the first to lose its independence to U.S. imperialism in the twenty-first century.

Originally intended to be a monarchy under Emir Faisal ibn Hussein, brother of the new ruler of neighbouring Jordan, Iraq also became the first Arab state to discover the wonders of the military coup, entering a period of extreme turbulence that was only really ended by the iron fist of Saddam Hussein. It also thrived thanks to the world's second-largest deposits of fossil fuel, discovered in 1927, but only fully realized during the oil boom of the 1970s.

In the Stalinist manner, Saddam became the state, the state became him. But, initially at least, Iraqis were sharing in the wealth; they travelled all over Europe and delighted in showing foreigners the phoenix of Baghdad once more rising from its ashes. Then came the long war with Iran, encouraged and supplied by America, Britain and others, and partly intended to defend Kuwait and Saudi Arabia from the ayatollahs.

The rest is, of course, news.

As it had been so many times before, Baghdad was back to zero. The city might as well be bulldozed now, a new one built. What is salvageable is not worth saving, and what lies in rubble is beyond repair. Not everything built by Saddam was monstrously Stalinesque, indeed many buildings were quite beautiful. No one will ever know that now. The destruction is complete ...

I thought of the later Egyptian pharaohs, who eradicated all trace of their predecessors or those they conquered. Yet in its place they generally raised up or embellished works of equal or even greater beauty. America cannot even return the supplies of electricity and water to normal.

I returned to the balcony, looking around at the darkened buildings held together by hope and nails. They had been bombed nightly until a few days earlier yet still somehow held up. I remembered the frightened eyes of the gaunt and grimy children in Bassim's neighbourhood, who jumped at the slightest unexpected sound, whose skin was yellowed by mild jaundice brought on by unsanitary conditions and stress. I remembered the old people with resignation stamped across their foreheads, who couldn't go on yet would go on. I remembered the young married couples who still hoped for a better life, yet did not hope too hard lest it break their hearts. I thought of the countless unremembered acts of kindness and of love that filled these desolate days, and I hoped — for all of Iraq's citizens — that America could still deliver on some of the many promises made before the war.

The bombs and gunfire, mostly far off, still sent waves of fear rippling through the darkness at this end of Iraq's five-thousand-year existence. Were there patterns and similarities in the ceaseless tide of events? Or is that just our desire to see some form in the chaos? I hoped in a way that the latter was true, because the only form I could see in this chaos as I gazed out wearily into swirling vapours and layers of dark upon dark, black upon black, was the ghost of Ghengis Khan, a mile high, one foot in the Tigris, the other resting upon Saddam's toppled statue, sneering with satisfaction at deeds of destruction that surpassed even his cruel and fevered imagination.

> *Boys and girls,*
> *And women, that would groan to see a child*
> *Pull off an insect's wing, all read of war,*
> *The best amusement for our morning meal!*
> *The poor wretch, who has learnt his only prayers*
> *From curses, and who knows scarcely words enough*
> *To ask a blessing from his Heavenly Father,*
> *Becomes a fluent phraseman, absolute*
> *And technical in victories and defeats,*
> *And all our dainty terms for fratricide;*
> *Terms which we trundle smoothly o'er our tongues*
> *Like mere abstractions, empty sounds to which*
> *We join no feeling and attach no form!*
> *As if the soldier died without a wound;*
> *As if the fibres of this godlike frame*
> *Were gored without a pang; as if the wretch,*
> *Who fell in battle, doing bloody deeds,*
> *Passed off to Heaven, translated and not killed;*
> *As though he had no wife to pine for him,*
> *No God to judge him! Therefore, evil days*
> *Are coming on us, O my countrymen!*
> *And what if all-avenging Providence,*
> *Strong and retributive, should make us know*
> *The meaning of our words, force us to feel*
> *The desolation and the agony*
> *Of our fierce doings?*

— SAMUEL TAYLOR COLERIDGE (1772–1834)[90]

PART TWO

Peace

CHAPTER SEVEN

BRIGHTNESS HIDDEN

Day comes and the brightness is hidden around me.
Shadows cover the light, drape it in sandstorms.
My beautiful mouth knows only confusion.
Even my sex is dust.

— ENHEDUANNA [91]

By Sunday afternoon, I had Paul Hackett sharing the two-bedroom suite with kitchen that I had scored for $30 a day in the Al-Arabie Apartment Hotel. Only now, it suddenly cost $60 a day. I assumed this had to do with the extra body, but the following day the room-rate went up to $90. The day after that it was $100. By the end of the week it was topping $200. It *was* a nice suite, but it wasn't *that* nice. I don't think anyone resented the owners making some extra cash, though. It had been some while since they had experienced a rush on rooms. America burst in upon this drought like a shower of spring rain. War is not just good for business, war *is* business.

For all the talk about the Palestine, you would think it was the best hotel in Baghdad. It was not, by a long chalk. That honour went to the Al-Rashid

Hotel, in which Uday Hussein had kept a suite. It was built right over one of Saddam's bunkers as well, with private elevators that went a long way down rather than up. The Rashid's greatest attraction, however, was the mosaic image of Bush I that you were obliged to walk over on your way into the lobby. Spelled out in little tiles — in case any visitor wondered about the significance of this presidential doormat — was a statement of fact with which no Iraqi disagreed: BUSH IS CRIMINAL. He looked like a war criminal in the mosaic too.

When I finally got to see the remarkably unscathed hotel again, its entrance was guarded by tanks, razor wire and soldiers, who were not letting in any scrivening riff-raff wishing to satisfy their curiosity that the Bush mosaic was no more. The whole Al-Rashid Hotel was no more.

"This is no longer a hotel, sah!" a soldier informed me. "It has been appropriated by the United States' Military Central Command and is off-limits. That is all I can tell you."

"It still have the George Bush doormat?"

"I couldn't say, sah."

"Is the cappuccino place still in the lobby?"

"I have given you all the information currently available. Please move along, sah."

> *What is to be is best descried*
> *When it has also been —*
> *Could Prospect taste of Retrospect*
> *The tyrannies of Men*
> *Were Tenderer — diviner*
> *The Transitive toward.*
> *A Bayonet's contrition*
> *Is nothing to the Dead.*
>
> — EMILY DICKINSON (1830–86)[92]

Philip Sherwell, by now a veritable hub of journalistic activity, moved into the adjacent suite. It used to be that only photographers had *equipment* — we scribes had a pencil and spiral pad — but Sherwell's room looked like the bridge of the starship *Enterprise*, fizzing, clicking and bleeping with electronica. The laptops and fold-out satellite dishes with battery-packs were more necessary than I had realized, too. There were no telephones any more in Baghdad. The plastic was still there, but it did not do anything. Even internal lines had ceased to function. In such a place, the man with a satellite telephone is king.

During those first days, you did not need to *search* for stories. They lay all around, crying out to be noticed, jockeying for attention; and the world's media came for them. Sherwell and Hackett organized a car with a driver-translator. I experienced envy. They did not even haggle over the price. But what is money when the Big Story stands like the morning sun upon one's horizon? With the mighty money-pit of the *Telegraph*'s aristocratic owners to dig in whenever more was required, the team was unstoppable. With *Harper's* there is no money-pit, just a damp coal cellar on Broadway where the humble magazine is edited and published by stooped and shabby figures huddling together around a candle for warmth and light.

The question I am most frequently asked about being in Iraq is, was I frightened? Was I not scared of dying?

Fear? Oh, yes, there was fear alright. That pitiless pelting of steel and explosives was still echoing around the houseless poverty of Baghdad, close enough to return, which was close enough to let those chill winds turn us all to looped and windowed raggedness at the thought of all that terror, noise, burning and death and the dark unlovely birds that swooped through the clouds of day or night to mete it out on those whom fate had chosen. Is the road untravelled because the traveller lies melted, blackened and crushed beside it? We all felt it, felt that the art of our necessities was strange indeed, and it was really nice to be around something familiar. On the edge of the abyss, we humans find our differences are not so great after all. We need hugging.

Everyone was asking himself where Saddam's Last Stand would take place. We had been conditioned by other wars, indeed by history, to expect a final decisive battle. It clearly was not taking place in Baghdad, so the rumour mill speculated that it would happen in Tikrit. Until Saddam changed the way names were presented, all but one member of his Revolutionary Command Council shared the clan surname al-Tikriti. Therefore, it seemed logical to assume they would choose the northern city as the site from which to stage their Waterloo. Discussing this like tourists looking for the best beach, we set out to find the U.S. front in its advance on Tikrit.

Baghdad's superb freeway system was in horrible shape — worse even than Montreal's. Whole sections had been blown away or riddled with gaping holes. Everywhere there were burned-out vehicles, mostly cars. Occasionally we saw areas littered with the blackened shells of Iraqi tanks and military trucks. Even beneath the flyovers where they had gone to shelter from the storm, rocket-launchers, tanks and lorries had been reduced to tangled balls of sooty steel. The antiquated Russian-built armour looked pathetic. It was as if a bunch of kids had tried to take on the might of the U.S. army with toy tanks and pretend missiles. Did any Iraqi commander really think he had a *chance* to win this war? During whatever war games they played, did anyone ever show Iraq's military what it would *really* be like to face off against American technology? They were zapped like Space Invaders in a video arcade.

We kept encountering U.S. tank divisions blocking off sections of the freeway. They often redirected us to roads that ended in three-metre-deep craters or overhead sections that had been destroyed. Fortunately John, the BBC's security man, had a road map of Baghdad. With it, we were able to find alternate routes by heading back off the freeway and zigzagging around the city streets.

Just before re-entering the freeway system, we came across several Iraqi civilians who seemed to be stopping traffic. A big burly man came alongside the car and started shouting angrily at our driver. Since I was behind him, sitting in the left rear seat, I rolled down the window to see if there was problem. The big man's eyes were bloodshot from rage or grief, or both. He reached into his jacket pocket and the next thing I knew was the barrel of his pistol prodding at my skull. I did not notice the gun's make.

"Easy, easy," said Hackett.

"Oh Jesus," said Sherwell. "Bassim," he asked our driver, "what does he want?"

"These men very angry," replied Bassim, usefully.

I was bracing myself, rather futilely, for the explosion that would knock half my skull away, glad that I had not paid off my credit cards. I clenched the muscles in my forehead so hard that it produced an instant headache.

The big man suddenly lowered the pistol and backed away, again shouting at Bassim the driver.

"Let's go, Bassim!" Sherwell said.

"Oh Jesus, that was too close ..."

"What was he so *ruffled* about then?"

According to Bassim, the man had berated him for driving us: *They destroy our city and you're driving them around!* They were also, he added, Ba'athi officials — the quintessential men whose time has passed. They were not happy about it. They did not seem resigned to it either.

But oddly enough, you don't much care *why* someone is going to kill you — and no cause having your death among its goals seems like a good one. It did occur to me, however, that being killed because you were mistaken for an American would be the worst of all possible deaths. To steady my nerves, I handed out maple-leaf pins to everyone. I had over twenty of them.

"Maybe you all want one of these to wear ... Eh?"

American journalists would seek me out to beg for these little lifesavers. The world is not a safe place for Americans any more, and they know why. A sense of shame pervades the language of decent Americans, the ones who know that the War on Terror will be no more successful or conclusive than other wars waged against abstract nouns — hunger, drugs, stupidity. A Canadian, on the other hand, now walks tall and safe through the alleys of hell, acknowledged gratefully by all as Friend to the Friendless, Refuge of the Refugee, Resort of Last Resort. Such was the genius of Jean Chrétien that no one knew any more where Canada really stood on the issue of this war, yet everyone thought we were on his side. *This,* I often told myself, is diplomacy!

Canada's actual role in the world, however, is what it always has been since the Korean War: to act as the conscience of America. It's a full-time job, a dirty job — but *someone* who speaks English has to do it. It is much like having a violent drunk for an older brother: you are ultimately the only one who can talk him down from his latest bender and the crunchy beating he is about to administer for no reason he will remember tomorrow.

The convoy kept doubling back, snaking through crushed freeway dividers to avoid bomb craters, heading inch by inch down steep pits to edge around burning buses or skirting rubble-strewn city streets to find alternate entrances to the highway. Every fifteen minutes or so, John would call for a halt to show drivers his map and explain where we were trying to reach next.

"See, the fuckin' prob' is 'ow to get from 'ere to vare. Okay? Now, we done *vat* — over vare to dare — but the fuckin' trick is 'ere to 'ere, eh? I been on to fuckin' U.S. CENTCOM *and* fuckin' U.S. SOCOM [U.S. Central Command and U.S. Special Operations Command], 'aven't I? They don't wanna be 'elpful this mornin', evi-fuckin'-dently. So we got a dilemma. See what I mean?"

The drivers did not see, but they nodded anyway.

Clearly, John was running out of options. And acronyms.

(One assumes an acronym exists because the words it represents are a mouthful yet need to be used frequently. A glance through the Pentagon's acronym dictionary is instructive in this respect. What are we to make of WOSB — Women-Owned Small Business — or YATS — Youth Attitude Tracking Study? What are they up to in there, immune from the vagaries of democratic election, watching administrations come and go while they quietly get on with the business of making the world safe and compliant for American business interests? For $431 billion a year.)

On what was basically a final attempt to reach the Tikrit highway via a section of freeway heading along the southeast of the airport, we came to a U.S. blockade with a couple of tanks and bored-looking soldiers, some of them stretched out to catch the rays of a weak yellow sun that had begun peeping through black clouds and grey air. John went up to them and established his ex-military credentials. Within seconds they were all laughing uproariously, and soon the Security Expert had his map out. After several minutes, he walked back.

"They'll let us fru," he said. "No one fuckin' told 'em anyfing 'bout *press*, so they don't 'ave a problem lettin' us fru. But the road's fuckin' 'airy, they say. So stick togevver, all wight?"

"All wight, John," we said, obediently.

We drove slowly past the tanks, waving and smiling at the soldiers, who waved and smiled back. I suppose this was the kind of welcome they had been given to expect here. The city had not greeted them like this, though. The city had not greeted them at all; it just lay back and opened its legs without a word. No man wants so easy a conquest, thus some of the soldiers were suspicious. Was it a trap? Would they catch some killer STD? But Baghdad did appear to be deserted. There were few cars on the streets, and fewer people anywhere. Nothing was open. It reminded me of those early Sunday mornings in big cities when you feel like the only person left alive after Armageddon — a bittersweet sensation.

A kilometre or so further on we came to an area at the extreme tip of the airport, where the road ran by some trees behind which there was a razor-wire fence marking off the airport perimeter. There was one stretch where the trees were entirely blackened. To the side of the road was the shell of a small Iraqi tank, incinerated. A little further on were charred branches from a tree. That was what I first took them to be. Then I thought they were oily garbage. However, closer, I realized they were legs, the lower part of a body from the waist down. The rest of the body was a black tar-like puddle. Something had melted it entirely, flesh, bones, the lot. Nauseating, sweet, the smell of roasted human flesh hung in the air. I could taste it at the back of my throat days later, as if nature wanted to emphasize that this taste and smell were not as others. These ones are forbidden to ye.

You could not even see the airport buildings from where we were now, but you did have an unobstructed view across the outer strips of runway. There were no signs of any battle going on, just thin black columns of smoke rising up beyond the horizon, the same columns we saw everywhere during those days in Baghdad. They increased in number daily, because they were largely caused by fires that started by themselves in bombed buildings, or were started as gestures of scorn by looters once they had finished emptying out the bastions of the old regime.

Further on still, we came to an area where there had recently been a battle between U.S. forces and some Iraqi troops fleeing in a military personnel carrier. The truck was on its side, fuming but not yet on fire. The road was littered with large-calibre shell casings, one of which punctured the tire of a BBC vehicle. While it was being changed, we got out and looked around. To the side of the road was a shallow ditch and all around were scattered very new-looking items of Iraqi army kit, gas masks, boots, uniforms, tin helmets and hundreds of rounds of live ammunition. People began collecting souvenirs.

There were also, scattered everywhere, dozens of tiny bottles of Tabasco sauce, some empty, some unopened. What lay behind this?, I wondered. A Tabasco sauce convention?

TABASCO 2003: BAGHDAD.

THE ONLY LOCATION HOT ENOUGH FOR THIS SAUCE ...

No one else found the enigma of the tiny sauce bottles anything like as intriguing as I did, so I wondered how common the phenomenon might have become on earth. Didn't anyone want to know why the bottles were there?

On the far side of the road, which from here on was the Tikrit highway, were some trees and, beyond them, a few scattered houses, the very last of Baghdad's unlovely urban sprawl. Some two hundred metres off, between the road, trees and houses, a group of people was burying dead bodies in a shallow pit. They were, someone told us, the bodies of Iraqis killed in the recent firefight. Those TV producers with us wondered about filming the no-frills funeral, but a translator said the intrusion would not be welcome. The producers gave each other puzzled grimaces — *Uh? Why on earth not? Duh!* Conceivably, they actually did not understand why anyone would object to having his grief transformed into entertainment.

"Tell them the world ought to know what's happening here?" one producer suggested.

The other shook his head.

"No, Jeremy, let's forget it. Abdul says they're a bit touchy — you know, *emotional ...*"

I sincerely doubt that Jeremy *did* know what he meant. But he'd certainly *heard* that foreigners in these parts had the emotional scaffolding of girls and often got weepy over nothing. Network television is unused to being turned away. But Iraqis, he was learning, found their lives authentic enough without the TV seal of approval.

Coming down the road towards us on the opposite side were small groups of men, some of them holding ragged squares of white cloth. I assumed they were locals uncertain whether or not it was safe to venture out — and indeed some were. Others were fleeing the fighting further north, although there was no fighting further north.

"Iraqi troops deserting," said Sherwell. "They've thrown away their uniforms and are walking home."

He scribbled a haiku on his spiral pad. Why did he not have a Gooseberry, or whatever those things were called that other journalists had? Or was this the next generation of Gooseberries? The Retro: they look *exactly* like spiral pads.

Some media had stopped one of the men and, with a translator, were questioning him. He had left Tikrit around 5 p.m. the evening before, he was saying. No, he was not *jaish* — army — he was just a civilian walking to Baghdad. Tikrit is about 240 kilometres from Baghdad. The man seemed nervous, his dark eyes darting around our faces, saliva scum in the corners of his mouth as he tried on a series of weak smiles. He was not sure who we were. He expected someone was going to hurt him. No one had bothered to reassure him that now he had rights.

A little later, a larger group of men appeared, this time carrying a black flag. Black, I should point out, is not the colour universally signifying surrender. White is usually that. This group of men were singing what sounded a bit like Sting's "Roxanne" but proved to be a hymn (the chorus contained "Hussein!"). None of the singing men had shoes or socks, walking over shrapnel, rubble and the bullet casings in the road. Indians may not wear shoes, but Iraqis do. They smiled at us as they passed by — *"Hussein, you don't have to put on the red light"* — and were soon gone.

"They'd thrown away their boots even," Sherwell remarked.

"I don't think *they* were deserting soldiers ..."

I thought they were Shia pilgrims on their way to Karbala. Hence the black Shia flag. This pilgrimage, Arba'een — a kind of Shia Easter — had been banned by Saddam since the Iran-Iraq war. It occurred to me then that it would probably not be banned this year.

"Well, as far as *Telegraph* readers are concerned," Sherwell said, "they're deserting Iraqi troops."

Not long after setting off again, we found so much Iraqi tank debris and rubble in our way that the road was impassable. Since everyone felt he now had a story to file — *Iraqis Bury Dead, Tikrit Falls Without Fight, Iraqi Army Deserts* — we decided to give up attempting to reach Tikrit. Taking a different route back, we decided to try heading out to the airport. Everyone sensed something was happening there, if only because we were being kept away from the place. At the first U.S. roadblock, we asked soldiers where the

American front was now situated.

"This is it," a sergeant replied.

"No, no, the advance on Tikrit. Where's *that* front?"

"Right here, sah."

"So where were we coming from, then?"

Evidently, we had been beyond the front lines. This did not make much sense, given what those walking back from Tikrit had said. Nevertheless, in the light of subsequent knowledge, it would seem that the U.S. divisions in Baghdad no longer felt any need to back up the 101st and 82nd airborne divisions in Tikrit.

"So the war's over?" I asked the sergeant.

"I wouldn't say that, sah."

Whether it was over or not, they were still not letting anyone get near the airport. The route to the main terminal buildings was completely sealed off by tanks and razor wire. Those soldiers we asked clearly had no idea why they were blocking the route — just that they *were* blocking it.

The streets of Baghdad were still more or less deserted, apart from the odd pocket of people gathered around a stall selling fruit or vegetables here and there, and those wheeling handcarts piled high with loot away from government buildings. Most of the loot now looked just like junk. Even when it was money.

The only thing resembling a crowd was the twenty-odd people gathered outside a bank to have a look at the money just stolen from it. The Iraqi dinars were stacked in a four-foot heap on a skid of rough-hewn wood that had been dragged through a shattered plate-glass window onto the pavement by robbers. The robbers lay on either side of it in pools of dark red blood. Apparently, they had been brothers. An altercation had arisen — presumably over division of the spoils — and both men had pulled guns, both also firing them. Both were now explaining this to an unsympathetic audience. According to Bassim the driver, later, the dialogue had gone something like this:

ROBBER ONE: He wants me to take only one third of the money. Rest is for him.

ROBBER TWO: It is my idea! He is too lazy to get out of bed in the morning; I had to force him to join me ...

CROWD: You are two numbskulls!

ROBBER ONE: Since we were children, he is bullying me!

ROBBER TWO: Otherwise, you would never do anything!

CROWD: You call robbing a bank "doing something"? Why don't you get a job?

ROBBER ONE: We are Shia. There are no jobs for us ...

ROBBER TWO: We are poor ...

CROWD: Poor Muslims, you mean! You are a disgrace!

ROBBER ONE: He shoots me!

ROBBER TWO: It was a mistake! But he shot me!

CROWD: You will now both die because your people have stolen all the hospitals too. Why don't you start crawling back to Saddam City now!

ROBBER ONE: I never fire a gun before this ...

ROBBER TWO: I tell him a hundred times not to squeeze trigger while moving the safety catch ...

ROBBER ONE: You squeezed your trigger too, you idiot!

ROBBER TWO: With me it is a mistake! You are the idiot!

CROWD: You are both numbskulls! Now you will die!

ROBBER ONE: I should not die. He shot me, so he must die!

CROWD: See what you have done!

ROBBER TWO: I was going to start my own business with the money. He would just spend his on booze and girls. Then he would come to me whining ...

ROBBER ONE: He is such a liar! He owes me money! He knows nothing about starting any business. The money-lenders would get all the money ...

ROBBER TWO: I do not feel so good. I need a doctor ... [dies]

CROWD: See, your brother is now dead. You are a lazy fool! What will your mother say?

ROBBER ONE: She will say I always get him in trouble. Then she will beat me ...

CROWD: This is the last trouble you two will ever be in! This was our money, fool! You are asking the wrong people for help.

ROBBER ONE: How can you let a brother die like this?

CROWD: Easy. We just stand here like this ...
ROBBER ONE: Get me doctor. I feel very faint ...
CROWD: Shall we look after your money for you?
ROBBER ONE: It is now all my money ... [dies]
CROWD: What a numbskull!

As we walked away, the crowd was debating whether it would be the right thing to divide the money among them and look after it until law and order was restored in Baghdad.

Further on a man was stealing the bricks from a new wall built over the pavement by a bank to shield its windows from looters.

Back at the Al-Arabie Hotel, Phil Sherwell called his desk editor back in London to announce what the Sunday story would be. Paul Hackett and I retired to our respective rooms. Minutes later, Sherwell came thumping in.

"Fuck!" he said. "They want a story on Stumpy instead. We've got to go over to Saddam City, c'mon!"

"Stumpy" was Ali Ismaeel Abbas, a twelve-year-old boy who had lost both arms and his entire family, including his five-months-pregnant mother, in a regrettable incident of collateral damage — indeed, the way the army had promoted it, perhaps the *only* incident of collateral damage of the entire war. Dragged from flaming rubble with third-degree burns to most of his body, Ali needed the best treatment medicine could provide. The U.S. army said that was exactly what he would be getting too. It had been the big story some days earlier, but now the media had moved on to other concerns. So had the army, and Ali had been left in the overcrowded Saddam City[93] hospital with whatever treatment it was able to provide him.

Readers of the *Sunday Telegraph*, however, had not forgotten Ali, it seemed. They had organized a fund for him, and now a follow-up story was required in response to all this interest.

Hackett collected his cameras, and the pair went off with Bassim the driver to Saddam City, the slum where most of Baghdad's poor Shia Muslims had been obliged to dwell. For Baghdad's Sunni masters, the place was synonymous with crime — any kind of crime.

I walked over to the Palestine to see if I could find any food. Apart from biscuits and candies, none of us had eaten in two days. Already, in front of the hotel, Iraqis had set up a few little stalls selling cigarettes, trashy souvenirs and candy. Every time I went to the hotel, there were more of them. They had a huge captive clientele, and someone was obviously making a pile from the concessions. I tried making a satellite phone call from the Palestine's driveway, without much success, and as I was heading back into the building, a young soldier with red hair and freckles stopped me.

"Esscuse me, sir. Can you call America with that phone?"

"Supposedly."

"I wonder if it would be a terrible imposition ..." He hopped from foot to foot. "But my wife is havin' a baby an' I don't know whether she's had it or not yet. I haven't spoken to her in three months ..."

"Of course," I told him, amazed that the army kept its boys on such a tight leash.

I showed him how to use the satellite phone, feeling certain he was in for a disappointment. He got through, however, with laughable ease.

I stood, looking around at all the TV and military equipment spread across the Palestine's forecourt. There were twice as many satellite dishes as there had been the previous day. As I stood there, another soldier came up.

"I don't s'pose ah could use that phone after him, could ah?"

"Sure."

When the fourth man approached, I told him it would cost.

"Sure, whatta y'want?" He pulled out some dollars.

"Not money," I said. "You have any food?"

"Food? Shit-yeah, we got food all right. I'll give ya 'coupla MRES for a call?"

"Done."

He ran off to get them. MRE is "Meal Ready to Eat," army rations. A million packs of these were consumed in Iraq every day then, so there were always plenty of them about.

"Hey, hey, hey!" the red-haired soldier on the phone yelled. "I'm a *daddy!* I gotta l'il boy! A son! I'M A DAD!"

"Congratulations. Here." I gave him a cigar.

Soon the second soldier was making a call. He too got through without a hitch.

"Ah'm *okay*, Mom!" he was saying, "Nah, I don't *eat* the Irakky food, Mom! We got MRES ... Honest, Mom ... Ah'm *fine*, Ma ... No, Ma, *honest* I do ... They *didn't* Ma, it's okay ... Ma! ... Ma, Put me onto Dad, will ya ..."

Ma was clearly bawling her eyes out.

The fourth soldier returned with three MRE packs, khaki plastic pouches about a foot square and six inches deep. They looked like they contained one helluva meal.

"I picked ya the best ones there," he said.

I had "Spaghetti Bolognaise," "Meat Loaf" and "Pepper Steak." The thought of Uncle Sam's home-cooking made my stomach gurgle and churn, rubbing its tentacles with glee.

Telling other inquirers my batteries were low, I managed to get away half an hour later. The *Telegraph* boys would be happy, I thought. There was a meal each.

But I ate Sherwell's meat loaf for him. I did not mean to, but when I opened the MRE to see what one was like, I was shocked by how little of it was actually meal. They were like loot bags, with many little sachets inside that contained amusements ranging from three leaves of toilet paper to herbal tea bags and a book of matches. At least it explained where all the tiny bottles of Tabasco sauce I had seen in the road came from, though: there were two in every MRE pack. With its ethnic diversity, the army tried hard to provide some spice for its food. Other dishes included such things as "Beef Enchiladas" and "Chicken Curry."

Intending to light a candle to dine by, I noticed that the book of matches stated its contents were designed to light in damp conditions, but they would not work in really damp conditions, and definitely would not work if actually wet. They were, then, ordinary matches? These meaningless instructions were just something to put on the otherwise blank khaki cover.

Indeed, everything was covered in unnecessary instructions written in prose so tortured its meaning was often entirely elusive. After deciphering one set, I realized that what it was trying to say was, *If you eat this meal and still feel hungry, eat another meal.* Another set said, *On active combat your body requires more food, which means you will need to eat more. Hunger,* announced another, *is nature's way of telling you that you're hungry* — good to know.

The most complex instructions were on the pouch designed to heat the pouch containing the actual meal. In this clear plastic pouch, there was a white plastic slab like a foam wafer. One should not eat this wafer under any circumstances, said the instructions. More than once they said it too. Every year, I learned, a few soldiers did eat the wafer, which was not a good thing to do. You had to put the food pouch into the pouch with the wafer, it said, then you added water, and then you stuffed the whole thing into the thin cardboard box that had contained the food pouch. This heated the food. In fact, it heated the food up *real* good. In seconds, the pouch had swelled like a balloon and was spurting steam. The water inside it literally boiled. I wondered what eating the wafer would do for one's stomach.

Ripping open the pouch, I found the meat loaf to be accompanied by noodles and tomato sauce. *Using the plastic spoon, scoop up some* MRE *and place it in your mouth.* As opposed to your ear. There was only a plastic spoon to eat with, and it broke on the third mouthful. I found a fork in the suite's kitchen, and a plate. It was scraping the pouch out onto this plate that emphasized how little food the pouch had actually contained. How could soldiers survive on this stuff? Still, it did taste a lot better than nothing.

The boys returned soon after I had eaten the humid slab called "Pound Cake" with my instant coffee and whitener. Sherwell went off to his room to write the revised day's article, and Hackett started downloading his pictures to the computer. The images were heart-breaking.

> Ali groans constantly from the pain, a wad of white bandages covering the stumps of his amputated arms. Cream is smeared across the horrific burns that blister his chest and stomach. He lies on a dirty bed in a squalid children's ward in Saddam City, a sprawling, Shi'ite slum quarter of Baghdad. The unhygienic surroundings are his greatest threat, his wounds leaving him susceptible to lethal septicaemia.[94]

In fact, the doctors confided that Ali was probably not going to make it. The *Telegraph's* readers would not want to hear this, though — and, in fact, they did not hear it.[95]

I left Hackett to work. Half an hour later, he came in to my room.

"I just spoke wi' my picture editor," he said. "D'ye know what he asked me?"

I shook my head. Hackett smiled ruefully as he told me what his picture editor had asked:

"'Don't you have any shots of him smiling?'"

> *There is no such thing as the State*
> *And no one exists alone;*
> *Hunger allows no choice*
> *To the citizen or the police;*
> *We must love one another or die.*

— W. H. AUDEN [96]

Or die.

The following day I was awoken just before dawn by an enormous explosion nearby, followed by a few short bursts of gunfire. Heart thumping, I went out onto the balcony. The streets below were still asleep. Nothing appeared to be unduly stirring the soldiery camped on the patch of land between the end of Sadoun Street and the Tigris. The odd dog was barking, woken like me and just as grumpy. The city seemed almost tranquil. But it wasn't.

The explosion had been U.S. forces blowing up an Iraqi ammunition storehouse in the city. It was situated near a residential area, and many civilians were wounded by the blast. This was just one among many incidents where the Americans revealed their lack of concern for Iraq's citizens, and it helped turn public opinion against them.

While ordering tea, I noticed someone eating an omelette.

"You have eggs?" I asked the kids who ferried up tea.

They nodded.

"And toast?"

I ordered some. No breakfast ever tasted so good. When Hackett saw me eating the eggs he went to order his own, but by then they had run out and did not manage to find any more for over a week.

I tagged along with the *Telegraph* again that day. I felt strangely listless, and in this passive state was easily able to persuade myself that gathering news about newsgathering was in fact my mission. There were rumours of journalists finding all kinds of interesting documents among the ruins of Baghdad's bureaucracy, so Sherwell wanted to poke around inside the Foreign Ministry, of which he believed that no one besides himself knew the location. On the way there, we drove past the Iraqi National Museum. I asked Bassim to stop for a moment. An American tank was stationed at the nearby roundabout, but in the forecourt not two hundred metres behind it, Iraqis were coming and going through the open windows and doors of the museum. In shopping bags or with their bare hands they were carrying objects pillaged from the display cases. One man's plastic bag had burst open and he was squatting in the dust scooping up little bronze or gold figurines.

"Hey, they're looting the museum!" I shouted to one of the soldiers in the tank at the roundabout, certain he must be aware of the fact.

He looked over at me then looked away without saying anything.

I went up to the tank.

"You've got to stop *this*!" I was angry.

"Not my job, sah," said the soldier, staring ahead.

Philip Sherwell did not mention the tank in his article, although he did quote the museum's deputy director saying, "The Americans were supposed to protect the museum. If they had just one tank and two soldiers, nothing like this would have happened. I hold the American troops responsible."[97]

I walked across the forecourt and into the museum through a door that had been torn from its hinges. It was very dark inside; broken glass squealed and crunched beneath my feet. Someone shone a flashlight at my face. There must have been fifteen or twenty people inside. Every few minutes I heard the noise of shattering glass coming from somewhere deeper within the building. The first display case I came to had been pushed over and half its contents still lay among the broken shards. Elsewhere, just one side of a case had been smashed open and a dozen little clay cups had been swept out of the way so the thief could reach something behind them. Already broken millennia ago and then glued back together, they were now broken again. Looking around at the wild-eyed faces, I realized they were all members of the underclass, poor Shia, ill-kempt and unshaven. It was almost as if they were being bred to develop a visual distinction, like the mark of Cain. This was almost certainly the only visit any of them had ever made to a museum. They would not know what was valuable here and what was not — unless of course they were looking at the 4,000-year-old silver harp from Ur. But you can't eat culture. Someone must have organized this particular bit of looting.

Recalling what had been in Baghdad's museum, the irreplaceable treasures of Sumer and Babylon, I began to grasp the enormity of this tragedy. It was not just most of Iraq's cultural heritage that was in this building, it was much of humanity's collective heritage. Now it was privatized, outsourced. The collection of cylinder seals from Sumer comprised the earliest examples of the written word on earth. Their value was secondary; no amount of money could ever replace them. As ill-lit and shabby as it may have been, the museum housed the world's largest collection of ancient artifacts still on display in the land where they were made — which says an awful lot about colonialism and imperialism generally, besides pegging America's culpability as silent partner-in-crime to this, the largest robbery of ancient artifacts in history: 170,000 utterly irreplaceable antiquities, gone.

But culture is low on the list of war's casualties. Amid the human tragedy all around us, the looting of the museum was no one's priority. The soldiers guarding the roundabout outside were implacable; they did not care. A tide of Ali Babas — as the Saddam City thieves came to be known — was sweeping away the glories of Iraq's cultural heritage just as surely as the floodwaters had when Genghis Khan's grandson destroyed the canal system's head-works.

Later in the day, when it was open, I managed to get through to someone's secretary at the British Museum's Near Eastern Department in London, leaving a message that stated what was happening in Baghdad. The person at the other end kept thinking I was in Bradford.

"*Baghdad*, not Bradford!" I yelled. "I'm in Iraq!"

"You're in *a raft*, are you?"

> International cultural organisations had urged before the war that the cultural heritage of Iraq, which has more than 10,000 archaeological sites, be spared. U.S. forces are making a belated attempt to protect the National Museum, calling on Iraqi policemen to turn up for duty. There is no pay, but 80 have given their services ... [The Museum's deputy director] added:

"They know that this is a museum. They protect oil ministries
but not the cultural heritage."

— *SUNDAY TELEGRAPH*

Although the spin-doctors and damage-controllers went to work when
news of the museum's ransacking got out, and although a few items were
returned over the months ahead, the great collection is no more. Like so
much else, it has gone forever. All the king's horses and all the king's men,
couldn't put Humpty together again ...

Someone lobs a child's shoe
into the furnace. Family photographs spill
from the back of a garbage truck;
they carry inscriptions:
Love from ... love from ... love ...

There's no way of describing these things,
not really. Each night I wake
and stand by the window to watch my neighbour
who stands by the window to watch the dark.

— GORAN SIMIC (1952–)[98]

The Baghdad Foreign Ministry was in the part of town that had been off-
limits to most Iraqis until now. It was a tall grey concrete monolith of some
ten or twelve floors, set back from the road with its own guard post and
gates. Smoke was wafting through windows on various floors and the whole
building was black with soot. When we reached its side, we saw the gaping
hole made by a Tomahawk missile that had exploded within. The structure
was probably still standing because it had been designed with an inner well
(to cope with the summer heat) that ran right up to the roof and thus
diffused the blast.

Broken glass creaked and cracked beneath our feet like a frozen lake as
we prowled around the floors. The air was toxic with fumes and as hot as a

sauna. Hundreds of electrical wires dangled dangerously and the occasional shafts of sunlight illuminated millions of ash flakes rising and falling in convection currents. This added to the feeling that we were exploring some underwater wreck, where quotidian existence had abruptly ceased. There is a vast difference between ruined buildings and buildings that have *been* ruined, just as there is between the victims of time and the victims of cruel fate.

The sticky stuff I kept treading on proved to be melting rubber from the soles of my own shoes. The ministry's floors were still hot from the missile's inferno. Most of the offices circling the central area were remarkably intact, though. From maps on the walls and signs that Bassim translated for us, we tried to work out what areas of the ministry we were in, as we groped our way up a windowless concrete staircase across all manner of unidentifiable rubble — including that which was somewhat soft and smelled sweetly of decay. By the time we had reached the third, it was apparent that each floor dealt with a different part of the world. We looked through filing cabinets and bookshelves and in drawers and cupboards, collecting a pile of interesting-looking documents that ranged from undersea maps of the Shatt al Arab waterway to microfiche copies of letters from various governments.

We were not alone in the building, either. At various points we came across the same unmistakable faces that I had seen in the museum — thin, ragged figures with a look of barely suppressed glee in their wild protuberant eyes. Here they were prying open doors or hefting entire desks to load on trucks we had seen waiting outside the ministry. I thought of those scavengers you see on PBS nature shows picking at the carcass of a beached whale: the best pickings were always to be had by the most courageous, before the whale was even completely dead. In the case of Iraq's beached whale, the best pickings went to the Big Oil scavengers who arrived along with the whale's murderers. Since they pay no income tax on the proceeds from wells dug on an exploratory basis, and since all wells are classified as exploratory, Big Oil — which is one company that disguises itself as several to avoid accusations of monopoly — is able to fund a lot of PBS nature documentaries.

As we reached the foreign minister's own office on the top floor, two men came out of it carrying a brown leather sofa. We nodded to each other with what struck me now as professional courtesy — for we were all looters in our own way. This topmost office was almost entirely unscathed, and it felt like a violation being inside the spacious sanctum where a very important man had spent many anxious days pondering Iraq's relationship with the world, and no doubt his own relationship with a regime that frequently purged senior officials like himself. There were photographs of him — I assumed they were of the minister — shaking hands with Saddam, walking a step behind Saddam along a row of dignitaries, sitting two rows behind Saddam at some event, and in a group of people standing near Saddam on an airfield. From these pictures, one got the impression that the foreign minister did not in fact know Saddam that well at all. They made me think of a photograph I possess that shows me at the rear edge of a group standing behind Samuel Beckett. My close friend Sam.

The room's sheer normality impressed itself most deeply upon me. By Saddam's gilded standards, it was not in the least opulent; it was the boss's office, no more than that. What stood out most was its attempt to avoid standing out at all. Other offices were merely smaller and contained less polished wood. When a foreign policy failed dismally, they would all be emptied of their occupants, who would beg the nation's pardon and Saddam's forgiveness for the disgrace they had brought down. This latest disgrace had unexpectedly brought along its own punishment, though, so the nation was spared their *mea culpa.* In a dictatorship, however, the foreign minister really just implemented policy; he did not shape it. That task, like anything else of importance, was the sole province of Saddam and his Revolutionary Command Council, and in particular Tariq Aziz, the man whom, more than any other apart from Saddam himself, represented the face of Iraq in the West. A few photographs showed the foreign minister sitting among a group of whom Aziz was one. There was, though, no suggestion that these two men knew each other well at all, either. The histories of kings and tyrants are a lot more straightforward than those of faceless bureaucracies, where villainy is spread so wide and thin it becomes almost invisible. *Everyone* can hardly be blamed.

How many offices like this — in Washington or Beijing or London or Paris — suspect that one day they will be abandoned, desolate, picked over by thieves and journalists? How many of those bare, ruined cubicles would reveal anything at all about their late occupants? These buildings, once so heavily guarded, in a part of the city that was itself restricted, in a country where not so much as a joke went unguarded by those who valued their lives, were all now prey to whatever the wind blew in.

~~However, the fact that no CIA~~ teams were already here carrying away files gave me the sneaking suspicion that there was nothing worth finding in the foreign ministry. Yet after hours of poring through folders, sifting through sheaves of documents, there were quite a few interesting minor discoveries. Not least of which was the catalogue from a Paris auction house I found that showed items from the Baghdad Museum put up for sale in June of 2002. I later gave it and other itemized lists of treasures from the museum to Mark McKinnon, the Toronto *Globe and Mail*'s man in Baghdad, who was then writing about the theft of Iraq's culture. The lists showed that a section of the foreign ministry was aware that someone from the old regime had been stealing and selling items from the museum long before the Americans even arrived. Unfortunately, there was no indication of the seller's identity. When I managed to get through to the auction house in Paris, they were understandably evasive. I still wonder who would have had the audacity to put such objects up for auction, knowing that the moment he was caught he would be as good as dead, if not better. It was either a fool, or else someone so close to Saddam that he knew he was immune from any consequences.

After showering off the soot and filth acquired in the ministry, I went over to the Palestine with the intention of swapping a few phone calls for some MRES. While waiting for a seven-foot soldier who, on calling Los Angeles, had just discovered his girlfriend was not home — at 6 a.m. LA time — I was approached by a well-kempt Baptist Viking type who said, in a Rhett Butler voice,

"Sir, could I ask you a favour? Not for myself but for this old Irakky man and woman. They seem like really decent sorta folk and they want to call their daughter in Syria. Would it —"

"No problem. When Romeo's finished."

"Thank you, sir. I will get you some MRES on their behalf ..."

The cost of my sat-phone calls, being such a bargain, was already widely known. A more canny man than me could have made many thousands of dollars with such a phone in Baghdad then, from the army alone.

I was admittedly deeply touched to find such a golden heart as this Viking possessed among the U.S. military. Yet there were in fact many of them, many,

many men and women who did not like what they had been made to do in Iraq, and whose good hearts went out to the suffering they found on all sides.

"She ain't *home*," said Romeo, handing back the telephone. "Six fuckin' ayem and *she* ain't home! What's the fuck wi' *that*?"

"Well, you were talking to *someone* ..." I said, thinking he was trying to wriggle out of the MRE deal.

"Yeah, her roommate. She *cute* ..." He laughed. "I'll get you some *food*, bro!"

Since "old" is always a generation ahead of oneself, the old Iraqis were not so old. A white-haired portly couple in their fifties, they had just been through too much and it had worn them down. With his clipped silver moustache, Western dress and spectacles, Nial was easily mistaken for the headmaster of a school. Haifa, his wife, had a kind of knowing beatific smile that concealed something impish, in spite of her knotted anxiety. Whatever else had happened to them, though, neither had gone short of meals over the past few years. After failing miserably several times to get them Damascus myself, I handed over the phone to Nial, who figured out how to work it with enviable ease.

"We are Christians," Haifa told me.

Estimates vary widely, but about one a million of Iraq's twenty-four million people are Christian.[99] Such distinctions were all-important within the complex social structure of Baghdad, where being Christian generally identified you as prosperous and an insecure ally of the Sunni Muslim ruling class, who took their religion no more seriously than we do ours. And if you were an Iraqi Christian, the only people you *trusted* in any degree were fellow Christians.

The statement of faith also explained Haifa's very Western appearance: you could not see knees, but she certainly had calves. Nial, I soon learned, had been a general and pilot in the Iraqi air force, not a schoolteacher. But he had retired and was "in business" now. It struck me as a most un-Saddam-like policy to allow air force generals to retire at this critical stage in Iraq's military history.

Just when I was wondering whether satellite links to Damascus were being blocked by the Americans, Nial got through. Yet it was brief; he was cut off quickly. I could see he found it hard to part with the phone when I went to take it back. I have never seen anyone want something so badly. The ancient oriental in me had half a mind to give him the phone.

By the time I had managed to extricate myself from their company, Nial and Haifa had offered all manner of tokens showing their enormous gratitude for the ten seconds of phone call, and their devout wish for further opportunities with the Iridium satellite. I said food was the only thing lacking in my life. They would bring me food. The general said he would bring a case of whisky too. When should he bring it? I told them I would be here at the same time tomorrow, and walked away not really thinking I would ever see them again.

> *Who brought this to pass?*
> *Who has brought the flaming imperial anger?*
> *Who has brought the army with drums and with kettle-drums?*
> *Barbarous kings.*
> *A gracious spring turned to blood-ravenous autumn.*
>
> — LI PO (701–62)[100]

There had been some signs of the city beginning to open its eyes. Here and there, a few little stores selling long-life milk, cigarettes, processed cheese and crackers were doing a desultory business, and the little street markets for vegetables grown in the rich alluvial soil of the Fertile Crescent were more numerous. People who had left the city to take shelter with relatives in the country were beginning to drift back. I had been trying to contact my friend Bassim since returning, and it was now that I found out what had happened to the family. Immediately, I thought of those soldiers sitting in the Palestine who had described a similar incident. How many such incidents had there been in this war? Rather than anger or sorrow, I felt a gnawing emptiness, as if I'd been up all night smoking cigarettes since the dawn of time, watching humanity's deadly tango with its own demise. It was all so shameful, so embarrassing to belong to a species so devoted to self-destruction, so committed to violence, so mindless in its general romp through time that the few specifics of its goodness, truth and beauty seemed scant indeed. I did not want to watch any more. The preciousness of life seems to beg for it to be cherished, yet all we have done is to squander it. I no longer feel we have a future on this planet — or not one worth the long and painful waiting. The fact that we can *imagine* something better makes what we have all the more unendurable. The images of Bassim and his family burning away like candles in a furnace haunted me. They cried out for justice. The whole world is crying out for justice, but there is no justice to be found. In Baghdad, there were not even lawyers.

> *I took one look at this world and said goodbye.*
> *I knew in a flash all that it had to offer.*
> *If you count my days, I vanished when I was young.*
> *But I was old if you add the things I suffered.*
> — ANDREAS GRYPHIUS (1616–64)[101]

Days were shaped for most by deadlines. Journalists would go out in the morning in search of the news, and then call in their suggestions to desk editors back in London, New York or Tokyo. Frequently, though — far more frequently than was once possible — these desk editors would say, *No, that's not the story — this is what I want* ...

I asked a few reporters how they felt about having someone sitting in an office back home dictating what was and was not a story here, but they sloughed off the question, either shrugging physically or verbally. That was the way things were. They had all worked hard to get as far as they had — however far that was. They were not about to jeopardize it now. It was not enough to have the dedication and sensibility of a Robert Fisk, either; you had to work for a newspaper that wanted a Robert Fisk. There are not many. Journalists tend to be left-liberal in their views — it's *that* kind of job — but they learned to put aside these opinions if they worked for one of the more right-wing papers. Those working for U.S. or British newspapers — with a few exceptions — knew better at this stage than to suggest a story revealing negative aspects of the war. And the vast majority of those "embedded" with the military had become PR outlets for their units.

Adam Lusher, also with the London *Telegraph* newspapers, had been embedded with one of the U.S. tank divisions that had driven to Baghdad from Kuwait. Tall, fresh-faced and lean, he looked far younger than his twenty-seven-odd years. He came up to take his first shower in three months. It was also the first time he had taken off his boots in three months, and the smell of them — of ripe goat's cheese and old locker rooms — permeated the entire floor. He was told to put the boots out on a balcony. It was soon clear from the way that Philip Sherwell treated him that Lusher was the office jester, the person everyone enjoys making fun of, and who himself enjoyed the attention in a taciturn sort of way. Lusher had spent three months imprisoned in a tank with — as he described them — an acidhead and a misogynist who had married his wife three times. His stories were hilarious, yet nothing of what he told us appeared in his articles, which were solemn paeans in praise of armoured militarism.

"The misogynist would look at me," Lusher related, "and say things like, 'Hey, Adam! You know those mornin's when you wake up and think to yourself, *What can I do to piss her off today* ...?'"

"To which you replied ...?"

"I told him I wasn't married ..."

"Lusher's now the division bitch," announced Sherwell, laughing.

I asked Lusher why he did not write a full account of his time, for *Harper's* or someone else less committed to victory.

"I don't think so," was all he said in reply, as if the suggestion was somehow out of the question, not possible.

Why would a person become a journalist if he were afraid to tell the truth? Lusher clearly enjoyed telling his stories verbally. What worried me was the tacit understanding he seemed to have that he could not tell them in print. Self-censorship is far more sinister than regular censorship, since it implies a climate of intimidation so effective it changes actual thought-processes. Soon, it even begins to make sense not to tell the truth. Then it makes sense to silence those who try to tell it. The slippery slope is always there, waiting for the fools who imagine they can use it to slide just a little way down.

There was a noise like someone dragging a bed over the floor above. Windowpanes vibrated in their frames. I went out on to the balcony and saw two U.S. Black Hawk helicopters flying some hundred feet from the ground, one slightly ahead and to the left of the other. They flew between the towers of the Ishtar and Palestine hotels, curving right to continue slowly along the road that ran by the Tigris. The skies were low and grey, the air filled with tension, anxiety. I kept hearing the phasing and skimming noise of a Stealth bomber too, coming from somewhere up above the cloud-line. Threads and columns of smoke were still visible all over the cityscape, so it was hard to see if there had been any fresh bombing; the noise of the choppers would have drowned out its sound. Without warning, gunfire started up somewhere down in the street below — so loud and near that instinctively I ducked. There was a brief silence, and then it started again, many kinds of gunfire too, from quick sharp bursts to the steady thumping of large-calibre weapons. On a lower roof of the Palestine opposite, I saw a U.S. sniper running to take up position at the edge facing the little park between the road and the river. Down in the street soldiers were running to huddle behind a big old tree, where they crouched, some firing, some scanning the park with field glasses. The noise was incredible. Was this the final battle after all? I wondered. But it was not clear to me if anyone was firing back at these troops. All the noise seemed to be coming *from* them.

I had grabbed the video camera and was filming the sniper opposite when he got up and walked quickly off the roof. At one point, he looked my way in exaggerated alarm and raised his gun. Mindful of other journalists whose cameras had been taken for weapons, I knelt down behind the concrete ledge. I thought his exit signaled the end of this conflict, but the guns started up once more, often so close I again had to move out of the way. A civilian car down in the street started blowing its horn: a tank had blocked the road but the Iraqi driver still wanted to continue driving through the combat zone. They were so used to war that a trifle like this hardly fazed Iraq's citizens any more. After some minutes, the man was turned back, shouting curses through his window as he reversed down the road for an entire block. Soldiers kept running to take up different positions in the park, including, I noticed, a unit with mortars. By now media were out on the roof where the sniper had been and on nearly all the balconies of the Al-Arabie and Palestine hotels, their cameras hoisted to capture the episode for suppertime viewing.

The gunfire kept up intensely for twenty minutes or so, and then ceased as suddenly as it had begun. Soldiers began walking back from the park, weapons hanging casually. No one knew what was going on. Urban warfare is always at best mere violent confusion. Some said a group of Republican

Guards had been discovered hiding in a foxhole, and made a last stand rather than surrender. At one point, there had been an explosion, which someone else said had been a mortar shell blowing up a small hut in the park. There were other explanations too. Yet, for some reason, none of them convinced me. I always found anything that took place around the Palestine highly suspect: it was just too convenient a place for a war to be fought. No official explanation was ever given for the meiotic battle, and I still tend to think it was just the U.S. army putting on a display for the cameras — as they had throughout this war — to impress the world with their weapons, and to impress upon the media how unsafe Baghdad still was. Just in case anyone thought it was now all right to go ferreting around out there and get in their way.

I am not a particularly sociable person, but I tried to keep abreast of things by taking up and handing out invitations for drinks. There were also parties, but the couple I attended proved to be just the usual decayed hotel rooms with the usual dozen over-stimulated men drinking in them, so I stopped going. In spite of what you may imagine, the combination of journalists plus war did not equal heavy drinking and wildness. Most people retired early and sober. While we were gregarious, we were also an introspective bunch. Everyone had people he loved and missed back home, and we had already seen enough to know that getting back there was not a *guarantee*. So we tended to grow melancholy when darkness fell, and were always asleep before midnight, as if in dreams we could return briefly to our other lives.

> *Display no more, in vain, the lofty banner.*
> *For see! where on the bier before ye lies*
> *The pale, the fall'n, th'untimely sacrifice*
> *To your mistaken shrine, to your false idol Honour!*
> — ANNE FINCH, COUNTESS OF WINCHILSEA (1661–1720)[102]

Of what, you may well ask, did Iraqis dream?

Dr. Ayoub, a psychiatrist connected with Baghdad's Dominican Hospital, told me that the most common and troublesome dreams he was finding with his patients were ones related to chronic insecurity.

"They dream their teeth falling out," he said. "They dream someone is chasing after them and they cannot escape — this kinds of thing."

What effect did the bombing and invasion have on people who were previously not suffering from psychological disorders?

"Anxiety. Stress. Worst are the *childrens*," said Dr. Ayoub, as if talking to someone who found all this hard to believe. "An adult has the rational intelligence to comprehend situation, that worst is over. But the child cannot understand this things. Some they will remain *permanently* anxious, fears-full. It is common after such events as the war, the earthquake ..."

"Permanently?"

"Yes. For rest of his lifes."

How many children would be affected like this in some way?

"At least two hundred the towsand. *At least ...*"

I suppose we should, in fairness, add these walking wounded to the five hundred thousand or more children who died from malnutrition because of the U.S.-led embargo. What does it take to indict on crimes against humanity these days?

The first casualty of war may well be truth, but the last will be these children, whose end has been seeded inside their beginning.

Children's wards are never cheery places, but this one was oppressive, sepulchral, the leaden silence only broken by muffled sobbing from adults and the occasional piercing animal wail. Little lives smashed to pieces were proving difficult to mend in a hospital now lacking narcotics, medicine, sterile bandages, supplies, electricity and running water.

"I was operate in the candles-light," Dr. Iohannes, the hospital's only surgeon, told me. "Now we have no more the candles so I do the surgeries in this passageway where I have some light ... In day time only, of course."

Beside him, on a narrow pallet on the floor, lay a little person resembling the parody of an accident victim from a cartoon. Both legs were in plaster casts and attached by wires to the radiator behind so they remained in the required position. The tiny arms were spread out bandaged to boards on either side; the torso area was covered by the hump of a wire cage over which a stained and ragged blanket had been spread; the head was entirely swathed in bloody rags, apart from an inch-wide gap through which one big haunting eye peeped unblinkingly.

Her name was Amina. She was four years old. A bomb had fallen on a house near where she lived while she was walking home from the market with her father. Shrapnel and flying glass had smashed and slashed her to pieces. She had not yet been told that her father had died of his own wounds.

"As you see, we have not any bandage here any more. Not plaster bandage too. We must use what we have. I apologize for our primitive method. You will think we are savage peoples. We have no anaesthetic to give her," said Dr. Iohannes. "And no anti-bio. She is in shock, you see, so is feeling nothing really." He paused and sighed. "She will die today. Yes, I am certain of it ..."

The brown pool of that eye in its frame of bloody rags was looking straight at me. Something leapt the space between us, some form of communication. There was a little girl in there, a little girl whose body had been broken and torn. A little girl about to die.

I had no adequate response to any of this. I just stood there nodding, but what I wanted to do was run out of that room and out of the hospital, down the road all the way to Jordan, and then onto the airplane that would take me far, far from sights like this, far from needless tragedies, far from all the evidence pointing to the flaw in us. Could anyone look at this little girl and say that what had happened to her was justifiable? I would like to see the manly men of Pentagon and White House take their photo-opportunity with little Amina, explaining to her that, painful and cruel as it may seem, the cost — *her* cost, not theirs — was worth it.

The words of all the poets and singers are true: her life was bigger than any big idea. She may have come to save George W. Bush's granddaughter from cancer, she may have come to paint a masterpiece, compose a symphony containing the voice of God, make someone happy, grow beautiful flowers, travel the world, improve the lot of women and the poor, or the lot of men. She may have come just to dream, love, breathe in and out ... We shall never know. Nor will *she* ever know — and that is what is *most* wrong here. When the manly men decide that what is right for them this week may well be wrong for Amina, they are violating the free will of a human being, violating the fundamental human right to live and to die in accordance with the body's nature. This is something we are told that even God is forbidden to do.

I look at little Amina and I know the difference between good and evil. I have partaken of the fruit of the tree and I shall never be the same again.

My journal makes for scary reading around this time. I am frightened to turn its pages, scared there is *something* in there. Something alive. Because what is in there is the truth, is REAL. Everything else is window dressing.

She is my compass, little Amina, and my true north. I cannot ever get lost as long as I have her. Did you know she was an only child? Yes, she was. And did you know that her mother committed suicide an hour after being told she was dead? Yes, she did. So I will always have her sitting in my brain like a broken sliver of mirror.

Think of Amina as your own child, or sister, or brother. Every time you send off your taxes to the war chest, think of Amina ... Think of her being ripped up and smashed into blood pudding every day while you look in the mirror and say you're proud to be an American. If you can do that, *then* bring it on. Not before.

> *but this is the problem: how to be alive*
> *in all this gazed-upon and cherished world*
> *and do no harm.*
>
> — JOHN BURNSIDE (1955–)[103]

The British Embassy in Baghdad had hired Samir — "Sammy" — over twelve years ago, a week before all British staff were ordered home in readiness for the start of the Gulf War. At first, he received his monthly $100 paycheck from the Swedish Embassy; when the Swedes left he got it from the Turks while they still maintained an embassy in Baghdad; after they had left, he received it via the Russian Embassy. He had not been paid in some months, however, and now he badly needed this money. There were debts. For a week or so he had been unable to sleep, he said, because of looters who came in the night to steal treasures they believed were kept locked inside the embassy. He showed us where he had nailed boards over doors, reinforced windows, put on new and larger padlocks.

"This is great," said Philip Sherwell. "Marvellous stuff! The faithful old retainer holds the fort ..."

The fort, however, did not look as if it would hold much longer.

Situated on a few acres of prime riverside real estate on the west bank of the Tigris, the British Embassy was, tellingly, one of Baghdad's oldest structures now, though dating back only to the eighteenth century. In a bijou area of shuttered merchants' houses from the same era, the embassy had a sleepy feeling about it as Sammy showed us what little he had done to preserve and secure it in twelve years. A group of Iraqi kids was playing soccer on the embassy's pitch — it looked like a regular event. The swimming pool, resonant with the ghosts of pink-skinned corpulent civil servants, was now as tattered as the beach umbrellas that stood around it like mad skeletons. Tampons from the embassy stores lay scattered in the dust — as I could not help but notice when a snot-nosed boy tapped my elbow and pointed to the one he had dangling from its cord.

"Hey, mister," he said. "You like this?"

"Careful, it could be Prince Charles ..."

"Gibb me money."

"Okay. Here."

I gave him a thousand dinars. He looked at it then at me with a you-gotta-be-kidding expression.

"When I first came here, that was worth nearly twelve hundred dollars."

"Yes, he came with General Maude," Sherwell added from some distance away.

"Jerrol Modd!" the kid exclaimed, laughing.

"Yes, you know General Maude?"

"Jerrol Modd coming this place, yesh?"

"That's right. Back when Turkey was your big cheese."

"You are Jerrol Modd?" the kid asked, brows knotted. "You beeg cheesh?"

"No, sorry. I am very little cheesh. Barely a cheesh at all. I'm the *vache qui rit*, the laughing cow cheese."

"Vashkeeree," repeated the boy. "Gibb more money?"

"Why not? But will you do something for me?"

He looked dubious but nodded anyway. I knelt to whisper in his ear.

"Understand?" I asked him. "You get the money when it is done."

"Promish, mister?"

"Yes, I promish."

In the supplies room itself there was a cupboard filled with jars of Imodium, for "Baghdad Belly." Another cupboard contained only Union Jack flags, huge ones. Another held application forms for various kinds of British visa. An adjacent room was bare except for a metal bunk bed. The wire webbing of the lower bed was, mysteriously, ominously, attached by jumper-cable clips to an electric wall socket the way you see beds used by pro torturers. I doubt if the British had been torturing people here — yet someone evidently had been. It did not look good.

"Look, here's the plan," Sherwell said.

He wanted to have Sammy raise the Union Jack from the embassy's rooftop flagpole for the first time in thirteen years — and he wanted to do it in time for the Sunday edition. Not before, though, in case someone snapped a picture of the building in the meantime. Were we all okay with this?

Since it would involve him climbing to the rooftop, Sammy was Sherwell's chief concern because the retainer was indeed "old" — seventy at least (he wasn't sure himself). Sammy shrugged. His arms were either very long or his legs were far too short, because he could have picked things off the ground without bending his knees.

Inside the main building we saw many pictures of the Queen but only one of Philip (the Greek, not Sherwell). There were a surprising number of pics showing Charles and Di, mostly cut from magazines and taped to office walls. The notice boards were filled with urgent communiqués about AIDS (and the impending draconian measures being introduced by Saddam to cope with what he clearly viewed as yet more Western perfidy). There were also serious and very official updates on Saddam's invasion of Kuwait (and the impending draconian measures being discussed by Bush 1 to cope with what he viewed as yet more of Saddam's perfidy).

The place had been frozen in time. It was still late in 1990 here. Princess Diana was alive. Bush's 1's "New World Order" had yet to be announced. And Saddam — not that many would have put money on his chances back then — still had over twelve more years to go as president of Iraq.

Dust lay over everything in an inch-thick crust that must have contained specks of carnage from every attack on Baghdad the Americans had launched since 1991. It was instructive to see exactly what happens if you don't clean your place for a decade — it's not so bad at all.

The ambassador's office must have had one of the best views in Baghdad. Iraq was no sinecure, however. Whoever ended up repping Britain there would have his work cut out for him. There was always some kind of problem. As I sat in the ambassadorial chair — which resembled the pilot's seat of a Vulcan V-Bomber, very fifties — my problem was the desert storm of dust I had dislodged. Lit by thick shafts of late afternoon sunlight, the dust showered down all around me. I could taste musty papers and mildewed carpet. I felt a sudden sense of panic: I was trapped, I could not breathe, I was choking to death in this dark mahogany room, where the weight of an oppressive bureaucracy and the British disease of class seemed to be bringing the ceiling down to crush the air out of me.

Pushing past the others, I said something about needing air and returned to the central quadrangle to breathe by the memorial to Maude's fallen soldiers. Yet even here, with the square of blue above me, I felt hemmed in, squeezed. My bones seemed to be softening, as if they were acutely aware of gravity's pull.

Only when I was sitting on the grass beyond the Oasis Club watching the river did I feel any respite. From that office, I told myself, many a dark deed was hatched and launched. The Brits had run the eastern part of their empire via Baghdad for a long time — though not long enough for Tony Blair, it would seem.

Shooting started up somewhere nearby. I got up to see where it was coming from, but it was impossible to judge exactly how far away it might be. A series of loud dull thumps from across the river made me turn. A building near the university had just been bombed and a huge black pillar of churning smoke was pouring upwards. There were at least ten or twelve other columns of smoke visible from here across east Baghdad's skyline, but none was as pronounced as the one just across the Tigris. I began videotaping. The kids playing soccer thought I wanted to film them, and every time I turned their way, they would halt their game to pose or play exhibition shots.

Only an ancient towpath and public right-of-way separated the embassy's low wall from the river, so I had noticed the very big man in a dazzling white *dishdasha* before. He seemed to be pacing up and down the length of the embassy's wall like a guard. A good four hundred pounds, he would from time to time stop children who were playing down by the river. Whatever he said to these children, it both scared and amused them. They would run off giggling.

As I filmed across the river, I realized that the big man was deliberately positioning himself in front of my lens, whichever way I turned. About to say something, I let it drop and sat back on the grass. The man was clearly a simpleton of some sort. There was no point in getting bothered by him. I remember vaguely thinking that the embassy wall, low as it was, still formed a symbolic boundary that no Iraqi would cross. The reason I remember it is that my next memory is opening my eyes to see the very big man standing over me.

He had been crying. His pupils were held in a web of red blood vessels and snot ran down his bloated cheeks. He reminded me very strongly of someone but I just could not figure out who.

"What have you done to my city!" he cried out, in English. "Look!"

He gestured back at the smouldering skyline.

His grief was infectious. I did not know what to say, and now felt like crying too. The city was a shabby smoking ruin from here, this spot where locals had probably once come to stand and admire its grandeur. Everything Saddam had built — and he had built everything one could see looking east from the embassy grounds — had been attacked. What had been a source of pride — and I remembered when — was now a humiliation.

"Look what you do! Why you do this? Why? Why? Why?"

He had been fumbling in the deep pocket of his *dishdasha* for some time now, and I finally saw what he was fumbling with as his hand emerged holding a pistol.

"Why you do this to our city? Why?"

The gun was about an inch from my left eye, so close I could not even focus on it. Ice seemed to flow through every vein and artery in me. I felt very calm, almost serene. Then it occurred to me that I wanted him to pull the trigger. I was ready for it. There seemed to be an immense amount of time to consider all this, too. I found myself weighing options, taking into account the horrors I had witnessed over the past several days, thinking about my family. Would they be better off without me? I inclined to "Yes," but an older me pointed to a younger me saying, "You know that is never true." All deaths are actually suicides, I realized, knowing without any doubt that I could decide whether this man pulled the trigger or not. It had nothing to do with him, although his feelings were understandable, perhaps even laudable.

The gun was now pressing against my eyelid as I looked way, way up to its owner's confused, grieving face and said in a voice that sounded calm, deep and resonant,

"It was not me, my friend. I am Canadian. I did not want this to happen. I am so sorry it did."

I felt the gun recede.

"*Kanadi*?" said the man.

"Yes."

"I think you was Inglishmans ... *Kanadi* good people. I sorry for this ..."

"You don't need to be sorry. I would do the same in your position ..."

"*Americani* are dogs," he stated. "We have nothing now. Where is the policemens? Who will stop these thiefs that are everywhere? We have no security here now. Who will protect us?"

"Allah?" I suggested.

The man affected a gesture of mock piety and said,

"Yes perhaps. I sorry for this, my friend *Kanadi* ..."

He had the pistol in his palm, holding it away from himself as if it had become a dog turd.

"Don't mention it. It is not a problem. I wish there was something I could do for you. But there is nothing any of us can do."

"You speak true. Thank you, friend."

He offered his other hand and I shook it, reassuring him that I did not think badly of him. Returning the pistol to his pocket, he went on his way, back through the gate in the embassy wall and along the towpath, turning to wave a couple of times — or perhaps to make sure I had not run to get the authorities. I would not have known where to run for that. There were no authorities.

As I was about to head back to find the others, I heard the unmistakable sound of an American fighter plane called the Warthog. It sounded as if someone in an attic above the clouds was hauling massive chains across the bare wood floor. I saw the plane, poised over the river about half a kilometre further down. It could remain almost stationary. With its snub nose and bulky torso, it did resemble a pig. But when its guns were fired, as they were now, it made the strange pig-like grunting sound whence its name derived. Hardly a moment later, tremendous explosions erupted. The building facing the Warthog on the east bank looked as if it was being sawn in half, as bullets from the plane's grunting guns ripped across an entire floor, causing fires and explosions inside. Within minutes, it was belching black clouds that made the day seem to skip all the hours between now and early evening.

The Warthog banked and rolled, inspecting its work. Then it darted off low over the Tigris. I wondered if there was any reason to fire at the building. Was the pilot just seeing what his little hog could do? After all, the chance to shoot up a real city does not come often.

"Wha' the fuck was *that*?" asked Hackett.

"Bit of stunt flying, I think."

"You okay? You luke terrible ... All pale an' sickly."

I told him about the big man.

"There's too many o' those guys aroond here for my liking ..."

"How many do you usually like, then?"

He narrowed his eyes.

"Sometimes I woud like to thump you ..."

"You should do it. I might like it."

He told me what the plan with the flag was, and how I must not breathe a word of it to anyone.

"Why, because it's fabrication of news?"

"It is nae *that*!"

"Just joking."

"Oh. Okay. Asshole!"

"But you can't be the one to raise the flag, because you're a Scot."

"Aye. Just another colony, we are. Like poor Iraq here. What the fuck are we doing to these people? It taint right, that I do know."

"Yep."

A candle for two lovers in a stripped apartment
A candle for the sky that has folded
A candle for the beginning
A candle for the end
A candle for the final decision
A candle for conscience
A candle in my hand.

— SAADI YOUSSEF [104]

CHAPTER EIGHT

THE THIEF OF BAGHDAD

And al above, depeynted in a tour,
Saugh I Conquest, sittynge in greet honour,
With the sharpe swerd over his heed
Hangynge by a soutil twynes threed.

— GEOFFREY CHAUCER (1343–1400)[105]

This terrorism is the 21st century threat. It is a war that strikes at
the heart of all that we hold dear, and there is only one response
that is possible or rational: to meet their will to inflict terror with
a greater will to defeat it; to confront their philosophy of hate
with our own of tolerance and freedom; and to challenge their
desire to frighten us, divide us, unnerve us with an unshakeable
unity of purpose; to stand side by side with the United States of
America and with our other allies in the world, to rid our world
of this evil once and for all ... Let us be very clear. America did
not attack al-Qaeda on September 11, al-Qaeda attacked
America, and in doing so attacked not just America, but the way

> *of life of all people who believe in tolerance, and freedom, justice*
> *and peace.*
>
> — TONY BLAIR, NOVEMBER 20, 2003 [106]

An Iraqi friend of mine, listening to Mr. Blair's speech, said:

"Let *us* be very clear, too. Iraq did not attack America on March 20th, America attacked Iraq, and in doing so attacked not just Iraq, but the way of life of all people who believe in tolerance, and freedom, justice and peace."

He then added that Blair — or Bliar, as the Brits now spell him — had a peculiar notion of how a belief in tolerance, freedom, justice and peace ought to best be expressed. Particularly to those whom, as it was, had their doubts about his integrity.

The civilian death toll in Iraq currently stands at around ten thousand. The latest figures are to be found at www.iraqbodycount.net, which also provides useful figures for the War on Terror generally: worldwide, there have been some fifteen thousand civilian casualties — mainly in Iraq and Afghanistan — as opposed to 2,752 deaths in the World Trade Center suicide attacks. Is this tolerance, justice or peace? There is a sickening tendency in the West to regard the lives of Westerners as more precious than those of other people. Far more attention was paid to the March 2004 attack on commuter trains in Spain, for instance, than was paid to the attacks in Karbala a few weeks earlier, although the death tolls were comparable. Although everyone was aware of the fighting in Fallujah, few in the West seemed to know that the Americans had killed six hundred Iraqis there, most of them women, children and old people. With the ubiquity of personal computers and internet access, not to mention Al Jazeera, our bias is increasingly available for all to see, and we are rightly despised for it, regarded as hypocrites and liars.

> *I hate that drum's discordant sound,*
> *Parading round, and round, and round:*
> *To me it talks of ravaged plains,*
> *And burning towns, and ruined swains,*

And mangled limbs, and dying groans,
And widows' tears, and orphans' moans;
And all that Misery's hand bestows,
To fill the catalogue of human woes.

— JOHN SCOTT (1730–83)[107]

Returning to east Baghdad from the British Embassy, I noticed a dead donkey lying across the sidewalk in the middle of Jumhunya Bridge — a victim of war that no one had claimed. A pair of pariah dogs was assiduously pulling its guts out of the way in order to reach the tastier parts. What remained of the donkey was still there a month later.

The Americans had now parked a tank and erected a razor-wire barrier at the end of Sadoun Street, so it was no longer possible to drive up to the Al-Arabie. A large group of Iraqis was gathered at the entrance to the sidewalk, some of them angrily waving documents at the four soldiers standing guard. Clearly, they were not able to get to homes, jobs or appointments on the street. I got out to ask if we could drive the truck in, since otherwise we would all be hauling Hackett's equipment back.

Whether by coincidence or design, the soldiers here all wore mirrored wrap-around shades that, with their tin helmets, made them resemble dangerously large bugs.

"Get that fuckin' thing outta my face!" yelled a soldier.

"Are you talking to me?"

I did not sound like Robert De Niro in *Taxi Driver* — I genuinely wanted to know.

"Don't point that fuckin' camera at me!"

"Are you talking to me?"

"Yeah, I'm fuckin' talkin' to you, asshole!"

My camera was not pointed at him but I was holding it above my head to avoid damage by the crowd. I decided to keep my mouth shut about his rudeness or else we would never get the truck in. I pushed until I was up to the barrier, resolving to report the soldier's rudeness to his co. This was the first time that I noticed something I was to see everywhere I looked for it: the U.S. soldiers on duty concealed the name and number stripes on their uniforms. The standard issue flak jacket handily concealed the stripe over a breast pocket; the other one on the helmet was usually hidden by sand goggles or a bandana. Combine this with the mirrored shades and the general anonymity provided by a helmet and uniform, and you have virtually unidentifiable American soldiers. Whether this practice was official army policy or just conventional barrack-room wisdom, I do not know, but it was certainly widespread enough to be policy. The Pentagon, of course, denied this, since it would violate the Geneva Conventions. When you consider how hard it would be to bring any kind of charge against a soldier without having his basic information, you can see why the code of war forbids unidentifiable soldiers. *He was a young man 18–25 ...* That narrows it down to everyone. *He was black ...* That excludes half of them. Unless the soldier was two feet tall, or had a spectacular birthmark or scar or a nose like a toucan's beak, he would be all but impossible to pick out.

"You got ID?" said the soldier.

I showed him my *Harper's* identification.

"'Kay, buddy, you can come on in."

His tone changed to that of a friendly guy. My anger melted as I realized that he was just a scared kid, who did not know where he was or even what he was supposed to do there. Anyone with a computer could have made my *Harper's* card. The fact that he accepted it as ID sent chills through me: if this was the level of security here, we were in trouble. Once through the barrier, I asked him about the truck. He genuinely wanted to help now, but I could see that he had no idea of how to open the road barrier without everyone pouring in, so I told him we would sort it out tomorrow. He seemed grateful. I offered him a satellite telephone call.

"That'd be great," he said. "But I can't, man. I'm on dooty ..."

His expression was a parody of inner conflict, so I told him not to worry: he could come to the hotel when he was off duty.

"Thank so much, man. I really 'preciate it ..."

I gave him my room number at the Al-Arabie, then I signalled a no-go to Hackett and Sherwell, who told Bassim the driver to park nearby. As I began to walk down Sadoun Street, a man's voice called out:

"Robert! Mister Robert!"

His face and belly pressed against razor wire, General Nial stood on the far side of the barrier holding up a huge plastic bag.

I told the soldiers that Nial and Haifa were friends of mine and, again disconcertingly, they were allowed through.

"All day she has been in the chicken cooking for you," said the general, introducing me to his wife as if we had never met.

"In the chicken?"

"He means the kitchen," said Haifa.

It took me a while to realize that her English was far better than her husband's, because Nial would never ask me to repeat anything I said, and would even nod when I asked him if he'd understood. If he thought he might *want* to understand something he would ask Haifa in Arabic what I had said. As a rule, however, he was only interested in what he had to say.

The general handed me his bag. It weighed a ton. Inside were several bottles of Scotch, a bundle wrapped in newspapers and four huge Tupperware containers. I could see him looking to ascertain if I had the sat-phone on me, deciding to see how long he could wait before asking for it: it was inside my shoulder bag.

"So, *Robert*," he said, smiling benignly, "how is it?"

"What?"

"You are having some interesting time in Baghdad, yes?"

"Oh, yes. Always an interesting time here ..."

"If there is *anything* you want to know, you just ask me, okay? *Anything!*"

"Just ask him for anything you want," added Haifa, fearing I had not understood.

"Where's Saddam Hussein?" I said.

They both laughed.

"*No one* he know this thing!" said the general. "*No one.* But any other things I can do for you ..."

"Okay," I said. "What about Tariq Aziz — know where *he* is?"

Expecting the same reaction, I was surprised to find the general coming close and whispering:

"This I *know.* He is near to my house ..."

Aziz was also, of course, an Iraqi Christian — though, as a Ba'athi, he was officially an atheist — thus his daughter, Zobeida, lived near the general, in an area of the city that housed, almost exclusively, wealthy Christians. The general had seen Aziz there earlier that day. As he spoke, I realized he was fairly well connected to the old regime. Even a bit *too* well connected. But I could tell that his anxiety to provide me this information was not unconnected with his need to make a telephone call, and all kinds of possibilities suddenly ran through my head. Such as: *he needs to use an untraceable phone in order to pass information on to someone like — Saddam! But he must know the phone would record any numbers he punches in? Maybe he did just want to call his daughter in Damascus.* The look of woe, of someone who has been through far too much, in Haifa's face, however, was what convinced me that the couple was genuine.

"Do you think Aziz would let me interview him?" I asked, assuming it was a ridiculous question.

I backed it up with some nonsense about it being important to send a message to all Iraqis that the war was over now, that the old regime was finished, to stop any more senseless killings. I would have said anything it took to convince, but before I needed to say more, the general told me,

"Yes, I think it is possible. I will ask the daughter of Aziz about this for you."

I was stunned.

"Would you like to make another telephone call?" I said, innocently.

"Is it okay?" said the general, just as innocently.

"It's my pleasure," I assured him, handing over the phone.

While he was preoccupied with Iridium's satellite, I took the opportunity to wheedle as much information as possible from his wife.

"It must have been hard, these last few weeks," I said.

"Oh! Oh! Oh!" she said, crossing her eyes and knocking herself on the skull, in a deft mime of befuddling severe times. "It was *very* bad ... very, very bad ..."

"But good to see Saddam gone, no?"

"Of course," she replied, sincerely. "We hate Saddam. He put Nial in the prison ..."

She looked down. I could see tears welling up in the big pools of her eyes. Either she was a great actor, or she was telling the truth.

"I'm sorry," I said, patting her shoulder — until I remembered you did not do that to someone's wife here. She did not seem to mind, though. "Esscuse me," she said, blowing her nose in order to dab away tears. Then she added, incongruously, "We have no widows in our house ..."

"I see ... No widows ..."

"*Win*-dows," she corrected. "The bomb is breaking all our *win*-dows."

"I hope no one was hurt," I said, instantly aware of how lame it sounded.

As I have observed, there is no easy way of apologizing for bombing someone's home.

"Just my son," she said. "His head ..."

I had visions of a small headless child, but it turned out that her twenty-four-year-old son had needed stitches to his skull after being hit by shrapnel from the bomb that had fallen a street away in their residential neighbourhood. Apparently, all the houses on both streets had lost their windows to this blast. It was still cold at night, so the very young and the old had suffered — one aging neighbour was now hospitalized with pneumonia; a baby had pleurisy.

General Nial, who had been talking enthusiastically all this while, held out the phone to Haifa. She excused herself again and was soon speaking on it with such obvious joy it was impossible to doubt that here was a mother talking to a child about whom she had been worrying.

"So, *Robert*," said the general.

"Yes, Nial?"

"When shall we meet?"

"Tomorrow?"

I saw him looking at my *Harper's* ID, which was now clipped to my shirt pocket.

"*Harper* New York," he said, looking at me quizzically.

"Yes. That's the *Harper's* office. In New York. But my *main* office, that I have to stay in touch with, is the CBC office in Toronto. It's the CANADIAN Broadcasting Corporation. In Canada there. Eh?"

"You are not American?" he asked.

He seemed disappointed, so I upped his spirits by telling him that I did write for an American magazine — the *only* one opposed to the war. Though not, of course, opposed to getting rid of Saddam. As long as it could be done peacefully. Or not too violently. And by Iraqis. With help if they needed it. But only if they asked for it. Politics, however, evidently held no interest for him. He had begun looking fretfully at the phone again, even though his wife was using it.

"You will come for dinner at my house tomorrow," said the general, quite specifically.

He was clearly used to giving orders.

"That's very kind of you. Thank you."

I told him he could make more phone calls if he needed.

"What time?" he asked.

I looked at my watch, but he explained he had meant what time would we meet the next day.

"Shall it be in the morning?" he asked.

I took this to mean that I should meet him in the morning, in case there was news about Tariq Aziz. We agreed on eleven o'clock.

To show good faith, I told him to take the phone back with him and make as many calls as he wished. I was deeply surprised when he adamantly refused to do this. All he wanted was one more call. Maybe he was not as easy to read as I had thought? Or could there be another reason he did not want the phone? When switched on, the Iridium provided a tracking signal — did he not want to risk me tracking down where he lived? As William Burroughs observed, a paranoid is simply someone with all the facts.

The aroma of food from the vast bag was making me start to drool, so I told the general to drop the phone at the front desk when he had finished, and, thanking them both profusely for the food, for everything, I backed away gracelessly and ran into the Al-Arabie, then proceeded up the four flights of stairs to my room.

At the second floor, I noticed they had got the television in the bar working. A couple of tired-looking soldiers were sitting there with beers, alongside a few Iraqi men. The colour image on the monitor was crisp and dazzling, hypnotic. I stopped to watch.

"This number one song in Iraq now," one of the Al-Arabie's many managers told me, nodding at the TV.

"Who's the singer?"

"His name Sa'ad," said the manager.

Unlike most MuchMusic or MTV performers, Sa'ad looked to be around seventy. He looked sad too, big bloodhound eyes drooping into skin as wizened as a dried-up lakebed. The song also was sad. It was very sad. You did not have to be Lawrence of Arabia to tell from the video that this song was about the hopes placed by the old in the young, who are none too happy about the world they have inherited. One of the Iraqis in the bar was ladling tears from his cheeks with both hands. The manager began to sniff and snort too. Boy, it was sad, this song. The plangent chords and the images of a guttering torch handed down the generations, the burden of hope in a peasant's bowed old shoulders, the look of pained expectation in the eyes of children, of wincing resignation in the old, especially in the context of all the shattered dreams and false hopes that was Iraq — the accumulation soon had me swallowing hard. The soldiers were paying no attention to the TV, however, talking among themselves, and occasionally laughing aloud. As this braying laughter rang out again, I noticed the weeping Iraqi look up briefly and scowl in the direction of the soldiers. It was not the best place to be insensitive, and I wondered how to covey this to the Americans without getting my face spread across the wall. I was just about to stride over and tell it like it was, plain and simple, when the manager slid a beer to me across the counter, although I had not ordered one. His face was a glistening mask by now, as if he had just come in from the rain.

"On the hiss," he said.

"What?"

"Beer is on the hiss. Churrs," he added.

"Cheers," I said. "What's the hiss?"

He sniffed loudly, wiping his nose with an elbow.

"Did you *weep* in this beer?" I asked him.

His expression crept more towards aghast as he shook his head slowly.

"Are you sure? Because I could swear I saw a tear slide off your face into it ..."

As I said it, I felt one of my own dewy creations careen down the slide of my nose and plop into my beer, vanishing under the foam.

He smiled helplessly, then made a baleful groaning noise.

"Saad?" I said.

He nodded, blubbering as he looked past me to the TV. I followed his gaze to see the massive overkill of the finale: the kindly old woman we had seen earlier is placed in a bleak coffin; the desolate child cries out, one of his tears falling slowly on the coffin lid; the mother-figure turns for solace to the father-figure, who fades into a photograph of himself in army uniform that bursts into flame and in seconds is dust blown by the wind; a little girl stands with parents who dissolve into the air around her until she is entirely alone in a vast and threatening city square, turning for comfort around and around, her little arms reaching out but finding no one and nothing; the little boy is handed a clock by the kindly old man, who melts into a puddle that instantly turns to vapour as he places the clock upon a desk behind him; when he turns back, the child is a middle-aged man with a cowed, defeated expression, standing in a place like a morgue with pale bodies on slabs as the rain beats down on them, on all the living and the dead; at which point we dissolve back to the woeful Sa'ad sitting at a lonely table by the river and singing lines that spoke of futility, waste, hopelessness, decay, sorrow, misery, defeat and doom.

It was about as upbeat a tune as Baghdad needed right now.

About a minute before the final bleat of despair, one of the American soldiers said, "So he fuckin' comes over to me with the fuckin' spear in his hand, don't he, and he says, 'Why the fuck don't you try one?'"

At which point he croaked and honked with laughter, inciting a similar kind of moronic seal's barking from his friends, who bent double and beat their thighs to express the impossibility of expressing such mirth. With a yelp of chair-leg against polished wood floor, the weeping Iraqi across the room abruptly got up. I thought he was going to hurtle over and murder someone, but instead he growled at the manager, flung some money on the bar and clomped out on lead feet.

"I saw *that* coming," I said, to anyone listening. Then I asked the manager, "What did he say to you?"

The manager seemed much paler than he had a minute ago. His skin looked translucent and glowing.

"He is say to me that I am deserving the death because I serve to *jaish Americani* here ..."

"Yeah, well we're all a little overwrought, aren't we? I'll see you later."

"Over rort?" he repeated solemnly.

"Ach!" said Hackett, as I walked in. "Are ye all right, mate? Ye luke *horrible* ..."

"I hate to tell you this, but you're no Brad Pitt yourself, you know ..."

"Baghdad-seriously, mate, is everthin' aright?"

I told him about Sa'ad and the Big Sadness.

"Sounds like tha fuckin' *Never-Ending Story* ... *You have your sat-phone wi' ya?*"

"Why?"

"Obviously I wan' tae use it!" he said.

I told him I'd left it with a couple of Iraqis in the street who were going to drop it off with the concierge when they were done.

"You might be interested in some swampland I got in Florida too ..."

"You've got to have more trust in people, Paul ..."

"Do nae call me *that* — I think you're talkin' tae yoursel' ... What the hell's in tha huge bag?"

"This is where you come to regret being such a mettlesome Scot —"

I took out the Tupperware containers and opened them: and, by God, had Haifa done us proud! Some kind of chicken dish, and another kind of meat stew, with some kind of vegetable dish and several rounds of flat bread.

"Are ye gonna eat that all by yoursel', now?," asked Hackett.

"She made it in the chicken ..."

"Did she now?" He picked up a bottle of the Scotch, saying, "MacHussein ... hmmm, *distilled in the highlands of Iraq ... aged for ten years in old cadavers* ... I'm nae familiar wi' it ..."

"And you'll not be having the pleasure, either ..."

I snatched the bottle away. It was not "MacHussein," but it was also not a familiar name, and it did say "distilled in Iraq," as well as "aged for ten years in oak barrels." I unscrewed the cap and sniffed.

"Ah," I said, "nice burning gasoline nose to it ..."

"They probably been cracking it in same place they do th' oil," Hackett said.

We ate like wild men, all but wiping the food across our faces. There is nothing like being hungry to make any food taste spectacular, but when the food is great to begin with —

"It's unbeatable!"

"Fantastic. Want some bread?"

"Yughwa, cnae yul ..."

"Eh?"

I told him about the general. Then I told him about the possibility of Tariq Aziz.

"Ya kuddin'?"

"'Swha-sed ..."

"Yull mak-for-oon wi' that ..."

"Thot so ..."

"Wha?"

So I asked him if he'd operate the camera during the interview, and we'd split whatever money came in. It *was* a bit too generous, true, but I could not even consider doing it any other way. I would be happy to get out alive with half of whatever money it brought in. I just knew that doing it any other way would be sure to end badly. I could see myself on fire, burning, holding the burning cheque, with Hackett, also aflame, looking reproachfully at me and at his own very little burning cheque.

"You can't tell Sherwell, though ... Okay?"

"Thass gonna be difficult ..." He agonized over it. "I'm primarily here for him ... If it don't mess wi' anything he wants tae do ... ye know?"

"Ah, what the fuck? He can come in on it too, if he wants. We'll just have to work out the details of when the *Telegraph* can print it, okay?"

"I'm sure it is. You'll hae t'ask him, though ... I feel a lot better 'bout it now."

"You're an honourable Scot, aren't you? Quite commendable, in fact."

It is rare indeed to come across someone this honourable in the face of money.

At that moment, Peter, a big, amiable journalist from New Zealand with cold pewter blue eyes, came in, so we cut the conversation short.

"Look what ah found!" Peter said, fanning a slab of dollar bills. "They was just lying in the dirt outside the Palestine ... Fuck! There mus' be five hundred here ... Aw Jeez, where you get that food? And where you get all that fuckin' *whisky*?"

A moment later, Peter was sitting with a plate of Haifa's food and a mug of Scotch, making the same rapturous noises. He had just found the money lying in the Palestine Hotel's drive. It did not really surprise me: there was so much money here right now, what with all the major networks arriving, and cash being the only currency. It was ironic that in this desperately poor land no one but Peter had noticed all those dollars lying there.

"Dis fuckin' brill," Peter said, chomping happily, and he proceeded to tell a complex, bawdy and somewhat mournful tale about being on a job in Scotland. It ended with him and a "chicky" going at it like stoats in some abandoned cottage.

Fortunately, another of the Al-Arabie's managers appeared at the door just then holding my sat-phone.

"There is America army to see you," he said.

"Well, it's been nice knowing ye," said Hackett.

"At least my trust in humanity paid off ..."

It was the corporal from the barrier wanting to use the phone. I told him to come up, since he would have to use it on the balcony.

"I don't s'pose I could use your shower, too, could I?"

"Sure."

His name was Terry, from Sevierville, Tennessee. None of the soldiers he knew, he told me, had been able to shower or bathe since arriving in Kuwait. Three months earlier.

"I'll clean it out for you real good," Terry promised.

"*Three* months, eh? Don't worry — it's a *hotel*."

The call was more important to him, so I led him out to the balcony and made sure he could get through, then rejoined Hackett and Peter and forgot about him.

A few minutes later Sherwell came in.

"Do you know there's a soldier on your balcony making a phone call?"

"Yes, we know that."

"Okay, just checking ... Oh, food! Where did that come from?"

Adam Lusher showed up very late with good news: he had persuaded the unit with which he was embedded to allow him to bring some colleagues in and show them around. His unit was now encamped in the grounds of Saddam's Republican Palace, so we would get a tour of that and a look at Michel Aflaq's mausoleum. Aflaq, a Syrian Christian, had been the founder of the Ba'athi movement, so this was Saddam's version of Lenin's tomb.

"By the way," said Lusher, "there's a soldier on your balcony — did you know that?"

"Yes, we know that, Lusher," said Sherwell, turning to me. "Long phone call, isn't it?"

Yikes! He had been on the phone for nearly an hour. I ran to the balcony, where Terry was crouched down, cradling the phone to his ear as if it was a baby. He had been crying a river, too.

"Don't worry, sweetheart," he was saying, "I'm okay, really I am, and I'm gonna be home soon ... I love you, darlin', an' I really miss you ... I gotta go now ... I will, I will ... Bye, sweet pea. Sorry," he said to me, "I guess I was on a long time. It's the first time I spoke t' her in three months ..."

"Don't worry about it. Ready for the shower now?"

He emerged oohing and ahhing about the virtues of being clean.

"Pity you didn't have some clean clothes to put on, hmm?"

"I tell ya, I feel grrr-eat all the same! This was so kind of you, I wish there was somethin' I could do for ya in return ..."

"*Nada ... niente ...*"

He went off into the night a new man.

"No showers, no phone calls, shit to eat — what kind of an army is this?"

For the first time in weeks, I went to sleep without profound misgivings about the next day. I have since been told that I was probably depressed, but I still cannot see why an appropriate response to something so deeply depressing has to be labelled a disease. I would have been more concerned, I suspect, if I had found myself in a good mood during the bombing and recolonization of Iraq.

> Now in my dial of glass appears
> the soldier who is going to die.
> He smiles, and moves about in ways
> his mother knows, habits of his.
> The wires touch his face: I cry
> NOW. Death, like a familiar, hears
> and look, has made a man of dust
> of a man of flesh. This sorcery

I do. Being damned, I am amused
to see the centre of love diffused
and the waves of love travel into vacancy.
How easy it is to make a ghost.

— KEITH DOUGLAS (1920–44)[108]

The part of Baghdad on the west bank of the Tigris between the Al-Ahrar and Al-Jadriyah bridges, housing the major ministries and Saddam's official residence along with the homes of his family members, had always been off-limits to most Iraqis — and it still was. The Americans had decided to use the Republican or Presidential Palace, with its extensive grounds, as their main base in Baghdad, so now they were the ones staffing the barricades, turning back vehicles. We drove along a wide boulevard that was entirely empty of other traffic, passing the Unknown Soldier monument and the military parade grounds containing a vast triumphal arch formed by two colossal arms holding scimitars. Supposedly, they were modelled on Saddam's arms. Beneath them now were rows of American tanks.

There had clearly been some savage fighting in this area. The sides of the road were littered with burned-out vehicles, most of them private cars. One rested on its rear bumper flat against the wall of a building, as if the driver had attempted to drive up to its roof. Many still smouldered. Occasionally, we saw sooty figures busy detaching usable spare parts from the wreck of a Mercedes or a BMW.

Obliged to get out at every roadblock and explain our presence, we took quite a while to reach the 14th of July Monument and Al-Kindi Street, which with the Qadisaya Expressway formed an inner ring road that ran between the Aflaq mausoleum and the Presidential Palace. Beyond the hedgerows on either side were now camped out thousands of soldiers, with Bradley Fighting Vehicles, tanks and military trucks of every description, many with washing lines strung between them and awnings made from khaki tarpaulins.

We pulled up and got out. Lusher was supposed to be meeting us, but there was no sign of him.

"Well," said Sherwell, "that's the palace over there through that gateway. I suggest we go on in."

We took our various pieces of equipment and walked across to where a stocky black soldier with a huge gun stood. Seeing us approach, he raised the weapon.

"This area is off limits," he shouted. "Get back in your vehicle and leave. Now!"

Sherwell carried on walking towards him, saying we had been invited by an embedded journalist.

"I don't give a fuck who invited you," yelled the soldier. "Get the fuck back in your vehicle and *leave this area. Now!*"

Sherwell must have thought he was in England or somewhere else reasonable, because he kept on walking, waving his ID card.

"Phil! Easy, easy," we said.

"You are one deaf mothafuck," said the soldier, his voice rising up an octave in disbelief.

"Let me just explain, sir," Philip Sherwell was saying.

The soldier took aim. His gun barrel was an inch in diameter. Whatever it fired would smash a hole through your body a foot wide. Finally, Sherwell stopped, though still waving his ID.

"Take your fuckin' ID, mothafucker, and just get the fuck back in your vehicle or otherwise I will fire at you."

"Oh, okay. All right," Sherwell said, backing away waving his arms like a conductor. "No problem ... Don't shoot me ..."

The soldier shook his head and lowered the gun, retreating into the shadows of a guard booth.

"Uncalled for," Sherwell muttered. "What an a-hole!"

"I liked the *or otherwise I will fire at you* ... So proper!"

"Isn't that Adam over there," Hackett said.

Lusher was standing a hundred metres away, languidly waving in our direction.

"Thanks a lot," Sherwell told him.

"They're *soldiers*," said Lusher. "What did you expect — a red carpet?"

We followed him into an area seething with troops and military equipment. Trucks were being refitted here, gassed up there. Oxy-acetylene torches roared into flame; wrenches tinkled against steel. There were orders being shouted out all over the place. Beneath an orange awning sat a group of embedded journalists pecking away on their laptops. One of them was ensconced in a huge white and gold-leaf chair like a throne, clearly taken from one of the nearby palaces — unless the army is *really* abusing taxpayers.

It was turning into quite a warm day — the first since I had been in the Middle East. We started our tour at Michel Aflaq's mausoleum, a round modernist structure with a clunking social-realist sculpture of Aflaq in the front.

I imagine one would have to be a fairly keen member of the Ba'ath Party before the prospect of seeing the founder's tomb would send chills down the spine, even though it did prove to be in a chamber decorated with pleasing Islamic simplicity. The Americans had announced at some point during the war that the mausoleum had been hit by a missile, but the only damage appeared to be a few broken stained-glass windows. The museum downstairs, however, was another story.

The damage here had been caused by off-duty American soldiers, but it was not immediately obvious, since there were no windows and thus no light at all. Lusher found us some flashlights, and it was then that I realized the place had been trashed. I had visited the mausoleum in 1996, when I had been a guest of the government and had little choice in what I did, so I vaguely recalled the little museum. It had contained Aflaq's desk and other items from his office, along with books and various pieces of Ba'athi memorabilia. The floor was now littered with broken glass from display cases that had been pushed over to clear the way while objects of furniture were being carried out. Like the gilded throne that one of the embeds now used as a chair. The items on display — mainly books and pamphlets — were still lying among shards of glass. I picked up a slim volume that proved to be a signed first edition of the Ba'ath Party's manifesto.

I suppose this is how my life of crime began: I did not feel I could throw it back into the glass on the floor, so I put it in my camera bag. Amid the atmosphere of war — which is nothing if not a licence to loot — it seemed a trivial thing to do, yet it is not, ultimately. I picked up Aflaq's ink blotter as well, and kept that too.

I am the Thief of Baghdad, as my confession in the *Globe and Mail* was called.

Aflaq's desk — a gilded rococo monster — was now being used by a Marine colonel, who had his computer and his feet on it as we walked past him on the far side of the mausoleum on our way out.

I realized when we stood at its entrance that I had in fact seen Saddam in the old Republican Palace, not this new one. Instead of going in, however, we continued walking south towards the compound of office buildings, one of which was Saddam's official office (since he maintained strict unpredictability in his movements and whereabouts, it is unlikely Saddam really had an office as such). The path led out onto a sort of towpath running along the edge of the river and then along a private canal. After the noise of the army camp, it was peaceful by the water, with just the ripples and wind in the trees to be heard. Near the boat slip and dock that led up to Saddam's office, a large satin Iraqi flag had been spread over a dead body that lay across the path. Only a hand was visible. It clutched for something, and was in bad need of a manicure. Americans, presumably, had covered the body with the flag — although any there whom I asked denied all knowledge of it. If fleeing Iraqis had covered it, why did they use this satin flag and not an ordinary one, or indeed any suitable piece of fabric? Was this someone important?

I went to peel back the flag and see who was under it, but the others prevented me: it would violate ethical codes. Not my ethical codes, but somebody's. There is no greater argument, I have always felt, for the existence of the human soul than the sight of a human corpse. Not for a moment do you think anyone is in there. Something profound yet indefinable is missing. It is like looking at a discarded overcoat. The Resurrection of the Body is not something we are going to want to be true.

The offices were either poorly constructed or else they had been attacked with particular severity, because the compound was now just piles of rubble in places — though Saddam's office itself was intact. A calendar on the wall showed that he would probably miss a couple of appointments over the next few days. Besides this, however, the year was, somewhat presciently, remarkably free. I took that calendar too.

To the north of the new Presidential Palace was a smaller palace used by Saddam's son, Uday. Returning along the towpath, we decided to see if we could enter it. From the rear, it looked like little more than a block of modern townhouses — a series of balconies, with big sliding windows behind them and staircases down to the walled garden. There was a gate at the northern end of the wall that led into the palace garden by a three-storey tower. This, we learned, had been Uday's shag-pad, the place he called his "Tower of Babylon" and to which he brought some of those hapless girls he had ordered to be seized on the streets of Baghdad after taking a fancy to them while driving by.

"Is that a kangaroo down there?" I pointed to the stuffed animal lying on its side in the garden.

"Nah," said Peter, knowledgeably. "Issa wallaby that is."

The French windows all around had been shattered by bomb blasts, so getting inside was not a problem.

"Jeez," said Peter, "this guy hid the taste of a Filipino whore — look it this shit!"

Looking around, I wondered whether bad taste was an hereditary trait. Saddam's penchant for Op-Art ties and white disco suits with bell-bottoms was legendary, but I have to admit that it was eclipsed totally by Uday's idea of cool. He is the only powerful person about whom I have *never* heard anyone say a single good thing. Not one — and there is *always* something. Perhaps his mother knows something good, but Saddam — who, I still believe, ordered Uday's execution — clearly disliked his oldest son as much as everyone else did. He had been demoted as heir-apparent in favour of the less flamboyant Qusay. This was after the 1996 assassination attempt on Uday that apparently blew off his testicles and left him with a limp — an assassination attempt that many believe Saddam himself ordered. I certainly had nothing to do with it, although I was in Baghdad at the time. In a letter found in the palace, Uday had this to say:

> My father wants to go down in history. There is nothing in my heart towards my father, not any love or kindness.

The feeling was unquestionably mutual. Saddam had previously thrown Uday in prison for killing a bodyguard who was also an old and close relative of Saddam's. It was a vitriolic relationship at the best of times, but over the past seven years or so it had gone steadily downhill. It was also the only relationship we know of in which Saddam is not the protagonist. One even feels sorry for him.

There were stuffed animals and animal heads everywhere. Uday loved animals, or rather loved killing them. I stole a fine antelope's head. His favourite hues appeared to be a particularly acidic turquoise and an especially florid pink, which were nowhere more in evidence than in the third-floor bedroom. With its mirrored bed, plastic flowers and panoramic water views, it was such a disco anachronism that you expected Austin Powers to come walking out of the closet. *Shagadelic, baby!*

Over in the main building, which had taken a direct hit by something big, soldiers were picking through rubble in one area looking for guns. It had apparently been the armoury, and there were weapons everywhere, all manner of weapons, from inscribed ceremonial swords and jewelled crossbows to gold-plated semi-automatic Kalashnikovs.

"Damn!" said the soldier looting alongside me, as he threw away an empty pistol case. "Fucken officers got here first: all the good handguns 're gone now. Shee-it!"

This did seem to be the case. Open and empty gun boxes were everywhere. So was live ammunition — thousands of rounds scattered in the crevices between clumps of concrete. I took a Kalashnikov and a superb English shotgun with gold filigree work on the stock. I do not like guns but I do appreciate fine machinery, and guns always involve beautifully hand-milled machine parts, precision tool-and-die stuff that functions with the dull metallic click of perfection.

In the lower rear of the palace, we stumbled across Uday's wardrobe room, where racks of custom-made clothing stood intact, just waiting for us.

"Christ," said Hackett. "This wee thing just has *party* written all over it, don't it now?"

He held up a collarless, puff-sleeved grey linen jacket emblazoned with large hearts and skulls in black and pink.

"I prefer something less conservative myself," said Sherwell, holding up a white silk jacket, around the collar and on the pockets and cuffs of which were sewn dozens of plastic flowers — the same kind that were in vases all over the palace.

"Man, that's bad!"

"Not as bad as this!"

Hackett held a garment that defied description. It was something like a floor-length kimono, the lower parts of which were padded tubes of fabric extending from armpit to ground, as if they were extensions of the sleeves. Every imaginable colour and shade seemed to be featured, in patterned and plain material, but the predominant ones were pink and turquoise. A feather boa had also been sewn into the collar and cuffs.

"That *must* be a chick's outfit ..."

"One way to find out ..."

I put it on. Uday was my girth, a big bastard, but about a foot taller than me. Besides its length, the garment fit me perfectly.

"There you have it: Uday was Mister Dressup ..."

"Look at the labels! *Christian Dior ... Dolce & Gabbano ... Yves Saint-Laurent* ... It's all designer stuff!"

"Original couturier designs? This stuff would be worth a fortune."

"I can't see Christian Dior making something like this, can you?"

"They see a rich idiot coming ... Yeah, sure they'd make it — as long as he paid."

"Wait a minute! Look at these pants — the label says *Dior* but the waistband says *Yves Saint Laurent!*"

"No, it doesn't! It says 'Yves *Sanit* Laurent'!"

"He's right! My God, they're all fakes, knock-offs!"

"That doesn't make sense ... Uday was worth billions. He didn't have to buy knock-offs in Hong Kong ... He could afford the real thing ..."

"Ye cannae argue wi' that label, though ..."

I later found that, among his many enterprises, Uday had a company that made French designer knock-offs for the Hong Kong market. Not all the stuff in the wardrobe was fake, however. I took a cashmere and wool suit by Lanvin that was unmistakably genuine. Not all the suits — and there were hundreds of them — came with trousers, either: when taken from the hanger, what had looked like pants proved to be a floor-length skirt in the same fabric as the jacket.

"Every ten years some berk tries to float a skirt for guys, doesn't he? I guess this last time he made a convert of old Uday ..."

"Or maybe when his balls were blown off he found skirts more comfortable?"

"Ouch!"

"This is a nice suit ..."

"Oh, I prefer the white linen and black plastic snakeskin look myself ..."

"This is gorgeous!"

I promised I would make it clear that Hackett and Sherwell took nothing, because the *Telegraph* would not like to hear otherwise — presumably, it only had room for one thief. So I confess that it was me: I did it, I took it all. The owner would not be coming back for it, would he? Why leave it for the army? But there was so much stuff — decisions, decisions! — that I had to find a huge plastic hamper in which to carry it all. Once I had crammed my loot inside, however, I could not lift the thing.

"Can you give me a hand," I said to two marines, half expecting to be busted for taking it.

"Sure thing, Bub ..."

They took the hamper from me and carried it to the drive in front of the palace, while the Thief of Baghdad continued his spree. I learned from Captain Cary Adams of the Marines, that, earlier in the day, U.S. Special Forces had found videotapes of Uday beating girls and tearing off their clothes. Another journalist had found over a kilo of heroin in ziplock bags in the palace.

In a sort of home office where Uday had his computer, we found more telltale evidence: printouts from Internet escort services, printouts regarding self-diagnosis for HIV-AIDS, printouts regarding early signs of liver cirrhosis. In a drawer, we found a large manila envelope emblazoned with the Iraqi eagle, the government crest. "Highly confidential," it said in Arabic. "Hand deliver only. For His Excellency Uday Saddam Hussein, may God save him."

Inside were dozens of colour negative filmstrips that showed Uday partying with lots of girls. In one picture, he was plying a girl with the huge cigar he smoked in a holder. I had been told that Saddam received from Cuba specially made cigars that had marijuana mixed with the tobacco — I do not know if this is true or not. In another picture, Uday shared a *narghile* water pipe with a different girl. In one, Uday fired a Kalashnikov from the balcony

— which probably means it was his birthday. In several pictures, he kissed various different girls.

Being a powerful little shit with no balls, Uday liked to demonstrate his omnipotence by forcing people to marry. Aware that the girls he had — and his weakness was for virgins — would no longer be able to find husbands, he married them off to the men around him, then endlessly baited the men with the fact that he had deflowered their wives for them. He was an unbelievable asshole. Later, I met a musician Uday had regularly hired to play at his parties. Although he did not tell me so himself, the man was married to one of Uday's girls. Before they played, he said, Uday would make each musician drink an entire bottle of ouzo, both so they found it hard to play — he was known to kill musicians for playing a wrong note — and so they did not remember much the next day. What had he thought at the time about what had to be one of the world's worst jobs?

"Hey, listen," he said, "it was about the only gig in Baghdad. I was glad of the work."

He had escaped to Jordan, but still lived in terror of Uday, and would not believe he had been killed. Even when the body was supposedly found, he still believed Uday was alive somewhere, waiting to take his revenge on those who betrayed him.

"In dreams," the musician said, "I see him. He comes running at me through windows, up walls. I try to escape but it is like swimming in honey. I see him behind me, then when I turn back his face is an inch from mine. You don't kill someone like Uday easily ..."

There are hundreds like him, scarred for life, eternally polluted from their contact with Uday. No amount of therapy removes this kind of contagion, which is like a rot in the soul. No story better sums up Uday than the one I heard in 1996:

Driving through the city, Uday passes a wedding group standing on the steps of a mosque for the photographer. He takes a fancy to the bride, and sends his bodyguard over to fetch her. It was like that in Baghdad: everyone knew that if Uday summoned you, you went, no questions asked. It was why people kept their wives and daughters at home until they were too fat to worry about. The bride went with Uday to his penthouse suite at the

Al-Rashid Hotel, on the 27th floor. After he had done with her, she put her wedding dress back on, walked out to the balcony, and threw herself off. I had asked my government minder, who had been very open with me about Uday, if she could confirm this story. *Yes*, she said sadly, *It was my cousin ...*

Beyond the faux-Babylonian gates in the palace grounds, we found Uday's pet lions — a male and two females. They had been very hungry and somewhat edgy when the army first arrived, but after a few dead donkeys had been thrown into their cage, they relaxed. Predictably, the soldiers had renamed them Simba and Nalas i & ii. A note on the cage said that anyone caught bothering these lions would be their next meal.

Mistaking their sphinx-like serenity for Disney docility, a female soldier put her hand through the cage to pat one of them while I was watching. She was lucky to be able to remove the hand in time. The male spun in a roaring blur and bit the wire fencing so hard it actually came away in his mouth.

Like a glum child with a broken toy on Christmas morning, the soldier walked away appalled, disillusioned for life with nature, just as she is no doubt disillusioned now with her life in Iraq. "Sonafabitch," she kept saying. "Sonafabitch!"

The Presidential palace was something of a letdown after Uday's treasure trove: the U.S. army had already picked the place clean of loot. A lot of soldiers were already smoking Saddam's Montechristo A's when we walked through the camp.

The most striking thing for a place that had taken a direct hit by a Tomahawk cruise missile was how structurally sound the building still looked. The missile had been dropped in through the dome like a dart, and it exploded inside. While the usual ribbons of steel, the wires and the dangling blocks of concrete hung down through the four floors, most of the dome itself and the outer walls had barely a crack in them. The army's high command had moved in immediately too, so the place had been swept, the rubble piled in corners, cables laid up the staircases, notices posted on the walls. The sole room of any interest was the one that seemed oddly familiar. It was the meeting room where we had most often seen Saddam in his pre-war appearances: the long table, the Gothic chairs. Everything still looked immaculate. On closer inspection, the glass in its windows proved to be over six inches thick.

"And lookee here," said Captain Cary Adams. "This one took a direct hit from an armour-piercing shell designed to penetrate ten inches of steel, and the *bastard's still intact!*"

The dent had formed a great blurred spider web, but there were no signs of a crack. A person deciding to weather out the storm in this room would have been unharmed — even though the building had taken a Tomahawk missile and the room itself sustained a direct hit by a depleted-uranium armour-piercing shell. You had to admire the artisanship and design. As an emblem of this, a model of Saddam's palace had been in a glass case directly beneath the dome through which the missile had come.

"It were the only thing left intact," said Captain Adams. "Glass case, the lot!"

"This is all turning into legend before our eyes," said Sherwell.

Back at Sadoun Street, Terry was on guard, so there was no problem in driving our truck past the razor-wire barrier — which was just as well, considering all the loot I had to carry. On my third trip back to the vehicle for more loot, a voice behind me said:

"*Robert*, I wait for you!"

The general. Shit! He must have been there for three hours — and, I came to learn, he was not someone you normally kept waiting even for five minutes. But this was not normally. I told him I had simply forgotten.

"What you carry here?" He looked at the shotgun wrapped in an overcoat under my arm.

"Just looted Uday's palace. Here, you want this shotgun?"

"No, no," he stepped back, looking around nervously. "Yes, but I take it later, all right?"

"Any word from ... um," I lowered my voice, "*Aziz?*"

"Yes, I tell you in car."

"We go there now?"

"Not now," he said. "You tell me you come my house for dinner?"

"I will. I can't wait."

"You come now?"

"It's only two o'clock ... How early do you eat dinner?"

He looked pissed off.

"I come for you at six, yes?"

"Much better ..."

"*Robert*," he said. "You don't be late for me ..."

"I promise. I've got you a present too. You will love it ..."

"At six I am here then?"

"Right."

He left.

Finally back in my room, I showered off the soot and dirt and, no doubt, radiation from all the armour-piercing shells hurled at the palaces. Then I took inventory:

- One signed first edition of Ba'ath Party Manifesto
- One piece of stained glass from Aflaq's tomb
- One handwritten letter signed "Aflaq"
- One ink blotter from Michel Aflaq's desk
- One tattered calendar from Saddam's office
- One stuffed gazelle's head from Uday's shag-pad
- One gold-plated toilet brush from shag-pad
- One gold coat hook from same
- One semi-automatic Kalashnikov from Uday's armoury
- One English shotgun with gold filigree on stock
- One flare pistol
- One crystal wine glass engraved with Iraqi crest
- One strip of film of Uday's party
- One silver- and gold-plated Babylonian lion
- Six jackets from Uday's wardrobe
- Four shirts from same
- Two suits from same
- One kimono party thing from same
- One Ba'athrobe from same
- One floor-length black velvet overcoat with fur collar from same
- One leather belt from same
- One portrait in pastel of Uday

- Five 9-mm bullets from Uday's palace
- Five Cohiba Corona cigars from same
- One photograph signed "Saddam Hussein" from same
- Three videocassettes from same
- Four CD-ROMs from same
- One Iraqi flag in silk from same

Not bad for a day's work!

"Ah, shit!" said Hackett. "Luke at all this stuff! What *are* you gonna do with it?"

"Charity auction?"

"Gude idea! Uday Fashion Show!"

"Proceeds to help Iraq's children, or something?"

"You're nae gonna try takin' those guns back?"

"Why not? Nah, '*course not* ... I have enough trouble with my *usual* luggage."

We paraded around in various outfits like catwalk models. I think we all needed this light-hearted playtime and banter after days that would otherwise have been filled solely with tragedies and disasters.

Peter, who had been punishing the Scotch, was now walking around with a Kalashnikov shooting MPEG video of himself to e-mail home.

"I'm one teff mother-ficker," he was telling the camera, waving the gun at it. "You den't wanter fick with this sin-of-a-betch ... One teff mother-ficker, yeh! I fickin' am, I fickin' am, mate!"

... with how like, how infinite
a lightness, man and shadow meet.
They fuse. A shadow is a man
when the mosquito death approaches.

— KEITH DOUGLAS [109]

CHAPTER NINE

OIL

It has nothing to do with oil, literally nothing to do with oil.
— DEFENSE SECRETARY DONALD RUMSFELD [110]

OIL, PART ONE

Since so little is ever said by the Bush II administration about oil, we need to be clear about the extent to which it is linked on every level to the oil and gas industry — the world's biggest business. The Bush family's connections to Texas oil culture need no elaboration. Vice President Dick Cheney, a Bush family friend, took office with a multi-million dollar retirement package in hand from his spell as CEO of Halliburton Oil, and once in office began to develop an energy policy chiefly under the guidance of a group of oil company executives whose names he attempted to hide from public scrutiny. National Security Advisor Condoleeza Rice was so deeply involved in the oil business that she once had an oil tanker named after her. Other representatives of Big Oil with key roles in the administration at one time or another include Thomas White, secretary of the army, who was a vice president of Enron, and Don Evans, secretary of commerce, who was president of Tom Brown, Inc., the oil exploration company, in which his shares were worth $13 million when he took office.

Ever-increasing consumption of oil — ideally cheap oil — is the fundamental theme of the Bush II administration's energy policy. It projects a thirty-three percent increase in U.S. oil consumption over the next twenty years. Although the White House has been busily encouraging greater domestic drilling and the opening up of places like the Arctic National Wildlife Refuge to the oil industry, it has also acknowledged that domestic oil production will fall by twelve percent over the next two decades.[iii] The result, therefore, is that American dependence on imported oil is set to climb to nearly seventy percent — from just over thirty percent in 1985, and the current fifty percent — by 2020.

Over the past thirty years, the U.S. has tried to seek alternatives to OPEC and Middle East oil supplies, and the current administration advocates increased production in places like West Africa, the Caspian, Venezuela, Mexico and Canada. Yet it is impossible to deny that the Persian Gulf region remains the world's principal supplier, or as the 2001 National Energy Policy Development Group report puts it, "Middle East oil producers will remain central to world oil security." The region currently accounts for about thirty percent of the world's oil production and over forty percent of its oil exports, and with sixty-five percent of its known reserves, it is still the only area that will be able to cope with the dramatic increase in world oil demand that the Bush administration predicts. According to the NEDPG report, Persian Gulf producers alone will be supplying between fifty-four and sixty-seven percent of world oil exports by 2020.

Saudi Arabia, the single largest producer, has always been the key player here, with a quarter of the world's total proven reserves. As they had done during and after the Gulf War, the Saudis were expected to raise production to compensate for disruption of Iraqi supplies and keep the markets calm. Unexpectedly, however, they have been keeping prices artificially high instead, with oil topping $40 a barrel in the spring of 2004 for the first time in more than a decade. The widening rift between the House of Sa'ud and the Ranch of Bush, which began in the wake of September 11 — after all, fifteen of the nineteen attackers were Saudis — was exacerbated by Washington's failure to help the Palestinians by pursuing the so-called "road map" plan for peace with Israel. The first Bush was persuaded by his Saudi friends to leave Saddam in power. Bush II has replaced Saddam with America: the Saudi princes can read the writing on their own wall.

We are accustomed to thinking of the Saudi fields, with 262 billion barrels in proven reserves, as the world's richest, and of Iraq, with 112 billion barrels, as a distant second. There is, however, reason to suspect that this situation may have changed. The Energy Information Administration of the U.S. Department of Energy, for instance, speculates that additional "probable and possible" resources in Iraq could raise its reserves to 220 billion barrels. Furthermore, because war, sanctions and politics have made complete exploration of Iraqi territories impossible, it is thought likely that as much as another hundred billion barrels lie under the western desert waiting to be found.

This would not just give Iraq the world's largest reserves: it would mean, because Iraqi oil is much cheaper and thus more profitable to produce, that Iraqi oil producers stand, in the long term, to dominate the industry. With the cooling of Saudi-U.S. relations — a distancing that can only increase — many in Washington have felt that regime change in Baghdad was a strategic necessity, in order to both develop and control the only alternative to Saudi oil. The sanctions imposed since Bush I were specifically designed to prevent any rehabilitation or expansion of the Iraqi oil fields, which were seriously affected by the 1980–88 war with Iran. Until their contract was cancelled in December 2003 because of an over-charging scandal, this job was given to Dick Cheney's old employer, Halliburton, and it was not merely lucrative: it also gave the oil giant a chance to explore and fully assess Iraq's potential reserves, placing it in a position of great advantage in the future of Iraqi oil production.

Analysts like Fadhil Chalabi, a former Iraqi oil official, claim that Iraq will be able to produce perhaps as much as twelve million barrels per day within a decade.[112] The impact of this on world markets will be immense, depriving Saudi Arabia of the ability to influence prices single-handedly. It will, in effect, hand Washington the capability of flooding world markets and driving down prices. This may well cause the OPEC alliance to unravel, as individual members engage in price wars against each other. It will definitely limit the influence over oil markets possessed by other suppliers such as Russia,

Venezuela and Mexico. The resulting lower prices — essential to the U.S. economy, remember — might also mean that Russian oil, which is expensive to produce, prices itself out of the market altogether, dimming the prospects for foreign investment to help exploit Siberian oil deposits. The feeble Russian economy is highly dependent on revenues from oil exports, and its federal budget is hinged around prices of $24–25 per barrel. Thus, as Aleksei Arbatov, deputy chairman of the Russian parliament's defence committee, has observed, "if a new Iraqi regime sells oil without limits, our budget will collapse."[113]

Until the OPEC revolution of the early 1970s, a handful of companies, often called "the seven sisters" or "the majors," controlled the exploration, production, refining and sales of the world's oil. Today, state-owned companies control most of the resources. Although the private companies still perform much of the actual work, their access to oil is regulated by prices and conditions established by host countries. While the private oil companies have managed to make a virtue of this necessity, adjusting to the situation by opening up new fields elsewhere, it has never been a secret that they yearn for a directly owned concession in the Middle East, both for the dramatically increased profits and for the flexibility it would provide them.

The chief private companies — known as "super-majors" since they are the result of recent huge mergers — are ExxonMobil and ChevronTexaco of the U.S., Royal Dutch Shell and BP of Britain and the Netherlands and TotalFinaElf of France. Together, they sell around 29 million barrels per day, only 35 percent of which comes from fields they own themselves. In spite of the billions they have poured into exploration and development of fields outside the Middle East, the proven reserves of the super-majors stood at a mere 44 billion barrels in 2001, or just four percent of the world's total, and, more to the point, only enough at current rates to keep producing oil for another twelve years. The other, smaller companies were in a similar situation when they assessed themselves in 2001. Thus it would have been apparent to anyone in the oil business that the Middle East in general, and Iraq in particular, was pivotal to the future of the whole industry.

Indeed, you could say that to be in the oil business at the turn of the millennium *is* to crave a way into Iraq. It is evident that Saddam had already signalled that Iraq was prepared to concede more favourable terms to foreign companies willing to invest in Iraqi oil production. He was willing to grant potential profits that were comparable to those of ownership, along with guarantees of tenure. Several European and Asian companies had signed deals with Baghdad giving them access to reserves of at least fifty billion barrels, with a potential output of four to five million barrels per day. Another estimate states that Russian companies alone had signed deals that involved some seventy billion barrels. A number of contracts had also been signed for exploratory work in the western desert.

Before the war, Russian, Chinese and French companies were poised to do the work now being performed, without any bidding process whatsoever, by American and British outfits. For example, Russia's Lukoil signed a deal in 1997 to refurbish and develop the West Qurna field, which has some fifteen billion barrels of oil reserves. The National Petroleum Corporation of China signed a similar deal for North Rumailah field, and France's TotalFinaElf was set to work on the vast Majnoon fields, with some twenty to thirty billion barrels.

It is no coincidence that France, China and Russia are permanent members of the U.N.'s Security Council. Saddam had tried using the lure of oil concessions to build political support for the end to sanctions, but opposition to this from Britain and the U.S. was tenacious and the ploy did not work. In December 2002, Iraq even cancelled contracts with three Russian companies because they refused to commence exploration work while sanctions were still in place. Even so, there is no doubt that U.S. and British companies would have been excluded from Iraq as long as Saddam remained in power.

For the first time in thirty years, American and British oil companies now have direct access to Iraqi oil. It is a bonanza worth hundreds of billions of dollars. Billions, not millions.

Before the passage of Security Council Resolution 1441 on November 8, 2002, Washington barely bothered to hide its threats to cut Chinese, Russian and French companies out of any future Iraqi oil concessions unless their governments supported the U.S. policy of regime change. The Bush administration's Iraqi tyrant-in-waiting, Ahmad Chalabi, leader of the Iraqi National Congress — which has since confessed to feeding the media and governments false information about Saddam's regime — had also provocatively announced that the INC would not feel bound by any contracts signed by Saddam's government and that "American companies will have a big shot at Iraqi oil" under a new regime. British and American oil company executives had been jockeying to secure future stakes in Iraqi oil in meetings with INC officials, and the State Department, meanwhile, had been encouraging Iraqi opposition members to create an oil and natural gas working group that involved both Iraqis and Americans.

There is no question that French, Russian and Chinese fears of losing access to Iraqi oil were behind their attempts to restrain U.S. belligerence, and rival oil interests were a key behind-the-scenes factor when the U.N. Security Council's permanent members argued over the wording of 1441, the resolution intended to set the conditions for any action against Iraq. Backroom understandings regarding the future of Iraqi oil probably played a major role in the political dance leading up to the resolution's unanimous adoption, so we are unlikely to see China, Russia or even France totally locked out of Iraq's oilfields. They are also unlikely to be thrown much more than unwanted scraps from the groaning board of the Anglo-American feast.

American policy in the Middle East has long depended upon building up proxy forces in the region and lavishly supplying them with arms. Iran, Iraq, Saudi Arabia and Israel have all played the role of surrogate at one time or another. But the Gulf War paved the way for direct intervention, by pre-positioning military equipment and gaining access to bases in Saudi Arabia, Kuwait, Bahrain and Qatar.

Access to oil in the Persian Gulf and outlying regions is now secured by an extensive U.S. military presence, running from Pakistan to Central Asia to the Caucasus and from the eastern Mediterranean to the Horn of Africa. Many bases have recently been added to this dense network of military facilities under the aegis of the so-called War on Terror. The presence of the U.S. military is not exclusively about oil, true, but oil is the main reason for it. In 1999 the then head of the U.S. Central Command, General Anthony C. Zinni, testified to the Senate Armed Services Committee that the Persian Gulf region was of "vital interest" to America, which "must have free access to the region's resources."

Why then is the Bush administration so coy when it comes to admitting that oil is one of the main reasons they waged war on Iraq? "It has nothing to do with oil," said Defense Secretary Donald Rumsfeld, "literally nothing to do with oil."

I beg to differ.

OIL, PART TWO

Speaking to the House of Commons, British prime minister Tony Blair was equally evasive: "Let me deal with the conspiracy theory idea that this is somehow to do with oil. There is no way whatever if oil were the issue that it would not be infinitely simpler to cut a deal with Saddam ..."[114]

We heard nothing about oil in Bush II's State of the Union Address, nor in Colin Powell's address to the United Nations Security Council. All we heard were endless repetitions of the big Bush lies: Iraq's illegal weapons programs, its attempts to hide those weapons from inspectors, and its links to terrorist groups.

We do not have honest leaders. Oil has been one of the most dominant U.S. concerns vis-à-vis Iraq in internal and unpublicized documents since the start of the Bush II administration, and indeed much earlier still. As Michael Renner wrote before the invasion began, "Washington's war on Iraq is the lynchpin to controlling Persian Gulf oil."[115]

The need to control Iraq's oil is also inextricably linked to the defence of the U.S. dollar. The dollar's strength is supported by OPEC's requirement — arranged through a secret agreement between the U.S. and Saudi Arabia back in the 1970s — that all OPEC oil sales be in U.S. dollars. However, this requirement was recently threatened by some OPEC countries, which expressed an interest in allowing sales to be paid in euros. This began in the autumn of 2000 when Saddam Hussein's government, supposedly as a protest against U.S. Middle Eastern policy, asked the United Nations for permission to be paid for its oil in euros. The permission, which was only needed because Iraq was then selling oil under a U.N.-supervised sanctions regime, was granted. Other countries, of course, did not need such permission, and Iran soon raised the possibility of following suit. Venezuela hinted it would follow and North Korea — not of course an oil producer — also stated an intention to conduct sales of exports in euros. All of this pointed to a potential change in the OPEC oil-pricing policy.

Pricing oil in euros rather than dollars might easily create a tremendous flight from the dollar, conceivably far more calamitous than the one that led to the collapse of the gold–dollar connection in 1973 or the one that prompted a plummet of the dollar in 1979–80. Like any other currency, the U.S. dollar is susceptible to the swift, anxious currency trades of the newly computerized world of global finance. However, it also has a unique vulnerability all its own. Because it is the dominant global currency, a large proportion of all U.S. currency — perhaps more than fifty percent — is held overseas by non-Americans. The U.S. gains a tremendous amount of financial power from this desire of foreigners to hold dollars, but this also makes it open to a much faster collapse if holders decide to dump their dollars. In such an event, the U.S. economy would suffer enormous damage.

Russia has also expressed intermittent interest in tying its economy closer to the euro, an eventuality only imaginable if there is a drastic deterioration in U.S.-Russian relations. If, however, the Persian Gulf oil exporters were to switch their pricing policy from dollars to euros in concert with Russia, a lethal multi-sided confrontation could easily develop. The extreme unilateralist tendencies of the Bush II government, combined with the Iraq war and the dire situation between Israel and the Palestinians, have brought out critical differences between the United States and the European Union, alienating France and Germany and contributing to the election of a socialist government in Spain. Relations with Russia and China, much improved since the end of the Cold War, have been strained once more. It is a dangerous confluence of events.

As far back as April 1997, a report from the James A. Baker Institute of Public Policy at Rice University was devoted to the issue of "energy security" for the United States. Specifying "the threat of Iraq and Iran" to the "free flow of oil from the Middle East," it concluded that Saddam Hussein still threatened Middle Eastern security and still had sufficient military capability to extend his reach beyond Iraq's borders. The Bush administration took up this theme as soon as it assumed power in 2001, by following suggestions laid out in a second report from the same institute, this one jointly sponsored by the Council on Foreign Relations in New York, yet another group long concerned with U.S. access to foreign oil resources, and signed by both Democrats and Republicans, which suggests that it represented a bipartisan consensus of ideas from energy experts of both parties.

Entitled *Strategic Energy Policy Challenges for the 21st Century*, the second report concluded: "The United States remains a prisoner of its energy dilemma. Iraq remains a de-stabilizing influence to ... the flow of oil to international markets from the Middle East. Saddam Hussein has also demonstrated a willingness to threaten to use the oil weapon and to use his own export program to manipulate oil markets. Therefore the U.S. should conduct an immediate policy review toward Iraq including military, energy, economic and political/diplomatic assessments."

The report was widely read by members of Vice President Cheney's own Energy Task Force, and when Cheney's own national energy plan emerged, it too declared that "the [Persian] Gulf will be a primary focus of U.S. international energy policy." It agreed that the United States was increasingly dependent on imported oil and that it might be necessary to tackle foreign resistance in order to gain access to new supplies. Anthony H. Cordesman, senior analyst at Washington's Center for Strategic and International Studies, later put it more bluntly: "Regardless of whether we say so publicly, we will go to war, because Saddam sits at the center of a region with more than sixty percent of all the world's oil reserves."

Behind this concern about the "free flow" of Persian Gulf oil lie other motives. In keeping with the recommendations of the Baker Institute reports, the Bush II administration wishes to increase international investment in the under-developed Iraq oilfields. This may well, of course, turn out to mean uniquely U.S. investment. On January 16, 2003, two months before the invasion began, the *Wall Street Journal* reported that officials from the White House, State Department and Department of Defense had been meeting informally with executives from Halliburton, Schlumberger, ExxonMobil, ChevronTexaco and ConocoPhillips to plan the post-war expansion of oil production from Iraq. (Before their nationalization, it should be pointed out, Iraq's oilfields were largely "owned" by U.S. companies.) The *Journal* story was subsequently denied by administration officials; yet, as the British *Guardian* newspaper observed on January 27, 2003, "it stretches credulity somewhat to imagine that the subject has never been broached."

The U.S. also wishes to continue exerting political dominance over all the oil-producing countries of the region. Secretary of State Colin Powell laid out U.S. intentions quite clearly when he told the Senate Foreign Relations Committee on February 6, 2003, that success in the Iraq war "could fundamentally reshape that region in a powerful, positive way that will enhance U.S. interests." Conceding, as it now does, that it will be necessary to keep U.S. troops in occupied Iraq for the foreseeable future, the U.S. is driving home the message to Iran and Saudi Arabia — both once secure bases for U.S. troops — that America is once more the regional Mister Big, walking very heavily and carrying a massive stick.

The dominance of Middle Eastern oil will entail maintaining dollar hegemony over the world oil economy. Henry Liu puts it unforgettably:

> World trade is now a game in which the U.S. produces dollars and the rest of the world produces things that dollars can buy. The world's interlinked economies no longer trade to capture a comparative advantage; they compete in exports to capture needed dollars to service dollar-denominated foreign debts and to accumulate dollar reserves to sustain the exchange value of their domestic currencies. To prevent speculative and manipulative attacks on their currencies, the world's central banks must acquire and hold dollar reserves in corresponding amounts to their currencies in circulation. The higher the market pressure to devalue a particular currency, the more dollar reserves its central bank must hold. This creates a built-in support for a strong dollar that in turn forces the world's central banks to acquire and hold more dollar reserves, making it yet stronger. This phenomenon is known as dollar hegemony, which is created by the geopolitically constructed peculiarity that critical commodities, most notably oil, are denominated in dollars. Everyone accepts dollars because dollars can buy oil. The recycling of petro-dollars is the price the U.S. has extracted from oil-producing countries for U.S. tolerance of the oil-exporting cartel since 1973.
>
> By definition, dollar reserves must be invested in U.S. assets, creating a capital-accounts surplus for the U.S. economy. Even after a year of sharp correction, U.S. stock valuation is still at a 25-year high and trading at a 56 percent premium compared with emerging markets.[116]

Yet even back in 2002, central bankers around the world did not expect either the U.S. dollar or the U.S. stock markets to sustain these levels. As William Greider pointed out, the "U.S. economy's net foreign indebtedness ... will reach nearly 25 percent of U.S. GDP this year, or roughly $2.5 trillion. Fifteen years ago, it was zero ... If the deficits persist around the current level of $400 billion a year or grow larger, the total U.S. indebtedness should reach $3.5 trillion in three years or so. Within a decade, it would total 50 percent of GDP."[117] Thanks to the so-called War on Terror and Iraq, it will get there sooner than that.

Japan's unresolved deflationary crisis also poses a major potential threat to the overpriced dollar. As analysts like Lawrence A. Joyce have commented, the dollar would take a major beating if the Japanese government were suddenly required to fulfill its legal obligations to bail out failed Japanese banks, which is quite possible.

Washington is well aware of these problems, but believes that overwhelming military strength and the will to use it will bully other countries into supporting the dollar at its artificial level. Professor Thomas Barnett of the U.S. Naval War College put it this way: "We trade little pieces of paper (our currency, in the form of a trade deficit) for Asia's amazing array of products and services. We are smart enough to know this is a patently unfair deal unless we offer something of great value along with those little pieces of paper. That product is a strong U.S. Pacific Fleet, which squares the transaction nicely."[118]

With friendly countries like Japan, whose defence costs have been lowered by the U.S. presence in Asia, there is some merit to the argument. However, the world's Islamic countries are probably not so able to appreciate the "great value" of a menacing U.S. presence. Indeed, the risk is that they will follow the example of Malaysian prime minister Mahathir Mohamad and look to the Islamic gold dinar as a means to weaken dollar hegemony in world markets. Malaysia is a small player, but it is also a partly Islamic country; if the Islamic nations in OPEC forced their allies to cease OPEC oil sales in dollars, the dollar would be in serious trouble.

If we accept these extenuating factors of oil and economy, it must be conceded that the Bush gang did not assault and batter Iraq on a whim. They have serious problems from the petro-dollar pressure drop, and Iraq appeared to be their only hope of a solution. The issue is entirely unconnected to "terrorism," which is not an especially big problem, though one now guaranteed to worsen. One thing is certain, though: the U.S. cannot and will not relinquish the Iraqi oilfields, even if it means taking on the entire Islamic world in the process. It will be dressed in some fancy talk, you can be sure, but if you realize that a renegade sector of American society is fighting for its very survival now, it is easier to understand the shamelessness of its actions and the miasma of lies cloaking its every move. The tragedy is that more decent Americans have not protested the atavistic notion that it is acceptable to rain down missiles and bombs upon the civilians of another country, who have played no part whatsoever in a crisis wholly of America's own making.

There are of course those who continue to investigate ways in which the oil and financial weaknesses of the U.S. can be lessened without wiping all of us off the planet, but their voices grow ever fainter as the war machine takes control of the state. As dire as these problems are, proposals have still been put forward for dealing with them in a civilized and multilateral manner. Just before the war, Ralph Nader wrote: "The demand is simple: Stop this war before it starts and immediately establish a sane national energy security strategy."[119] Indeed, a key component of such a strategy — the restriction of demand — can even be found in the less megalomaniacal sections of the Baker Institute reports. Naturally, these were the parts that Bush II and his grey neo-con eminences chose to ignore.

Yet no one pretends that a viable energy policy for the U.S. can be created without a major change in attitude towards the rest of the world, since it cannot be achieved without global cooperation. Regarding the dollar's more arcane problems, the economist and futurist Hazel Henderson has written that "a more balanced world order must center on reforming global finance, taxing currency exchange and reducing the dollar's unsustainable role as the world's de facto reserve currency (which is destructive for all countries — even the U.S. itself). I favor a global reserve currency regime based on the parity of the U.S. dollar and the euro. The fundamentals in the U.S. and the EU suggest that the G-8 has an opportunity to peg the dollar and the euro into a trading band. This ... would lead to more stable currency markets."[120]

The "free" market is a myth promoted only by those who can benefit from it, while they are able to benefit from it. In reality, every market is and needs to be regulated or else it will tear itself apart. For capitalism to continue, it must recognize its limitations. Like religions, all economic systems contain elements of truth, but none of them is THE truth.

It would seem to be clear that the only route to dealing with America's dilemma is a multilateral approach. The United States may be able to dominate the planet with its military machine, but economically it is fading, increasingly less competitive and daily deeper in debt. The current administration seems to be sold on the notion of sheltering economic realities beneath military ones, much as the Roman empire did. Rome itself should provide ample evidence of the risks being taken, which is the provoking of economic retribution. If not Rome, then Britain should serve as an example. If anyone in Washington reads about the ignominious British retreat from Suez in 1956, the parallels cannot fail to strike them. The retreat was imposed upon Britain by the United States as a condition for propping up the ailing British pound.

Rather than enhance and enlarge the legacy of good will that America once enjoyed in the world, the Bush II regime has chosen to further unveil the ugly face of America that many suspected was the real truth behind the PR facade. The criminal attack and invasion of Iraq will now abide as an emblem of this greedy and violent reality. That such shoddy, barbaric thinking can prevail over all of the alternatives available ought to give all modern nations pause, just as all Americans should look at their current leaders and wonder if these are the best democracy can provide. No one doubts America's military strength; yet its financial and economic health depends on peaceful cooperation with other nations. These are the realities of the new world order, which forces one to wonder which order Bush the First imagined he was hailing. For his son seems to believe it was a very old order indeed, one abandoned during the waning of the Middle Ages.

CHAPTER TEN

THE CURFEWED HEART

I saw stones take flight
I saw dewdrops become weapons
When they slammed shut the door of my heart
When they threw up barricades
When they imposed a curfew inside me

— MAHMOUD DARWISH (1942–)[121]

The general arrived fifteen seconds early. Fortunately, I was already waiting. He had a six-inch stack of bank notes and a pistol on the tray between the seats — *don't leave home without it*, as his friends all said. A large crowd of Iraqis had gathered in front of the Palestine to protest against the conditions under which they were now obliged to live. What bothered everyone most was the total lack of security. The term "security" had a particular meaning in Baghdad. It meant protection from the poor Shia in Saddam City. With the collapse of the old regime, there was no police force to perform this role. There was no Law — only whatever the occupying forces imposed; and, besides a curfew, the Americans were very vague about this. As a result, anarchy was descending. Having looted the ministries and other government buildings, the Saddam City thieves had turned their attention to the largely abandoned homes of high officials and the Republican Guard. Now, however, they were beginning to swarm into any upscale neighbourhood. There ought to be soldiers stationed at every street corner, people complained.

They also wanted electricity and water services restored, and an end to the chronic gasoline shortage. This was one commodity that Iraqis were not accustomed to going without. Now, few gas stations were open at all and at the ones that were open, you could line up for three hours only to find no gas left. Increasingly, we would see petrol sold in plastic jugs at inflated prices on street corners by ragged, grimy figures who would refill their containers by siphoning from their own beaten-up cars. By the end of the day, they would be reeling drunk from the petrol they had inadvertently consumed. While there was a gas shortage for Iraqis, the Americans were giving away fuel to accredited foreigners at the Baghdad refinery. Many expressed the view that Iraq's oil was not America's to give away.

"These people very angry," said the general, as we drove past the crowd. "They know America comes for the oil, not for them ..."

There are no secrets in Iraq. Accustomed to the restrictions on information imposed by Saddam, the people had their own ways of finding out what really went on. As the U.S. military was learning, Iraqis are an unusually well-informed and educated people. As a result of the highly attuned information networks that had evolved over thirty years, Iraqis were also fully aware of what the invaders were doing. They were aware that the army had largely retreated to bases in the desert, which were being furnished and fitted out for a long stay. They were aware that the oil and interior ministries were the only structures of the old regime not targeted during the bombing. They were aware that security for the oilfields had been an American priority. They were aware of being pawns in the game.

But in spite of the information they had, I think the average Iraqi was still prepared to give the invaders the benefit of the doubt, still prepared to wait and see. It was only when they began to realize their worst fears were true — that this *was* about oil, not about them — that they turned against America. Had adequate security been provided and services restored, this might never have happened. The hearts and minds were waiting to be won over, but no one tried, no one wanted them. No such battle was ever fought. Iraqis felt betrayed, abused. After all they had been through, for their basic needs to be scorned in this way was monstrous. For Iraqis are also implacable and deadly enemies, utterly fearless, and consequently brave as martyrs. Their vast history is a charnel house of furious and bloody battles fought to defend this turf, often against the greatest armies on earth. Even when their ancestors lost these battles, as they frequently did, you could not really say they had lost because, further along the road, another generation had sprung from the blood and dust to continue fighting for the right to be free in the land of their birth.

The shops might not be open yet but I noticed that the sidewalks were beginning to do a brisk trade. Besides food, there was one other commodity that everyone seemed to want: TV satellite dishes. Someone had been busy too. Wherever I looked, homemade dishes were for sale. Crudely constructed from sheet tin, they varied in size and did not seem to be accompanied by any electronic apparatus. According to the general, everyone had the boxes already — it was the dish that gave you away. Under Saddam, satellite dishes, and indeed any device that would allow even one-way communication with the world, were banned. Now nothing was banned. Everything was so unbanned.

The general pulled up at a hectic little strip and got out, telling me to wait. Nearby was a store called THE DUBAI CENTRE FOR TRADING ITALIAN OFFICE FURNITURE. You had Swedish or German office furniture, they weren't interested. Just Italian. The general hopped back in, handing me some bottles of orange soda.

"What do you think goes on in the Dubai Centre there?"

He gave me a perplexed look. "They sell office furniture."

"But only *Italian* office furniture, eh?"

"The Italy make good furniture ..."

"There's something fishy about this ..."

"Feeshy?"

"It smells ..."

I asked him about his arrest, how it had occurred. The Mukharbharat had just come for him one evening and taken him away. Why? Earlier on he had refused to let two other secret policemen into his garden so they could enter the house next door. The owner of that house had been a secret-police chief.

Only in Saddam's Iraq, where there were so many different levels of secret police, half of them spying on each other, would this have made sense. Nial had been thrown in a jail cell and kept in the dark for six months, fed only soup. Then one night they let him go. Just like that. No explanations. His wife did not recognize the thin bearded figure at her door, so she would not let him in at first.

We arrived at an area of opulent-looking houses with high-walled gardens, stopping at the entrance to a street that had been blocked with a tree trunk. The general sounded his horn and two men with Kalashnikovs slung over their shoulders emerged from the shadows to drag the tree trunk aside. They waved to the general as we passed by.

"They guard the street," the general told me.

It was a pleasant residential neighbourhood, with elaborate, well-kept gardens and clean streets. The houses were larger and newer than I expected. There were no signs of people about, though, and many homes were boarded up.

"The daughter of Tariq Aziz she live here," the general said casually, pulling up by wrought-iron gates that blocked a short driveway.

He got out.

"Shall I come?" I said.

"Yes, come."

I walked over and stood beside him as he rang a bell in the wall. From the corner of my eye I saw a curtain move in the house, which was an ornate monstrosity in sandy stone, indebted to several architectural styles from Ottoman-Gothic to Bauhaus-Rococo. But no one answered the bell. The general rang again.

"We will come back later," he said.

Further along the same street, we came to an area that had been devastated. An entire house had been reduced to grey rubble, and the houses facing and adjacent to it were pocked with indentations from flying debris and shrapnel. Trees had been smashed down or blown into driveways. A parked car lay squashed beneath a slab of concrete four feet thick. A man in what had been the garden was carrying a cardboard box full of broken china collected from the rubble.

"You want to meet this man?" said the general.

"Sure. If he wants to meet me ..."

The general rolled down his window and shouted a neighbourly hello. The man put down his box and waved, dusting himself down. He could have been in the middle of gardening rather than rescuing what little was left of his possessions from the ruin of his bombed house.

His name was Ayaad Fardis, a Christian. He was a professor of engineering at Baghdad University. A big bear of a man, his eyes were red and his hands shook as I asked him about the bomb. It had fallen at 11:45 a.m. Everyone was home at the time, yet only his son had been injured, both legs broken. I looked at the jagged piles of concrete where the house had been. This surely was incredible.

But no, I was wrong. The pile of rubble was his sister's house. His was the house next door, the one still standing. Just about. His sister and her whole family of thirteen people were in hospital with serious injuries. Of course they were. One of them had died in the rubble, the second floor collapsing on top of him and crushing his rib cage into powder.

Professor Fardis took me inside his house.

"This is my study," he said. "Here are my books, my hopes and my dreams ..."

One wall was ripped out. The bookshelves spilled through the hole. The desk had been crushed. A computer keyboard protruded from plaster and rubble.

"This is my daughter's room ..."

Apart from deep cracks, it was unscathed, the little bottles of perfume still in a row on the bedside table, a nightgown hanging behind the door.

"This is my bedroom."

It too was intact but the furniture was shattered. Suits and shirts had caught the shards of a dressing mirror and been slashed to ribbons. A crack two inches wide ran right around the room just below its ceiling, as if something had tried to tear off the whole third floor

"This is my son's room."

A poster of Manchester United was pinned to a wall as cracked as an old boiled egg. A wardrobe had been reduced to matchwood by a bed-sized slab of the roof, which had then knocked out an entire wall and slid down to crush the professor's car.

"This is the room for television."

It was gone, this room. We were standing on the roof now, looking down at the squashed car in the drive.

"Is that your car?" I asked.

"Yes," he laughed. "Yes, that my car. Canadian made — Malibu ..."

The details were important to him. They were all he had left now that the wholeness of things had melted into air.

"I'm so sorry ... for this ..."

"Yes," he said. "It is okay. We are strong. We shall rebuild Iraq ..." His eyes filled with tears. "We want nothing, nothing from the pocket of America ... We have our oil ..."

His students at the university, he said, were about to undergo *viva voce* exams on their theses. He did not know where any of them were now, though — if they were alive or dead. It was a wasted year.

"Yes," he said. "I do not know now who will pay my salary. There are nine people in this house. What will we do? Hmmm? What will we do?"

Had any aid agencies contacted him?

"No one," he said. "No one. We hear from no one."

He began sweeping with a threadbare broom. It was a futile task: there was more rubble than there was house, and what house still remained was way beyond repair. Yet he was used to tidying up the place, used to finding it possible to tidy it up. But everything was smashed to atoms — clothes, furniture, cups, plates, pictures, sinks, all the things it takes a lifetime to accumulate, from keepsakes to quotidian functional items, all gone. He looked forward, if he ever received another paycheque, to the task of restocking an entire life — an impossible task. The brush came away from his broom handle as he swept, and he knelt, trying to reattach it with duct tape. But he had reached the end of his tape roll, and his shaking hands did not seem to know what to do with all the items they clutched. Carefully, he lay the old broom down and smoothed its bristles as if it were a dying relative. Grief had nearly driven him insane. Seeing all this, my heart began to feel like an infected wound, raw, aching.

His mother sat in what had been the kitchen, peeling vegetables for an incredibly battered and bent pot that perched over a little fire made from wood that had been a chair.

"___"

I do not know what I intended to say, but it would not come out. The words fled rather than attempt to say the unsayable.

This is what you do when you go to war, I thought. *This is what your tax dollars achieve. This is the noble enterprise. Even those who merely kept silent when the wickedness, the non-feeling and non-thinking began, share guilt in this ...*

The professor tried to end my visit on an upbeat note:

"When I think of where each person was when the bomb fell," he said, "in a position that would save his lives, each of them ... I get an equation ... You know what is the answer?"

I shook my head.

"God. Only God can do this ..."

The noise must have been extraordinary, I said.

"No," he said, ever the professor. "At the centre of explosion it is silent because the sound wave travel outwards. We hear nothing. And all we feel is a great shuddering like earthquake ..."

You don't meet many people able to attest to this fact.

"Don't worry for us," said the professor, his lip trembling. "We will be fine. My faith in God is strong. Yes ... I *know* my God!"

Our end drifts nearer,
the moon lifts,
radiant with terror.
The state
is a diver under a glass bell.

A father's no shield
for his child.
We are like a lot of wild
spiders crying together,
but without tears.

— ROBERT LOWELL (1917–77)[122]

"Your eyes have water," said the general, as we drove away.

"It's so sad, so awful ... I don't know what to say," I said.

"People they notice you is crying," he said. "It is good they see this."

I wasn't sure what he was getting at.

All the houses on both sides now, I noticed, had lost their windows. They were closed off with cardboard, blankets, planks, and they felt subdued, like wounded monsters.

We drew up by a small house with a big hedge and dangling wisteria. The general blew his horn and a slim young man with sad, smiling eyes came to slide open the gate.

"This is my son," said the general.

His name was Firaz. I would get to know him well. He was at that age where you have your whole life stretching out in front of your mind like a glittering diorama, the tree of your life and all its fruit, yet he acted in the manner of a tired old man, cowed and care-worn, the best now far behind him. He was slow and listless. He had been born in time to know nothing but war and troubles, and the wars had shaped him to their own design, and the troubles had made a man out of chronic fear, biting anxiety, sorrow and timidity. He was as much a victim as the dead were — indeed, perhaps more so.

I had not been sure where we were going since leaving the hotel, and I thought all the stop-off points might be ways of seeing if we were followed, so it was a surprise to find we were actually at the general's house, that not everything rested in deception. Haifa came out to say hello, followed by two yappy little dogs. It was almost normal.

"Their names, Uday and Qusay," said the general, bending to pat the little dogs, smiling.

They had probably just been renamed. A joke like this would have cost you your life under Saddam's regime.

It was a modest little house. All the windows were covered with new cardboard from Dell computer boxes, making it gloomy inside even at noon. I was seated in a living room full of photographs. Here, I was told, was the general, with sandy-brown hair, in the cockpit of a fighter jet; there, he was seated at the controls of a helicopter. That is he in Russia. There he is in Switzerland. I would not have recognized him, even in pictures taken barely four years earlier. He had suddenly become an old man: an air of resignation had perched on his shoulders like a vulture and was looking out of his eyes. There were three different sets of wedding photographs: Haifa and Nial's, from the sixties; their daughter's, from the eighties; and Firaz's, very much from the Millennium — Iraq's sixth, as Firaz reminded me.

"You want Scotch?" asked the general, standing at his bar in a pose so familiar to his limbs and torso that they appeared to be melting into the polished mahogany.

"Please."

For all his glib banter, you could tell he had not entertained in a long while. There was dust on the presentation cases of Johnnie Walker Blue Label. Although there was plenty of alcohol on the shelves and in the cabinets, it was obvious these people were not drinkers. The ceramic kegs and celebratory figurines still had their caked wax seals. The crystal tumblers had to be dusted off. No one knew where the ice tongs had gone. Firaz went around lighting oil lamps that barely changed the deep shadowy gloom in which we sat. When he reached the lamp nearest his mother he was roughly seized by the collar.

"Look," Haifa said, parting the hair on her son's head. "See his injury?"

There was a deep cut that had taken three or four stitches to close up.

Firaz left the room and came back seconds later like a child holding a heaping handful of shrapnel he had found the day after the bomb. They were ugly grey blobs of steel with edges as sharp as razor blades. One of them — he wasn't sure which one — had taken the chunk out of his skull. Any of the pieces could have done this, and there were many of them, carelessly flung here, a street away from where the actual bomb had fallen.

This is not the collateral damage of bombs, either, not an unfortunate but unavoidable consequence of explosive devices dropped from the air. *They are designed to do this*, intended to break apart into hundreds or thousands of tiny pieces of scalpel-sharp steel. These are then flung out with the velocity of bullets hundreds of metres from the "target." The one that hit Firaz did so while he was sitting in his house, at the same time all the windows shattered. He could have been a baby lying in its crib — shrapnel is not particular. The pilot in his jet was many kilometres away by then.

Since we are on the subject of bombs and cowardice, I will now unburden myself of an especially sickening piece of information. On page 3 of the *Jordan Times*' Sunday edition for May 4, 2003, there was an article headlined: JAPANESE JOURNALIST SUMMONED BEFORE MILITARY TRIBUNAL. It concerned a man named Hiroki Gomi:

> *The 36-year-old photo-journalist from the Japanese newspaper* Mainchi Shimbun *was taken into custody late Thursday after an unidentified metal object screened in his bag exploded in the hands of airport security official Ali Sarhan, killing him and injuring three others. Gomi was later questioned by prosecutors in the presence of the Japanese consul.*

Gomi had been on assignment in Iraq, the article went on to say, and "had picked up the explosive device as 'a souvenir of the remnants of war on Iraq, but was unaware it was an explosive device' ... The journalist 'picked up objects, shaped like bells, in debris around an abandoned car on April 11' while travelling to Amman from Baghdad."

The article is somewhat inconclusive, since we do not discover Hiroki Gomi's fate. Why a military tribunal?, you may also wonder. Or, what kind of idiot takes home bombs as souvenirs?

Back in Jordan I heard the real story. At Amman airport, the security scanner did not like the look of something in Hiroki Gomi's luggage. He was asked to take it out. The object seemed to be a child's spinning top, but it had an unusually thick shell so inspectors were suspicious. While they were examining it further, it exploded. Gomi was running around screaming hysterically. When authorities finally found someone who could speak Japanese it turned out that the journalist was saying: "There's another one. I gave it to my cab driver for his kids." A frantic hunt ensued. When finally the cab driver was found, the other device, fortunately, had not yet exploded. During questioning, Gomi said the objects had come out of another device that had been dropped by an American plane near Ramadi, on the outskirts of Baghdad. There were many more, all looking like children's toys, and he had assumed they were gifts — part of the "winning-hearts-and-minds" campaign. In fact, they were cluster bomblets.

Jordanian authorities immediately hushed up the incident — hence the closed military tribunal. A very thorough search of all travellers coming from Iraq was then put in place, as I found the next time I crossed the border. There were even signs up saying that souvenirs of the war were illegal. Nothing happened to Hiroki Gomi — which, I think the reader will agree, is unusual for someone who has exploded a bomb in an airport and killed a security inspector. He was sent home to Japan, where his newspaper, which imagined it had lost face, demoted him to some clerkly role where he currently keeps a low profile. Presumably, Washington applied the same pressure to the Japanese as it applied to Jordan. It is not hard to see why, either. If it got out that America was using cluster bombs in which the bomblets resembled children's toys, someone, somewhere might object. After all, it does violate the Geneva Conventions, which proscribe the targeting of children and non-combatants.

I have tried and failed to find a good spin for this. The bombs look like children's toys because ... so that ... in order to ... But all I come up with is, so that children pick them up or adults take them home for their kids, and then while the kids are playing with them — Zap! In a land as deprived as Iraq has been for over a decade, too, new toys are only something a very wealthy child has known. On the outskirts of Ramadi, those toys would have quickly been scooped up. We know that ten thousand Iraqi civilians have been killed since March 21, 2003; if we knew the details of these deaths, we might better understand Iraq's hatred of Americans.

As with so much else about this ignoble, squalid war, there is no adequate response to a bomb that targets children, deliberately or not. What can one say about such atavistic barbarism? It is one of the most repugnant things I have ever heard of an army doing. It is also not a matter I feel ought to be dropped. I want to meet the man who implemented the use of these diabolical creations, who can defend his actions, quoting some facile report or theory. I want to *know* my enemy.

> *When you see millions of the mouthless dead*
> *Across your dreams in pale battalions go,*

Say not soft things as other men have said,
That you'll remember. For you need not so.
— CHARLES HAMILTON SORLEY (1895–1915)[123]

"You were in Russia?" I asked the general.

"*Many* times, I show you ..."

While he was rummaging through a drawer, a young woman entered the room. She was very beautiful: thick black hair, full sensual lips, big dreamy eyes, and she had clearly just woken up. She yawned and stretched, tousling her hair, pushing it over in front of her face. She was dressed like any American college student, T-shirt, loose shirt, jeans.

As I stood to introduce myself, the general said, dismissively,

"This Tara, the wife of Firaz."

"This *Paul*, the friend of general Nial," I said.

She proffered a soft limp hand, saying,

"I just waked up ... Oh, you say waked or woken?"

I was about to pronounce on matters grammatical, when the general interrupted.

"Tara," he said, "tell Firaz to bring my spectacle."

"Spectacle?" said Tara.

The general told her "reading glasses" in Arabic. She made herself a mental note of the wrong word, all but writing with her index finger upon an imaginary pad.

"Look," said the general, handing me a black-and-white photo from the top of a large stack he was holding.

Expecting him in front of the Kremlin, I was surprised to find myself holding a photograph showing a peroxide blonde in garter belt and stockings sprawled on a tiny bed. She had a face like a potato and a smile so humourless it could well have been her first.

The general affected a proud "not-bad-eh?" posture, saying,

"She is my girlfriend in Russia."

I made manly sounds of approval.

"I *do* with her there ..."

He rubbed the palms of his hands together in the Arab gesture for fucking (it does not mean making love, or even having intercourse).

I was not sure what my response to this should be. It is not always easy, being a guy. The general held out another picture, which actually did show him (and the girlfriend) standing in front of the Kremlin.

"Mosque," he said, pointing to the Kremlin. "Russian *chairch* ..."

"Church? Oh, I see ... Yes ..."

Just then, Haifa came in holding the general's glasses. I felt as if I had been caught masturbating, and wondered if I ought to hide the pictures.

She gave the general a *look*. "Oh," she said, with great disinterest, "*her!*"

Then she placed her palm to one side of her mouth in stagey confidentiality, saying in a loud whisper to me:

"I *hate* her."

"She's ugly too," I said.

Haifa brightened. It was like the sun emerging from cloud in England. I had made a friend. Giving the general a different kind of look — the one that said, *See! Even your friends think she is ugly* — she sailed proudly from the room like a royal barge.

"She does not like my girls," said the general, as if this quirk of his wife's was impossible to understand. "One time I *do* with three of these Russian girls," he continued, adding, "I speak effluent Russian."

"You speak Effluence?"

"Not this," he said, waving it aside like a fly. "Russian. Many times I go Russia."

"Why?"

"To buy ..."

"Buy?"

I looked into his stained grey eyes.

"Buy what?" I asked. "Weapons?"

"Airplanes," he said. "MIGs."

If he went on purchasing sprees like this for Saddam, I told myself, he could not have been such an insignificant cog in the regime's wheel, could he?

"When can I interview Aziz?" I asked.

"He will see you," said the general, in a very low whisper. "But when, I don't know."

People here had become accustomed to speaking like this, or going for a drive to have a conversation. It was assumed that everywhere was bugged. It was safer to make this assumption than the opposite one. An excess of caution never harmed anyone.

"Where will he see me?"

"This I don't know. Maybe here, maybe outside of Baghdad. I cannot say."

Tara came in holding a tray.

"Do you like juice?" she asked.

I took a glass of murky greenish liquid. It had an extraordinary nutty taste followed up by an effervescence of fruit.

"Incredible juice! What is it?"

Tara smiled, genuinely pleased that I liked it.

"Dringe," she said.

"Dringe? It isn't *orange* ... so what is *dringe*?"

"Special to Baghdad this," she said.

"She's very beautiful, Tara," I told the general when she had gone.

"What?" he said, absently, leafing through his photographs.

"The wife of Firaz — she is very beautiful ..."

"Tara," he said, looking puzzled. It was as if I had asked him her name. He really could not grasp what I was getting at. He simply did not see it — which was probably just as well.

Tara reappeared, clearly dispatched by Haifa to terminate the general's Russian confessions.

"Would you want to see my wedding photograph?"

"I would love to see your wedding photographs."

"We go for the *cerque-Russe*," said the general, showing me another picture, undeterred.

"The *cerque-Russe*?"

"Yes," he said. "*Cerque-Russe.*"

The picture showed him with the Russian tart again. Behind them were the vague forms of elephant and a man wearing a top hat. The *circus!* Presumably he had confused the word with the French term for "Russian circus" ...

"Do you speak French too?"

"*Mais qui!*" he said, rather unconvincingly.

"*J'espère qu'une fois vous me diriez la verité concernant votre travail avec Saddam ...*"

"Haha," he said. "*Qui qui.*"

Quite possibly, he did not understand because my French was no better than his.

Tara returned with five huge photograph albums bound in yellow leather with dangling tassles. She sat on the sofa heavily. She had hastily applied eyeliner and lipstick in the interim.

"Come," she told me, patting the cushion beside her.

The general would not concede defeat, holding out another pic.

"Sorry, Nial. Beauty calls ..."

I sat beside Tara. She smelled of warm fabric and soap. She placed half of the first album on my lap, then wriggled across to close the gap between us.

"Ah," said Firaz, puzzling into the room with a plate of cheese and crackers. "She is showing you ..."

"Yes, she is," I said, embarrassed.

She was not showing me wedding pictures, I realized later, so much as pictures of herself on the day she looked as beautiful as she was able to look. And this was beautiful indeed. But she clearly did not know whether it was beautiful enough or not. In her innocence, she blamed an unresponsive husband on herself: she was not sexy enough, she was not pretty enough. It was an old story. And it was an area where Arab society could use a little reformation.

"You look very beautiful here," I said to Tara.

"Do I?" she asked. "My mother she make the dress ..."

"You know something," I said. "You are one of the most beautiful women I have ever seen in my life. Firaz is a lucky man ..."

I could see that she did not know how to take this. Was I just being polite? The full tragedy of Tara only came out over time, and even when it did I had to read between the lines to understand it. There was a cultural divide between what I was told and how it could be interpreted. In Arab societies, men are shielded from criticism more than women are.

On March 21, 2003, the squalid day of shock and awe, when the whole city shook and the night sky blazed with the light of fires and bombs customized with pyrotechnical flair to sparkle and crackle or throw up fountains of coloured stars, Tara had miscarried her baby. Firaz had not been understanding. It was her fault. It seems that the thought of having to make another baby was not something he relished. A component in him was missing. It left him devoid of passion, which, ironically, was the one component Tara most needed from him. It all amounted to a family tragedy of Greek dimensions, the kind of sorrow that no one who saw this couple in public could possibly suspect.

At dinner, I was fed like a Strasbourg goose. Haifa had gone to a lot of trouble. She must have been in the chicken all day again. All I could do was express my gratitude. And eat enough for four.

By the time I had polished off a fifth dessert, I felt like Orson Welles. I could scarcely even reach the table over the hemisphere of my gut.

"*Robert,*" said the general. "Eat. You must *eat ...*"

"I have. I've eaten ten suppers ..."

"You have eaten nothing. *Robert ...* eat!"

"I can't."

"Robert-Robert-Robert," he said.

I think he liked the way it sounded in his mouth. He would often say what he imagined was my name for no apparent reason.

We tottered back to the sitting room. The skin over my stomach was stretched as tight as a drum. If someone had kicked it, I would have exploded.

"Robert," said the general, behind me. "You must have chocolate ..."

He lowered a box of chocolates the size of a bed onto the crest of my belly, where it perched unsteadily while he poked through the contents and even unwrapped several in search of his favourite: strawberry crème.

"Not me," I said. "Not for a million dollars. I have no room, no room at my In — and little at my Out. I have less than no room."

"A million dollars, Robert!"

"Not for a million."

"I have a million dollars," said the general. "You want to see it?"

"Yes. Show me now."

"Okay, Robert. Come ..."

I staggered to my feet and hauled the cauldron of my belly off in the general's wake. We ended up in what was clearly his bedroom, where he unlocked the cupboard in a small desk and tugged open its door. Inside were bundles of American dollar bills.

"I'd have to count it," I said.

"Yes. Count it, Robert."

"I trust you ..."

Why was he showing me this? I am still not entirely sure. It may have been just to impress me. It may have been to show me he could afford anything he asked me for — and he *did* ask me for many things over the next few months. It may have been to demonstrate that he could counter any offer of bounty I was promised by the Americans to take them to Tariq Aziz. Or there may have been another reason. He was an inscrutable fellow when all is said and done, an inscrutable fellow hiding inside a transparently scrutable one.

"You will stay here tonight," he announced, when we had returned to the sitting room.

"Okay. Thanks."

It was illegal under the rules of the occupation to go out between sunset and sunrise. The Americans had trouble enforcing this rule, however, largely because they obeyed it themselves.

> *And I must enter again the round*
> *Zion of the water bead*
> *And the synagogue of the ear of corn*
> *Shall I let pray the shadow of a sound*
> *Or sow my salt seed*
> *In the least valley of sackcloth to mourn*
>
> *The majesty and burning of the child's death.*
>
> — DYLAN THOMAS (1914–53)[124]

I woke the next morning from a horrific and particularly vivid dream to see the general and Haifa hovering over me. She had brought me a cup of mint tea.

"There was an old lady standing here," I said, still half asleep.

"That is my mother," said the general. He explained that she lived upstairs with his father, but neither of them had spoken to the general in nine years.

"What about Jesus? He live upstairs too?"

Haifa crossed herself. "You saw Jesus Christ?" she said.

"It was a dream."

"You will go to church on Easter?" Haifa asked.

"Oh, yes, no doubt I will ..."

"You come to our church, yes?"

"I would like that, thank you ..."

"Robert, Robert ..."

We were walking down the street towards the house where Tariq Aziz's daughter lived.

"*Everyone* knows Robert ..."

"Why hasn't she spoken to you in nine years? What did you do?"

He frowned and grew gravely serious.

"She told Saddam to put me in jail, that I am bad ..."

"She told *Saddam*?"

"Yes, she know him. But he send a man to ask neighbour people about me. And everyone they say 'Nial is good man,' so Saddam does not put me to prison ..."

"Why did she say you were bad?"

"She always too much like my older brother. She never like me ..."

"Still ..."

"She always think bad of me ..."

"Yeah. I know what you mean ..."

"You meet him ..."

"Who?"

"My brother."

He asked me if I had noticed the old man who had appeared briefly during dinner to collect a plastic bag full of bones. I thought he was a servant. The general had been very curt with him, and the old man acted very obsequiously.

"Were those bones his food?"

"No. Bones are for Max ..."

"Who's Max?"

"Max is the dog."

An old man with a kind face approached, greeting the general, who told me this man had also been imprisoned for no reason.

"Did they torture you?" I said.

"Just little bit," he said, holding his thumb and index finger a millimetre apart. "But you know what their little bit is like ... I told them, 'Bring the list of my crime and I will confess.' They bring in some papers and I sign without even read them. Yes, I did them all ..." He laughed, but it was not funny.

"I am sorry for all your suffering here," I said. "I wish it was better now. I hope it will be better soon."

"Thank you, my friend," said the old man with a kind face. "We have no hopes for that. We are, how do you say, *realists* ..."

He went on his way.

We arrived at the daughter's house. The general told me to wait outside the gate, which was open, while he went in.

A man across the street stared at me. A child walked by in a great arc to avoid me. I felt conspicuous.

"Robert, come!"

The general pulled me through the high metal gate.

"You do not talk with him," he said.

"With whom?"

"Talk only with the daughter."

He pulled me through another gate and I found myself standing in a garden with about twelve other people. They had just eaten breakfast outside in the weak spring sun. Tariq Aziz was still in his pyjamas. His skin was pasty and, when he removed his tinted glasses, he had black circles beneath his eyes. But if you didn't know it you would never have guessed this was the second-most important figure of the old regime, or that he was a fugitive on the run.

People tended not to survive for long around Saddam, who trusted no one and suspected betrayal in all. The sole exception was Tariq Aziz, whose roots in the Ba'ath movement went as deep as Saddam's. They were imprisoned together in the 1960s and knew life on the run as wanted men, travelling by night and sleeping rough by day. They shared the kind of memories that bind men close, and most important of all, Aziz never forgot who was boss. This modesty and loyalty earned him twenty-four years as Saddam's deputy prime minister and chief advisor. He seems also to be the closest Saddam ever got to a pal.

He was born Michael Yuhanna. Like Ba'ath Party founder Michel Aflaq, he was a Christian, and he changed his name to Tariq Aziz when Saddam suggested he adopt a more Islamic name. A thoughtful, scholarly man, his rumpled suits stood out among the well-pressed uniforms of his colleagues on the Revolutionary Command Council; like Saddam, Aziz had never been a soldier, but unlike the boss, he did not intend to become one. He seems to have been content with his role as Number Two, which made him as recognizable in the West as Saddam, and much more respected. The only senior member of the ruling council to speak decent English, he was also the only one to have been educated above the fourth grade. On February 14, 2003 — Valentine's Day, three weeks before the invasion was launched — Tariq Aziz met with the Pope in the Vatican, where he communicated "the wish of the Iraqi government to co-operate with the international community, notably on disarmament." Even those Iraqis who yearn for the day when Saddam will stand before his judges can find it in their hearts to forgive Tariq Aziz. Excessive and misplaced loyalty seem to have been his greatest crime.

The general immediately became involved in an argument with a group of four men and two women. They were all shouting at each other. I sat on a low wall and stroked a cat that had begun weaving around my ankles. I have no talent for small talk, and in this situation I had even less. I hoped the cat would not abandon me.

"You have some proposal for me?"

I looked up. Tariq Aziz sat down on the edge of a nearby chair.

"Yes, sir ..."

I gave him my best pitch: how it would save lives if someone representing the old regime told Iraqis that the war was over, how the confusion and uncertainty would just prolong the occupation, how he was the best person to do this, et cetera.

"You think I am best person for this job?"

"Yes," I said, not sure where this would lead.

"Why?"

"Well, you're the only one who speaks English ... I mean, good English ..."

"Yes ..." He made it sound as if he had just realized this himself.

"I have, um, some concerns about security right now ..."

"Of course, sir ..."

"And it is unlikely that, um, I will be knowing the answer to many of your question ..."

"Would it help if I gave you the questions in advance?"

"Yes, that would be most helpful, thank you ..."

He was running on empty. The last few weeks had presumably been hell, and now that it was all over, he could not take it in. His big protruding eyes darted this way and that. He kept tugging at his dressing-gown sleeve, then rubbing at the stubble on his chin, then cleaning his glasses repeatedly.

"I will accept any conditions you impose on the location of the interview, of course, but it must be suitable for filming, I —"

He cut me off.

"Tell me," he said, "do you think the Americans would grant me asylum in England if I surrender to them?"

I had no idea and told him so. "I could ask if you want ..."

It seemed an absurd thing to say, given the situation, yet he was polite enough not to say so.

"You know my daughter?"

"Yes, well, sort of ..."

"She will make the arrangements. I must go now. It was nice to meet you."

I shook his damp little hand as he rose. He seemed suddenly disoriented, looking around on all sides.

"Here, Papa ..."

A handsome woman in her forties took his arm.

"I am Zobeida," she said. "We appreciate your help. Here —"

I thought for a moment she was handing me a tip, but it was a piece of paper with a satellite phone number written on it.

"Call me tomorrow evening," she said.

"Okay, I will. Thank you."

"Yes, er ..." said Tariq Aziz, as she steered him away across the garden.

"Robert, Robert," said the general, when we were on our way back to his house. "Is it all right?"

"Oh yeah," I said. "It's all right all right ..."

He pulled me close and said quietly, "You must not tell anyone, *anyone*, that you see him here. You understand me? If you do I am —" He put an imaginary gun to his head and pulled its trigger.

"I understand."

"Come," he said. "We take some tea."

"Is he a good man, Tariq Aziz?" I asked him.

He thought, screwing up his mouth for a moment. Then he said, "Yes."

"You don't sound very sure ..."

"He is a good man," said the general. "Yes. But there are ... no, nothing. He is good man."

> *The way of killing men and beasts is the same*
> *I've seen it:*
> *truckfuls of chopped-up men*
> *who will not be saved.*
>
> *Ideas are mere words:*
> *virtue and crime*
> *truth and lies*
> *beauty and ugliness*
> *courage and cowardice.*
>
> *Virtue and crime weigh the same*
> *I've seen it:*
> *in a man who was both*
> *criminal and virtuous.*
>
> — TADEUSZ RÓZEWICZ (1921–)[125]

Outside the Palestine, when the general dropped me off, there was another demonstration by angry Iraqis. High above the lake of bobbing noisy heads was a large banner in English for the benefit of the media. It read:

BLOODY LIBRATION MOVIE IS BEGIN — BAD DIRECTORS

The only advantage to living under a brutal military dictatorship, as far as I know, is that there is very little crime or disturbance of the peace. The punishment for doing nothing in Saddam's Iraq could be death, so you can imagine what happened to real criminals. One estimate said that during the first week of the occupation there had been more crimes committed in Baghdad than there had been during the entire decade preceding it. Women were being raped and abducted while out shopping. Carjacking was a booming business. Break-ins were the rule not the exception. People drove around in their servants' cars because it was not a good idea to let strangers know how wealthy you were. Iraqis wanted protection, they wanted a police force, they wanted somewhere to go for help or with complaints. But the Americans were either too incompetent to set up a police force, or they were deliberately stoking the furnace of anarchy. Whenever the subject came up, Iraqis were not sure which explanation was right, though initially they were inclined to accord the invaders more intelligence than they did further into the fiasco. What we have seen ever since is the manifestation of their anger. The so-called insurgency is not limited to pro-Saddam elements; it represents the feelings of all Iraqis. No Iraqi wants the Americans there.

The journalists, meanwhile, were growing restless. Their desk editors now demanded more than just coverage of the invasion. The embedded journalists now had steadily less to write about as their regiments settled into the diverse humdrum tasks of occupation. After the excitement of war and the advance on Baghdad, life was suddenly dull. So the possibility of an interview with Tariq Aziz was seized upon hungrily. In retrospect, I should have kept it to myself.

Because it was now impossible to check out the general's connections to the old regime — no one admitted knowing anything, and the bombing and fleeing Ba'athists had destroyed most records — I decided to see if I could find out more about what he had been doing in Russia. To this end, I befriended Ilana Ozernoy, a Russian-American journalist who worked for the Moscow office of *U.S. News and World Report.* Dangling the carrot of Aziz, I asked if she would meet the general and see what she could pry out of him. He seemed to like Russian women, after all, and often said his Russian was far better than his English. Ilana was more than keen to get a shot at Tariq Aziz, but first she had to clear it with her office. I had, of course, entirely forgotten the once-widespread suspicion that *U.S. News and World Report* was owned by the CIA.

I called Zobeida, Tariq Aziz's daughter, around 4:30 p.m., but no one answered the ringing, not even a machine. Before I could try again, the general appeared, as arranged, to collect me for dinner. I told him that I had not been able to reach Zobeida.

"Tomorrow we go to Samarra," he said.

"That's where he wants to do the interview?"

"Yes. There is some important news in Samarra for you."

Although I had previously made sure it was all right to bring along other people, I asked him again. He looked less than enthusiastic this time, however, so I said that the others would come with us in the same SUV — which seated six.

"And one's a very pretty Russian girl," I added.

I was not sure he had understood, but he eventually told me it was fine to bring three more people.

"I shall tell them to meet us here at 9 a.m., okay?"

"Nine sharp," he said. "We go direct to Samarra."

After my gluttonfest at the general's table, the idea of food repulsed me, so I was happy to beg off dinner, saying I needed to pack and make arrangements with the others.

"But Robert, Robert," he said, "you will be there at nine o'clock, yes?"

"I promise."

"Good thing I told Bassim to come at 8:30," said Sherwell, when I informed him.

"Bassim can't come," I said. "I promised we would all be in the same car. They're not going to be happy if a convoy shows up ..."

"It isn't a convoy — it's one car ..."

"Sorry ..."

"How are we going to get back?" he said.

"He'll bring us back."

"What if he doesn't?"

"Why wouldn't he?" I said.

"I don't know. But I don't want to be stranded there."

"Look, Phil ... They're risking their necks doing this and the deal is one car, okay? If you don't like it, don't come ..."

I think I wanted Sherwell to be more grateful than he was, and I know I did not want him challenging my arrangements, because the extra car was not such a big problem as I made it seem. It was, after all, my suggestion that we go in one vehicle, not the general's. All the same, I felt that any change of plans at this stage would have caused suspicion. I also assumed that the general was really in charge of arrangements to meet Tariq Aziz, not Zobeida. The habitually furtive nature of conversation in Saddam's Iraq meant that everyone was used to taking evasive measures when discussing anything forbidden, so the general's low voice and guilty manner were not as remarkable as they seemed to me, and did not necessarily indicate that he was especially fearful of electronic eavesdropping. But this was how I took them, and consequently I was careful not to state anything to do with Aziz openly. It prevented me from asking the general the kind of questions I would normally have asked him, and made me read between the lines of what he said more than was necessary.

The three of them were already waiting at the agreed-upon spot when I arrived there just before nine. I could tell something was afoot. They had the look of conspirators.

"We want to bring another car," said Ilana, who only seemed to possess a denim shirt and jeans, since that was all I had ever seen her wearing.

"No," I said.

"We'd feel more com-fort-able," said the traitor Hackett.

I gave him the evil eye and he looked sheepish. They had clearly decided on a united front before I arrived; it was this that angered me as much as anything else.

"Then I go alone," I said, hoping to split the ranks. "I am not going to jeopardize this just because you want your own car ..."

Hackett was red in the face and looked down. I don't really blame any of them for wanting independent transport, but I did at the time.

"Then fuck the lot of you," I said, as the general's car arrived.

"What happen with friends?" the general asked, when I told him that I was coming alone.

When I explained, he immediately said they could bring their own car, but I sensed something in the way he said it that was testing. Was he trying to ascertain if I could be trusted after all? I was not sure, and he was never easy to read at the best of times.

"The arrangement was made," I said. "I don't like them breaking it this way. We will go alone."

He remained parked, however, and the three rebels remained standing on the sidewalk staring. I wished he would give me a clearer indication of what he thought, but he was leaving it all to me. I decided that a change in the arrangements at this stage would not send the right message.

"To hell with them," I said. "Let's go."

"Sure?"

"Yes."

As we drove away, I squinted sideways at the three faces waiting on the pavement. They were willing to give up the chance of a real scoop interview for a car? For nothing! What were journalists made of these days? Pah! Then I started wondering if they were right. Was I the one making a mistake, going to Samarra — a city some 240 kilometres north of Baghdad — all alone, with no independent means of transport, no way of returning if I needed to return? I had thought at least one of them would crack and coming running after us, but they simply stood there staring.

"You friends they wanting to come with us," the general said. "Now they sad."

If he had directly stated that he wanted them to come in their own car, I would have relented, but he merely questioned my determination and made the incident seem to be a test of my reliability. I felt very alone as we drove away from the Palestine, and I wondered if I would live to regret bitterly not backing down. After several minutes of seemingly testing my resolve on the matter, the general changed his mood as if it were a hat, so I told myself I had done the right thing. I even convinced myself that I was happier alone.

CHAPTER ELEVEN

MAKING RED WAR YET REDDER

All nations striving strong to make
Red war yet redder. Mad as hatters
They do no more for Christés sake
Than you who are helpless in such matters.
　　　　　　— THOMAS HARDY (1840–1928)[126]

Soon, the low clouds that made the city seem grey and depressing blew away and the sun turned bricks and concrete yellow, made green leaves look far greener, and even changed the care-worn expression on the faces we passed. Probably because one is used to areas of destruction and desolation being contained, the continuous vistas of Baghdad's ruin were unnerving. Ruin was the norm here now. Even what had already been in ruins was ruined again, re-ruined. Presumably, much of what I saw was even the ruins of ruins of ruins? A good deal of Old Baghdad, for instance, had been ruined by Time, the British, and then at least twice by the Americans. Much had been ruined ever since the Gulf War's massive bombardment, but now the city had gone from being a ruined city, or city in ruins, to being a city of ruins.

Just when I thought the devastation was limited to downtown, we would pass something else reduced to a pile of smouldering rubble. Everything was broken. Although the Americans had openly stated their intention to destroy everything connected with the old regime, I was still amazed to find post offices, sports stadia, water works, train yards, registrars' offices, local town halls, state banks, bus terminals and so on smashed to dust. These were the kind of structures around which neighbourhoods are centred, so every time it looked as if an area might have been spared, we would suddenly pass through the ruins at its core. The effect was deeply disturbing. It prevented anyone from clinging to a sense of normality, of life going on. There was literally nowhere to go that gave respite from the war. There were no beautiful buildings any more, because the ones there had been were all owned by the government and had thus been destroyed. The mosques had been spared, but Baghdad did not really have any major mosques. Ba'athism frowned on religion in general, and did not encourage religious centres in the capital, so there were few. The only institutions left untouched had been schools and hospitals, but these had become targets of the looters and many had been set on fire by thieves anxious to cover their tracks.

During the first three months after the war, America provided nothing to alleviate the suffering of the people of Baghdad, so many of whom had lost homes and families, not to mention incomes and security. I was there, I saw nothing — and I was *looking* for it. I am told little has changed in the year since. Unemployment alone is currently around fifty percent. Roughly half the population worked for the government, so it should have come as no surprise to the invaders to find that, with the government gone, every other person was without a job. Which is to say without a paycheque — which in the West would mean far more serious a situation than it does in the East, where extended families can absorb a financial disaster for quite a long time. But not indefinitely. Nearly everyone has reached his or her limit now. If more had witnessed Iraq as it was before, more would be outraged by what is happening there.

The best-kept secret is the profound level of discontent among the invading army itself. I first noticed this as the general and I drove to Samarra. The traffic had been very light until just outside of Baghdad, when we turned off one freeway to join another and found ourselves at a complete halt in a kilometre-long line of vehicles waiting to cross a bridge that no longer existed. The U.S. army had installed one of its temporary single-line bridges at this crucial junction, and several soldiers were now allotted the task of directing traffic. This entailed getting Iraqi drivers to grasp the concept of lining up and waiting their turn. Every time the barricade went up in either direction, forty or fifty vehicles would scramble to drive through, all them coming to an untidy halt at the entrance to the narrow strip of steel, where two soldiers stood guard on either side. These soldiers looked as if they had been at their task continuously for years. They were hoarse from shouting and exasperated by the ceaseless tide of people refusing to understand that the bridge could only handle five at a time. They were even tempted to let everyone drive on in a mass, but the officer in charge would not permit it. The bridge would break, and it belonged to the American taxpayer, not them. The day was becoming hot and sticky too. These young men were at the end of their tether.

I walked up waving my *Harper's* ID.

"Goddam fuckin' country," said a flushed red-haired boy from the South. "Whassa matter with these fuckin' people?"

I said I would get the general to explain the routine to as many people as he could.

"Appreciate it," said the soldier. "Appreciate it. We was told they'd be glad to see us — they ain't fuckin' glad to see us. They shootin' at us!"

"You've been shot at?"

"Not us. But lookit these fuckin' animals! Why cain't they see that they's gotta wait in laan? I'm fuckin' pissed, man, I am! Wait'il I get home, I tell ya ... They fuckin' lied to us, man, they fuckin' lied through they teeth. That fuckin' Rumsfeld ..."

His partner was a dour-looking black soldier with bookish spectacles. His mouth turned down at the edges and he glared.

"Tough day, huh?" I said.

"Don't fuckin' get me started, man," he said. "You don't wanna hear it, I tell ya ..."

I wondered if they thought I was an American journalist writing booster pieces for the war. Didn't they realize most journalists *wanted* to hear soldiers complain?

"Yeah, *Harper's*," the black soldier said. "Mah l'il brother reads it ... I don't give a shit who hear this, my friend, 'cos they can't do nothin' to me that I don't want ..."

"Rufus's more pissed than me," the other soldier added.

"Yeah you take this down, Mista *Harper's* ..."

"Can I get your names?" I said.

The tags, as usual, were covered.

"Woh, no, not mine!" the white soldier said. "Mah Daddy's in the army ..."

"Private Rufus C. Freemont," said the black soldier. "Third Expeditionary. Yeah! You can say that I am not happy about the lies I was told before comin' here ... Yeah, say that. And I am leavin' this fuckin' army the moment I gets home. *Whenever* the fuck that is ..."

"Yeah," said the white soldier. "We was told three month, but now it's six. I ain't heard from mah wife since I been here!"

"What he said," said the black man.

I made my way back to the general, past a turmoil of vehicles and grumbling Iraqis. He got out and told several uncomprehending faces the news about lining up five vehicles at a time. Nevertheless, when the barricade went up, fifty vehicles spat dirt trying to get into a space for six or seven. An hour later, we finally passed through ourselves.

"I tried," I shouted to the soldiers. "Good luck with it."

"Be safe, man," the perspiring black soldier shouted back.

"Yeah, say hello to New York for me," said the white man. "Fuck this!"

I thought of them standing there all day, never imagining when they were sent out here that they would find themselves trying to direct Iraqi traffic at a desolate spot in the middle of nowhere.

Further along the road, we came across a massive American supply convoy heading north. It moved very slowly and when we went to overtake it we found it was over three kilometres long. Twice we had to pull in between huge khaki trucks to avoid buses coming the other way. Each time, the soldiers bristled with suspicion, hands gripping rifles, eyes narrowing. I felt certain we would be pulled over and checked out, if only to make sure we were not armed. The fact that no one saw fit to do this boded ill for the army, I thought.

During the following two hours, the general was evasive about the Aziz interview but seemed happy to talk about Samarra, where he evidently had many friends, one of whom, Sheikh Adnan, was now by all accounts the city's guardian or custodian. Saddam apparently hated Samarra and had promised to reduce it to an impoverished village. It was the city in between Tikrit, Saddam's home, and Baghdad, so I reasoned that alone would have been sufficient to arouse ire in Saddam, who had an inferiority complex that supplied him with a chip on his shoulder the size of the Black Forest — very much like his hero, Stalin. Thus Samarra, the general claimed, had always been a hotbed of anti-Saddam plots and sentiment, which better explained the leader's animosity. It was one place where the American army would find itself welcome, he added, but they had not yet arrived. To me, Samarra was mainly memorable for its unique twelfth-century spiral minaret, a high tower with a staircase that wound in a corkscrew up the outside. It had an eerily modernist feeling. The city also had a spectacular glittering Shia mosque and, on the outskirts, the mathematical miracle of a ruined Umayyad palace, which was all that now remained to remind Iraqis that Samarra once —very briefly — surpassed Baghdad and was the seat of the caliphate.

You had to turn off the main highway and take a small two-lane road to reach the city, which created the impression Samarra had been shunned by Iraq's highway system. There were no signs of Americans at all. Indeed, besides the local telecommunications and post office building — reduced to tangled rubble by a Tomahawk missile — there were no signs of the war itself. It was a tiny city, with a sleepy, underpopulated air about it. Only along a main drag did there seem to be any activity. Over the town hall hung a banner proclaiming NATIONAL SALVATION MOVEMENT. Around it were a dozen or so men in paramilitary gear holding Kalashnikovs. They showed a little interest as we drove by, but not much.

The National Salvation Movement, the general told me, was a nascent political party led by Wafiq al-Samarrai. Wafiq had been Saddam's director of army intelligence from 1980 until he fell from favour in 1992. He had managed to flee Iraq with a considerable fortune, and went to live in London. At this stage, he had not yet returned to lead his party, however, but was believed to be on his way — as were many other exiles hoping to move into the power vacuum.

"We not want him," said the general. He added that Iraqis did not want new leaders who had been in any way connected with Saddam. Nor did they want exiles who had not shared their suffering over the last decades. They did not want leaders from the military, either. And most definitely they did not want anyone the Americans chose for them as leader.

"We want same government you having," said the general. "If bad, then — pffft!"

He clapped his hands, and we nearly ran over a small boy.

Turning off the main road into a small cul-de-sac, we came to a halt in front of a large old house surrounded by a high wall. Many other cars were parked nearby, and through the wrought-iron gates I could see many people milling around in the garden.

"This Sheikh Adnan house," said the general. "Come, Robert. He is now the big man. My friend."

The interior of the house was very gloomy, and it took a while for my eyes to adjust. We were shown into a huge room that had chairs placed around the walls. On the chairs sat men in traditional Arab dress, smoking and drinking tea or coffee from tiny cups. They looked with curiosity at the Westerner.

"Come, Robert."

Sheikh Adnan was an enormous mountain of flesh swathed in white cotton, with a red-and-white checked *keffiyah* cascading down around jowls that wobbled when he spoke. He must have been in his eighties, but thanks to liberal use of hair dye his neatly trimmed moustache was jet black. His red flecked eyes drooped like an old bloodhound's, and those teeth that were not gold were barely more than nicotine-stained pegs.

A small boy brought us thimble-sized cups into which he poured a half inch of pungent black coffee flavoured with cardamom. I had no idea what to discuss with the sheikh, so I asked him how he felt about the war. He nodded and offered me a very fancy gold-tipped cigarette. His gaze was penetrating, with something lascivious about it. I felt decidedly uncomfortable.

He was a cautious man, so, although he talked at length, he said little. No one was unhappy to see Saddam go, he said, but no one wanted the Americans here. Everyone was now worried about security. Would he be supporting Wafiq al-Samarrai?

He stared at me without blinking for a long time. "I will see," he said, lighting another cigarette. "Most people will not vote for him." Then he laughed.

The general then introduced me to another sheikhly old man, and I ran through the same questions, receiving largely the same non-answers. After this man there was another, and another. I had experienced this kind of thing before. It had become a matter of prestige, once Sheikh Adnan was interviewed, that others were seen being interviewed by the Westerner. It became a measure of their importance, and I could see, when at one point I made motions to leave, that there was considerable anxiety among those yet to be interviewed, who had drifted over to my corner and were sitting trying not to make their interest obvious. We were back in the old tribal world, and I knew I would have to go through the motions with everyone or risk generating ill will. I relied on the general to let me know when I had reached the echelon of no importance. Islamic societies are in some senses more egalitarian than we in the West can imagine, and it is often hard to sort the leaders from the followers, yet it is important to accord the right people the appropriate respect.

As an ancient toothless man scurried over to sit next to me, the general rose and came over.

"Come, Robert," he said. "We must leave now."

When we were in the car, I asked him what the whole ordeal had been about.

"They are *sheikhs*," said the general. "It is good you show them respect."

I knew what he meant. These men were the local tribal patriarchs. Nothing happened in the area without their knowledge or their approval, even though none of them held any kind of formal office. By meeting each of them and taking tea or coffee, I was paying respect to their authority and allowing each one to inspect me. Bedu pride themselves on being able to judge a man's true intentions merely by looking into his eyes. Saddam always went to sit with the sheikhs when he needed their support. He came out of that world himself and knew how vitally important it was to the governance of Iraq. For once the local sheikh was on your side, the whole tribe could be relied on for support. One of the last broadcasts from Iraqi state television had been a call for the tribes to arise and throw out the invaders. The biggest mistake Paul Bremer, the American head of the Interim Governing Council, made when he first arrived in Baghdad was to summon the sheikhs for a meeting. Had he gone to see them, as custom demanded, and humbly requested their cooperation, the situation in Iraq today might have been very different. The sheikhs were deeply offended, and few attended the meeting. It is yet another measure of the ignorance and arrogance that went into the war's so-called planning.

We drove back to the main road and stopped again about a block away in front of a brand new, excessively ornate house.

"What about Tariq Aziz?" I said.

"Yes, yes, Robert. You must wait."

I was taken into another large room with chairs around it. This one was empty, though. The general left me alone and went into another room to talk with someone. Ten minutes later, he came back with three men. I shook hands:

Brigadier Ziad al-Samarrai

Omar T. Ali al-Samarrai

Sabbar Ahmed Mohammed al-Samarrai

As the reader may have noticed, everyone from Samarra carries the city in his surname, as do those from other cities and areas. I shall generally just use their first names.

Ziad, a thin and nervous man, was a brigadier of police. Omar, bald as an egg with wise, sad eyes, was his brother. Sabbar, a big soft man with immaculate greying hair, had been a Mukharbharat officer, and seemed to be a friend of the brothers.

"These are the men, Robert!" said the general.

"No doubt. What men, Nial?"

"We rescue the American prisoners," said Omar, whose English was good.

On April 11, 2003, seven Americans — two pilots and five soldiers — captured in Nasiriya were freed in Samarra. I had read the news reports, which made it sound as if U.S. troops had rescued the captives. Ziad, the police chief, had been given orders to kill the Americans, but instead he and Omar had sought out the nearest U.S. troops and led them to where the prisoners were being held. It was a noble deed and I felt sure they would be handsomely rewarded for it. Indeed, they had a note from Staff Sgt. Beretz of 3/4 Marines, the U.S. commander they dealt with, identifying them as the men who had freed the captives. What did they want from me? It seems they had more information that would be useful to the U.S. army, and they had endeavoured to seek out the right intelligence officer in Baghdad to convey it to, but, in spite of their letter, they had been treated badly and turned away.

What was this other information?, I asked. It seems that the U.S. prisoners were brought to Samarra as hostages by General Ali Masjid — "Chemical" Ali — who no longer had any use for them and thus turned them over to local authorities. Ali, however, was supposed to be dead. It had been announced early in the war that he was killed during an air raid on the villa near Basra where he was staying. I asked how the brothers could be certain he was still alive. Ziad told me Ali had come to one of his captains, Abdullah Mohammed, with dozens of phony ID cards, requesting that they be officially stamped. Being a police officer, Ziad had arranged this himself. I later confirmed these details with Captain Mohammed. Ali, it seems, was still in the area, holed up at a farmhouse outside of town and protected by a dozen or so Syrian mercenaries.

The brothers offered to show me where Chemical Ali was hiding. I asked them if they thought he would be willing to allow an interview. They seemed dubious. Well then, what did they want me to do with this information? I realized they were frightened of Chemical Ali, and assumed they may just have wanted him gone.

At this point Sabbar, the other man, cut in. They also knew, he said, where Kuwaiti civilians were buried.

Kuwait had long claimed that Iraq still held some of its people who were taken prisoner during the Gulf War. Iraq had officially denied it. This was the first evidence that indicated otherwise. Sabbar told me that there had been 78 Kuwaiti citizens, most of them women and children, who had been captured in a bus and brought back to Iraq during the retreat from Kuwait, presumably to use as human shields. They had been held in various places and were finally sent to a military post somewhere near Samarra. In 1992, when their presence, if known, would have been an embarrassment, the order came down to kill them. They were buried alive. Some of the women had been raped first, Sabbar said. He then offered to take me to one of the killers, who would then show me where the Kuwaitis had been buried.

It seemed simple enough, though the term "buried alive" poured acid into my soul, slow-acting but bitter as gall.

"Also," added Omar, "I can show you where there are weep-ons buried."

"What, like atomic and chemical weapons?" I said.

"Yes, I think," said Omar.

"Why are you doing this?"

The short answer was because they were glad to see Saddam gone, and wanted to convey this to the Americans. There was other information too, but my head was spinning, so I told them to let me think. Sabbar then added the most salient detail: the government of Kuwait was offering a million-dollar reward for any information leading to the recovery of its citizens in Iraq, alive or dead. He wanted me to make sure that the three of them received the reward.

"How can I do that?"

For three pillars of Samarran society, a secret-police chief, a police chief and a police chief's brother, they were like nervous schoolboys. They seemed unfamiliar with the ways of the world too, and the idea of just picking up a phone and calling Kuwait was quite beyond them. You don't depressurize from tyranny that quickly, though, and under Saddam no one called outside the country unless he wanted his calls monitored. I came to see that they felt powerless. Their country had been invaded; they were scared that the Shia would take over, scared for their lives; and they thought that with my help they would not get shafted over the reward. I agreed to help. Sabbar, the big soft man with perfect hair, then invited us all for lunch at his house.

When people had been buried alive, lunch seemed somehow inappropriate, wrong. I had no appetite. But these were my emotions, not those of Iraqis. If they had missed lunch every time they heard about an atrocity, lunch would not exist by now.

Behind a high wall in a small lane, Sabbar's house was more modest than those I had previously seen, and his women were in a purdah section of their own, only visible when they brought out food. After taking tea, the general announced that he was going back to Baghdad and I would stay here.

"For Aziz?" I managed to whisper when no one was paying attention.

"Zobeida she know you here," he said, hardly moving his lips.

"Thanks ..."

"Yes," said Sabbar, who had changed from pants and shirt into *dishdasha*. "You are welcome, Mister Bull."

His expression perpetually suggested guilt — someone who has erred and is trying to make up for it in the hope that the error will be forgotten. His character was very much that of an overgrown child, though, so one could not dislike him. As a secret-police official, I imagined, his days were not exactly devoted to philanthropy. Those soft pudgy hands were capable of immense cruelty. Yet everyone had acted in ways they regretted under Saddam. Those who had not were the ones towards whom the regrettable actions were directed. What Iraq needed now was a version of the South African Truth and Reconciliation Commission, a forum for confessions and amnesty. A man cannot be punished because he was too weak to resist a corrupt regime. Most of us would be too weak to resist. Most of us *are* too weak.

I saw the general to his car and, when we were alone, again asked about Tariq Aziz.

"Yes, Robert," he said. "You must wait here."

I was glad the others had not come. They would not have had the patience to go through this waiting period, and their impatience would have been interpreted as both rudeness and unreliability. The East taught me patience. It took years to learn as well, for I was not a patient person.

Sabbar offered me a shower. I was hot, and engrimed with dust, so it was welcome. He gave me a *dishdasha* to put on after showering, so that his wife could wash my clothes. They were rather filthy, I suppose; I had not changed in a week. Clean and in the *dishdasha*, I felt suddenly less of a Western eyesore. Arab dress is so comfortable and sensible compared to the trussed-up effect of ties and trousers — clothing that speaks of stress and pressure. As usual, the Arabs were delighted to see me in their traditional garb. It was something Westerners rarely did.

"It is for you gift," said Sabbar, referring to the white cotton *dishdasha*. "And this."

He handed me a *keffiyah* and showed me how to tie it as a flattened turban, in the local manner.

"Now you Arab," said Omar.

His brother Ziad, the police chief, had gone home. Ziad's wife was very ill with kidney failure. She badly needed dialysis, but Iraq had no machines, and even if it did, it would have been unable to run them because the electricity was intermittent and dialysis needs a reliable power source. Ziad wanted his share of the Kuwaiti reward to pay for a kidney transplant performed by U.S. surgeons. He did not want local men doing the job. It struck me that just freeing the American soldiers he had been ordered to kill merited someone giving his wife a transplant free of charge. How much are seven lives worth?

"Yes, Sheikh Bull," said Sabbar.

Arab hospitality never fails to overwhelm me. I always try to imagine how Arabs would be treated in America if the situation was reversed. After September 11, Sikhs were being gunned down just because they wore turbans. There was something deeply gratifying about the warmth and kindness I have always been shown in the Arab world, something we have lost almost entirely in the West. We may talk about all of humanity being our brothers and sisters, but we do not act as if they are. Increasingly, we treat each other with cold suspicion. People are assumed to be thieves and robbers. Stores view all customers as shoplifters, parents assume all strangers are child-snatchers. Generosity of spirit is not gullibility. It is the implementation of that truth we hold self-evident, that we must treat everyone as we want them to treat us. This we can learn from the Arabs.

An extraordinary meal was produced, stew, flatbread, a huge fish, several roast chickens, radishes, onions, and we ate seated on the floor in a circle. On the wall was an enormous photograph of the Ka'aba in Mecca in a gaudy gold frame. Thousands of pilgrims circled the huge cube draped in black, while beyond the brightly lit interior of the vast open-air mosque a new moon hung like a dagger in the star-speckled night. It was a remarkable sight. Beside it hung framed photographs I saw in many Iraqi houses. They showed scenes from the Canadian lake country: wood cabins at the edge of cool blue lakes surrounded by dense pine forests. These landscapes were there because they correspond with descriptions of the Islamic paradise. Arabs do not like the desert. They yearn for forests, rivers and lakes.

After lunch, I called a friend of mine, Julie Chappell, at the British Embassy in Amman. I had to go up on Sabbar's roof to get the sat-phone to work. I told her where I was and to pass on the information about "Chemical" Ali. Then I asked about the Kuwaitis. She had heard of the reward offered and, after consulting with someone, gave me the phone number of Rabia Adifani in Kuwait City. He was in charge of the unit dealing with missing Kuwaitis and the reward for information. She said she would call him first to introduce me.

I conveyed all this to Omar and Sabbar, who seemed satisfied with the results. Then I called Zobeida, the daughter of Tariq Aziz. She answered after one ring, cutting me off before I could speak.

"I know where you are," she said. "It is good, understand? It is a good place for you."

I got the point, and quickly hung up.

After talking for a while with Omar, whom I immediately liked, I found that Wafiq al-Samarrai was his wife's brother, and that he was due back from exile in town the following day. Why not, I suggested, ask for his assistance, since reporting all this information would be good PR for the National Salvation Movement? Omar seemed slightly reluctant, but agreed anyway that it was a good idea.

"Come, Mister Bull," said Sabbar. "We go now to Muhi Atta house, yes?"

Atta and Ibrahim Alawi were the two people identified by Sabbar as killers of the 78 Kuwaiti civilians. Clearly, they were colleagues of his from the secret police. It seemed an unusual step for him to turn them in like this.

I kept the *dishdasha* on and tied the *keffiyah* into a turban. It came as a relief to be taken for an Arab. There were no longer stares, indeed my presence aroused no interest at all. I wished I had embedouined myself earlier. Life was so much simpler — with other Arabs, at least.

Muhi Atta's house was not far away. When we rang the bell in his wall, no one answered the door. Sabbar pushed open the gate — an unusual act in this part of the world, where a man's space is sacred — and the three of us walked into the garden uninvited. Sabbar knocked roughly with his fist on the front door. A curtain moved slightly to the side, which Omar noticed and told Sabbar, who began shouting for Muhi. At length the door opened to reveal a bleary-eyed man in his late thirties, unshaven, greasy greying hair and moustache, wearing his sleeping *dishdasha*. We were shown into a rather opulent sitting room, with fitted mahogany cupboards and sleek polished furniture. Tea was brought by yet another small boy. I had asked Omar if they could get Atta to describe the killing as well as identify the place where bodies had been buried. This they did, in Arabic of course, and I still have it on videotape. Atta did not implicate himself, naturally, but he did describe what had happened, and he drew a map showing where the murders took place.

He looked tormented, as well he might, and at one point was clearly pleading with Sabbar.

"We want him to show us the place himself," Omar told me later. "But he not want to do this."

"He's not in much of a position to refuse, is he?" I said.

Back at Sabbar's house, I called Kuwait City and got through to Rabia Adifani without any trouble. He was an urbane, highly educated man who spoke faultless English. Julie Chappell had briefed him, so I merely had to fill in the details. It was when I mentioned that the Kuwaiti civilians had been captured in a bus that he really began to take interest. The bus was travelling near the Iraq border, and Iraqi soldiers, then occupying Kuwait, seized all the passengers, who were mainly women and children, and drove them to Iraq. It was a piece of information that had been withheld from the media in order to make the verification of reports like mine easier. Adifani was anxious to come himself to verify the discovery, so we agreed to meet the following day at a well-known restaurant on the outskirts of Samarra. He would fly in by helicopter.

Sabbar had some business to attend to, so I went for a drive with Omar, who immediately told me he did not trust Sabbar. It seems that Sabbar's family knew the family of Muhi Atta, the killer, and were putting pressure on Sabbar to keep quiet about the dead Kuwaitis. They had, in fact, threatened to kill him.

I told Omar, who seemed a good and decent man, that it was far too serious a business to keep quiet about, although I understood Sabbar's position. We agreed that, whether Sabbar was in or out, we would carry on with the plan. Omar then opened up to me a little more, confessing his interest in starting a political party of his own. He had assembled a group of people, he said, who shared his political views. They were all professionals, doctors, lawyers, teachers, and they wanted a party that represented their interests. Like the general, Omar said Iraqis did not want leaders from the military or the old regime, or from exiles who had escaped what they had suffered.

He paused, as if deciding whether to go on. The wrinkles on his forehead spread across his shiny bald pate when he thought deeply. He sighed, then told me that he had planned a coup against Saddam in 1995. It had been very elaborate, involving aircraft and divisions of the army, and it may well have worked, but at the last minute, it had been nixed by Wafiq, Omar's brother-in-law, who was then in London. It was not clear to me why Wafiq had called it off, although it seemed to involve army units still loyal to him. The only answer appeared to be because the coup did not involve Wafiq, or did not involve him sufficiently. I sensed that Omar's relationship with his brother-in-law was a little rocky, but I did not press him on it.

We passed a wall on which was daubed some old graffiti:

ISRAEL AND ZYNIST AMERICA MUST GO TO HILL

"Which hill would that be?" I said.

Omar laughed.

We warmed to each other greatly over the following hour, confessing hopes and dreams like old friends. Omar embodied almost everything worthwhile about human beings. His hopes were unselfish, but not impractically utopian. He just envisaged a better tomorrow for his people, where the emphasis was on education and achieving potential, not on making money. It turned out that he intended to give his share in any reward to his brother Ziad, for the wife's kidney transplant. Omar had lived on the edge for many years, I realized, with little more than his good intentions and decency to get him through. The years had taken their toll, and worry had riven its indelible marks on his kindly face. A business he had been partners in was seized by Uday, too, leaving Omar with much debt. But you took that on the chin in Iraq and moved on. Getting angry did no good, and getting even was impossible. Yet debt did not prevent him from being generous — I had to fight to pay for anything. When I looked into his big pained eyes, sorrow and anger would well up in me against the gang of thugs in Washington, men who were not worthy to lick Omar's shoes. For a man who had lived an extraordinarily hard life and somehow remain upright, he was extraordinarily humble and self-effacing. If there were twenty more men like him, I thought, the country would survive. It was the Omars of Iraq who ought to have been sought out and appointed to the interim council, not self-seeking convicted felons like Ahmad Chalabi, who merely want to step into Saddam's huge shoes, then get even for past humiliations, then get even richer.

"You know, Mister Paul," Omar said, as we stood watching the murky Tigris flow by, "it is my wish that when all this war is over you will come back to Samarra as my guest."

It was a nice thing to say, and I knew it was meant as a gesture of affection. He was a sincere man. He just led a life of such Byzantine complexity that it frequently baffled even him, and made commitments and allegiances difficult.

I had dinner that night at Omar's house, where the women were not in purdah and things seemed a little more Westernized. Afterwards, Omar said he would show me the new house he was building. On the way, we passed an area of lavish new homes centred around a brand new mosque.

"This Saddam Mosque," said Omar. "The weep-ons are buried underneath this mosque."

"How do you know?"

He had evidently seen them being buried when the mosque was being built. Army trucks had arrived at night and a cargo had been unloaded which was then stacked in a sub-basement beneath the main basement.

"How can we get permission to look in there?" I said.

"We must ask imam."

"Would the imam allow it?"

Omar shrugged. Who knew?

While we were inspecting the smart new house he was building in a new part of town, the general arrived. As I have observed, people always know where you are in the Middle East.

"Robert, come," he said.

Thus summoned, I told Omar I would see him later.

The general drove back past the spiral minaret towards the old part of the city. We stopped at a high-walled house not far from Sabbar's home. Zobeida answered the door.

"Come in," she said.

I followed her down a corridor, while the general went off into a sitting room. It was a large old house, with linoleum floors and an excess of decorative ceramic urns. They were everywhere, on shelves, on the floors, on windowsills.

Tariq Aziz sat alone at a square wooden table upon which many papers were scattered. He looked sick. His eyes were red and watery, he was unkempt and unshaven and his hound's-tooth sports jacket looked as if he had slept in it. There was no sign of a bodyguard or any kind of military presence. I am sure he was alone, with his daughter.

"Sit down," he said, his voice hoarse. "You said you would give me the list of your questions ..."

"I was not able to get it to you," I said, taking the list from my case. "Here it is, sir."

"You look fine as an Arab," he said, taking the list.

His lips moved as he read the questions.

"How would I characterize Iraq's relationship with the U.S. before 1990?" he read aloud, adding after a pause, "It was excellent. We were an ally."

I wondered if this was the interview.

"No, no," he said. "I wanted to see if I could help you ..." He looked back at the sheet of questions. "Did the U.S. supply Iraq with weapons of mass destruction?" he read. "The million-dollar question, eh?"

"Yes, sir."

"Well, yes, of course they did, as did others," he said. "But we have none now."

I could not resist asking the question that followed it: "Were you ever warned, by Donald Rumsfeld or anyone, not to use these weapons against Iran?"

"No one warned us," he said. "Why were they given to us if not to use? But it is not a straightforward issue ... When Rumsfeld came here it was not to warn anyone. He came to offer encouragement and assistance. His excellency, our president, is not someone America can push around or warn."

I agreed that Saddam did not seem to be this kind of person. A phone bleeped nearby and I heard Zobeida answer it. She said something in Arabic and came immediately into the room, handing her father the phone.

"We will have to cut this short," she said.

"No problem."

"Thank you for coming at such short notice," she said, showing me out.

The general was already sitting in his car.

"It is all right?" he said.

"I don't know. I think they got bad news."

"No, it is all right," he said. "We will come tomorrow."

As we drove away, I saw in the wing mirror that the gates of the house had opened. A vehicle emerged.

The general left me at Omar's, where I slept until dawn. At one point, I awoke to the sounds of distant gunfire, learning the next day that looters were at work in Samarra too.

Wafiq al-Samarrai had arrived in the night, coming from the north through Turkey. People were flocking to the National Salvation Movement building to pay their respects and offer allegiance, just as they did to the sheikhs. Despite the family connection, Wafiq kept us waiting a long time and, when we were finally shown into a large bare room, it was made clear by an armed guard, who stood at the door throughout our meeting, that we had five minutes.

Wafiq, a stocky middle-aged man with a thick black Stalin moustache and glossy hair, was dressed all in black. As his new PR consultant, I thought, I would have to have a word about his sinister appearance. Omar spoke to him in Arabic. It seemed to be a harsh conversation, but I could not really follow what was being said. When they were through, Wafiq turned angrily to me and said,

"You. What are you doing here?"

There was something fairly unpleasant about him. He was one of those people who are more dangerous when they are nervous, and he did seem to be on edge. As I came to learn, his reception had not been what he had expected. Iraq after Saddam was not what he imagined it would be.

I told him I was covering the war and the reconstruction of the country.

"So you want to interview me?"

I did not, but I assured him I did, saying I was not ready to do it yet and wanted to give him time to settle in. I could tell he resented the suggestion that he was not settled. He gave me his sat-phone number and I promised I would call in the next couple of days.

When we were outside the building, I asked Omar how Wafiq had responded to the suggestion about turning over the information about the Kuwaitis to the Americans.

"He is not interested," Omar said. "He was very angry with me for bringing you."

"Why?"

"He is a bad man, a killer," said Omar, looking sad. "My wife is willing to testify in court that he killed nearly one hundred Shia prisoners."

"Her own brother?"

"Yes."

"That says something about him ..."

"Yes, Mister Paul. He is a bad man."

I pondered Wafiq's reluctance to use the information about the Kuwaitis, asking Omar if it was possible Wafiq had anything to do with their murder.

"I think he did," said Omar. "As we talk there I see his eyes and I know he is hiding something."

A chill ran through me. I recalled Wafiq's black pitiless stare. "It was not a very good idea to bring the subject up, was it?"

"No, Mister Paul."

We went for our meeting with the man from Kuwait.

The place — which Omar had chosen — was a restaurant that had been reserved for Ba'ath Party members. It was a large low building of red brick beside a man-made lake that adjoined the Tigris. It was an obvious novelty for Omar to enter the grounds. He told me no one had been allowed to build anything by the river — Saddam had a fixation with keeping the Tigris to himself. It transpired that another of Omar's dreams was to build a hotel on this spot for tourists visiting Samarra. Omar had a lot of dreams. The dreams had seemed very possible then, and we fantasized a very different future for Iraq, one in which Westerners would once again flock to see the birthplace of civilization. Just thinking about our little fantasy makes my heart heavy now. Omar loved his hometown. He was proud of it, and he took great pride in showing me around.

We asked the restaurant staff if any Kuwaitis had been in. They were puzzled by the question. I assumed we would notice a helicopter landing. When Rabia Adifani was an hour late, we began to realize he was not coming.

I called his office in Kuwait City, but only got through to an unpleasant, haughty woman who chastised me for not speaking Arabic to her. All she would say was that Mr. Adifani was not available. I left a message.

As we drove to Sabbar's house, Omar turned into a small side-street. "We meet someone, come," he said, getting out.

"Who?"

"Let him use your phone," Omar said. "But do not say I tell you who he is. You can say you recognize him, okay?"

"Who are we meeting?"

"He is the private secretary of Saddam — Ahmed Hussein." (Not to be confused with the general of that name.)

A woman answered the door. She had a worried expression that lifted when she saw Omar. We were shown into an inner courtyard garden where an older woman and a fat man were sitting. As I was introduced, a tall older man in Arab dress appeared. He had neatly groomed grey hair and the ubiquitous Ba'athi moustache. His face was very familiar, and I realized I had met him before, and seen him in countless pictures sitting beside Saddam. We shook hands and I offered him my phone. He was calling a number in Syria, and I had to show him how to punch it in.

I sat with the others while he called. The older woman turned to me and said, in English,

"It's atrocious, isn't it?"

"What?"

"What the Americans are doing here."

I wondered if there was news I had missed, but she meant the invasion generally.

"You miss Saddam?" I asked.

"Terribly," she said. "We all do. The country will fall apart now. What we shall do, I don't know ..."

"The Shia will kill us," said the fat man, and then he laughed.

When Ahmed Hussein handed me back the phone, I told him I recognized him. He had introduced me to Saddam in 1990, in fact. He looked faintly embarrassed.

"I am no one," he said. "Just a servant. I have no information."

When had he last seen Saddam?

"I have not seen him," he said. "I know nothing. Mistakes were made ..."

"Mistakes?"

"The party made many mistakes, wrong things. I am sorry for that, and now we must pay the price. But I have no information."

I asked if I could interview him on camera. He made self-deprecating, apologetic gestures. They were all in shock, I realized. It was hard for people his age to be forced to adjust to new realities. I was surprised at his frank admission that "mistakes" had been made. Even in 1990, I had the impression that Saddam had lost touch with what was going on. People were scared to tell him the truth, and even less likely to tell him that mistakes had been made. As he said himself, Ahmed Hussein was of no importance in the regime. His opinion did not matter to anyone, and would only have brought him trouble. One could not expect the people close to Saddam to take the blame for anything. They had merely been concerned with their own survival.

After tea, Omar and I left. On the road, we passed Sabbar and Muhi Atta. They stopped and backed up. Sabbar looked sheepish, guiltier than usual. Omar and he had a brief exchange, and then we drove off in opposite directions.

"What's going on?" I asked.

"He does not want Muhi to show us where the bodies are."

"This is terrible. You cannot allow this killer to escape justice, Omar."

"I think Sabbar is not so innocent," he said.

This was getting convoluted. Was I dealing with a group of killers all trying to blame one another? I wondered. I asked Omar if he still had the map that Muhi had drawn. He pulled it from his jacket pocket.

"You and I will find the place," I said.

Omar nodded. There was something about his sad eyes and gentle manner that I found reassuring. He was not involved in any murder, I felt absolutely certain of it.

The place where the Kuwaiti civilians were buried alive proved to be some distance from Samarra, near the resort town of al-Habbaniyah, between Ramadi and Fallujah, on the shores of the second of Iraq's three huge lakes. To get there, we had to drive through a hundred and fifty kilometres of desert. To while away the time, I helped Omar draw up plans for his political party. We named it the People's Democratic Party, the PDP, and made a list of laudable objectives. It might as well have been called the Utopian Party.

I had sounded out various people about the possibility of Jordan's Prince Hassan becoming king of Iraq. Reactions were mixed. Some thought a parliamentary monarchy under Hassan a good solution, providing a sense of continuity while democracy took root. Others were violently opposed to the idea, denouncing it as another attempt to deprive Iraqis of self-rule. Omar was more mildly opposed to a monarchy, viewing it as just another form of dictatorship.

"We are ready for democracy," he said. "We are hungry for it. Why should we not be allowed to make it for ourselves? We will make mistakes, and we will learn from them. Just as you did. But it will be our democracy, not anyone else democracy."

Just outside of al-Habbaniyah, we came across American troops with several armoured vehicles. They flagged us down. I got out, conscious of my Arab clothes.

"I'm a British journalist," I said, waving my ID card.

"Keep your hands up," someone shouted. "Don't move."

Guns were pointing at me. The soldiers were Special Forces, so it did not take them long to work out that we were legit. They searched the car, frisked us, and then everyone relaxed. A Major Gregg asked what the hell I was doing out here alone. I told him about the Kuwaitis. He seemed interested, but it was not his mission. He asked why we were going into Habbaniyah City, which he described as "not secure." Omar told him we were going to ask a friend of his, a doctor, for help locating the burial site. Major Gregg asked me to keep him informed of what we found. I asked for his telephone number. The major wished us luck and a safe trip, and we went on our way.

Omar was impressed by the courtesy with which we were treated. His previous experiences had clearly been different, so I told him that Special Forces were the exception not the rule. They were better educated and more intelligent, and operated with more reason than fear.

The entrance to Habbaniyah City was barricaded and a group of armed Iraqis stood by it. I thought we were in for trouble, but Omar shouted something through his window and the barrier was pulled aside, allowing us in. It seems the Iraqis were merely defending their city from looters. So much for Special Forces' warning.

We drove to a small hospital where Omar's doctor friend worked. The man gave us tea while examining Omar's map. After explaining where we should head next, he went back to his patients. The city was like any resort out of season, sleepy and largely closed up. We drove along a road that skirted the lake about a kilometre from its shore. About twenty minutes from the town, we came to a large area behind barbed-wire fencing and turned into its long driveway. Out of sight from the road was a series of long low brick huts with corrugated tin roofs.

"These are for killing," said Omar.

The place was deserted, and an oppressive stillness hung over it that reminded me of Auschwitz. We looked inside the huts. Most contained just one long room. In the first hut, we found a huge pile of rocket-propelled grenade launchers, complete with grenades. There must have been three or four hundred of them. In the next hut, we found the back wall riddled with bullet holes. In the ceiling were ominous-looking hooks. To the side were oil drums full of gravel that were also riddled with bullet holes. It was an awful room. People had been brought here and hung by hooks, then tortured and shot. The floor and walls were stained dark red. There were three more such rooms in the other huts, and outside was a metal frame to which people had been tied then shot. A watchtower stood by the rear fence, beyond which was the broad lakeshore. It was a beautiful spring day and the surface of the blue lake rippled with whitecaps. Yet a great chord of doom seemed to hang over this place. Terrible things had occurred here, and those responsible for them had clearly fled the moment they heard the regime had collapsed.

"Many, many they kill here," said Omar.

We walked through a gate in the fence onto the shore. Omar's map indicated that the Kuwaitis had been buried out here beneath the sand. It was obvious from the assorted mounds visible that bulldozers had moved a lot of sand out here. Omar had brought a shovel from his car, so I took it and began to dig in a spot where there had been a large square pit. The sand was loose and easy to move. On my second shovelful, I uncovered a tattered brassiere and a large pair of women's underpants. They had obviously been in the sand for years, their fabric half-rotted, the colours faded. After ten minutes' digging, I realized that any bodies were going to be a good deal deeper.

Omar took over, finding more women's clothing.

"They pull off the clothes," he said, "and have the womans first ..."

"Yes."

It did not bear thinking about, what had happened to these people.

Before long, we uncovered a partially rotted human head. It was in a hideous state.

"Okay," I said. "That's enough for me. We've found enough. Let the Kuwaitis come for their people."

"Yes," said Omar.

His eyes brimmed with tears. I led him away. We continued on the same road, heading towards Fallujah rather than returning the way we had come, and soon we crossed the bridge of a small dam. Beyond it lay a little village. Omar stopped, saying there was someone to whom he wished to speak. While he was talking with a wizened old man, I telephoned Kuwait City.

Rabia Adifani was now there. I asked him why he had not come to meet us, but the answer was vague. He had run into some sort of bureaucratic problem, but he would not say what it was. There was something in his voice that I did not like, a sense that he was not being truthful. I told him we had now found the burial site, and what did he want to do about it? Before he could reply, we were cut off, and I was unable to get through when I redialled. I told Omar we would try again later.

He had asked the old man for some details about the death camp, but beyond confirming that it was a death camp — something we hardly needed anyone to do — he was unwilling to say more without permission from his sheikh. The sheikh was away, however, so although he had information, he would not help us.

The attitude suddenly angered me. How could they apply tribal codes to something like this? It was futile thinking this way, though. The answer was that they did, and they did because they always had done.

"Perhaps we must go to army?" said Omar.

"If you want. They should probably be told about 'Chemical' Ali, but it's not my job to help the American army."

"You will help me?" he said.

"If you want me to, but I'm not sure what I can do. My main concern is to interview Tariq Aziz."

This was not among Omar's priorities.

Back in Samarra, we went to see Sabbar, telling him we had found the murder site. He became very solicitous, hugging me several times with soft, pudgy arms. Then he offered to bring me items taken from the Baghdad museum — not by him, he hastened to add, but by Shia. They were for sale. Thinking I would hand them over to the authorities, I agreed to see the items. That was the last I heard of the matter for some time.

While we were sitting talking, the American army arrived in town. The 3rd Brigade Combat Team pulled into the old Ba'ath Party headquarters and barricaded themselves behind rolls of razor wire. We drove to take a look. The faces staring out from huge tin helmets were those of terrified teenagers. I realized that in my turban and *dishdasha*, I was just another Arab staring back at them, and for the first time I saw the hatred and fear in their eyes. Had no one told them that Samarra was one place they would be welcome? Obviously not, because by morning they had shot and killed three men whose crime had merely been carrying rifles. Many people carried guns now, not surprising during a war. Within a day the Americans had alienated the whole city, which had been prepared to fête them as liberators. It was a pity.

The following morning, I accompanied Omar to the old Ba'ath Party HQ. He parked in the road outside and we walked to where a U.S. tank now blocked the entrance. Peering out from behind the armour, the U.S. army looked like a bunch of poorly educated, very scared teens from a distant planet, beamed down into what they believed to be very hostile terrain and absurdly over-armed.

"Hey!" shouted one of these space invaders as I approached. "Stop right there!"

The *dishdasha* and turban had obviously thrown him, so I reached for my *Harper's* press card, saying, "It's okay, I'm a Brit journalist."

"I said, 'Stop,' fucker!" he growled, pointing his enormous rifle at me. "You understand 'Stop'?"

I nodded.

Another soldier appeared and asked me in Arabic worse than my own what I wanted.

"I do speak English," I pointed out.

"Get this motherfucker!" the first soldier shouted to no one in particular. After the grace and warmth of the Arabs, this jolt of American culture unnerved me. I removed the turban in an attempt to convince them I was friend not foe, but the combination of tightly wound cloth and the heat of the day, I noticed a little later, had left my hair looking far from friendly. I now resembled one of the medieval churls in *Bride of Frankenstein.*

The second soldier patted me down roughly, then scrutinized my ID card minutely. I had just prepared myself to defend its authenticity when he said, "What the fuck is *Harper's?*"

I told him, making it sound more like the *National Enquirer.*

"It have naked chicks in it?" he said.

"Not as many as we'd like ..."

"Am I gonna see my name in it?"

"If you tell me what it is, I guarantee it."

As usual, his name flashes were hidden beneath the flak jacket and, this time, under sand goggles on the helmet. He said nothing, turning the ID card over to read the two dense paragraphs on its back. I realized I had never read them myself.

"Who the fuck is Ben Metcalf?" he said, after two minutes.

"Editor. *Senior* editor ..."

The expression on his face made me wonder if I'd said "pimp" or "crack dealer."

"You report to him?"

"Yeah. He's like the general. And I'm like ... you guys. The ground troops."

I thought this inspired.

"I never talk to no fucking generals," he replied, bitterly.

I quickly demoted Ben Metcalf to sergeant.

"Sergeant he'd fucking be here. Like me."

I wondered how he even knew about Ben, soon discovering that the tiny print on the card's rear declared that all questions regarding the ID should be directed to Ben. I hoped Ben knew about this.

"What the fuck is this?" the soldier then demanded, thrusting the card under my nose and prodding at the second paragraph angrily, as if it contained something terrible. Maybe it did ...

Mercifully, it proved to be a French translation of the former paragraph.

"Why the fuck is that there?"

"Good question," I said. "Maybe it's because I live in Canada?"

"Let me get this straight," he said. "You gotta British passport, you live in Canada, and you write for an American magazine ..."

"Right."

"You gotta admit it sounds fuckin' weird."

I admitted it did.

"So why you dressed like this fucking scum?" He indicated the growing crowd of locals, some of them clearly concerned for my welfare.

I told him I found his remark deeply offensive.

"Thatta fact?"

"Yep."

"Fuck you."

I was about to walk away, back to the "scum," when brigade commander Colonel Frederick Rudesheim showed up. Tall, humourless, with a face so dry and blotchy from the heat and dust it looked camouflaged like the rest of him, the colonel at least asked, and in English, what I wanted.

As I rattled off the embarrassment of intelligence riches and mentioned the POWs freed by Omar, I could see more than a flicker of interest in his ungenerous eyes. He sent me to fetch Omar, who had been anxiously waiting in his car outside. Clearly, I had not been receiving the kind of welcome he envisaged for us.

We were taken up into the Ba'ath Party building, which reminded me of a Chinese restaurant I knew, cut-out friezes around the walls and recessed strip lighting. As we sat down, I realized Rudesheim was now interrogating us. It was not a chat. Also present was a giant Kurdish translator wearing a U.S. army uniform and a demonic pair of wraparound shades.

"Why concern yourself with Kuwaiti civilians dead when so many Kurdish people also dead?" he demanded at one point, in a booming angry voice.

I was not sure what the right answer to this might be. Kuwaitis, it must be said, are not the most beloved of Arab peoples. Kurds, of course, are not Arabs but do rank high among the most oppressed of peoples.

The Kurdish translator then flashed a smile his face had appeared incapable of seconds earlier, and I realized that he was joking. Kurdish humour is probably something worth exploring.

Half an hour into the grilling, Colonel Rudesheim announced, somewhat surprisingly, that he had a lunch appointment. Omar and I said we would go back to Omar's house for lunch, but that did not suit Rudesheim.

"You're the best intelligence assets I've come across," he said. "I'd rather not let you out of my sight."

What did that mean? Were we being arrested?

"I'm just concerned for your safety," the colonel said, unconvincingly. "I'd prefer you just wait here. Then we're gonna fly you up to Tikrit so the CI guys can talk with you. Okay?"

CI is Central Intelligence — the CIA in uniform. I made another futile attempt at persuading him we would be fine driving back and forth to Omar's, but I could tell that if we tried to walk out we would be arrested.

"Well make sure you're fed," Rudesheim said. And with that he was gone.

An hour later saw Omar and I tearing open heated pouches from MRE boxes. I had Country Captain Chicken; Omar got Chicken with Salsa. He dug his plastic spoon into the red sludge gingerly, and I think was genuinely surprised to find that it had no taste at all.

By the time Colonel Rudesheim returned from lunch, Omar and the Kurdish translator were behaving like old friends. They had hit it off big time — something the colonel clearly did not like. He told us a Black Hawk helicopter would soon be arriving to take us up to Tikrit, and then he resumed his questions.

At the point where I mentioned Wafiq and said his National Salvation Movement had little support in Samarra, Rudesheim bristled.

"I've just attended a big lunch hosted by him," he said, "and all the local sheikhs were there. Looked to me like he had a ton of support."

I told him the two most prominent local sheikhs — Adnan and Fadhel Hassan — had assured me the other day that Wafiq would be lucky to get ten percent of the vote in any election. He had three strikes against him, the sheikhs had pointed out: he was a military figure, and no one wanted the military involved in a new regime; he was a close associate of Saddam from 1980 to 1992; and he had been living in exile, which meant he had avoided the suffering in Iraq yet now expected to return as a leader. True,

Omar had told me more of this than had the sheikhs, but it did accurately represent local opinion.

"Looked like a popular guy to me," said Rudesheim, making me realize how ignorant he was of the customs and social norms in the land he occupied.

"The sheikhs are there out of courtesy," I said. "And no one would show disrespect to his host. But they will also support the candidate they think will win. It's that simple."

"They're two-faced?" Rudesheim said.

"If you like, yes. But in different ways than we are two-faced ..."

"We?" the colonel narrowed his eyes.

"Like when Bush says this war is to liberate Iraqis ..."

"S'right." He was daring me to go further.

"We all know he's lying, don't we?"

"I don't believe the President of the United States is a liar," said Rudesheim, his voice eerily low.

"Wafiq is trying to impress you."

"And he succeeded."

I told him Omar's wife was Wafiq's sister and that she was willing to testify in court that her brother was guilty of mass murder.

Rudesheim was clearly rattled by this, but determined not to show it.

I briefly recounted Wafiq's past for him.

"Put it this way," I said. "If this war had been fought in '91, Wafiq would have been on your deck of cards."

"I'm sure CI will be fascinated," said the colonel.

By the time our transportation to Tikrit had arrived we could have driven there and back twice. Omar bid farewell to his new pal, the Kurdish translator, and followed me outside. The expression on his kind face seemed to be wondering whether he would like the experience awaiting him.

It was not, in fact, our transportation to Tikrit that had now arrived, but rather our transportation to that transportation. Colonel Rudesheim announced that we would be riding in separate Hummer vehicles, which sounded sinister to me (*keep them apart so they can't confer*) yet proved to be merely pragmatic: there was barely enough room in them for a driver let alone passengers.

The interior of my Humvee resembled the tiny basement workshop of an electronics buff too absorbed by his hobby to bother with basic hygiene. It smelled like an old sneaker, and besides being painted the colour of sand was liberally basted with real sand and mud. The computer bolted onto its dashboard looked as if it had lain in the ground for several years. Rudesheim wiped its screen clear, revealing a complicated map with a flashing blue dot in its lower left hand corner. Evidently, we were that dot.

"You'll like our toys," he predicted.

It seemed a friendly enough statement.

I supposed that this was the army's idea of a fully "loaded" vehicle: there was so much stuff clamped, bolted, hooked, clipped or glued onto the Hummer's roof, walls, floor and dashboard — a caddy for tools where the cup holder would have been, a short-wave radio in the glove compartment, a metal-detector and five cases of bottled water on the rear floor — that the doors had been removed to make leg-room while the rear seats had been sacrificed for more storage space.

When the driver turned his key, metal quivered and tractor-like engines growled as all four Hummers in our convoy lurched into life at once. But none moved. We sat vibrating lustily. Soldiers looked around anxiously; one face nodded uncertainly to another, which, a beat later, nodded back with knitted brows. The roll of razor wire was dragged back across the Ba'ath Party HQ's entrance by guards who stepped backwards in unison. Suddenly, we moved. These rituals of safety are commonplace in the army.

The puzzled faces of locals, riven with both mirth and concern, spotted Omar and me inside the snarling dun-coloured vehicles and grew more baffled than before. Children ran alongside us shouting. I felt part of something mighty and impressive, yet I also felt horribly vulnerable. This is what soldiers must feel all the time: a part of something larger and nobler than themselves, yet also, because of this increased stature, easy prey for forces that are cunning, swift and few in number. The lone gunman is a far greater threat than any enemy battalion. I felt like Gulliver in Lilliput.

Had any in our convoy hoped for happy, cheering faces lining the liberated streets of Samarra, they would have been disappointed. The men who watched us pass did so with sullen looks, extreme skepticism the only identifiable idea in their dark bright eyes. The driver seemed nervous, edgy, glancing from side to side behind his wraparound shades, looking more like a naive twenty-year-old cast ashore in a strange land than an ambassador of liberty bringing good news of freedom. The U.S. Army had received the message quite soon: Iraqis were not happy to see them, not happy to be freed of tyranny by blitz and invasion, not certain of the invaders' motives at all. I wondered if the invaders were even sure of their own motives, which, in the case of soldiers, were always someone else's motives — for theirs was but to do and die ...

We finally turned off the main road onto a dirt track that ran alongside the spiral minaret, bouncing and roaring some five hundred metres and throwing up a thick fog of dust before coming to an abrupt halt. Soldiers leapt out and took up positions in a farcical, familiar manner, weapons trained on imaginary foes, faces squinting in a parody of combat readiness. After a minute of this ritual posturing, it was deemed safe for the rest of us to get out. I wondered idly why we had been transported to this barren, dusty spot, but thought better of asking. There were certainly no helicopters anywhere to be seen.

I struck up a conversation with one of our defenders, a five-foot sinew with mirrored insect eyes and a curious protrusion jutting from the reddened skin on his chin. It looked like a second set of lower teeth extending from the first one, and made the chinstrap of his helmet appear to be cradling an alien mandible.

"Bin trahn t'git me some o' that Eye-Rakky currency," he confided. "Th' wife, she klects bank notes, she does ..."

"They all do," I said.

He squinted up at me uncertainly, the mandible moving further out below its thin, taut skin — as if it was about to burst through and come snapping at me.

I took out my wallet and gave him a few 250-dinar notes. They looked like bad counterfeits, scanned and printed out on copy paper, which is understandable: the printing process would have cost more than the cash it produced. Iraqi money had inflated nine thousand percent over fifteen years.

"Thass real nice o' you," he said, genuinely grateful. "How mush this worth then?"

"Approximately nothing."

He nodded, assessing. Then he ejected a spurt of black saliva from between his lips and the mandible moved from side to side in his chin urgently. I realized only then that it was a wad of chewing tobacco packed between his gums and lower lip. I had never seen someone chew tobacco.

I had never met this kind of American before, either, I decided after we had talked for another ten minutes. Of the rank and file, the grunts, many of those who weren't black were much like him. Small — around five foot two — and wiry, he seemed unaffected by the quantity of "kit" strapped, clipped, tied, buttoned and buckled somewhere onto his torso. Packs, pouches, wallets, holsters, a knapsack, belts, guns, knives, a water canteen, the flak jacket, a gas mask, walkie-talkie paraphernalia — he was as fully loaded as the Hummers, yet this extra seventy or eighty pounds did not prevent him from seeming coiled and ready to spring into action at a second's notice. The army places little value in contemplation. It's all about knee-jerk-yessir-will-do reaction. *Into the Valley of Death rode the five hundred* ... Not their commanding officers, though. The thought of "canon-fodder" again stuck obstinately in my mind — because this man was it! He was the one Bush II blithely condemned to death with the phrase, *Bring it on* ...

"Yo!" he yelped suddenly, bouncing into his action-man defensive stance, hunched over, poised, flicking off the safety catch. "Who the fuck those assholes?"

Three curious locals had appeared further down the dusty track, probably wondering why the U.S. forces were so interested in their field. When they noticed that twenty soldiers were now aiming big guns straight at them, however, they backed off and walked hastily across a distant field and vanished, in gun-sights all the way.

"Paranoia?" I asked him.

He spat, knitting sweaty brows.

"Cain't be too careful," he said.

It struck me that you could easily be too careful — you might kill a few less innocent Iraqis.

We got around to why he had joined up. It was the old story: Mom and Dad couldn't afford no education. The army dangled its carrot. No one had mentioned no war ...

"Bet you'll be glad to get back home?" I said.

"You fucken said it there," he said, envisioning the moment with wistful eyes. "Oh yeah. I'm gonna sit me out on that fucken porch looken out over them woods, a bottle o' Jack in one hand, fucken glass o' ice in th'other, and ... I'm juss gonna chill. Yessir! Chill ..."

I imagined the word, in this heat, had suddenly taken on new meaning for him.

"Yo!"

I thought we had more hostiles approaching.

"Here come your ride," he said.

The air was suddenly filled with the ominous *thwack-thwack-thwack* of chopper blades. First one Black Hawk appeared, turning in a narrow circle then descending like some great bird of prey and disappearing in a huge, swirling cloud of dust as it landed in the field. Seconds later, a second chopper mimicked precisely the motions of the first, landing some thirty metres ahead of it.

"Good luck," said Colonel Rudesheim, when we were okayed to approach the Black Hawks.

I felt we were on a mission now (how a kindly word from the Father Figure *always* fires one up!) and badly wanted to say something like, *Thank you, sir. It's been a privilege working with you gentlemen* ... We were in a movie, after all, and for most people back home, this war would only make sense as a movie, or the memories of many movies. Soldiers are invariably heroic if they are lead roles. So is the war they are fighting, in spite of all the evidence available to counter this notion. Children are still being told the old lie. *Dulce et decorum est pro patria mori* ... Bullshit!

"The front helicopter," someone told us.

"No, they'll travel in the other one," someone else said.

"Watch your head!"

I clambered up the ladder and fell into what looked like a basement tool closet. The army did not believe in frippery, to be sure. Its vehicles all had interiors of relentless pragmatism — all one saw was the skull beneath the skin. There was not much room, either. I was buckled into the harness seatbelt, then handed a huge set of headphones with a spindly mike attached. Omar, receiving the same treatment, looked merely embarrassed. He glanced over at me and smiled wanly, but I could not tell whether he was enjoying this or wishing he had never met me.

Few of us travel often by helicopter, do we? It needs to be stated, therefore, that the take-off is, if not vertical, certainly diagonal — a somewhat exhilarating experience. This is quickly doused by the sheer volume of engine noise. They were not headphones, really — they were noise mufflers. If you wanted to converse you had to do it by microphone.

Flying low along the line of the Tigris, I was struck by how peaceful the land below looked from this serene height. It must be *something* to unleash bombs and death on such a tranquil prospect. It must take *resolve*. Here and there, huge dense columns of black smoke from burning oil made it look as if the clouds were starting to invade earth. The land seemed tired, though; everything had a wasted appearance, as if it had been used up, as if the juice had been sucked out of it.

Inside twenty minutes, we began to circle over a vast complex of palatial buildings sitting high on a promontory over the river. From the Black Hawk's vantage point, you could see the intricacy and profusion of security walls, with concealed roadways and hidden gates. This was Saddam's greatest of fortresses outside Baghdad, built near the village of his birth, which had also been the birthplace of Arabia's greatest warrior, Salah-ad-Din, who drove the Crusaders from the Holy Land and reestablished Muslim supremacy over the whole region. Saddam made much of the association.

The soldier strapped in opposite me cradling his M16 had been grim-faced throughout the trip, and I wondered how we had been described to our escorts. Were we prisoners for interrogation? Were we to be considered friend or foe? It was hard to say, and the sheer noise of the chopper's engine made any conversation impossible. Soon we began to descend, landing in what looked like a soccer field.

I had videotaped as much as possible of the flight, and continued when we were summoned out of the Black Hawk. I could tell it irritated the soldiers but

I resolved to continue, mainly to assert my position, that I did not consider myself a prisoner. I was soon told I couldn't film here, though, with no further explanation. We waited for half an hour or so, without being told why. Omar looked nervous, probably thinking he had made a big mistake in trusting me. I tried reassuring him but I did not feel particularly reassured myself.

Eventually, a convoy of Hummers arrived and we were loaded on board with assorted crates and boxes. After the usual combat rituals, the vehicles wound out of the soccer field into the city, which seemed deserted, and then through the formidable gates in a high wall and into the palace complex.

As I had seen from the air, the interior was a labyrinth of walls, and everywhere in the extensive grounds there were U.S. soldiers camped. We cleared three checkpoints, passing dozens of armed guards and small buildings, then ascended on a smaller road towards an extraordinary structure. It seemed to be part Moghul palace and part geodesic dome. It was, I learned from Omar, Saddam's Salah-ad-Din Palace, designed a decade earlier by one of the president's girlfriends who was an artist from Samarra. The domed central area was supposed to resemble the helmet worn by Salah-ad-Din. On two sides, there were classical Moghul balconies with protruding turrets at the corners, and below them carved stone pillars of intertwined hands and arms, the top one of which was supposedly modelled on Saddam's hand and appeared to support with its palm the balcony above. The soaring pillars of the entrance had something Egyptian about them, yet despite this mélange of architectural styles the overall effect was one of tremendous harmony and beauty. For a modern building, it was breathtaking, and I felt glad that it had been spared from the bombing.

"This where y'all gonna be staying," said our driver, pulling into the drive that led past an equestrian statue of Salah-ad-Din in a small garden to the palace entrance. Omar and I were led through the orange marble of the entrance portico into an enormous hall which rose right up to the domed roof. In its centre hung a large gilded birdcage lacking a bird. A grand staircase flanked by strange phallic capstans spiralled up to the second floor. There were ornate mirrors everywhere, large modern paintings on the walls, and intricately patterned marble inlay on the floors. The overall effect was one of inordinate grandeur. Omar gazed around in awe, walking as if across eggshells.

"This way, gentlemen."

We were led across the hall and down a dark corridor. There was no electricity. The soldier opened a door and showed us into a vast wood-panelled room ringed with custom-built sofas in wood and silk.

"Nice place you've got here," I said.

"We like to take care of our guests," said the soldier. "Just wait here. The CI guys'll be with ya in a minute." He indicated a pile of MREs. "Help yourself to food, if you want ..."

He went out, closing the door.

Omar looked at the polished wood, the gilded sculptures, the Persian rug covering the entire floor, the man-sized fireplaces, the silk cushions, and he shook his head slowly.

"If Iraqi people see this," he said. "They not believe ..."

"You didn't realize Saddam lived so luxuriously?"

"No. We not told this. All the time we suffer and he is live this way ..."

He was weeping at the thought.

Behind the wood panelling, I noticed, there were at intervals spaces for guards to sit concealed, with small grilles through which to observe. Saddam had not felt safe anywhere. Looking at the giant vases and carved lions, at the Chinese lamps and ormolu side tables, I realized that most of the furnishings were just the kind of overpriced trash one saw for sale in shops catering to those with more money than taste. They were big and gaudy yet essentially worthless. Many items were overturned or broken, and several of the windows were smashed. Evidently, looters had been through here the moment the Republican Guard had left the palace complex.

All Omar saw was the opulence that had been sucked from the bones of his people. Their poverty versus this ostentatious wealth. I had not realized before now how little Iraqis actually knew of their leader's lifestyle. They assumed that Saddam lived well, but not this well. Tears running down his cheeks, Omar kept shaking his head in disbelief, perhaps matching every deprivation he had suffered with every surfeit he saw around him.

I dug through some of the opened MREs and found some sachets of juice crystals. Obviously, the room had been used as a mess hall. As I was mixing Omar up some grape juice, the door opened and two men in combat fatigues came in. They were in their late twenties, one fair-haired and fresh-faced, the other probably Hawaiian.

"Sorry to keep you waiting. I'm Agent Stewart," said the fair-haired one.

I did not catch the other's name, and neither wore name flashes at all, just as they had no apparent rank.

Agent Stewart's colleague was there as interpreter, we were told, but his Arabic proved to be worse than mine, so it was fortunate Omar spoke good English. They were both extremely polite, solicitous of our welfare, that we had eaten lunch, and so on. They were also anxious to "debrief" us separately. I told Stewart that Omar was the one with the information they wanted, that I was just along for the ride, but it made no difference to his interrogation.

Because I was not sure what Omar would say, and because I assumed we would be flown back to Samarra later that day, I was fairly frank about my encounters with Tariq Aziz. As I told Agent Stewart, I did not care what happened to Aziz after I had interviewed him, since I had no reason at all to be fond of the old regime.

After about two hours of questioning, Stewart announced a break. He and his colleague disappeared. I made Omar and myself some more juice. Half an hour later, a captain appeared and told us we would be needed for more questioning the next day, so we would have to stay the night.

"I guess you will have to stay here," he said.

I told him I was sure we had told the agents everything, that we wanted to return to Samarra, that Omar's wife would worry since he had not been able to tell her he was leaving. The captain shrugged. There were no helicopters going back today. I said we could get a taxi in town.

"You can try leaving," he said, "but you won't get past the first gate."

"Are we under arrest?"

"No. You've been detained for questioning."

"Is there a difference?"

He shrugged. "You may as well enjoy it."

Then he said he would show us to our rooms. We followed him back into the entrance hall, then up the twisting staircase to the second floor, which, amazingly, contained only two bedrooms.

"Which of you wants to sleep in Saddam's bed?" said the captain.

I was ready to give Omar this satisfaction, but he positively did not want it, so the captain showed him into the first room we came to, then escorted me to the far end of the huge landing.

"There you go," he said, opening the only door left. "Someone will bring you food in a while. Make yourself at home." He walked off.

We were the birds in that gilded cage downstairs, I thought.

I went through into a small sitting room furnished with reproduction French Empire furniture, wingback chairs and a monstrous desk. Beyond it lay the bedroom, which had French windows leading out to a vast balcony overlooking the river, with huge fireplaces at either end. This was the highest point of the promontory and the view over the other palaces and the rapids below was spectacular. The rooms were littered with broken glass from where the French doors had been smashed. Curtains, pillows, bedcovers, everything was pink and turquoise. It gave the room a girlie feeling that belied its occupant. But Saddam spent little time anywhere, and this suite with its magnificent views had probably seen as little of him as all his other suites. I have often observed that those who possess the places of which others can only dream rarely seem able to spend much time in them.

The bathroom was of preposterous grandeur, a built-in marble tub, toilet like a throne, shower overlooking the balcony, and all the fixtures solid gold. But there was no longer any running water, as the overflowing toilet amply proved, which makes even the grandest bathroom utterly irrelevant. As darkness fell, the lack of electricity was also beginning to turn the whole palace into a vast haunted house. A strong wind had started up and blew through the smashed windows, sending lace curtains billowing into the room, making the open door of the wardrobe creak on its hinge and rattling the glass beads in the chandelier. As comfortable as the linen sheets on Saddam's bed promised to be, I sensed it was going to be a long night. I lay back on the pillows with the curtains fluttering inches from my face. It was like a parody of a spooky room. Even the sashes going up from the headboard to the ceiling were rustling. Why, I asked myself, did they need to keep us here for the night?

"Bastards!"

I stood up.

How dumb could you get? They were going after Tariq Aziz! Of course they were. With what I had told them, they did not need me to lead them there. And they certainly did not care about my interview. I dashed out onto the balcony and tuned into the Iridium satellite.

Mercifully, Zobeida answered on the first ring. I told her what had happened, where I was, and that the Americans would almost certainly be coming. I could not tell whether she was angry with me or grateful for the warning. She said simply, "I see," then hung up.

The following day, I learned later, Tariq Aziz surrendered to the U.S. Army. He tried offering all the information he possessed in exchange for exile in England, but the Americans were not buying. He was imprisoned at the airport, where by all accounts he spent many days crying his eyes out. His family, including Zobeida, were flown to Jordan with their Mercedes and $250,000 in cash, which was immediately confiscated. As far as I know, they are still in Jordan, where several members of Saddam's family have also lived since the invasion and occupation of Iraq.

When Omar came, I told him what I had done, but he showed little interest. It had by now grown quite cold, so we set fire to the logs in one of my balcony's fireplaces, dragged two solid-silver Indian chairs outside and sat there watching the manic shadows dancing as a night full of stars was unveiled over the gushing waters of the Tigris.

"Hey, this is cozy," said Private Richard Feldran, the soldier who brought us a dozen MRE boxes.

The orange flames and their shadows, the moonlight glazing the sculpted stone and glinting off the rapids below, reflecting from domes and cupolas — it was an evening of such profound beauty that the war, indeed all the doings of humanity, withdrew to insignificance. As if we were three guys on a fishing trip, Dick Feldran from Nebraska, Omar and I sat there, eating our way through all twelve meals and conjuring up a better world for all of us. Differences were forgotten, and I think each of us realized how much more natural it was to be at peace, and how much more we all had in common than we were supposed to have.

Even when two more soldiers, Alan and Tim, joined us, there was scarcely a word out of joint. I tried hard to think what it was that set human beings snapping at each other like dogs, and could only come up with "ideologies." It wasn't even ideologies, the five of us decided, it was people trying to shove ideologies down each other's throats.

"You believe what you want," said Tim. "I don't care. Just let me believe what I want, we'll be *fine* ..."

"I agree," said Dick. "Hell, we only gotta short time here as it is. Why not enjoy what we have?"

"Always some asshole like Rumsfeld gonna stick his snout in," said Tim.

"Well, slam the fuckin' door on it!" said Alan, and we all laughed.

"I jess hope," said Dick, "that one day I gets the chance to see somethin' of ol' Omar-here's country under different circumstances is all ..."

"Yes," said Omar, "and you come as my guest to my house."

"Thanks Omar, you all right, you know that?"

An eavesdropper would never have known the hostilities that supposedly tore between us existed at all, and I don't believe they did that night. Instead — for there is always something — every time there was a lull in the buffeting wind, we felt ourselves being eaten alive by mosquitoes. Considering how cold it still was at night, and how windy it had been nearly all evening, and how much smoke the fire gave off, this did not bode well for the summer mosquitoes.

When everyone had left, I lay in Saddam's bed, as he must have once or twice, watching the firelight flicker across the balcony and listening to the river rush past far below. Had he sat on this promontory, which was a short walk from the village where he grew up, as a boy, and dreamed of building a palace here? Or had he just been dragged along in the tide of events and granted precious little time for reflection like most of us? I must have dozed off, because when I awoke to a loud noise, the balcony was just cold silver moonlight framed by darkness. The curtains blew in rippling waves at the bedside. With a jolt, I realized there was a dark figure standing just beyond the foot of the bed. I remained still. Perhaps he had not seen me? All manner of foolish ideas flooded through my sleep-addled mind: Saddam had hidden himself among the many secret passages in this palace, and was now outraged by my presence in his bed ... But the figure did not move, and as reason returned I realized it was just the bronze statue of Cupid that stood there. Cupid! In Saddam's bedroom!

Bang! It was my outer door pushed shut then heaved open by relentless gusts. I went to wedge it shut, conscious of how much fear a shadow held, and how night was nothing but shadows. I know I slept, but it was an uneasy sleep fraught with phantoms, and I was truly grateful to find the room flooded with rosy light.

A thermos flask one of the soldiers had brought last night still contained enough hot water to make two instant coffees from MRE sachets, so I took one over to Omar's room. He was already up and dressed. He even looked washed, though he could not have been. How did he feel about things?

"It is okay," he said. "They are good to us. Good people."

He felt he was doing the right thing. The real pity was that he came to regret it. He imagined that this act of trust would receive a hand of friendship from America in return. He was making a brave gesture of friendship and he expected something similar back. The whole city of Samarra had seen him flown away by helicopter. They could see he was not being punished, so they would put two and two together and realize he was collaborating in some way. It was that simple. Omar was easy enough to check out. He was not a member of the Ba'ath; he and his brother had freed the American POWs. What more did anyone want? Someone should have asked what America could do for Omar, because Omar had done more than his share for America. I suppose it is the raw naivety that bothers me, the schoolboy notion that someone risks his life to give Uncle Sam valuable information *because that's the right thing to do ...*

But back then, sitting on Saddam's balcony looking out over the rose-tinted flood plain and the palaces below still in shadow, Omar thought he had done the right thing. And what he came to regret was not what he had done but rather what America had not done. It breeched both good manners and common sense. I blame myself for agreeing to take Omar to the U.S. army. If I had refused, there would at least be one slightly less bitter Iraqi today.

These are the facts, such as they are: Omar was grilled for five more hours by several agents from Central Intelligence. No one offered him breakfast or lunch. The information he gave them helped in the capture of "Chemical" Ali, facilitated the surrender of Tariq Aziz, led to the uncovering of a mass grave and to the discovery of a military communications centre deep below the Shahin Hotel in Samarra. It may have helped with other arrests and discoveries too. In return, when the agents had concluded and gone for lunch, Omar and I were told we were free to go. There were no helicopters this time; we walked from the palace gates all the way into town, where Omar purchased a packet of biscuits for our lunch and we eventually found a taxi willing to drive us back to Samarra. I know he felt as if he had been raped and dumped out with the trash, because, in his own way, he said so.

CHAPTER TWELVE

WHEN THE SOUL LIES DOWN

[U.S. soldiers in Vietnam] raped, cut off ears, cut off heads, taped wires from portable telephones to human genitals and turned up the power, cut off limbs, blew up bodies, randomly shot at civilians, razed villages in a fashion reminiscent of Genghis Khan, shot cattle and dogs for fun, poisoned food stocks, and generally ravaged the countryside of South Vietnam in addition to the normal ravage of war, and the normal and very particular ravaging which is done by the applied bombing power of this country ... Yes, I committed the same kinds of atrocities as thousands of other soldiers have committed. I took part in search and destroy missions, in the burning of villages.

— DEMOCRATIC PRESIDENTIAL NOMINEE JOHN KERRY [127]

America, America!

By their deeds shall you know them. When you hear Bush II talk about "freedom" or "democracy," it is tempting to believe him, but the words don't count, they are labels, hollow cyphers. It is deeds that count. I would like to be shown one deed that does not bear the stamp of bullying neo-imperialist policy. It is not what they say but what they do. Are Iraqis really in control of Iraq? Have there been free and fair elections? Are the rulers elected representatives of the Iraqi people? Has America, having freed Iraq from Saddam, now left it to find its own way? Is Iraqi oil controlled by Iraqis who are respected and trusted by their fellow countrymen? Has the U.S. army left its bases and quit the country? When we can answer yes to these questions, I will stand corrected. By their deeds shall you know them.

Along these lines, I consoled Omar during the hour it took to drive back to Samarra. I found many, if not most Iraqis had given little thought to the pros and cons of other countries' political systems while Saddam's boot was their roof. Any system had to be better than the one they suffered under, so calibrating the degrees of betterness seemed superfluous. Now that they had only the stars for a roof, however, people like Omar were keenly interested in the political process of democracy, the checks and balances, the strata and branches of government. I walked him through the systems with which I was somewhat familiar: the Indian, British and Canadian parliamentary systems and the American system. Of them all, he liked the Canadian best, saying it would best suit Iraq, and he liked the American least, saying it would not work in Iraq.

Whenever things would not work in Iraq, Omar eventually blamed the Shia. Nearly every Sunni I knew did, as did most of the Christians. It had become a habit of mind with the ruling elites, and it will be hard to break. It was one of Saddam's myths too: that he was all that stood between the nation and its self-destruction. Iraq was effectively an apartheid state, where the Shia were treated in much the same way as the Israelis treat Palestinians. They were second-class citizens, mostly poor, uneducated, with little future beyond that offered by the mosque, and little hope that their children would have better lives. The other Iraqis, especially those in the higher Ba'athi circles, had come to think of them as subhuman, which is the only way you can continue treating people like animals. The Sunni Muslims and Christians of Iraq will have to wash their brains of these old ways of thinking.

Back in Samarra, Karbala and the Shia were suddenly at the forefront of Sunni consciousness too. For the first time in a generation, the Shia were allowed to make the ritual pilgrimage of mortification to celebrate the festival of Arba'een at Karbala. Millions had descended on the city, processing there in a macabre dance that entailed celebrants cutting themselves with knives and swords until they were drenched in blood, scourging themselves with metal-tipped whips or beating themselves with their own fists in a reenactment of the tragic slaughter of Hussein and his family. Every television channel carried the images. The Sunni, whose branch of the faith did not contain such excesses, watched with scorn, fascination and dread. The pictures from Karbala seemed to contain a message about their future, and they certainly underlined the enormous gulf between the two halves of Islam — the gulf that would have to be bridged by a partnership of mutual respect and forgiveness if Iraq was to continue as a single sovereign state.

I watched the pilgrims in Karbala on television at Sabbar's house. His wife sent out plates of hors-d'oeuvres from the kitchen, including those celebrated sheep delicacies, the eyes and the testicles, which, since I was guest of honour, were replenished on my plate as soon as they disappeared, in spite of my objections. They disappeared into the deep roomy pockets of my *dishdasha*, where I was glad indeed to find them much later that day. I did once try eating them, finding that their taste was unremarkable but their texture was that of grapes made from coiled gristle which writhed against the tongue as if seething with wriggling life. It was enough for me to wish never to repeat the experience.

Sheikh Adnan was also visiting, accompanied by a nephew who was courting one of Sabbar's daughters. This entailed hanging out with her dad, and so was not much of a date. As Karbala's pilgrims appeared on the TV screen, Adnan said something in Arabic and then trailed off in a spluttering cough.

"He says they are animals," said Sabbar. "He wants to know what you think."

"*Chacun à son goût*," I said.

Most educated Iraqis understand a little French — and a little French is exactly what I have.

The general arrived during this. He looked ashen and blurred at the edges.

"Robert, Robert," he said. "I look for you, I wait for you!"

I told him where Omar and I had been.

"Tariq Aziz he surrender," the general said. "The Americans they have him."

As he said it, magically, the story was announced as a special news flash on television, which made it seem as if Aziz had merely recognized he was up against a superior foe and decided to throw in the towel. There was mention of his attempt to negotiate asylum in England, but it was made to sound as if this had occurred after his surrender, which was like paying for something then trying to haggle over the price.[128]

"You make trouble for me, Robert?" asked the general.

"Of course," I said. "I told the CIA that you were Mister Big, the man behind Saddam. They're coming to get you."

"Ah, Robert, Robert. Always you joke."

"Not always."

"Come," he said. "We go Baghdad, yes?"

At this point, Sabbar came over, guilt spilling from his eyes.

"Mister Bull," he said, "you have interest for the items?"

"Items? What about Muhi Atta?"

"Muhi he is ... ah ..." He rattled off something in Arabic to the general, who translated.

"He say Muhi now not want to help with this problem."

"Muhi," I said, "is a mass murderer. He doesn't have a lot of options."

Sabbar spoke at length in Arabic. I could make out some of what he said, which concerned the threats made by Muhi's family.

"He say," the general translated, "that it is not good now for him with Muhi Atta."

"Yeah, I heard what he said, and I appreciate his situation, but this guy is a killer and if his family is threatening Sabbar then as far as I'm concerned they're killers too and the Americans can take all of them away. Understand?"

"Mister Bull —"

"Yes, Sabbar?"

"Muhi Atta family, my family ..." He wove his fingers together.

"I understand," I said. "They're close. But you can't let that prevent you from doing the right thing. It makes me suspicious. I think sometimes that maybe you are involved in killing the Kuwaitis ..."

He was the very image of righteous indignation, eyes widened, mouth puffing and popping, hands pushing at the air in front of me.

"I ... I?" he said. "I not do this thing. I have childs —"

"Okay, okay, Sabbar," I said. "I believe you. I just said when you protect Muhi it makes me think ..."

The general anxiously added that Sabbar could not afford to get himself murdered by Muhi's family because he owed the general money.

"Who doesn't owe you money?" I asked.

This remark broke the tension, and we all laughed.

"Tell me," I said, "does Muhi think I will just forget about his involvement if you ask me to?"

Sabbar and the general spoke back and forth in impenetrable Arabic.

"He says," said the general, "that Muhi tell him it is Ibrahim Alawi that is doing this killing."

"Maybe the Americans should just come and take all of them away?"

"Robert, forget about it ..."

"They were women and children," I said, angrily, "and they were raped and buried alive! I don't want to forget about it. I wish I *could* forget about it ..."

I realized I was behaving badly. A guest does not offend the host in his house. But my frustration with these codes of conduct in the face of mass murder, of women and children, was making me boil over with rage. Tears welled up in my eyes. My emotions seemed mixed up and beyond my control. I took a few deep breaths, but they just made the tears roll.

"I'm sorry," I said. "I know I should be more understanding ... I —"

I excused myself and went to the washroom, which was outside between the house and the front wall. I took a few more breaths, then began sobbing mightily, wrapping my face in a towel to muffle the sound. After ten minutes, I felt much better. Iraq was an emotional rollercoaster at the best of times, but this time the ride from horror to hope to rage and frustration was debilitating. The country was an open wound with exposed nerve endings. For some reason, I cared about it deeply, cared about the people. I had cared about them during Saddam's reign, even before America began its long persecution. I wanted them to be free. Perhaps part of me believed the empty promises made by Bush and Blair. But when the bombs began falling, I suppose I had to face the truth. You don't bomb people you care about. The worst part of all, I think, was knowing that, now that they had done this, now that they were here, the Americans could not leave. Much as most Iraqis loathed them for what they had done to the country, they also wanted them to stay now to prevent the country tearing itself apart. They would prefer a U.N. force, or the French or Russians, but they would rather have the Americans than no one at all. It was an Iraqi conundrum, the lesser of two evils. And the situation itself, the impossibility of it, fed into the rage and frustration.

"Are you okay, Robert?" asked the general, when I returned. "You have red eyes."

"Sweet of you to notice, Nial. I'm fine."

"I show you the items?" said Sabbar.

"What items?"

"You say you see them ..."

I assumed he meant the items stolen from the Baghdad museum, so I agreed I did want to see them.

"Okay, Robert. I go," said the general.

I told him he should not be driving after the curfew, but he just shrugged. He had handled Saddam, the shrug said, so he could handle the Americans and their curfew.

> *Here is a broken city,*
> *And the wind throws the screams of gulls on your grave*
> *When I am talking with you.*
>
> *What is poetry which does not save*
> *Nations or people?*
>
> — CZESLAW MILOSZ (1911–)[129]

Before long, I was in the passenger seat of Sabbar's brand-new Ford flatbed truck. It still had the shipping documents taped to the windshield, and I noticed it possessed no licence plates at all. He said he had taken delivery that morning, dismissing my query about the plates — after all, there was no government to issue licence plates. Before leaving Samarra, we picked up a crony of Sabbar's, who sat in the rear for a while, then got out near the highway. I noticed that he had handed Sabbar a rifle, which, as Sabbar placed it on the floor near my feet, I realized was my Kalashnikov, the one I had taken from Uday's palace. I had given it to the general as a gift, and he had complained that it lacked a clip. Now it had a clip that did not match the silver plating on the rest of its metal. I told Sabbar that I recognized it, but I do not think he understood me.

After fifteen minutes on the highway, we came to the ditch full of burning oil that Omar and I had passed when it was still light. At night, it was a far more arresting spectacle, a blinding gold turret of flames surrounded by a billowing black fleece of dense smoke that zigged and zagged across ten metres. Just as we approached it, a hedge of fire shot out in front of us across the road. Sabbar was clocking 190 kilometres an hour. He tried avoiding it but went into a partial skid before heading straight into the inferno. The flames blew out all around us for a second. It was blinding, and all I could hear was rushing wind. Then there was velvet blackness and silence. The truck rocked from side to side as Sabbar corrected the skid. Then he continued at the same speed north.

"Oils burning," he said.

"I noticed."

For a few minutes I kept thinking the truck would explode or be engulfed in flames.

A little later, Sabbar yelled something and stamped on the brakes. We slithered to a halt, and I could see ahead of us a U.S. army roadblock, three vehicles and a group of soldiers waving flashlights and pointing guns.

I fumbled for my ID and went to get out of the truck.

"Stay inside the vehicle," said an amplified voice. "Do not leave the vehicle."

"I'm a British journalist," I shouted. "It's okay."

The light was in my eyes and I could not see anything ahead of me. Good job someone speaks English, I thought.

"Stop. Don't you fuckin' move or you're dead!"

I could hear the safety catches click off.

"Whoa," I shouted, backing away. "Okay, okay, don't shoot!"

It felt very vulnerable, pleading not to be shot.

I climbed back into the passenger seat. Sabbar did not seem particularly worried.

"We have problem?" he asked me.

"Just stay very still," I said.

"Keep your hands where I can see 'em," yelled the voice. "I am approaching your vehicle."

The blinding light wobbled closer.

"Maybe gun is problem?" Sabbar speculated.

"Maybe. I will say gun is mine, okay?"

"Yes, Mister Bull."

I felt my door open at the same time as Sabbar's door opened. Lights shone in, and to one side of the lights were gun barrels.

"Here," said the voice near me. "Don't you fuckin' move! Gotta gun! I am taking the gun ... Okay, get out!" I felt my arm nearly yanked from its socket as I was pulled from the car.

I was turned and placed against the truck then frisked very thoroughly and very roughly. It made me conscious of the Arab clothes I wore, because the soldier had clearly been trained in frisking someone wearing a *dishdasha*. The same thing was happening to Sabbar on the other side. Someone was inside with a flashlight, pulling out seats and opening compartments. There was a crash and I realized the soldier had thrown out my video camera case.

"Hey!" I protested.

"What's in there?"

"It's a fucking camera, okay?"

"Open it."

I opened the case and the soldier stepped back as I went to grab the camera. Then he recognized what it was and relaxed. After searching through the compartments, he picked up the Kalashnikov.

"Who owns this?"

"I do," I said.

The enormity of it all suddenly hit me. A loaded semi-automatic rifle with no gun permit: they send people to jail for that.

"It's just a souvenir," I said, pathetically.

"I'm sorry, Buddy," the soldier said, in a reasonable voice, "but I gotta take it. We'll give you a receipt, though. Take it to CENTCOM in Baghdad and they might give it back to you. Okay?"

"Yeah, thanks ..."

Right, I thought. We're in Iraq not the U.S.A. There *are* no laws, so they can't send me to jail for having a gun. I imagined what it would have been like if I had been an Arab, without a clue what was going on.

I grabbed the camera and started to videotape the rest of the search.

"Hey!" another voice said. "Put the fuckin' camera down or you'll lose that too."

"This is my job," I said, to the darkness and light. "I have a permit from you people saying I can do it."

"That don't mean shit. Put the fuckin' camera down!"

"If it don't mean shit," I said, "we have a problem, because the permit's issued by your central command."

"I warned you, fucker!"

I saw a light come bobbing towards me and then felt the camera ripped from my hands.

"That's the way you want it, fine by me," said the other soldier.

I grabbed for the camera, but could see two other soldiers start towards us, so I let it go. I was about to insist they take the case, but realized all my tapes were in it. I quietly took them out and took the case over to the soldiers, insisting they store the camera in it.

Twenty minutes later, I was heading north again with Sabbar, reading with the help of a cigarette lighter the document I'd been given by the soldiers:

DEPARTMENT OF THE ARMY
HEADQUARTERS TASK FORCE 1-66 ARMOR
1ST BCT, 4TH INFANTRY DIVISION
SAMARRA, IRAQ

MEMORANDUM FOR RECORD

SUBJECT: Receipt For Confiscated Weapons etc.

1. In accordance with the CENTCOM commander's directive dated 16 April 2003, all military weapons and equipment will be seized at Coalition sponsored checkpoints by Coalition forces until further notice.

2. This document is an official receipt sponsored by Coalition forces for the confiscated weapons and should be retained for an indefinite time.

This was then repeated in handwritten Arabic, below which my gun —
MP5 KAL 9mm X 19 — and the camera were listed. It was signed SSG Quill,
TASK FORCE 1-66 AR, 1BCT, 4ID.

What did it mean, that the receipt was "sponsored" by Coalition forces?
Surely they meant "issued"? It should be "retained for an indefinite time"? I
still have it, but I am not sure how long I can keep this up. I did attempt
trying to get the camera back, but after two days of run-around from the
army in Baghdad, I could not even discover where I had to go to make the
request.

"It was good gun," said Sabbar, back at 190 kilometres an hour on the
pitch-black road.

"It was a good camera, too," I said. "And they were both mine so I don't
know what you're upset about ..."

He did not understand a word.

A few minutes later, we swerved off the highway onto a side road, and I saw
a signpost reading al-Awja.

"Isn't that Saddam's village?" I said.

It was about ten minutes south of Tikrit.

"Yes," said Sabbar, as if the coincidence had just struck him. "Saddam born
in the Awja. Live here when small ..."

"So Awja is where we're going?"

"Yes, Awja ..."

"Just checking ..."

If there was one place in Iraq that was definitely not happy that Saddam
no longer ruled, it had to be Awja. Nearly every member of the Revolutionary
Command Council came from within a few kilometres of here. The place
must have enjoyed all manner of special privileges over the past three
decades; now it was going to be enjoying all manner of special persecutions.
I had seen a photograph of the "house" where Saddam was born. It made
Elvis' tarpaper shack look opulent. It was a kennel, a sty, a crate.

We pulled up outside a swank series of red-tiled, three-storey structures. A
sign read BA'ATH PARTY HEADQUARTERS. I wondered if any of Awja's villagers
were *not* members. If Saddam had bothered with elections, he would have
done well in this area. The last time I had been in Iraq, in 1996, a referendum
was held. People had to answer yes or no to the question, *Do you want*

Saddam Hussein to continue as president of Iraq? Since no other candidate was mentioned, if you voted no it presumably meant that you did not want a president at all. But Saddam needn't have worried, because 99.6 percent of the ballots said Yes. That 0.4 percent was all he could give to the cause of credibility. The voters were probably asking themselves who this plucky 0.4 percent were, since no one in his right mind would vote against Saddam. No matter what was said about the secure and tamper-proof nature of the ballot-boxes and the anonymity of the voter slips, everyone believed the Mukharbharat knew how each person had voted and would have the dissidents strapped to a wire mattress plugged into the national grid before sunset. Compared with such crude techniques for encouraging consent, the American system for rigging elections is awesomely sophisticated. Like all the best confidence-trick stings, the marks never even know they have been conned. Iraq has much to learn before it catches up with the twenty-first century.

Sabbar hammered on the main door with his fist.

"My friend is here," he said, peering around anxiously.

"Glad to hear it," I said.

Since this Muhi Atta business had started, I found it increasingly hard to conceal my scorn for Sabbar. He knocked again. The place seemed to be deserted. We had not passed a soul driving in, and I could not see any signs of life inside any of the new villas or chalets. Maybe everyone had fled with Saddam? Yet if on that night in December Saddam really was where they say they caught him — in his so-called spider hole — he would have been no more than three hundred metres away from where we stood.

Suddenly, there was a rattling of chains behind the door followed by a sliding of bolts, then it inched open and a head peered out.

"Ah, Sabbar!" said the head, in a voice bubbling up through tar.

The door was thrown open, revealing a man who may as well have worn a sign around his neck saying BEWARE, SMALL-TIME CROOK. Sixtyish, squat, his greying hair was parted just above his left ear then hauled up over his skull and down the other side, where its last six inches were looped around his right ear. Perhaps the weight of its own grease kept it plastered to the top of his head — either that or it was glued there — for it was motionless and had the texture of bacon fat. His eyes were so bloodshot they looked like fake

Halloween eyeballs. His nose had the appearance of honeycomb dipped in chocolate, and pieces of it were missing, rot had set in — where had he been putting it? His eight teeth resembled old gold-tipped cribbage pegs. He had not shaved recently, and his cream silk *dishdasha* with mother-of-pearl buttons had a thick brown crease at the back from where he had been scratching the crack of his arse — something he did so frequently it must have been obsessive or compulsive, or both. The final flourish to this appetizing persona was the belt he wore around what would have been his waist and the enormous handgun stuffed into it.

"This Hamid," said Sabbar, after kissing the man on both cheeks. "This Mister Bull ..."

Hamid gave me a bloodshot knowing look, offering a hand that felt like a bunch of rubber pipes.

"Hamid very good man," said Sabbar.

"I'm sure you are applying the usual lofty criteria," I said.

"Ah, ofti right here ria," Sabbar said, nodding.

I realized that he was trying to impress Hamid with his English.

We followed Honest Hamid down a corridor and into an enormous room, which stretched up three floors to the roof, with chairs lined around its walls and no other furniture anywhere on the flagstones. At one end was a vast fireplace in which a fire of hazardous proportions was snapping and roaring, the flames occasionally licking around the outside brickwork. It had been a fairly warm night, so why anyone felt the need of a fire at all, let alone a fire of this size, was beyond my comprehension. Hamid motioned for me to sit, and as I did, a shadowy figure shot out from a side door and threw the best part of a tree bough into the fireplace, where it instantly began crackling and hissing. Soon, I began to sweat profusely. It was like a colossal sauna.

"Why the fire, Sabbar?" I asked.

He was sweating too.

"They making fire for they self of wood ..."

"Yes, you noticed that, did you? Why are they doing it, hmm? Why?"

"For ... ah ... this ..." He held his thumb and index finger in the gesture of A Very Small Thing, then he waved the hand around his head, adding, "This one ... small ..."

"A small reason ... They're lighting the fire for virtually no reason at all?"

Just then I became aware of three or four biting insects on my ankles, bending to brush off several mosquitoes that were so large they were nearly birds.

"Jesus!" I said, aware that more were biting around my calves.

"Ah yes, Mister Bull! This for fire ..."

"Oh, I get it. The fire is to keep the mosquitoes away ..."

"Ah!"

I recalled the beasts on Saddam's balcony. That was high above ground, too. But Awja was a swamp. All these centuries and the best anyone here could do was light a huge fire in the summer to keep from being eaten alive? Is that what had happened to Hamid's nose?

"This is *terrible*!" I swatted at my legs, my elbows, my shoulders. "You tell Hamid he had better hurry it with his 'items' or there won't be much of me left ..."

"First we take tea," said Sabbar.

There was no way around tea. Nothing happened here without a preface by tea.

A boy who had to be Hamid junior appeared with a giant pot that had a spout like a flamingo's beak, offering me a cup the size of an acorn, then pouring a centimetre of cardamom coffee bitter as earwax.

"Delicious!" I threw it back. "Now let's get on ... Yikes!" The thing that bit me must have had a proboscis like a rapier. I felt it sink through many layers of skin in my waist and prick internal organs.

Hamid leaned towards me and started speaking Arabic in the kind of furtive voice used to offer the services of young boys or hashish, then realized he was speaking to the wrong person.

"He say," said Sabbar, "he have for you rolly sills ... You like?"

After much agonized miming and guessing I managed to work out that what he had meant were "cylinder seals." The Iraqi National Museum had possessed the largest and most important collection of cylinder seals in the world, some of them amounting to the earliest examples of writing ever found — and thus literally priceless. It seemed tragic that any had ended up in Awja with Honest Hamid.

I told them that I was willing to have a look.

Hamid barked at the boy, who ran off the way we had come in. He returned with an old leather shopping bag which he handed to Hamid, who tossed it on to the flagstones, where it landed with a worrying crack. I reached over and pulled it open. It was filled almost to the top not just with cylinder seals made of stone, copper, bronze and clay, but also with little statues, oil lamps, tiny bowls, ceramic tiles and three British Museum coffee mugs. I wanted to hit Hamid for leaving everything in this old shopping bag, totally unprotected, but I realized how delicate this negotiation was going to be. So delicate, in fact, that I did not know whether to offer him $50 or $50 million. Beyond knowing what they were, I knew nothing about cylinder seals. When I said some were priceless, I had no idea whether that figure would be thousands or millions. Or billions. I picked through the bag trying to get an idea of what was there, trying to burn certain pieces into memory. Hamid made a tutting noise and grabbed the bag from me, turning it upside down. The contents fell hideously, some pieces rolling several metres away, others almost reduced to dust.

"For ... Why does he have to do that?" I asked Sabbar, wanting to add something about importance and value.

Then it dawned on me that if he could treat the contents like that he must have no idea of their value. This started up a daydream about buying the whole bag for a hundred dollars, then discovering it was worth billions. The ending was problematic: either I smuggled them out and auctioned them off in London, or I handed them over to curators from the British Museum who rewarded me lavishly.

"If he can give me a good price," I said, "I would take the lot. I like old stuff ... But the price has got to be right ..."

After conveying this information to himself, Sabbar conveyed it to Hamid. I knew what he was going to say, though:

"As you like," he said, in English he had memorized but did not understand, bowing towards the bag.

"No, no, just give me a price. I don't want to insult you with a low offer."

Just as he did not want to insult me with a high one. Neither of us knew the value of this trade, so how would it take place?

"A hundred," I said.

Sabbar looked baffled, giving Hamid the figure. Hamid gave me his bloodshot knowing look. Then he took a folded piece of newspaper from his pocket and gave it to Sabbar. It was in Arabic, but I could read the photograph, which showed a display of cylinder seals.

"Say the sills value for me-lee-ons," said Sabbar.

"Right. But they're stolen and will be impossible to sell easily. So I think a hundred thousand is fair."

"Hunnerd towsand? You say hunnerd."

"We don't say the thousand part. It's assumed ..."

"He say you he will ask if it is okay to his friend," Sabbar told me.

I was relieved. Hamid looked like he could turn nasty if a deal went sour. We agreed that he would contact me through Sabbar in a few days.

The mosquitoes had enlarged their pincer attack to include my whole body by now. Between the biting and the itching, I could not think straight. I got up to leave, thrashing at the air around me, but Sabbar told me there were other "items." Clearly, he stood to make a hefty commission, and sources of money in Iraq after the war were not to be treated lightly.

The main "item" was outside, it transpired. We left by a rear door and walked across a field to where a group of people was standing around with flashlights on a patch of coloured stone. It was not actually stone, but I did not notice until we drew quite close that stretched out on the grass was a huge Persian rug. It had to be a hundred metres long and forty or fifty wide. Flashlights were shone wherever I stooped to look. As I did, I found the carpet oddly familiar, suddenly remembering why.

"How the hell did you get this out?" I asked, laughing.

It was the rug from Saddam's Salah-ad-Din Palace in Tikrit, the one that had been in the room where Omar and I were interrogated. There were not two rugs of this size and design in the area, of that I felt certain. It was a Kashan, and must have been made to order. No one makes a carpet that size on spec.

The people laughed with me, but no one was volunteering the details of how it managed to be in Awja a day later. These were Saddam's kin, I told myself, so if anyone deserves to have the carpet, they do.

And they deserved to sell it to me.

Half an hour's merciless mosquito biting and vintage haggling left me shaking hands, the proud owner of a $5,000 carpet that was a hundred metres long. I had to break the bad news to Sabbar gently: I did not actually have five thousand dollars, so I would have to arrange to get it in Baghdad, and then pick up the goods. I could tell he was miffed. He sulked all the way back.

> *The father continues he does business*
> *The son is killed he continues no more*
> *The father and the mother go to the graveyard*
> *They find this quite natural the father and mother*
> *Life continues life with knitting war business*
> *Business war knitting war*
> *Business business business*
> *Life with the graveyard*
>
> — JACQUES PREVERT (1900–77)[130]

We did not go directly back to Samarra, however, because Sabbar noticed that his gas tank was on empty. He knew a gas station further along the highway towards Tikrit, but the chronic fuel shortage and the lateness of the hour made it seem unlikely that the place would be open. When we reached it, we saw another sign of the Coalition's priorities: an American tank parked behind the pumps. This indicated that there must be gas available. But were the Americans protecting it for themselves or just protecting it? Most gas stations were owned by the government, and the ones that were still open were run by their old managers now acting as owners. Their legality was dubious, but after the illegal war and invasion, Iraqis could be forgiven for wondering if the rule of law even existed any longer. I told Sabbar I would see if the soldiers in the tank minded us taking enough gas to get us back to Samarra. We pulled up just off the road. I got out and walked towards the tank. Immediately, a bright flashlight clicked on and nearly blinded me.

"Go back to your vehicle and drive on," said a voice.

I stated who I was and that we were out of gas.

"I don't give a fuck who you are," said the soldier. "Get back in the car and fuck off."

The arrogance and the abusive language sickened me.

"It's not your gas," I said. "You don't have the right to refuse it."

"Take one more step, motherfucker, and I'll fucking waste you. Complain about *that*!"

I stopped, but I was very pissed off.

"Give me your name and regiment," I said. "I am going to report you."

"Go fuck yourself, asshole!"

"Are you refusing to identify yourself?" I asked.

"No, I'm telling you to go fuck yourself. Now get back in your car and get the fuck outta here!"

"I am going to put some gas in the truck," I said. "Then we will go."

"Touch that gas, I'm gonna fuck you up, buddy."

"Go ahead," I said. "I'm going to take some anyway."

I approached the pumps, looking around for a container. There were none, and I did not think it wise to drive the truck in.

"You couldn't lend me a gas can or something for a few minutes, could you?" I asked the darkness.

"You're in violation of the curfew order issued by authority of the United States army," he said. "Put your fucking hands up. You're under arrest."

I was in no mood for this, and I could see a long night ahead, so I told him to fuck off, and added some disparaging comments about his country and president for good measure. Then I walked away, careful to keep the pump between the soldier and my back. They would not risk igniting ten thousand gallons of petrol just to spite a hostile journalist.

There was a deafening crack of gunfire. My heart jumped, and I ran for the truck. I was almost certain he had fired into the air, but I had no desire to prove the thesis, telling Sabbar to get out of there ... *fast*! I could hear laughter as I slammed the door, so I was sure we were okay. Assholes!

Sabbar acted like a naughty boy, full of glee.

"Mister Bull," he kept saying, "they shoot you?"

He told me his wife's family lived in Tikrit, so we would have to go there and get them to siphon some gas from one of their cars. He kept looking in his rearview mirror to see if the tank was coming after us. However, I think the incident reassured him that I was not a Yankee spy.

And death shall have no dominion.
Dead men naked they shall be one
With the man in the wind and the west moon;
When their bones are picked clean and the clean bones gone,
They shall have stars at elbow and foot;
Though they go mad they shall be sane,
Though they sink through the sea they shall rise again;
Though lovers be lost love shall not;
And death shall have no dominion.

— DYLAN THOMAS [131]

The countryside is supposed to be dark at night, but cities are not. Tikrit without electricity was oppressive, a warren of shadowy forms that deceived the eye: the hull of an ocean liner proved to be a high-walled garden; the mujahedeen pointing a grenade launcher at us was only a small tree. It seemed deserted, the cafés and chai houses closed and in darkness, but we would occasionally pass houses whose gardens or courtyards overflowed with people. They sat in rapt conversation by candle or oil lamp. As we drove by, people stopped in mid-sentence, every head turning to look at the vehicle approaching. Seeing it was not from the U.S. army and only carried a couple of Arabs, they resumed discussions that I assumed were about the war and occupation.

By now the fuel warning light had come on and we expected to splutter to a halt at any moment, so we were silent, willing the truck on. Behind us, somewhere across town, there were intermittent bursts of small-arms fire. Looters, I imagined, until the *thump-thump-thump* of a large calibre weapon sounded out, echoing around the hills.

Sabbar's in-laws lived in a large house concealed behind high walls at the end of a steep road. The ancient studded door in the wall was opened by an old man with one eye. Where the missing eye had been was a scabrous reddish-black hollow. Sabbar kissed the man on both cheeks, and he led us in across a dark forecourt to the door of the house. I could just about make out the dim glow of an oil lamp inside, but the sound of women crying was unmistakable. Sabbar told me to wait outside while he went with the old man to find his father-in-law. The man who let us in, I later learned, was his wife's grandfather.

After a few minutes, I started to walk around the house, which was larger even than it seemed. The forecourt turned into an immaculate flower garden, with climbing frames, arbours and an intricate maze of beds, some of them freshly turned over. Near the back, I came to some shuttered windows behind which a cadmium yellow light pulsed dimly. Peering through a large crack, I saw a bare room with a thin mattress on the floor. On it, cross-legged, sat a young woman reading a thick book, presumably the Holy Koran. She wore jeans and a T-shirt. Her long dense black hair hung down in gleaming spirals, and she brushed it laconically as she read, pausing for long periods in knotted concentration while she put down her hairbrush and followed the text with her index finger. At one point, she threw back her head, shaking the hair off her face, and I could see she was crying, her eyes big wet pools in which the flame from her lamp seemed to be constantly flaring up and dying in a dozen minute fires. It was an image of extraordinary truth and beauty as well as tragedy, and I was transfixed.

When I felt the urgent jab of a finger on my leg, I nearly jumped out of my body. Ready with a thousand apologies and excuses, I turned to find no one, just the wind in the leaves ... and a bow-legged brown dog looking up at me with mad eyes. Some kind of Teutonic attack dog, its spring was wound so tight it resembled one large velvet sinew, and when I started to make *nice-doggy* noises, it bared its fangs and made a sound like a small well-tuned motor. Then it prodded my thigh again with its damp rubbery nose, looking up with pure malice. At first, I thought its nose had left a large greasy stain on my *dishdasha*, and then I realized what it was after.

It watched my hand intently, its motor revving, as I slowly went to reach deep inside my pocket and fish out one of the sheep's eyes I had hidden there earlier. I was not sure whether to throw the eye or hand it to the beast, which looked ready to leap at my fingers.

"Good boy," I whispered, placing the eye in front of its nose between extended fingers. "Here ..."

It looked at me, then at the eye, then at me again, then back to the eye. I was sure it would snap off my fingers, but instead it opened its mouth and extended a long pink tongue beneath the sheep's eye, carrying it back in the loop. It ate with great delicacy, evidently appreciating the dish enormously. As it chewed, I began to edge away, but it immediately started growling again. I dredged up another eye — or was it a testicle? Wondering if it was a big mistake to give the thing a taste for testicles, I removed all the gourmet organs from the pocket, along with several thousand dinars now glued to them, placing everything on the flowerbed near the dog's feet.

"That's the lot," I said. "Honest."

It looked up, then down at the eyes and testicles, then up at me again, assessing whether I was telling the truth or not. I started to move away, it bristled for a second and then relaxed, digging in to the snack.

I arrived back at the door just as Sabbar was coming out.

"Is everything all right?" I said.

"There is problem. Come, Mister Bull."

"Where are we going? We have no gas ..."

His father-in-law was at the hospital, apparently, as a visitor, not a patient. Sabbar seemed troubled, but I did not press him on it, nor did I ask why the women were crying.

The hospital was not far, which was just as well, since the truck began coughing and hiccupping as we approached its entrance. I did not want to see another Iraqi hospital, so I said I would wait for Sabbar outside.

"No, Mister Bull," he said, urgently, "you come!"

Reluctantly, I accompanied him towards the dark building. It was a small utilitarian modern structure surrounded by well-kept gardens with neat hedges. It looked more like a school than a hospital, but the moment Sabbar opened one of the main doors the smell of surgical spirit was overpowering. Oil lamps burned behind the reception desk and figures moved in the gloom, but what caught my attention immediately was the odd noise. A low warbling kind of hum, it rose and fell in waves, coming from everywhere at once yet also seeming far off. Sabbar appeared to know his way, for he did not stop at reception, striding on through two more sets of double doors. Following him, I only realized we were in a ward when the doors swung to behind me. This was the source of the noise.

I suppose it had originally been a children's ward, but the exigencies of the war had changed that. Injured parents were crammed in beds next to their injured children. The noise was the sleepy moaning and crying of dozens of wounded children in pain mingled with the hums and lullabies of exhausted parents trying to put them to sleep. It was endless, the peaks and lows in its wave deceiving the ear into thinking the sound was fading or swelling, but it was neither. It was constant and felt like a claw scratching my brain.

There seemed to be no doctors or nurses, but the ward was full of visitors, many of whom were changing dressings and diapers, even sweeping the floor. In a room built for perhaps twenty little beds, I counted sixty-seven sleeping arrangements: inflatable mattresses, camp beds, cots, pallets, piles of blankets, carpets. Plates bearing the remnants of food were stacked at the foot of many beds. There were oil lamps and flashlights everywhere. The air was hot and dry and it smelled of ether, kerosene and vomit. Every so often some poor little mite would erupt in a feline howl of pain, eliciting an increase in the volume of a lullaby and an outbreak of grumpy sobs from the half-wakened kids nearby.

I followed Sabbar down the central aisle. He looked from side to side at the groups around each cot, finally locating his father-in-law near the end. He was with three or four other adults gathered around a bed that held a woman and a girl of five or six. The woman's face was black, yellow and blue with bruises. Her left arm ended at the elbow in a stump covered with a white powdery substance that was dark in places with congealed blood and whatever else it is that we ooze when badly injured. The girl lying beside her had lost both legs, one below the knee, the other just above it, and her left arm from the shoulder. The legs were bandaged but the shoulder was not, its crater covered with the same whitish powder. The left side of her face was entirely covered with gauze pads and bandage strips that vanished into her hair, and her right eye was covered with a pink patch. The injuries seemed very fresh.

The pair were Sabbar's sister-in-law, Fatima, and her daughter, Dazi. Eventually, I learned that they had been brought in earlier that day. They had been helping to clear the rubble at Dazi's school, which had been accidentally bombed during the American assault on Tikrit, when Dazi picked up something that had been lying under the bricks. Fatima told her to put it down. She did not like the look of it, although it was brightly coloured and seemed to be made of plastic. Dazi would not put it down, so she went over to see what the object was. When she noticed some writing in English, she pushed it from Dazi's hands and it exploded upon hitting the ground. Now she blamed herself. Dazi would never walk again and it was uncertain whether she would be able to see out of her one remaining eye.

The U.S. and Britain together launched thirteen thousand cluster munitions in Iraq during the war,[132] most of them from the ground. These contained nearly two million submunitions, or bomblets, which are scattered in a wide area after the initial blast. The submunitions have an unusually high failure rate of between five and sixteen percent, which means that at least ninety thousand unexploded "duds" were left lying around after the war. These continue to act like landmines, maiming rather than killing the civilians who stumble across them. The U.S. air forces used cluster bombs extensively in the first Gulf War and in Kosovo in 1999 and Afghanistan in 2001 and 2002. At least eighty U.S. casualties during the 1991 Gulf War were attributed to cluster munition duds, and more than four thousand Iraqi civilians were killed or injured by cluster munition duds after the end of the war.[133] In this recent war, there were at least fifty strikes against the Iraqi leadership in crowded civilian areas, none of which succeeded in killing its target, all of which caused a high civilian death toll. The U.S. based its targeting upon coordinates derived from the use of Thoraya satellite phones by the leadership, which only narrows down the target to a radius of one hundred metres, as well as corroborating ground intelligence that proved to be highly inadequate. As a result, at least a thousand civilians were killed or wounded.[134]

The mother was insane with grief. She kept indicating her daughter with a toss of her head, and asking the relatives gathered there to forgive her. No one knew what to do or say. I think our arrival was a relief in this respect.

I hastily introduced myself to Ahmed, Sabbar's father-in-law, fearing that Sabbar had neglected to say where in the West his Western friend was from. This was another place where you did not want anyone thinking you were British or American.

"Welcome," said Ahmed, a stately old man with white hair and glasses whose English was excellent, "you are welcome. I wish to thank all Canadians for their refusage to join America in this horrid war ..."

"I think we did the right thing ..."

"Look around. Can you doubt it?" said Ahmed, who in fact taught English at college. "Everyone in here is a casualty of Bush. It is all children and parents with wounds from the war. It is as you say, a bird hand is not worth two bushes ..."

He told me what had happened to his daughter and grand-daughter.

"I am too old to be this angry," he whispered. "But I want to go out and kill American soldiers. Forgive me, but I don't know what else to do. Look at that little girl!"

"I'm so sorry ..."

"Does she look happy to be liberated, hmm? I wish the George Bush Younger could stand here and tell me his lies to my face. Every Iraqi they know why America is here: the oil, my friend!"

"Yes ..."

"They are just like the Crusaders, who claimed to come for God, but really came for what they could steal — is it not so?"

"Yes, it's true ..."

I recalled reading in a history of Venice about the blind octogenarian Doge, Enrico Dandallo, who carefully instructed his Crusaders who had joined in the sack of Constantinople to avoid the fighting and head for places containing only the best works of art, which they were carrying back to the Piazza San Marco before the Crusade was even over.

"They are pirates," said Ahmed. "Like Long John Silver and his parrot."

"The parrot was innocent."

"But even pirates were honest enough to admit that they were pirates, isn't it? The Bush wants everyone to think he is the angel. Am I not right?"

"You are," I said. "How can you stand it?"

"What?"

"What's happening to Iraq ..."

"Nobody asks us if we can stand it. Nobody asks us if we want it. Nobody asks us anything. But I tell you, my friend, Iraqis will not forget this. Even if it is in a thousand years, we will take our vengeance on America for this. And I can tell you, they will not find it so much a sliced cake here as they think." He looked me in the eyes and with a voice of cold steel added, "You cannot put the snake back in Pandora's box."

I could not remember what Pandora had kept in her box but I knew it had not been a snake.

"No, she won't like that," I said.

"That Tommy Blair does not look old enough to be prime minister of Britain, does he? How old is he?"

"My age."

"There used to be fine leaders in the West. Where did they go?"

"I don't know."

"Shakespeare was a fine writer," he said.

"Yes, he was."

"The quality of mercy is not strained," he said, "it droppeth as the gentle rain from heaven upon the place beneath. It is twice blest: it blesseth him that gives and him that takes. 'Tis mightiest in the mightiest: it becomes the thronèd monarch better than his crown; his sceptre shows the force of temporal power, the attribute to awe and majesty, wherein doth sit the dread and fear of kings; but mercy is above this sceptred sway, it is enthroned in the hearts of kings, it is an attribute to God himself; and earthly power doth then show likest God's when mercy seasons justice. Therefore, Jew, though justice be thy plea consider this, that in the course of justice none of us should see salvation: we do pray for mercy; and that same prayer doth teach us all to render the deeds of mercy."[135]

"Bravo," I said.

"I have remembered that for all these years," he said. "He was a wise man, that Shakespeare."

"Yes."

"You must know some, being a literary man?"

"Yes."

"Recite!"

"Well, I don't think it's ... er ..."

"You are helping me enormously," he said, in a desperate voice. "I need to keep my mind on something else ..."

"Poor naked wretches, whereso'er you are, that bide the pelting of this pitiless storm, how shall your houseless heads and unfed sides, your loop'd and window'd raggedness, defend you from seasons such as these? O, I have ta'en too little care of this! Take physic, pomp; expose thyself to feel what wretches feel, that thou mayst shake the superflux to them, and show the heavens more just."[136]

"Oh," he said, quietly, "Lear ... I am a man more sinned against than sinning — like Iraq, eh?"

"Except Iraq has been out on the heath under that dreadful storm for twenty years, not just one night ..."

Tears were streaming down his cheeks. He turned away from the bed so no one could see him. I put an arm around his shoulder.

"Let's go outside for a breath," I said.

I steered him down the ward and then out into the garden through a side door, muttering calming words and rubbing his back. As soon as the door closed behind us, he fell to his knees, wracked with sobs, heaving for air. I knelt beside him, just holding on. I did not know what else to do. We are so inadequate in the face of real tragedy.

After several minutes, he asked for a cigarette.

"First time since I was a child," he said, sighing out smoke.

"First cigarette?"

"No," he laughed. "First time I have cried since I was a small boy ..."

"No disgrace in it."

"I feel a lot better," he said. "Thank you, my friend."

"Please!"

"You do not have a Canadian accent," he said.

"No," I admitted. "I was born in Britain."

"I thought so. We Iraqis have long known not to blame a man for his leader," he said.

"Right."

"Except the Americans," he added. "They have too many bad leaders not to be at fault themselves."

He wanted to walk in the night air, so we went to the car park, and then drove his car down to Sabbar's truck. Ahmed produced the length of rubber tubing that all Iraqis seem to have in their cars, and proceeded to siphon gas from his car into the truck.

A burst of gunfire a mile or so off caused him to spill some gas on his shoe.

"More killing," he said.

EPILOGUE

Consider whether this is a man,
Who labours in the mud
Who knows no peace
Who fights for a crust of bread
Who dies at a yes or a no.

—— PRIMO LEVI (1919–87)[137]

I attended the Easter Sunday service with the general, Haifa, Firaz and Tara. Mass was conducted entirely in Athurian, the ancient local dialect of Aramaic, spoken in Mesopotamia long before the time of Mohammed, may peace be upon him. Besides the two priests, I don't think anyone in the packed congregation understood a word of it. But we all knew the story.

Death and resurrection, it was all about death and resurrection. With nothing else to do for two hours, I pondered the subject of death and resurrection. I'm sure everyone in that little old church was as heartily sick of death as me and could have used some resurrection for a change. The general was doing his bit, though. Through the agency of Clint, a Lebanese-American soldier he had met, the general had a deal to import Budweiser beer into Iraq. He was importing machinery from Romania with the help of two ex-SAS carpetbaggers. In partnership with an enormously fat Turk, he was importing raw materials for the pharmaceutical business via Azerbaijan. He had something going with the Israelis too.

One day, while driving, we had passed a new five-storey hotel in a quiet square near Karradah that was completely surrounded by white Toyota Landcruisers.

"Israelis," said the general.

He did not like Israel.

Apparently, the Landcruisers had driven all the way from Israel. They carried Iraqi Jews, or their descendants, who were returning to reclaim property confiscated by the Ba'ath regime, which came to power with a wave of anti-Jewish activity, show-trials, public executions, lies. It seemed a good sign, an indication that things were improving. Baghdad had once possessed a huge Jewish community, which had contributed much to the culture and society of Iraq, and the thought of it returning was synonymous with Baghdad reviving, resurrecting.

The general thought otherwise, however. "Jews give nothing," he said. "They just take. They do only for themselves, and they make the peoples fight against each other." He was an old-style medieval Jew-hater, and I found it almost quaint to hear. But it did not stop him from hatching some kind of business deal in the small hotel surrounded by the white trucks.

He was a survivor, the general, and his every other thought was of how to make a buck. He knew there were uncertain times ahead, especially for the small Christian minority. I had told him repeatedly to change his attitude towards the Shia and he knew he would have to do that, because Iraq's Christians had always tried to ally themselves with whoever was the top dog. However, his main concern was money. He urged me to go into the tourist business with him; he urged me to go into the oil business with him; he urged me to get into the used-car business. But Iraq needed this sort of thing now, needed to get back into the world, and allow the world to get back into Iraq.

Helping with his various schemes, in whatever little ways I could, gave me a reason to remain in Iraq. What I was really waiting for was some kind of decisive event, something that would signal the Resurrection. But none came.

Though I kept telephoning Rabia Adifani in Kuwait City, I was never able to catch him in and tell him where Kuwait's civilians were buried. I assumed Kuwait was not really interested. The dead still lie there, in the sand. Hamid never contacted Sabbar, either. He probably got cold feet after numerous people were arrested for selling stolen antiquities. Omar never started his political party; he ended up supporting Wafiq al-Sammarai, whose party made no impact and has since crumbled. Ahmed Hussein surrendered. "Chemical" Ali was caught. No one ever looked beneath the mosque where Omar said weapons were buried. The helicopters prowled the skies. The U.S. soldiers grew disillusioned with their mission, and became even more trigger-happy. Iraqis, who had been prepared to give America a chance, saw little but violence, greed and stupidity from them, and grew to hate them. Spring turned to a hot summer of discontent, and with the heat came disease. There was no effort to repair utilities destroyed by the bombing. The water was not potable. The electricity was too unreliable for anyone to use a refrigerator, and lights came on and off at random. The gas shortage even made it difficult to run generators. The only improvement, everyone said, was that you could freely watch satellite TV — when the electricity was working.

Instead of diminishing, the lawlessness increased. All night long there was gunfire, near and far; everyone locked away their garden chairs, their lawn sprinklers, their plastic gnomes. Women ceased to go out, and men rarely did alone, and never without a gun. Carjackings became commonplace. What little business there was dwindled to a halt. The cars and trucks that had poured back and forth across the Jordanian border, enjoying the benefits of paying no duty, all but ceased — the road had become too dangerous. Sand pirates from Fallujah and Ramadi were hijacking anything and everything. The morgues would fill up every night with victims of the carnage, of gun battles with the army, of firefights with thieves, of altercations between Sunni and Shia. And the soldiers made no attempt to provide security, which was the only thing anyone wanted from them.

It was an unqualified fiasco, deeply saddening, and entirely the fault of America, which had made one of the greatest misjudgements in history. Even the Israelis began to worry that the region had been destabilized for another generation, and their future was now less certain than it had been when Saddam ruled Iraq.

I spoke with many soldiers, mostly rank-and-file grunts, who were the only ones willing to talk, and their opinion was all but unanimous: they had been misled, the war was wrong, the president and his advisers had seriously fucked up and the army was paying for it. They could not wait to get home. When they do, America will hear a little of the truth about this monstrous war crime from a source it may be willing to believe. As many soldiers have come to see, what their country has done in Iraq over the past dozen years will rank alongside history's greatest tragedies. Over twenty million people have had their lives destroyed. Most may still be alive, but they sometimes wonder if that is not the worst part of all.

> *You would think the fury of aerial bombardment*
> *Would rouse God to relent; the infinite spaces*
> *Are still silent. He looks on shock-pried faces.*
> *History, even, does not know what is meant.*
> — RICHARD EBERHARDT (1904–)[138]

As the dignified old priest read the story of the passion of the Christ, the sun came out from behind sombre grey clouds that had cloaked Baghdad all morning, sending a shaft of light through one of the church's stained-glass windows, spraying the polished wooden floor with colours, and somehow changing the energy in the room.

I had been thinking of how long Easter Mass had been said in this part of the world, of how many deaths and resurrections had been witnessed here. Ur, Babylon, Baghdad, these primal cities were resilient, and when they were not, other cities sprang up nearby that were. Life would go on. If a few stupid greedy men could interfere with that, where would we be? Not only would life go on, we would all be wiser for it. If from out of all this misery and error we could extract one pearl of wisdom, it would not have been in vain. If this atrocity makes us wonder about the nature of democracy, politics and leadership — wonder and then change — it would not have been for nothing. But if we fail to learn, then we are adding idiocy to misery, compounding the errors of time's wreckage, guaranteeing the misery of our children and the futility of our own lives.

Haifa insisted I come to meet the priest on our way out. I could tell it was a matter of social prestige to be seen chatting with God's representative, like going backstage after a rock concert. He sat in a little storefront office off the walkway leading to the street, a grave old man with shiny iron-grey hair pressed to his skull and a huge horse-like face riven with deep fissures, creating the illusion that his job was unimaginably hard, back-breaking toil and inner conflict on a scale we mortals could barely conceive.

Haifa introduced me. It was clear she believed that this was as close to the Architect of the Universe as she would ever get. Even the general behaved like a schoolboy summoned to the headmaster's study; he kept straightening his tie and bowing. I did not know what to say. *You were great ... Fantastic show ...* It has been a long time since we in the West have looked up to the clergy. I remembered my stepfather actually apologizing to a friend because there was a priest in the house, although he was only trying to sell my mother raffle tickets. We have come a long way; but then, we are the ones with the bombs and planes, unleashing hell in the name of a god no one believes in.

It took me a while to realize that I was there with this priest because Haifa thought I was a Christian far from home who would appreciate the spiritual succour. It was like the Rotary Club or the Masons, or an American Express card: membership has its privileges.

We talked of this and that, mainly of how everyone was surviving. The future is always uncertain, but there are few communities in the world whose joint future is as uncertain as that of Iraq's Christians. All Iraqis fear for their future, the Sunnis more than the Shia and the Christians more than both. Few of them understand that religion plays no role in the decisions of Washington or London, or rather plays the role it has always played since the Roman Empire became the Holy Roman Empire and God's will a reflection of geopolitical expediency.

"Without the Lord, there is no survival," said the grave priest, in faultless English.

"There often isn't any with him, either," I said, reassuring myself that honesty was always the best policy.

The priest did not react. Rather, he turned the idea over in his big horse's brain, as if it were entirely novel. Finally, he looked at me and smiled.

"Are you confusing me with the local witch doctor?" he said. "Because if you are, you have the wrong man. I am not here to prop up the tattered tent of an irrelevant faith. If Haifa here comes to me and says, 'Father, I've lost my faith. Can you find it for me?,' I will tell her No. She'll have to live without it ..."

Haifa beamed silently, looking back and forth between us, pleased to be the agent of such fine conversation. The general seemed similarly happy, picking his fingernails and pondering some money-making scheme. Merely sitting here was doing his community status a power of good, and that could only help business.

"But she's never going to do that," said the priest. "Is she? Because faith has to be a very important thing to a person before they can lose it, yes? You lose your spectacles, you'll get over it. You lose your daughter, it will destroy your life. Am I wrong?"

How did he know I was always losing my spectacles and had a daughter?

"Right," I said, understanding that this was not just theoretical. "When did you lose your faith?"

His eyes flickered, trying to decide which of my eyes was the window to my soul. Then he smiled weakly and said,

"Good. I did not think I was wasting my words, but one never knows ..."

"So what tent are you propping up?" I said.

"No," he said. "Wrong question. Ask me if I want it back ..."

"I assume you do."

"Put it this way," he said, sighing and searching for the words. "I know what it was I lost, which is something I never knew when I still had it. So I know what all these people who come here still have, and although I am the poorest of the poor, I can at least provide them with the structures of nourishment."

"Structures of nourishment" struck me as an extraordinary phrase. Only in Baghdad could you have a conversation like this with a priest. It was so free of bullshit that I missed bullshit.

"Sounds more like a dark night of the soul," I said, feeling like a doctor diagnosing flu. "Misplaced, not lost ..."

"After twenty-five years, you are forced to admit to yourself that it is not coming back."

Although I knew the soul's dark night lasted longer than the day's, I had no idea whether a quarter of a century was too long or just average. What was I supposed to say to this man?

"I am not seeking reassurance," said the priest. "Not from you. I have come to see things all too clearly here. So clearly that I once began to write a book. I only stopped writing when I found I saw things too clearly for words. That is what I like about this country: everything is clear. I see it in the eyes of your soldiers, and I want to tell them: You ought never to have come here if you are not ready for the truth."

"What truth?" I asked.

"Whatever we hide from is the truth. Saddam was our truth, and we were his. We hid from our lies and our violence when we hid from him. And in us, Saddam hid from himself. But in the end he confronted who he really was ..."

"Who was he?"

"Just another man who wanted to be loved like a god, and found it was easier to make people fear him than it was to make them love him, without noticing that he had forgotten the difference between love and fear. He thought he was loved. You are just the same ..."

"Me?" I thought I had misheard.

"Americans, British — it's all the same. You thought we would not notice what it was you really wanted if you freed us from Saddam. But you misjudged us. You may have forgotten what things like freedom really mean, but we have not. You thought that moving us from one prison into another, no matter how modern and luxurious, would make us forget we are in prison. It will not."

"Maybe it is just the transition that is hard. Things will improve ..."

"I look into your eyes," he said, "and I know you do not believe what you are saying. Iraq is just an American colony now. That is all you will ever allow us to be. You will never allow us to run our own country, but you will make it seem as if we are running it. I told you, here things are much clearer. You will never fool the Iraqi people the way you can fool your own people. You mock the suffering we have endured by even trying to fool us."

I knew he was right. A year later and he seems more right. The handover of power means only that a quisling government will operate, with every ministry controlled by U.S. officials, with an army of stooges and a stooge police force. State security will be run by people who were prominent in

Saddam's secret police, under the direction of the CIA. The U.S. military will have the same "status of forces" agreement that has been imposed on host nations of their 750 bases around the world, an agreement that basically puts them in control. Iraq is just another colony, like Haiti.

"What I do not understand," said the priest, "is why you have this need to fool yourselves. I read the papers — yes, we get what we need here. I remember how forthright and truthful they were about Saddam's regime. I remember how passionately they wrote about Vietnam. American papers in particular. They felt no need to support an unjust war. Now they do. Why?"

A year later again, I ask myself the same question, along with other questions. Ten thousand Iraqis are being held without charge in concentration camps. Why? Many of them have been tortured. Why? Entire villages have been corralled with razor wire. Why? The activities of the media are severely curtailed inside Iraq. Why is this tolerated? Every Iraqi knows that Israeli intelligence agents played key roles before, during and after the war, and now operate openly within the country. Why is this alliance never investigated or denounced? Why has the Atomic Energy Agency not been allowed to send in experts to assess the effects of the depleted-uranium weapons deployed in the war, which it describes as "a catastrophe?"[139] The uranium-tipped shells deployed in 2003 left areas so "hot" with radiation that the army survey teams sent in to assess them wore full protective clothing, yet Iraqis were never even warned of the dangers and children now play there. I have been almost constantly plagued by odd ailments since my return, finding out only recently that many of the places I visited in Iraq clocked up to four thousand times the normal amount of radiation. Where is the outrage of a world allegedly pledged to outlaw such weapons? Every day, unexploded cluster bomblets claim their victims, mostly children: where is the humanitarian concern of a world that has supposedly denounced the use of such horrors? Why do we have this need to fool ourselves about American intentions and actions? Do we even care?

"It is a sickness," said the priest, "this non-thinking that comes from non-feeling. But even this is not what I mean by seeing clearly. Do you know what I mean?"

I shook my head. I did not have any answers.

"Simple things," he said. "These are the answers I see clearly. We have got to learn to love one another. We have got to understand that all wars are wrong. Any war for any reason is wrong. If you think there is a just war, you are wrong, wrong, wrong. It is wrong to kill. Wrong. You do not need God to tell you this, and if you do not believe it, you do not need God at all, because he does not need you. Treat other people the way you want other people to treat you — is this not the only answer there is?"

"A Christian answer ..."

"No!" He straightened in his chair, eyes widening, voice like thunder. "I hammered this answer out in the forge of my own soul without God or Jesus. I *know* this is true. It may be *all* I know. But I can tell you that if it was not in the Bible, I would put that book away. If it was in the Holy Koran I would be a Muslim by now. It is just an irony that the God who has abandoned me is also the only one I want to believe in. Get out of here!"

I rose instantly, thinking he might leap at me.

"No, no," he laughed. "Not you. Sit. I meant your armies. Get out of here, and come back when you have something to teach us that we need to learn ..."

I sat obediently, like a dog. Haifa and the general were looking a little perplexed. They could not follow the conversation and were wondering why I had stood up, then sat down again.

"Time to go," I told Haifa, smiling.

"Ah, Robert, yes," said the general. "You are liking our priest, I think?"

"An understatement. You should tell him I am from Canada, though. He seems to think I am American."

When he learned where I was from, the priest perked up a notch, recalling the places and names of his student years in Toronto an age ago. He had always wanted to go back, but it had not been possible. Still, he could always hope, couldn't he?

"It is a country that does not yet think it knows everything," he said. "We do not understand what a blessing is, do we? A blessing is God's way of filling the space that evil wants to occupy. That's what I have learned. Do you see?"

"Alas," I said.

"You are blessed to live in Canada, my child," he said. "Truly blessed. Is that so hard to understand? Now go in peace ..."

Out beyond all wrongdoing and rightdoing,
there is a field. I'll meet you there.
When the soul lies down in that grass,
the world is too full to speak about.

— MEVLANA JALALUDDIN RUMI (1207–73)

PWR

Baghdad and Toronto, March 2003–April 2004

AFTERWORD

Misrule, you see, has caused the world to be malevolent.

— DANTE (1265–1321)[140]

As I write this, exactly two years have now passed since the statue of Saddam Hussein in Baghdad's Firdos Square was pulled down and the world given to believe that the war had ended, Iraq was free, America's "mission accomplished." When I started writing this book it was still necessary to prove that the invasion was a disaster and the war unjustified. Now everyone knows this — and those who pretend otherwise have only lies with which to bolster their arguments. The war's principal theoretician, Paul Wolfowitz, has left his position as assistant secretary of defense to head up the World Bank. The move from warmonger to philanthropist is something of an American political tradition and should surprise no one: Robert McNamara, chief architect of the Vietnam War, also ended up running the World Bank, whose main activity consists of loaning ravaged countries money with which to hire reconstruction and development specialists like Halliburton. War is a business.

For all their soul-searching in the wake of the war, the American news media still on the whole continue to serve as propaganda outlets for a government that, in its disregard for truth and the historical record, more closely resembles a Stalinesque tyranny than it does the Jeffersonian ideal. Its control over the institutions that rule America is now total and, according to the few Democrats still willing to go on record as the "opposition," abusive in the extreme. A nation that once embodied the noblest aspirations of the human soul now seems scarcely different from the kind of totalitarian fundamentalist theocracy from which it purports to be saving the world. Even highly credible sources like Brent Scowcroft, National Security Advisor to both presidents Ford and Bush Sr., tell us that President George W. Bush believes God is on his side and guides his mission. The folly of this seems apparent to no one in the administration, which, as serious magazines like *Foreign Policy Review* confess, is essentially controlled by the offices of vice-president Dick Cheney and defense secretary Donald Rumsfeld, a man Henry Kissinger once described as "the most ruthless politician I have ever met."

Late last year, I happened to be in Halifax, Nova Scotia, when George W. Bush swept through the city, ostensibly to thank Nova Scotians for their hospitality to American air travellers during the September 11, 2001, crisis, but really to deliver what was termed "a major foreign-policy speech." Watching the snipers on rooftops, the droves of police with walkie-talkies, and the sealing off with barricades of entire streets, I was reminded not so much of a superpower flexing its imperial muscles as of a small medieval city-state preoccupied with its own vulnerability and weakness.

My anger, directed at the figurehead of Bush over the war, has now abated, replaced by sorrow and a sense of shame that evokes something like pity. Whenever I watch this American president, I am struck by his awkwardness, his permanently bemused expression, his painfully inarticulate manner of dealing with unexpected questions and his utter inability to convey anything approaching intelligence, even when reading a speech he did not write. I cannot recall any world leader who has ever displayed so few signs of competence, yet so much certitude. Indeed, as Admiral Stansfield Turner, ex-director of the CIA, told my friend Chisanga Pute-Chekwe at a private dinner, "The problem with this administration is its certitude."

(Chisanga had asked him why there were New York taxi drivers who had predicted the consequences of the Iraq war better than most in the U.S. government.)

I think the United States will be forced to leave Iraq fairly soon. To remain there would entail a full-scale draft, and I am not sure the political will exists to break what was a key promise of the 2004 presidential election. The $100 million or so a week currently poured into the occupation is also crippling the U.S. economy. A relatively small force will be left to maintain some of the desert bases the army has created in Iraq, so that troops can be flown in again if the Iraqi government requests assistance, or the now U.S.-controlled oil fields — already protected by their own militia of mercenaries, hired by Halliburton and others — are ever threatened. The game of "grab" was won some time back.

I have remained in almost constant touch with various Iraqis from different walks of life who are still in Iraq, 27 of them in all; and I have developed 23 contacts in the rank-and-file echelons of the U.S. military, most of whom I first met when there. For a variety of fairly obvious reasons, none of these people wishes to be identified. I often send them news reports on Iraq from U.S. media for comment. Not one has ever been deemed wholly accurate, and of the last hundred such reports sent, only one was said by *both* categories of communicant to be more than 20 percent accurate. We use websites and internet chat rooms mostly, and occasionally e-mail. The two areas where I have found unanimous agreement are these:

1. All the Iraqis agree that the only good result to have come from the war is the end of Saddam Hussein's rule, and that every other aspect of life in Iraq is worse now than it was before the invasion.

2. All the soldiers say that morale within the military is at an all-time low. Many of their colleagues talk openly about desertion, and some even discuss mutiny.

Most soldiers feel betrayed by their senior officers, yet all reserve the most scorn for Donald Rumsfeld, who promised they would be home within three months and, once they arrived in Iraq, cut both their salaries and benefits, also denying them adequately armoured vehicles and other life-saving luxuries. Many say they've come to realize they are regarded by the Pentagon as little more than cannon-fodder. Most agree the actual death toll among military personnel is far higher than the official figures. Few have any love for Iraq or Iraqis, and indeed many say they've come to hate the place and its people. Not one expressed any respect for their commander-in-chief, and only two voted Republican in the 2004 elections — whereas all 23 voted for Bush in 2000.

I do not claim that my 23 communicants in the military represent all American troops in Iraq. Their views are simply the opinions of 23 ordinary soldiers who have been stationed in what they have come to regard as hell for over two years now, and who live solely for the moment they can return home.

Meanwhile, in the shadows of the mighty, the ordinary people of Iraq still suffer under appalling conditions. Materially, little has changed since I left in 2003. Electricity supplies are still erratic; tap water is not potable; food is scarce and expensive; there are no jobs except in the security services; public transport is all but non-existent; and although Iraqi oil production is up to three million barrels a day there is still a chronic gasoline shortage. A British Medical Association report has now estimated the civilian death toll since the war began at well over 100,000.[141] Around one million unexploded cluster bomblets litter the country, daily claiming more lives and limbs. Few schools or colleges are open, and parents are reluctant to send their children to the ones that are for fear of kidnappings or attacks. Women are scared to venture out alone, and no one goes out after dark. The poor suffer most, and poor children are the hardest hit of all. Indeed, Jean Ziegler, the U.N. Human Rights Commission's special expert on the right to food, recently confirmed that Iraqi children were actually better off under Saddam Hussein's rule than they are now. The number of children under five suffering from malnutrition has doubled, from four percent in 2002 to nearly eight percent by the end of 2004.[142]

Since 1991, the United States has been directly responsible for the deaths of over one million Iraqi civilians, more than half of them children. They still run daily bombing missions, flattening entire blocks of buildings where resistance fighters are alleged to be hiding, yet where innocent people also live. This is a form of collective punishment, and is illegal under the Geneva protocols. Cities known to be centres of the Sunni resistance have become ghost towns; the worst example is Fallujah, where some seventy percent of the buildings are now rubble, under which bodies still lie crushed. Of the 350,000 inhabitants living there before the U.S. military launched its campaign of terror in which even the quisling Allawi government admitted at least 2,000 civilians were slaughtered, only 25,000 have so far returned to occupy their homes, or to pick through the rubble for whatever can be salvaged of their possessions and whatever remains to be buried of their loved ones.

Iraq is still largely a tribal society, where traditional codes take precedence over everything, including religion. When a brother, sister, mother or father is murdered — no matter why or by whom — these codes dictate that the remaining sons or brothers must avenge the death or else bring shame upon the family. With 100,000 civilian dead, a large number of them killed by American bombs or guns, it is not hard to do the arithmetic and work out where Iraqi resistance groups are getting their recruits. As *Time* magazine's correspondent in Baghdad reported late last year, "the U.S. military here are merely acting as wet nurses to the next generation of al-Qaeda terrorists."

The devastation of Iraq's cultural heritage by U.S. forces has also continued. The National Museum's irreplaceable treasures have vanished forever — perhaps one percent were recovered or returned; the National Library has lost most of its rare books to theft or fire; the library of ancient manuscripts at Ur was looted by U.S. soldiers, who also sprayed ancient scrolls with graffiti; the ceremonial road of Babylon, made from bricks bearing a cuneiform inscription by Nebuchadnezzar, has been completely destroyed by U.S. tank treads; and 2,500-year-old tiles from the ancient city's gateway were pried out by army souvenir hunters while their commanders looked on. Babylon is a World Heritage Site, so the barbarians are stealing from all of us and from generations unborn. This is also the case with the latest cultural casualty, Samarra's unique ninth-century spiral minaret, which Omar had once so proudly shown me. It was partially destroyed in a mortar attack after U.S. troops had been using the roof as a sniper position — yet another war crime according to the Geneva protocols, which provide for the protection of historic sites by occupying armies. Omar and his brother

archives

Zaid are also believed to be dead now, victims of the city's siege by U.S. forces last year. The reader may recall that Samarra was the one city ready to welcome the invaders, and Omar and Zaid had freed American soldiers held hostage there. I can only imagine these good men's final thoughts as the people for whom they once risked their lives laid waste to their home town.

Whatever happens in Iraq, no American will be welcome there for decades to come. If something good is to come out of all this misery, it ought to be a recognition that, in an increasingly multicultural world, where few nations do not contain large populations of non-indigenous peoples, war and military force of any kind are no longer viable solutions to political problems and need to be removed from the quivers of leadership. In a sense, all future wars will be civil. The wars already waged will forever remain as the most shameful aspects of our communal past, and their lessons must be studied and learned until the end of time. We are better than this now, I believe, and we will need to be in order to deal with the more global concerns that lurk in the shadows beyond time's bend.

We all live on this beautiful blue and white ball, and the sooner we realize it is our only home the better off both we and the planet will be. There are no unilateral actions in the Third Millennium. Anywhere is everywhere, and the effects from any cause hit us all. I think, too, that America is going to need the world's help and goodwill sooner than anyone believes possible. That help would be so much easier to guarantee if Washington awoke from its evil enchantment, remembered its Constitution and once-glorious destiny, and became determined to lead the world in eradicating forever the scourge of war — if only as penance for its deeds over the past half century.

It needs only to be added here that the money spent on destroying Iraq could have been used instead to give Americans the kind of health care and education systems that most other civilized nations regard as basic rights, not privileges for the oligarchy. Of course, it would also have been sufficient to permanently end AIDS in Africa and feed for a hundred years every one of the world's two billion human beings who go to sleep each day hungry.

"Defending democracy"… but to defend democracy by military means, one must be militarily efficient, and one cannot become militarily efficient without centralizing power, setting up a tyranny, imposing some form of conscription or slavery to the state. In other words the military defence of democracy in contemporary circumstances entails the abolition of democracy even before war starts.

— ALDOUS HUXLEY (1894–1963)[143]

PWR

Toronto, 9 May 2005

NOTES

1   From "A Vision," translated from the Arabic by Khaled Mattawa.

CHAPTER ONE

2   "Myth has been our time-honoured technique for virtualizing experience. Life rarely takes on the shape of formal tragedy, but the effect of horrendous events can be dramatized without the actual facts of death and disaster. In fact, it is the virtual form that makes such events fully meaningful. This relationship between the virtual and the real still exists, except that the techniques of aural culture have now given way to the technologies of mass media." Frank Zingrone, *The Media Simplex: At the Edge of Meaning in the Age of Chaos*, Toronto, 2001, p. 55.

3   Statement to John Pilger recalled in interview, *Socialist Worker*, November 20, 2003.

4   Press conference, U.S. Government Archives, February 24, 2001.

5   Statement, May 15, 2004.

6   Speech to Senate Foreign Relations Committee, July 17, 2001.

CHAPTER TWO

7   Archives of U.S. State Department, 1947–48, SDPP.

8   Transcript of meeting between U.S. Ambassador April Glaspie and President Saddam Hussein, U.S. Government Archives.

9   Interview with the author, April 6, 2003.

10   Saddam was on the CIA payroll for some years following the coup that placed his predecessor in power.

11   When the empress asked her friend, the wife of Egypt's president, Anwar Sadat, for refuge, Madam Sadat inquired why she did not seek help from her friends the Americans. The empress replied, "I think we have had enough American help to last us a lifetime." The shah was taken in by Egypt after a nightmarish period on an island in Panama under the watchful eye of another CIA casualty, Manuel Noriega, who was about to become Panamanian president before eventually ending up in a Florida jail.

12   He was specifically told that the Voice of America broadcast had been a mistake and that the person responsible had been fired.

13   The most respected report was compiled in 1992 by Beth Daponte, a demographer at the U.S. Commerce Department, who was threatened with dismissal for publishing her findings. Now a Carnegie Mellon professor, she updated her estimates in 1993, concluding that nearly 205,000 Iraqis died in one year as a direct and indirect result of the U.S.-led bombing campaign and the ensuing uprisings in the north and south. About a quarter of the casualties, 56,000, were Iraqi soldiers; the rest were civilians, including 35,000 Kurds and Shiites killed by Saddam's troops. Many more civilians — about 111,000, including 70,000 children under 15 — died after the fighting, mainly because of "postwar adverse health effects" caused by the massive destruction of water and power plants.

14   Ibid.

15   "As has been documented by United Nations agencies, NGOs, humanitarian and human rights organizations, researchers and political leaders, the sanctions upon Iraq have produced a humanitarian disaster comparable to the worst catastrophes of the past decades. There is broad controversy and little hard evidence concerning the exact number of deaths directly attributable to the sanctions; estimates range from half a million to a million and a half, with the majority of the dead being children." Marc Bossuyt, *The Adverse Consequences of Economic Sanctions on the Enjoyment of Human Rights*, UN report by the Economic and Social Council, Commission on Human Rights, E/CN.4/Sub.2/2000/33, June 21, 2000.

16   A fact confirmed by the Pentagon's own reports on these weapons.

17 Robert Fisk in the *Independent*, November 21, 2003.

18 Interview with author, September 2002.

19 National Security Strategy, September 20, 2002.

20 Ibid.

21 "Rebuilding America's Defenses," Project for a New American Century Report; September 2000.

22 In an interview with Eleanor Wachtell on *Writers and Company*, aired by CBC Radio, January 11, 2004.

CHAPTER THREE

23 Quoted in Manocher Dorraj, *From Zarathustra to Khomeini: Populism and Dissent in Iran* (Boulder, CO: Lynne Rienner, 1990), p. 50.

24 Quoted in Thesiger, *The Marsh Arabs*, p. 43.

25 Abdulaziz Abdulhussein Sachedina, "Activist Shi'ism in Iran, Iraq, and Lebanon," in *Fundamentalisms Observed*, ed. Martin E. Marty and R. Scott Appleby (Chicago: University of Chicago Press, 1991), p. 425.

26 Figures from the *Iraq Body Count* website, www.iraqbodycount.net.

27 Kamel became reconciled with Saddam and was persuaded to return to Iraq, where — according to the official record — he was put to death by members of his own family. I never believed the story at the time, finding it highly improbable that a man of Kamel's obvious intelligence could have been fooled into believing Saddam had forgiven his defection. After all, Saddam had murdered far closer relatives than Kamel before this, and for far lesser offences.

28 February 1998, town-hall meeting on Iraq.

29 See note 7.

30 John Barry in *Newsweek*, February 23, 2003.

31 Reuters, February 26, 2003.

32 The document can be seen at www.casi.org.uk/info/unscom950822.pdf.

33 Lt.-Gen. Sir Stanley Maude, *Proclamation to the People of the Vilayat of Baghdad; 1917*. Archives of the British Foreign Office.

34 Some petro-geologists believe that the Saudi oilfields have been so depleted by rapacious exploitation over the past thirty years that the Iraqi fields are now the world's largest repositories of Arab D-grade oil — the champagne of oils, most coveted, and only found in Saudi Arabia and Iraq. American oil is very poor in quality and unsuitable for refinement into high-octane fuel.

35 One should remember that U.S. oil companies have managed to designate every well as "exploratory," rendering its profits tax-exempt.

36 Quoted in Kenneth Rose, *Superior Person: A Portrait of His Circle of Late Victorian England* (New York: Weybright and Talley, 1969), p. 215.

37 The British forces were left with this task while U.S. units headed for Baghdad almost immediately.

38 The legendary caliph of *1001 Arabian Nights* fame, who largely created the old city of Baghdad.

39 Churchill was then British secretary of state for war and air. Quoted by Phillip Knightly in "Desert Warriors" (*M Inc.* magazine, November 1990).

40 Quoted in Randall Baker, *King Husain and the Kingdom of the Hejaz* (New York: Oleander Press, 1979), p. 51.

41 Quoted in Peter Mansfield, *The Arabs* (New York: Penguin Books, 1985), p. 165.

42 Quoted in Milton Viorst, "The House of Hashem," *The New Yorker*, January 7, 1991, p. 46.

43 T. E. Lawrence, *Seven Pillars of Wisdom: A Triumph* (New York: Anchor Books, 1991), p. 649.

44 Quoted in Phillip Knightly, *Imperial Legacy* (New York: Touchstone, 2003), p. 9.

45 Quoted in Lewis Lapham, *Theater of War* (New York: The New Press, 2002), p. 4.

46 T. E. Lawrence, *Collected Letters* (London: Faber & Faber, 1961), p. 287.

47 Quoted in Knightly, *Imperial Legacy*, p. 14.

48 As reconstituted by Evan S. Connell in *Deus lo Volt! Chronicle of the Crusades* (Washington, D.C.: Counterpoint and London: Secker and Warburg, 2000).

49 Within a year, the Spanish elected a Socialist government that, by spring 2004, had fulfilled its key election pledge to withdraw the country's army from the so-called "coalition" in Iraq, where the situation had deteriorated badly.

50 All CNN quotes from broadcasts transcribed on March 25, 2003.

51 Quoted in *Extra: The Magazine of FAIR — the Media Watch Group*, vol. 16, no. 3, June 2003.

CHAPTER FOUR

52 All available on the Pentagon and Department of Defense websites alongside much else that would once have been "classified" information.

53 For more information on all the journalists killed and injured during the war, visit www.cpj.org, the website of the Committee to Protect Journalists, a large independent nonprofit organization for journalists by journalists.

54 From his masterpiece, the title track of *The Future* (Columbia Records, 1992).

55 Prince Philip went on to become head of the World Wildlife Fund.

56   Interviewed by V. K. Ramachandran of *Frontline*: "Iraq is a Trial Run" (April 2, 2003).

57   From the title track of *The Future* (Columbia Records, 1992).

58   Department of Defense Press Release, March 9, 2003.

59   On April 8, 2003, for example, a U.S. tank fired an explosive shell at the Palestine Hotel killing two journalists — Taras Protsyuk of Reuters and Jose Couso of the Spanish TV network Telecino — and injuring three others. Earlier the same day the U.S. launched separate but virtually simultaneous attacks on the Baghdad offices of Al Jazeera and Abu Dhabi TV. Both outlets had informed the Pentagon of their exact locations (see letter released by the Committee to Protect Journalists, April 8, 2003). These airstrikes killed Al Jazeera's main Baghdad correspondent, Tareq Ayuoub, and injured another journalist. Al Jazeera's camera crew was fired on by British tanks on March 29 and its offices in Basra were shelled on April 2. On April 7 a car clearly marked as belonging to Al Jazeera was shot at by U.S. soldiers (source: Reporters Without Borders, April 8, 2003). The U.S. military has a pattern of deliberately targeting broadcast operations going back to the Kosovo war, when it attacked the offices of state-owned Radio-Television Serbia. During the U.S. invasion of Afghanistan in 2001, Al Jazeera's Kabul offices were destroyed by an American missile. In an interview with the BBC's Nik Gowing (April 8, 2002), Admiral Craig Quigley, the Pentagon's deputy assistant for public affairs, claimed the compound was being used by al-Qaeda — a charge strongly denied by Al Jazeera — and was thus a "legitimate target." The U.S. "evidence" consisted solely of Al Jazeera's use of a satellite uplink and its regular contacts with Taliban officials — both thoroughly normal activities for a news outlet. Quigley even made the claim that the U.S. had not known the compound was Al Jazeera's office — which is totally unbelievable — then asserted that in any case such information was "not relevant" to the decision to destroy it. The BBC concluded that the U.S. made no effort to distinguish between legitimate satellite uplinks and those belonging to "the enemy." It cannot be stated too often that attacks on civilian institutions, whether or not they are being used for "propaganda purposes," violate the Geneva Conventions and are thus war crimes.

60   *Poynter Online*, April 11, 2003:
see www.poynter.org/content/content_view. asp?id=29774.

61   In *Jarhead*, a Desert Storm memoir by former Marine Corps sniper Anthony Swofford, we learn that Swofford's unit was given a stern warning by the instructor who taught them how to use the .50-calibre Barrett sniper rifle: "By

the way, you know you can't hit a human target with a .50-caliber weapon, right? It's in the Geneva Convention. So you hit the gas tank on their vehicle, and they get blown the hell up, but you can't target some lonely guard or a couple of towlies in an OP calling in bombs."

62   *Boston Globe*, April 24, 2003.

63   *Poynter Online*, op. cit.

64   This information is based on my conversations with the British SAS officer known by the *nom de plume* Andy McNab, who led several unsuccessful "Deniable Ops" missions to assassinate Saddam Hussein — an act that, I might add, is illegal under both British and American law. He has written several books about his experiences, starting with the bestseller *Bravo Two Zero* (1993).

65   McNab's wife has written an account of why their marriage broke up in which she speaks of her horror upon realizing she had married "something inhuman."

66   From "The Second Coming" (1921).

67   Al Gore in a speech to the Commonwealth Club, San Francisco, September 2002. See "Text: Gore Assails Bush's Iraq Policy," *Washington Post*, September 24, 2002.

68   "The War Prayer," in *Mark Twain on the Damned Human Race*, ed. Janet Smith (New York: Hill and Wang, 1994), p. 67.

69   Press Conference, October 12, 1998. Source: CNN news.

70   Quoted in James P. Pinkerton, "Forget Elway — U.S. Is Throwing the Long Bomb," *Newsday* (New York), February 2, 1999, A36.

71   In "The Chance for Peace," a speech to the American Society of Newspaper Editors, Washington, D.C., April 16, 1953.

CHAPTER FIVE

72   National Security Strategy of the United States, September 2002.

73   For more information, and some grisly photos, on specific breaches of the Geneva Conventions by the U.S. forces in Iraq, visit: www.informationclearinghouse.info/article3450.htm.

CHAPTER SIX

74   Barton Gellman, "Allied Air War Struck Broadly in Iraq," *Washington Post*, June 23, 1991, A1.

75   See the report by Beth Daponte, note 13.

76   Ibid. "U.S. Bombs Missed 70% of Time," *Washington Post*, March 16, 1991, A1.

77   Quoted in Howard Zinn, *Terrorism and War* (New York: Seven Stories Press, 2002), p. 85.

78   A recent example was during the summer of 2003, when three Special Forces soldiers stationed at Fort Bragg, NC, murdered their wives shortly after returning from Afghanistan. Two went on to kill themselves.

79   From "September 1, 1939."

80   Chalabi is the billionaire banker wanted for fraud in Jordan who managed to convince certain gullible factions in Washington that he was the best bet for new Iraqi strongman. His family left Baghdad thirty years ago when the Ba'ath Party first came to power, and Iraqis universally despise him for his involvement with the U.S. Cronies of Chalabi now control Iraq's oil, no doubt on BushCo's behalf.

81   From "America, America" (1995), translated from the Arabic by Khaled Mattawa and P. W. Roberts.

82   Some of this information in a variant form can be found on www.debka.com, which is notoriously a web site that utilizes both Israeli intelligence information and *dis*-information.

83   Source: Debka Files: www.debka.com/article.php.aid=462.

84   Ibid.

85   www.debka.com/article.php.aid=463.

86   Ibid.

87   From "America, America," see note 81 above.

88   George Roux's *Ancient Iraq*, 3rd edition, 1992, though what follows is largely derived from Arabic sources and paints a somewhat different picture of the history than one gets from the writings of Western historians.

89   This was the old Iraqi dinar, replaced in 2004.

90   From "Fears in Solitude" (1798).

CHAPTER SEVEN

91   Believed to be the first female poet in history, she was daughter of King Sargon of Akkad, and high priestess of the Moon-God temple in Ur, near Nasiriya, Iraq, c. 2300 BC.

92   From "My Triumph Lasted Till the Drums," written during the American Civil War; exact date unknown.

93   Saddam City was renamed Sadr City, after a deceased Shia cleric, some time after the war.

94   Philip Sherwell, *Sunday Telegraph*, April 13, 2003.

95   Soon after Sherwell's article appeared, Ali was moved to a hospital in Kuwait City, where U.S. specialists began treating him.

96   From "September 1, 1939."

97 Elizabeth Day and Philip Sherwell, "Looters Strip Iraqi National Museum Of Its Treasures," London, *Sunday Telegraph*, April 13, 2003.

98 From "The Sorrow of Sarajevo," English version by David Harsent (1996).

99 Many of Iraq's Christians are Chaldeans, whose faith is similar to that of the Assyrian Catholics of Syria and Lebanon; they conduct their liturgy in Aramaic, the language of Christ. Hundreds of thousands of Christians have left Iraq in the last fifteen years.

100 From "Lament of the Frontier Guard," translated from the Chinese by Ezra Pound (1915).

101 From "Epitaph for Mariana Gryphius, His Brother Paul's Little Daughter," (1660), translated from the German by Christopher Benfey (1995).

102 From "All is Vanity" (1713).

103 From "History" (2002).

104 From "Night in Al-Hamra," translated from the Arabic by Khaled Mattawa and P. W. Roberts.

CHAPTER EIGHT

105 From "The Knight's Tale" (c. 1387).

106 November 20, 2003, as he stood side by side with U.S. president George W. Bush in London.

107 From "Retort on Mordaunt's 'The Call'" (1782).

108 From "How to Kill" (1943).

109 Ibid.

CHAPTER NINE

110 On *60 Minutes*, December 15, 2002.

111 National Energy Policy Development Group report, May 2001. The NEPDG is headed by Vice President Cheney.

112 *Foreign Policy in Focus* policy report, January 2003.

113 Ibid.

114 *Times* (London), January 15, 2003.

115 *Foreign Policy in Focus*, February 14, 2003.

116 Online *Asian Times*, April 11, 2002.

117 *Nation*, September 23, 2002.

118 From "Asia: The Military-Market Link," an article published by the U.S. Naval Institute, January 2002.

119 www.citizenworks.org/admin/press/feb4-rn.php.

120 www.hazelhenderson.com/Bush's%20unilateralism.htm.

CHAPTER TEN

121 From "Poem for the Land" (1977), translated from the Arabic by Sarah Maguire with Sabry Hafez.

122 From "Fall 1961."

123 From "When You See Millions of the Mouthless Dead" (1915).

124 From "A Refusal to Mourn the Death, by Fire, of a Child in London" (1945).

125 From "The Survivor" (1947), translated from the Polish by Adam Czerniawski.

CHAPTER ELEVEN

126 From "Channel Firing" (1914).

CHAPTER TWELVE

127 Testimony before the Senate Foreign Relations Committee in 1971.

128 At the date of this writing he has now been jailed for over a year, allegedly in Room 32 at the Baghdad Airport, still unaware of the crimes for which he will one day have to offer a defence. Just before the missiles began to roar and thunder over Baghdad, Aziz was heard to tell a friend that he would rather die than be a U.S. prisoner of war.

129 From "Dedication" (1945).

130 From "Familial" (1946), translated from the French by Lawrence Ferlinghetti (1970).

131 From "And Death Shall Have No Dominion" (1936).

132 Human Rights Watch: www.hrw.org/press/2003/12/us-iraq-press.htm.

133 Human Rights Watch: www.hrw.org/press/2003/04/us040103.htm.

134 International law does not entirely forbid the killing of civilians but it does require armies to take every measure possible to prevent such deaths. By using a method of targeting known to be flawed, the U.S. and Britain cannot claim to have taken the required preventative measures. They are thus in violation of the Geneva Conventions and international humanitarian law, and must be charged with war crimes for many of these incidents, not to mention all the other violations I have listed, as well as those mounting up in the reports of humanitarian agencies around the world.

135 William Shakespeare, "The Merchant of Venice," Act IV, Scene I.

136 William Shakespeare, "King Lear," Act III, Scene 4.

EPILOGUE

137 From "Shema" (1946).

138 From "The Fury of Aerial Bombardment."

139 Dr. Doug Rokke, director of the U.S. Army depleted uranium project, in an interview with journalist John Pilger, May 2004.

AFTERWORD

140 From *Purgatorio*, the second cantiche of *The Divine Comedy*, written between 1308 and Dante's death in 1321.

141 From a report published in the prestigious medical journal *The Lancet* in October 2004. "From a purely public health perspective it is clear that whatever planning did take place was grievously in error," wrote Dr. Richard Horton, the journal's editor, in an accompanying editorial. "The invasion of Iraq, the displacement of a cruel dictator and the attempt to impose a liberal democracy by force have, by themselves, been insufficient to bring peace and security to the civilian population. Democratic imperialism has led to more deaths, not fewer." See www.iht.com/articles/2004/10/29/news/toll.html

142 See www.commondreams.org/headlines05/0331-08.htm

143 From *Letters of Aldous Huxley,* first published in 1936.

INDEX